T0374516

THE ZAKIR HUSAIN MEMORIAL LECTURES 1992–2004

THE ZAKIR HUSAIN MEMORIAL LECTURES 1992–2004

**Zakir Husain College
University of Delhi**

 Tulika Books

Published by **Tulika Books**
35 A/1 (III floor), Shahpur Jat, New Delhi 110 049, India

© Zakir Husain College, University of Delhi

First published in India 2007

ISBN: 81-89487-11-6

Designed by Ram Rahman; typeset in Sabon and Univers
at Tulika Print Communication Services, New Delhi; printed at
Pauls Press, E 44/11 Okhla Phase II, New Delhi 110 020

To the memory of

SALMAN GHANI HASHMI

1939–2004

'Monotheism of reason and the heart, polytheism of the imagination and art, this is what we need. ...'

(*Die älteste Systemprogramm des deutschen Idealismus*, by Hegel, Hölderlin or Schelling)

Contents

Foreword

Zakir Husain College stands on the deep foundation of a three-hundred-year-long history, one that speaks of a vibrant tradition of knowledge-building in the Indian subcontinent. This is as much an inspiration as a challenge to the institution. While the strength of its foundation offers tremendous scope to reach great heights, it also constantly demands a dynamic engagement with contemporary ideas, life and education. This volume is one of our modest attempts to meet this challenge.

The Dr Zakir Husain Memorial Lecture, held at Zakir Husain College each year, honours an eminent educationist, nationalist and distinguished President of India. Zakir Sahib was well aware of the historical contribution and contemporary significance of Delhi College for higher education in modern India. The Memorial Lecture commemorates the vital role he played in the governance of the Anglo-Arabic College in the pre-independence period and its successor, Delhi College, in 1948.

The lecture series collected here constitutes a significant tribute to an institution that has, for three centuries, retained a sense of enduring identity through institutional changes and historical vicissitudes alike, and fulfilled its commitment to the students entering its premises.

For decades this College has been at centrestage in inspiring its faculty and students to chart new paths in rising to the intellectual and cultural challenges posed by a civilization encountered as a colonial power. Whether during the turbulence of 1857 or, later, the upheaval of Partition in 1947, this place of learning has persevered stoically and survived in its steadfast commitment to education under different titles. The fortunes of the College have been inextricably linked with those of the city, the northern region and, in fact, the country. Despite some grave setbacks and threats, this institution has demonstrated the great resolve of the people and optimism in its energetic revivals.

A quick review of the history of the College fills us with a sense of pride, but it also endows upon us the responsibility of steering the great tradition forward. We must cognize the progressive ideals demonstrated by this institution, for instance, in its concern for women's education or through its stress on vernacular education alongside the learning of the English language. It is pertinent

here to remind ourselves of how this College played a pioneering role in emphasizing scientific awareness through education and in making western texts accessible through translation into Persian way back in the eighteenth century. From
as long back as the threshold of the eighteenth century to the present times,
decade after decade, this institution of learning has upheld the values of a composite culture, asserting the need for imparting education of relevance. Situated
between the old walled city and New Delhi, the traditional and the modern, the
College continues to nourish its distinct identity with a forward-looking vision
negotiated rationally with its cherished past.

It is such a perspective that provided the motivation for instituting the
Memorial Lecture after Zakir Husain College moved to a new location in the
vicinity. As the lectures included in this volume amply demonstrate, this is what
also guided the choice of distinguished speakers and hence found a resonance in
the content of the lectures they have delivered.

It is a matter of honour for us to present to the reader this first volume of
the Zakir Husain Memorial Lectures, which I believe, offers a significant glimpse
into some areas of intellectual engagement in contemporary times.

I wish to record here my sincere thanks to all those who pooled in their
time and effort to make this volume possible.

M. ASLAM PARVAIZ
Principal
Zakir Husain College
University of Delhi

Three Hundred Years of History

Madrasa Ghaziuddin – Delhi College (1824) –
Anglo-Arabic College (1924) – Delhi College (1948) –
Zakir Husain College (1975)

Zakir Husain College is heir to a rich and versatile academic and cultural tradition. Its origins can be traced to the closing years of the reign of Emperor Aurangzeb with the founding of the Madrasa Ghaziuddin. This is the only madrasa of the Mughal period that is still an institution devoted to education. 'It was founded by the father of the first Nizam, Ghaziuddin Khan, who died in 1710, and himself lies buried there. It has been in turn an Arabic madrasa, an oriental college, a police station, a high school, and it is now a college again' (Spear 1945: 11). For twenty-five years, Ghaziuddin Khan served Aurangzeb gallantly. He was made Governor of the Deccan and given the title of Firuz Jang. 'Ghaziuddin Khan who built the school and mausoleum during his lifetime was one of the leading Umaras and influential grandees during the reigns of Aurangzeb and his son and successor Shah Alam I. . . . His son, Mir Qamruddin, entitled "Nawwab Nizam ul-Mulk Asif Jah Chin Qalij Khan Fath Jang", rose to the rank of Wazir (Prime Minister) during the time of Muhammad Shah' (*Monuments of Delhi* [1919] 1997: 2). The complex containing the tomb of Ghaziuddin Khan, a mosque and a madrasa,

> immediately beyond the Ajmer gate, is the largest and best preserved. . . . The school, today housing Zakir Husain College, has been one of Delhi's leading educational institutions since its establishment and is the oldest continuing school in the city. The patron, Mir Shihab al-din, came to India from Bukhara in 1674. In 1683 he received the title Ghazi al-din Khan Bahadur for his successful campaigns in the Deccan. Sometime after this date and before his death in 1709 he built his complex in Delhi.[1]

The location chosen as a final resting place was situated in the vicinity of the dargah of a thirteenth-century Sufi, Hazrat Hafiz Sadullah. The Madrasa

This account of the history of the College was to have been written by the principal Salman Hashmi. His tragic and untimely death a day before his retirement, when he had promised to devote himself to the task, necessitated the present essay. Although, like many other colleagues, I shared his knowledge and love of the institution, I am aware that I cannot match it. I am grateful to his wife, Jennifer Hashmi, for allowing me to benefit from his extensive notes.

fulfilled the desire of the devout to be buried at a place of learning. Following his
death at Ahmedabad in Gujarat, the body of Ghaziuddin Khan was brought to
Delhi and interred there. His wife and grandson are buried beside him, their
graves being on the west and east side, respectively, of the main tomb. Tradition
assigns the two graves found 'inside the enclosure of Ghaziuddin's college some
130 yards to the west of his tomb', to Muinul-Mulk Rustam-i-Hind, commonly
known as Mir Mannu, and his wife. Mir Mannu's wife 'is said to have been the
daughter of Ghaziuddin Khan II, the grandson of Ghaziuddin Khan I, who was
the founder of the college, and the eldest son of the celebrated Nizamul Mulk
Asafjah' (*Monuments of Delhi* [1919] 1997: 3).

H.C. Fanshawe confuses the patron of the Madrasa with his grandson
when he asserts that 'Ghazi-ud-din was son of the first Nizam-ul-Mulk of
Hyderabad. He became a leading noble of the Delhi court when his father returned to the Deccan after the events of 1739, and died in AD 1752, on his way to
assert his succession to the Hyderabad territories' (Fanshawe [1902] 2002: 64).
This is responsible for conflicting accounts of the date of the Madrasa's establishment, as Fanshawe also states that 'the Mausoleum and College of Ghazi-ud-din
Khan . . . one of the few remaining specimens of a religious endowment . . .
comprising a place of worship, the tomb of the founder, and a residence and
place of instruction for those who were to have charge of both, [were] all built in
his lifetime.' Pernau asserts that 'British sources quoted by standard histories of
the Delhi college hold that it was founded in 1792 as a traditional madrasa by
Nawab Ghazi ud din II' (Pernau 2003: lxiii). However, Ghaziuddin Khan II had
died forty years earlier. Carr Stephen, although mistakenly referring to the founder
of the Madrasa as the 'son of Nizam-ul Mulk', is more accurate in identifying
him as 'one of the leading Amirs of the court of Aurangzeb and of his son and
successor, Shah Alam Bahadur Shah. He built this mausoleum during his lifetime
and . . . his death occurred at Ahmedabad in 1122 AH [AD 1710]' (Stephen [1876]
2002: 263).

Not much is known about the progress of the Madrasa from the early
1700s onwards, although Firuz Jung's name has been 'associated with a college
which he founded in Delhi about 1711', and the Madrasas Ghaziuddin,
Sharafuddaula and Raushanuddaula were identified as 'three noteworthy educational institutions flourishing in Delhi under private patronage' during the reign
of Bahadur Shah I (Jafar 1936: 140–41). Delhi passed through terrible upheavals
during the ensuing period. Seven bloody battles of succession were fought between his descendants in the thirteen years following the death of Aurangzeb,
weakening the grand empire of the Mughals. The Maratha standards were seen
outside the city walls for the first time in 1719 and they repeatedly attacked the
city in the coming decades. In 1739 Nadir Shah's soldiers ravaged Delhi, followed by Ahmed Shah Abdalli in 1757 and Ghulam Qadir Rohilla in 1787. The
Marathas eventually defeated the latter, restored Emperor Shah Alam II to the
throne and occupied Delhi themselves.

Not surprisingly, the Madrasa is said to have closed for 'want of funds' in the early 1790s.[2] As a traditional Madrasa it had offered conventional Islamic education, and fresh resources and support led to a speedy revival. Instruction was provided in prose, literature, rhetoric, logic, philosophy, jurisprudence, astrology and medicine.[3] The *Punjab Gazetteer, Delhi District 1883–84*, reports that it 'was originally a college for the education of Musalmans in Oriental literature, science and art, and was established in Delhi in 1792, and supported by subscriptions from the wealthy residents of Delhi belonging to that creed'.[4] This report has often been taken to confirm 1792 as the date of origin of Madrasa Ghaziuddin, but the high noble status of its founder makes it unlikely that its establishment would have been left dependent on public subscriptions, and that too some eight decades after his death.

In 1803 Lord Lake captured Delhi, rescuing Shah Alam from the Marathas and bringing him under the East India Company's 'protection'. Delhi's population, which had reportedly been about 15 lakhs in its days of greatness, was hardly 2 lakhs when the British captured the city. British administrators found that the complex of Madrasa Ghaziuddin, located outside the city walls and fortification, served as a convenient headquarters for the Marathas who continued for some time to threaten British control over the city.[5] Decades later, a report to the Commissioner and Superintendent, Delhi Division, stated that

> when it first passed into the hands of the British Government, orders were passed for its destruction, but the British finding the work of destruction costly owing to the solidity of the Masonry and the building also being one of great beauty, settled on maintaining it and including it within the city wall and ditch.[6]

In 1824, when the oriental Madrasa was made the foundation of a superior college by the East India Company, it comprised nine students and a single teacher, Maulvi Abdullah. The decline was symptomatic of a widespread malaise: 'a number of private schools existed, which had been established, as was customary among the Muhomedans, from benevolent motives. . . . The Teachers received no fixed remuneration. They derived their support entirely from presents tendered and accepted as such. . . . It appeared that several public educational Institutions had formerly existed, the whole of which had fallen into a state of "deplorable neglect". The funds for their support had been swept away during the political changes that had taken place, and were now almost wholly beyond the reach of recovery.'[7]

The East India Company launched the project of providing Anglo-Oriental education by opening colleges at Delhi and Agra. Oriental learning was undertaken together with modern scientific education. English was cautiously and selectively introduced. The notion that European sciences and arts should be gradually 'engrafted' on to traditional education lay at the heart of the Company's education policy during the 1820s. This approach, based on the notion of education as the provision of 'useful knowledge', reflected the growing confidence of the British, and can be distinguished from the early orientalist strategy adopted by the Company in the late eighteenth century when the Calcutta Madrasa for instruction in Arabic and Persian was established by Warren Hastings in 1781, and the Benaras Sanskrit College by Jonathan Duncan in 1791. Aware of the fragile base of British power in India, Hastings had preferred to rely on the presence of an elite corps of acculturated British officials, who, through their knowledge and sympathetic understanding of Indian institutions, laws and customs, would exercise power in the manner of traditional Indian rulers.

The General Committee of Public Instruction at Calcutta issued a circular calling for proposals to spread education and enquiring about available resources. The local Agents at Delhi responded with the suggestion that a college could be started, and Rs 3,500 per annum could be locally mobilized for the purpose out of the revenue 'realized from the rent of Lawaries, Escheats and Waqf lands and tenements'.[8] The reply concluded with an eloquent appeal to the members of the Committee to

> recognize Delhi as the once splendid metropolis of this vast empire, celebrated as the chief patroness of the arts and the sciences throughout the eastern quarter of the globe, crowded by the youth of her flourishing dominions, resorting to her as the nursery of oriental literature, and sending forth from her classic soil those poets and philosophers who to this day adorn the pages of her annals, and place before their imagination the wreck of so many Academic Institutions, most assuredly those remains of the princely munificence bestowed on the cultivation of letters all desolate and in ruins, those venerable monuments of the learning of an age gone by now mouldering into decay, will awaken the sympathy of your Committee, . . . and secure to Delhi her portion of the boon set aside by the beneficence of the Government.[9]

Accordingly, Delhi College was started with J.H. Taylor as its Secretary and Superintendent.[10] A sum of Rs 7,115 was utilized from the Town Duty Fund in 1824 for repairing the Madrasa, 'an edifice of great beauty and celebrity'.[11]

The Committee of Public Instruction fixed the grant for the College at Rs 3,000 per annum. In response to Taylor's appeal for increased funding, a further sum of Rs 250 per mensem would be provided two years later 'as a fixed money equivalent for the receipts available for education under the head of Waqf and Lawaries property at Delhie'.[12] Apart from Taylor, who received a salary of Rs 175 a month, there was a Head Maulvi who received Rs 120 and two other Maulvis who were paid Rs 50 a month. The rest were employed at salaries of Rs 25 to 30. The College started admitting pupils in 1825. Unlike the Sanskrit College at Benaras, admission to the Delhi and Agra Colleges was unrestricted and open to members of all communities.[13] Initially, instruction was imparted chiefly in Persian and Arabic. There was also a Sanskrit department.

On the advice of the local Agents, students were given stipends as was customary in indigenous schools, and the number of stipendiary students rose from forty-nine with an allowance of 3 rupees in the first year, to 80 in the second year. By 1828, 209 students received stipends with those in the junior classes getting from 1 to 3 rupees, while senior students received from 4 to 6 rupees.[14] At the time, following the indigenous system of organization of instruction, a college contained classes in which the alphabet was taught under the same roof with pupils reading advanced texts. 'Except that there were forty or fifty advanced students, and that its discipline was more perfect, it did not differ from the secondary schools which sprang up between 1820 and 1854 in the more important towns, such as Allahabad, Meerut and Bareli.'[15] In 1845, the Principal, the renowned orientalist Dr Alois Sprenger, suggested dispensing with some of the junior classes by establishing a preparatory school for those wishing to enter the higher level, and there was even some talk of discontinuing junior classes altogether. These suggestions were rejected but, from 1846 onwards, junior fellowships were 'freely thrown open to out-candidates, no distinction being made between them and the College students. Intimation of the Annual Examination is publicly given to the students of private schools.'[16] The scheme attracted talented aspirants, and in 1848–49, 62 out-candidates competed for scholarships in Persian and thirty-two for those in Sanskrit.

The 'study of astronomy and mathematics on European principles' was introduced alongside the Oriental sciences in 1827, and was enthusiastically received by teachers and students of the college.[17] Instruction was provided in Urdu, the vernacular, and lecture notes were extensively circulated to compensate for the absence of adequate textbooks. 'Though the syllabus and interests of the major intellectual centres of the north and west became . . . less susceptible to European influences after 1857, in the early nineteenth century they still remained avid for the new learning, especially in astronomy, medicine and chemistry' (Bayly 1999: 139).

In 1828, an English class open to all students of the College was started under orders from Charles Metcalfe, the Resident at Delhi, causing much consternation among the local population amidst fears of conversions to Christianity.[18] The initiation of the English section led to a marked decline in the intake of pupils. Numbering 204 in 1827, the student strength, which had risen to 209, dropped to 199 during 1828 and 152 in 1829.[19] Educated Hindus and Muslims of the city 'were worried that this might be an indication of the intention of the Government to depart from its policy of patronizing oriental learning and holding up religious neutrality'.[20] The agitation among Delhi citizens was not with foundation. The evangelical movement, which became increasingly influential in the Company, Parliament and British public life towards the last decade of the eighteenth century, was at the forefront of the campaign to anglicize Indian education and society. The authorities were urged to introduce English as the language of government and to set up free schools for providing instruction in the language. Proposals to open India to the proselytizing and educational activities of missionary societies were rejected by Parliament in 1793 when the Company's charter came up for renewal, but gained a significant foothold twenty years later with the inclusion of a clause legalizing missionary activity in British India.

An endowment by a prominent Muslim nobleman, Nawab Itmaduddaulah, the Oudh Vazir, specifically for the Oriental section of the College, seems to have allayed anxieties at Delhi. According to Dr H.W. Wilson's Report of 1831, 'it was subsequently considered expedient to separate the establishment and found a distinct English Seminary (although under the control of the Oriental College Committee and its Superintendent), which was accordingly done in August, 1829'. J.R. Colvin's *Note* of 1840 is more explicit: 'in 1829, when the large accession of funds was obtained through the Nawab's grant, the English class was separated from the Muhammadan or Oriental College'.[21] The Delhi Institute, as the English section was known, would remain a distinct seminary until 1844.

A tablet set in the wall of Ghaziuddin Khan's tomb some years later commemorates the munificence, and states that Nawab Itmaduddaulah Ziaul-Mulk Sayyid Fazli Ali Khan Bahadur Suhrab Jung 'entrusted the Honourable English East India Company with one lakh and seventy thousand rupees for the advancement of learning at this school'.[22] The Nawab's Will of 1830 clarified that the endowment was for the institution

> which the late Ghaziuddin Khan had established in Delhi, my native place, for the development and teaching of Arabic and Persian, which are the disciplines of my religion and the fountainheads of morality. The income accruing from the endowment is to be used for the welfare of the students and teachers.[23]

The endowment apparently helped the College to win back local allegiance and, aided by the many scholarships that could now be provided, it began to attract students from all over north India.

Following a visit to the 'college of Ghazeeood Deen', a prominent British official observed:

> Perhaps there are few communities in the world, among whom education is more generally diffused than among Mohomedans in India. He who holds an office worth twenty rupees a month, commonly gives his sons an education equal to that of a prime minister. They learn through the medium of the Arabic and Persian languages, what young men in our colleges learn through those of the Greek and Latin – that is, grammar, rhetoric and logic. After his seven years of study, the young Mahomedan binds his turban upon a head almost as filled with the things which appertain to these three branches of knowledge, as the young man raw from Oxford – he will talk as fluently about Socrates and Aristotle, Plato and Hippocrates, Galen and Avicenna, alias Socrate, Aristotalees, Aflaton, Bocrate, Jaleenoos, and Booalee Sehna, and what is much to his advantage in India, the languages in which he has learnt what he knows are those which he most requires in life. He thinks himself as well fitted to fill the high offices which are now filled exclusively by Europeans, and naturally enough wishes the establishments of that power would open them to him. (Sleeman 1844: 283–84)

This glowing contemporary account is supported by later official reports:

At this time (1829), the Delhi College was the best institution of its kind then existing in the N.W. Provinces. . . . Its range of study was as high as that of the present (1877) M.A. Degree of the Calcutta University. In the Oriental Department the standard was the same as that recently adopted by the Punjab University College for its higher examinations. It rendered distinguished service for the country by training young men for Government Services.[24]

It is, however, at variance with the views expressed a decade later by James Thomason, then Visitor of the Oriental Colleges of the North-Western Provinces, to whom the Bengal Committee of Public Instruction entrusted the general superintendence of the Colleges at Agra and Delhi, and requested reports on 'such changes as might be necessary'. The Delhi College was cause for special concern due to the persistent complaints of mismanagement by Syed Hamid Ali Khan, son-in-law of the donor of the large endowment to the College. Thomason's Minute of 8 April 1841 stated that the attainments of the students of Delhi College were 'very low'. The discrepancy can be explained by the fact that Thomason's reference is to the impact of the government's policy of withdrawing stipends for Oriental learning after 1835. A majority of the students could not progress beyond the elementary level in the Arabic, Persian and Sanskrit departments.

> There are on the list 75 students of the Arabic and Persian languages and 24 Sanscrit scholars. This number is however nominal. Many are absent and have been so for a considerable period whilst the attendance of those who are said to be present is very irregular and uncertain; several attend only for an hour or two in the morning and are then compelled for the remainder of the day to occupy themselves in some other employment which will serve to support them. Their attainments as may be supposed are very low.[25]

That Thomason's concern was primarily focused on policy can be seen from his complaint that the College 'has now been in existence only 16 years and during that time numerous plans and systems have been successively tried, more especially as regards the means for drawing students and attaching them to it'. The discontinuation of stipends and scholarships had, in his opinion, caused 'the College to sink to its lowest state'. The solution he offered, since 'it seems now to be the wish to *restore* the College to efficiency as rapidly as possible', was to reintroduce stipends for as many students as possible, and only then reward the progress they could be expected to make with merit scholarships. Thomason would in fact incur the displeasure of the General Committee of Public Instruction and the Governor-General by unilaterally implementing this decision and notifying it to the public in the Urdu Gazette.[26]

Defending his action, Thomason drew attention to the importance of the College for British initiatives to succeed in Indian education, and argued that a departure from the policy being adopted elsewhere was warranted.

The Oriental College at Delhi has been the subject of much discussion. It occupies a prominent part in the eyes of a large and influential body of the native community, whom it is most important to convince of our liberality and sincerity. Special measures had been adopted for the restoration of the College, and the inducement held out to all connected with the College to exert themselves to the utmost. Those hopes had not been disappointed. Great and successful exertions had been made and these it would be unjust and unwise to disappoint.[27]

Delhi College 'was a unique institution where the Oriental literatures of the madrasa regimen and a Western-style curriculum were both taught through the medium of Urdu' (Minnault 2005: 115). Development of Urdu as the principal medium of instruction was the defining feature of the College. Persian gradually became 'secondary in importance to the vernacular, through which Science, Philosophy and Mathematics were taught'.[28] This was so not only for Oriental learning, but also for the study of the European sciences. Drawing on personal accounts provided by Zaka Ullah (1832–1910), C.F. Andrews testifies to the way in which the initiative sustained itself. 'In the first instance a single English book was taken by the pupils themselves and translated page after page into Urdu and then revised by the college staff. Written copies of these translations were handed round, or dictated, and thus the New Learning spread' (Andrews 2003: 44).

The refined and Persianized form of the language of north India, enriched by popular and regional variations, evolved into the highly flexible and accessible vernacular, Urdu or Hindustani.

> There was a particular variant for the use of women, for court camp and army, for local officials and village registrar. Particular professions, sub-castes and even bands of criminals had their own argot. Sometimes the specific blend of language forms could be used to exclude and monopolize. This, for instance, was the claim commonly made about court and bazaar writers. But the abiding impression is of linguistic plurality running through the whole society and an easier adaptation to circumstances in both spoken and written speech. (Bayly 1999: 193)

The turn towards Urdu in the courts and camps of north India in the eighteenth and nineteenth centuries represented, according to Bayly, 'a deliberate populist strategy on the part of the elite'. It both facilitated and was encouraged by the socio-political changes that were taking place. The gradual disintegration of the weakened Mughal empire led to a sharpening of debate between the Shias, Sunnis and Hindus. Its range extended well beyond doctrinal principles to political, social and ethnic issues.[29] The polemic deepened after 1750 as Shia or Sunni influence alternately grew or declined at Delhi. There was also a strong historical basis for this rigorous debate. The north Indian elite had

> their own tradition of cultural re-examination and reform. This tradition went back to the work of Shah Waliullah of Delhi in the eighteenth century, or perhaps further back to Sheikh Ahmed Sirhindi and Abdul Haqq Muhaddith

Dehlavi in the seventeen century.[30] The Madrasa-e-Rahimiya in Delhi carried on the work of Walliullah's line of scholar-sufis who sought . . . to re-examine the sources of the faith . . . for new sources of strength and inspiration, both political and religious. (Minnault 1986: 289–90)

The Delhi Sunnis, led by Shah Walliullah's son Shah Abdul Aziz and the Lucknow Shia institution of Maulana Dildar Ali, consolidated their following and refuted their opponents through campaigns of public debate and exchange of tracts. In both cities the contest converged with the disputes between rationalist Islamic purists of both sects and their more conservative co-religionists.[31] The religious conferences, public disputation and pamphleteering that ensued 'were governed by certain standards of conduct which implicitly acknowledged the existence of a critical public sphere'.[32]

The popular base of this 'critical public sphere' was strengthened because Urdu or Hindustani had taken on the character of the public tongue of learned elites. Spread among the people by the Sufi scholar-saints, it was also the language of the court and the discerning literati. Bayly is emphatic in concluding that

doctrinal debate and campaigns of purification amongst urban citizens there-fore preceded and accompanied the Christian missionary and the 'reform' cam-paigns of the early nineteenth century. . . . Missionaries were often surprised by the vehemence with which not only religious teachers, but also local officers, *thanadars* (superintendents) and kotwals, engaged them in debate. . . . In the 1830s the Muslim police chief of Buxar, for example, revealed to a passing missionary that he had often put a stop to widow burnings within his jurisdic-tion and denounced the Company for cowardice in failing to confront the issue.[33]

Doubts have been cast on the question of linguistic allegiance and its relevance to a sense of 'community' in pre-colonial India. The dominance of the nineteenth-century European preoccupation with language as the socially cemen-ting bond of races or nations situated in set territorial locations, has resulted in underestimating the importance of pre-modern linguistic identities.[34] 'Although peasants may not have consciously named the language they spoke, poets and scribes were indisputably aware of their linguistic heritage, as were the wealthy patrons who financed their literary production. In pre-colonial India, as in other pre-modern societies, social identities were most strongly developed among the privileged' (Talbot 2003: 102). Throughout the nineteenth and well into the twen-tieth century, the multi-denominational and multi-racial 'community' that evolved around Urdu in parts of north India would not merely display its brilliance, but also repeatedly demonstrate its awareness of constituting a particular linguistic culture.

Delhi College was an integral and significant part of this culture and its history. The surprising longevity of the shared linguistic, cultural and service traditions of the north Indian elite which held through till the first quarter of the twentieth century, has been attributed initially to 'the strength of the tradition (Mughal court culture)' following the acceptance of Persian, the court language, by the Hindu elite as early as the fifteenth century. However, by the nineteenth century this strength was seen to lie elsewhere. The Urdu vernacular, which replaced Persian as the language of the courts and government offices in the 1830s, became a dynamic instrument for strengthening anew the bonds among the elite. 'Many of them were graduates of Delhi College, who for all their fluency in English and familiarity with the Europeans, continued to publicly defend and privately treasure that cultural heritage' (Sender 1986: 329).

In the early nineteenth century, Delhi College became the focus of the composite urbanity that characterized the premier city of north India.

> In the years before 1857, in sharp contrast to the subsequent period, relations between the prominent Indians of the town and the British officials were char-acterized by an easy conviviality, because Englishmen as well as Muslim umara and Hindu kayasths and khatris all subscribed to the vibrant Urdu culture and etiquette. (Gupta 1981: 8)

From the 1830s onwards, *mushairas* convened by Munshi Faiz 'Pursa', poet and mathematics teacher at Delhi College, were held fortnightly or monthly at the Madrasa Ghaziuddin.[35] Ajmeri Gate would be left open till late into the night to facilitate attendance of the city's residents. The practice of holding poetic assem-blies not only at the court, but also in homes, public institutions and even in bazaars, popularized aesthetic standards and forms of language. By the 1840s, proponents of Urdu 'were often less consciously aristocratic than the champions of Persian and were more influenced by Indian forms' (Bayly 1999: 195).

Aided by the establishment of the first Indian press for Persian and Urdu lithography, and the publication of some of India's first Urdu newspapers and journals, Delhi College, its teachers and students became the centre of a scientific and literary flowering, referred to as the 'Delhi Renaissance' by C.F. Andrews.[36] The weekly *Delhi Urdu Akhbar*, probably the first printed Urdu newspaper, ap-peared in early 1837 and survived till 1857. The paper and its lithographic press, a successful enterprise located at their Kashmiri Gate residence, were associated with the family of the learned Shia Maulvi Muhammad Akbar. His son, Maulvi Muhammad Baqir (1810–1857), a tehsildar before he turned to journalism, was long-time editor and, for a while, manager of the newspaper. Its printer and pub-lisher was Pandit Motilal who had been educated at Delhi College. Muhammad Baqir's son, Muhammad Husain 'Azad', who was also educated at Delhi Col-lege, worked with his father at the paper in the 1850s. Delhi College received attention in the paper even prior to Baqir's son becoming a student. Maulvi Baqir's press published textbooks and translations for the College before it set up its own press in the mid-1840s. In 1857 the paper backed the Revolt, and when Delhi was retaken by the British, Muhammad Baqir was among those who were executed.[37]

Among the earliest Delhi College graduates to excel were the munshis Mohanlal and Shahamat Ali, who would later become prime minister of Indore,[38] and Master Ramchandra, whose brilliant record as a student was followed by an equally successful career as professor of mathematics in the vernacular section of the college, and as author and translator of significant mathematical texts. A distinguished group of alumni followed – the founder of the Muhammadan Anglo-Oriental school and college at Aligarh, Sayyid Ahmed Khan, apparently as a private student of Mamluk Ali; mathematician and historian Zakaullah; leading Urdu prose writer and novelist Nazir Ahmed; Mukund Lal, one of the first highly reputed doctors in northwest India to be trained in western medicine; the renowned Urdu litterateurs Ziauddin and Muhammad Husain 'Azad'; the Kashmiri pandit Motilal Dehlavi, later to be appointed translator of Persian texts at Lahore; Maulvi Karimuddin, who authored several literary biographies; and Munshi Pyare Lal 'Ashob'.[39] The renowned poet Altaf Husain 'Hali', who taught Persian at the Anglo-Arabic School, was a prominent member of the Delhi College circle. This 'rapid efflorescence of men's minds . . . represented the renaissance in the north of India'.[40]

These intellectuals were characteristically prolific over a wide range of subject matter, extending from mathematics and science to literature and the values and norms of civilized conduct. Their conception of their work was evident in the style and content of their writing. They saw themselves as *educators* and were dedicated to the spread of education in the vernacular, although many of them occupied administrative positions with the British at different stages in their careers.

> The thinking of Delhi renaissance men can best be understood in relation to their attitude toward vernacular education . . . . Though most had a traditional education, they came into contact with western ideas in translation in their lives. They were not averse to learning English, but saw it as a subsidiary subject in a revised vernacular curriculum.[41]

They founded schools, wrote books and textbooks, translated works into Urdu, and edited journals. Conversion to Christianity did not make Master Ramchandra desert Urdu and Delhi's cosmopolitan culture. He edited two of the city's earliest Urdu newspapers – the *Fawaid-ul-Nazarin* for general readers and the *Kiran-us-Sadai* which was devoted to scientific subjects. His opposition to Macaulay's Minute on Education is evident in the title given to a translation published in July 1847, *Dekhiye Hindustan ke dinen kab phirenge?* (When will Hindustan's days of greatness return?). As authors and scholars, Delhi College alumni fostered the development of Urdu as the lingua franca of northern India.

Distinctively modern in their outlook and often impatient with ancient dogmas and irrational religious observance, they nevertheless nurtured the awareness that the 'new learning' should be used for rejuvenating and strengthening their own society. Master Ramchandra's articles in Urdu aimed not only at scientifically demolishing the popular superstition and theological dogma 'generally laughed at by advanced students' of both sections of the College, but at enabling Indians to make the achievements of science their own.[42] The commitment to Urdu, the vernacular and hence more natural medium of instruction, for acquiring scientific knowledge underlines this concern; 'for Ramchandra and the generation of Indian scientists that followed, science not only offered itself as a catalyst of change in the nineteenth century, but also served as a weapon in the still nebulous struggle' against an imperial power whose contours were yet to be fully articulated (Raina and Habib 2004: 14). The use of *begamati zuban*, the language of women, and the focus on women's education by both Nazir Ahmed and 'Hali', were similarly symptomatic. The former saw women as true managers of the family, and feared that the decline of vernacular education would result in their capabilities and influence being undermined both in society and in the home. 'Hali' emphasized the socio-cultural role of women in a colonial situation. As economic considerations pushed men towards acquiring the cultural trappings of British education, women as channels of a cultural continuity played a significant part in instilling self-confidence in the younger generation through the training they received at home.

This was clearly a turning point in the educational and cultural life not only of Delhi but all of north India. The intellectual history of the time was one of ambivalences. The desire to acquire western scientific knowledge was juxtaposed with fears of its detrimental impact on religious beliefs, customs and values. Mirza Abu Taleb, the Lucknow munshi who was one of the earliest educated Indians to travel in Asia, Africa and Europe between 1799 and 1803, was of the opinion that many of the customs, inventions, sciences and ordinances of Europe, the good effects of which were apparent in those countries, might with great advantage be imitated by Muslims as they were not 'inconsistent with or opposed to the laws of Islam'. Yet he was highly critical of the English for want of religious faith, for their pride, insolence and an unseemly passion for acquiring money (Mujeeb 1967: 494). Such anxieties were neither unique to north India nor specific to the Muslim community. The patriotic Henry Derozio, poet and assistant headmaster of Calcutta's forward-looking Hindu College (now Presidency College) was dismissed in 1831 for criticizing Hindu customs and espousing heretic views. Even that ardent enthusiast of modernization and western education, Raja Ram Mohan Roy, was embroiled in theological controversy, penning under a pseudonym, 'a vindication of Hindu religion against the attacks of Christian missionaries' in 1823.[43]

> The early years of the nineteenth century were a transitional time for Delhi, a time when two worlds co-existed, their antithetical natures not yet fully evident. This period came to be recalled and idealized as the Delhi Renaissance; years of exceptional prosperity and what, in retrospect, appeared exceptional communal harmony.[44]

The Delhi Renaissance 'achieved something which was qualitatively very different from the contemporary Calcutta "Renaissance". Delhi had a well-defined and broad-based school curriculum and a native language. On to this were grafted European philosophy and science' (Gupta 1981: 6). C.F. Andrews states that, 'by far the most popular side of the education offered in the Old Delhi College was that which dealt with science. Here the interest was paramount, and it soon extended into the homes of the students within the city, where the new experiments would be repeated.' Recalling first-hand accounts given by Maulvi Zaka-ullah, he writes of

> how eagerly these scientific lectures were followed, and how, after each lecture, the notes used to be studied, over and over again, and copied out by many hands. It was like entering into a wholly undiscovered hemisphere of the human mind. The young students were also taught by enthusiastic teachers. They were allowed to try astonishing experiments . . . [and] invited to dip into the mysteries of magnetism. (Andrews 2003: 46)

The Frenchman Felix Boutros, Principal of Delhi College from 1839 to 1845, outlined the perspective that emerged from this experience.

> To be desirous of receiving what in India is frequently called an English education – that is, instruction in the sciences of modern Europe, – is very different from a desire to learn English. The wealthy classes of the Mofussil are more anxious about the former than the latter, . . . From all the inquiries I have made among Pandits and Moulvies, there is apparently no objection on their part to have the treasures of European knowledge communicated to them through Vernacular class books, without any reference to their sacred languages. Besides, this proposed connexion between science and Religious authorities, particularly when no such connexion is absolutely necessary, is, I think, objectionable on several grounds, and might become inconvenient.[45]

During Boutros's tenure as Principal, the Oriental section of the College extended instruction in Urdu not just in mathematics, philosophy and the sciences, but also in history, geography and law. 'The subjects expressly mentioned are Arithmetic, Geometry, Algebra, Natural Philosophy, Geography, History of India, Political Economy and Jurisprudence.'[46] The policy was continued with the same dedication by his German successor, Dr Sprenger. This bold and revolutionary step opened wide the intellectual horizons of the students and teachers to modern education, and Urdu rapidly developed as a vehicle of modern ideas and education. The policy was favourably reviewed in the Annual Reports of the General Committee of Public Instruction based in Calcutta.

> There is one feature by which Delhi College has been for many years distinguished from all the other Colleges both in the Upper and Lower Provinces, namely in the extent to which instruction is communicated through the medium of the vernacular language. This applies particularly to the subject of Mathematics in all its branches, and in a somewhat lesser degree to history and moral Science. This plan was steadily acted upon by Mr Boutros . . . [and] continued

with equal zeal by his successor Dr Sprenger; and it is now recognized as part of the established system of instruction at Delhi. It is very desirable to allow this system to develop itself freely. After some years, we shall be able to compare its results with those of other systems.[47]

In 1852, Principal Cargill acknowledged in his Annual Report that, on the basis of classroom lectures and translations from works in English and Persian, the

students of the Oriental Section are much ahead of the students of the Western or English Section in Knowledge of Science.[48] Recently some distinguished educationalists, which included some highly knowledgeable military officers and some deeply experienced teachers, came on an inspection visit to this college. They tested the students of the Oriental section in Science, Astronomy, Ethics and other subjects during conversation, and came to the conclusion that this Section had made remarkable progress. They also expressed the view that there was no such arrangement anywhere in India to teach Western modern subjects in the vernacular, Urdu. (Quoted in Ali 1999: 11)

In 1853–54, the Resolution on the General Report on Public Instruction, listing enquiries and observations following an 'inspection of the most important institutions of education in the North-Western Provinces', stated that 'Dr Mouat, . . . speaks highly of the amount of scientific instruction communicated at the Delhi College through Treatises in Oordoo.'[49]

The policy of imparting education in the vernacular received a great impetus after Delhi came under the control of Agra, capital of the North-Western Provinces, in 1840. Thomason, who became the Lieutenant-Governor in 1843, responded to differences in conditions prevailing in Delhi, Agra and Oudh from those found at Calcutta,[50] and established a network of Urdu-medium schools. Reacting favourably to the widespread circulation of books by agents of 'native' presses that had sprung up in the region, he noted: 'the native mind in this part of the country is undoubtedly making great advances now. A popular and useful Oordoo literature is now forming . . . and it is becoming the vehicle for conveying practical and useful knowledge to all classes of the people.'[51] Thomason's enthusiasm for the promotion of 'useful knowledge'[52] led him to advocate a restructuring of the indigenous system of imparting education. He claimed that it was both a waste of time and of limited funds for the College to provide

instruction in the elements of the vernacular languages [which] can easily be obtained outside the walls of the College, and its attainment is daily becoming more easy. Simple Reading, Writing and Arithmetic according to the Native system as far as Division, are taught by the Natives themselves in a way which England adopted from them and designated its national system. . . . The desireable object would be to take up the best Native boys at this point and give them a superior education in the branches of learning in which we wish them to excel.[53]

Delhi College had already set up a Vernacular Society in 1832 for the translation of scientific treatises, Greek classics and Persian works into Urdu. Norms for translation were laid down and translators were paid from 6 to 12 annas per page, depending on the nature of the book. Maulvi Abdul Haq has provided an impressive list of 128 books translated and published by the Society within the space of two decades.[54] Its remarkable achievements were supplemented by the Society for the Promotion of Knowledge in India through the vernacular. Felix Boutros, Thomas Metcalfe and Dwarkanath Tagore were prominent among its executive committee members.

The success of the policy of instruction in Urdu medium had the added benefit of laying to rest the suspicions of the local people about Anglo-Oriental education. Students flocked to the College. In 1840, following the withdrawal of stipends, the number was 166; five years later, when Boutros left the College, student strength had risen to 460, of which 418 were in the Oriental section while 245 students were also learning the English language. C.F. Andrews's claim that the English section had demonstrated its popularity by 1831 as 300 students were enrolled in that section, was contested by Maulvi Abdul Haq who pointed out that this was the total strength of both sections in that year (Haq 1989: 21n). However, both appear to be well off the mark. The first report of the General Committee of Public Instruction of December 1831 includes a table of the number of pupils and the cost per annum of the fourteen colleges under its superintendence. It shows that Delhi College, that is, the Oriental section, had 309 students at a cost per annum of Rs 16,800, while the English section had 100 students at a cost per annum of Rs 9,600 (table provided in Howell 1872: 22). Detailed records (provided in *Public Instruction in Bengal*, Part II, p. 202) show that in 1833, a total of 279 students were in the Oriental college, and 152 students (the Secretary's Annual Report, p. 200, scales this down to 116 students) in the English institution. The Secretary's Report (p. 206) notes that 'no place has been found in the foregoing statements for the number of students who are reading Urdu. It may be sufficient to mention that it comprehends nearly all of every class who are attending the College.' Even as late as 1837, 91 students were enrolled in Arabic and Persian, and 32 in the Sanskrit department and 84 students in the English section.[55]

The demographic composition of the student body was equally significant. It demonstrates that Delhi College was an institution answering to the needs of the city as a whole and not only serving students of a particular denomination. The 460 students in 1845 included 299 Hindus, 146 Muslims and 15 Christians.[56]

The educational reports throughout the college's history show that inspite of some leading Muslim scholars on the staff, and occasional examples of lavish Muslim patronage, the founder's original intention of attracting to its classrooms the sons of the displaced Muslim elites had never really been fulfilled. Although the Muslim students made up 44 per cent of the roll in 1833–36, a higher proportion [than] for any government college in north India. [57]

Whether this was indeed the intention of the founder is open to question. Hamid Ali Khan, son-in-law of Nawab Itmaduddaulah, tried to exercise greater control over the institution after 1835, protesting that the government's policy of discontinuing stipends for Arabic and Persian, and promoting English at the expense of classical oriental learning, ran counter to the intentions of the benefactor of the institution. Stopping stipends would prevent 'the children of the poor' from getting the education for which the nobility traditionally donated funds. Further, Hamid Ali charged that the College management was incompetent to handle an institute of oriental learning and that funds were being mismanaged. Taylor's removal and the appointment of persons of the stature of Boutros and Sprenger were obviously aimed at countering the Nawab's charge. The question of financial mismanagement proved intractable and indeed the Itmaduddaulah Fund was not used to augment government funds but to permit transfer of the latter to the English institution, while the common management costs and the principal's salary were taken solely from the Fund. To support his demand for a greater role in the superintendence of the College, Hamid Ali claimed that the Nawab's objective had been the utilization of the endowment solely or primarily for the minority Shias of Delhi, an interest that he, as a member of the sect, was expressly qualified to protect. The claim was not sustained by any written evidence, and would meet with determined resistance from the Delhi elite, including Shias, Sunnis and Hindus, when it was used later to divert funds from Delhi College. The attempt to interpret the terms of the endowment to restrict its use only for educating Muslim students would be selectively exploited by the Committee of Public Instruction. 'The application of the endowment was the subject of much discussion; but it was finally resolved by the Committee that the Delhi College should be made an efficient institution of Muhammadan learning. This resolution was not, however, carried into effect. . . . The Delhi College always attracted a large preponderance of Hindus' (*Report of the Education Commission, 1882*, Chapter II, p. 21). Hamid Ali Khan's appeal to the Supreme Government ultimately received a favourable response from Lord Mayo. The Anglo-Arabic School, attended almost exclusively by Muslims, was founded in 1872 and a substantial part of the Itmaduddaulah Fund was transferred from Delhi College. This was just five years before the imperial government, citing lack of funds as the principal reason, decided to abolish Delhi College.

The study of English language, literature and philosophy did not thrive at Delhi College. 'Old Delhi College was in full flourish, but, in the society in which I was raised, knowledge was linked only with Arabic and Persian. English education, on the contrary, was not seriously regarded as learning. At the madrasa in which I was educated, teachers and students alike regarded their counterparts in the College as ignoramuses. In the one-and-a-half years that I spent in Delhi, I never visited the College or interacted with its students' (Altaf Husain Hali, *Maqaalat-e-Hali*, Vol. 1, p. 264, quoted in Haq 1989: 18). Hali would also caustically comment that 'we regarded English as a means of getting a job, not an education' (quoted in Gupta 1981: 7). Most students pursued literary studies in

Arabic and Persian, which had become very popular due to instruction in the Urdu medium, with the Maulvis Mamluk Ali and Imam Baksh of the Oriental section.[58]

All the same, Delhi renaissance men served the British administration as officials, judges and teachers, and as inspectors in the Education Department. The early establishment of Delhi College, an institution that attracted the traditional elite and also provided for familiarity with English, made it the 'most crucial' of all institutions with which the British were associated. 'As an instrument of transition and transformation, . . . like the city itself, the College preserved one cultural heritage while gradually introducing a new one' (Sender 1986: 324). The claims of its alumni for administrative positions and key employment as munshis and translators attached to British officials and various Company offices, were favoured by English officials.

However, if relations formed at the College led to close personal bonds with British patrons, they also served 'to strengthen the ties of members of the traditional service class at a time when the weakening of the court culture contributed to a lessening of those ties in other realms' (ibid.: 325). The significance of this ambivalence and the multi-layered perceptions of the role of Delhi College by its alumni, by Delhi's learned elite and by British administrators, are central to understanding the importance of the College. Delhi College was an institution established in accordance with the Company's anglo-vernacular educational policies and controlled by the Company administration; yet, even the British recognized the importance of its claim to traditional legitimacy and celebrity. 'The state of the population at Delhi and Agra is very different. At Delhi there is a large, intelligent, haughty but indigent Muslim population, well able to profit by instruction and capable of estimating its value. . . . (Agra College) works on a less educated and intelligent people than the Delhi College.'[59] The British were never entirely comfortable with the institution, and their discomfort often bordered on suspicious hostility. The College alumni, for their part, cultivated an intellectual independence frequently verging on arrogance, which sat uneasily with their dependence on the British government for stipends and employment. The parallel with the city and its genteel classes was undeniable and it is little wonder that they regarded the institution as their own.

In 1844 the College was shifted to the 'more commodious' Residency at Kashmiri Gate.[60] There were, of course, other considerations.

> Ghazee-ood-deen's Madrassah, where the College is at present fixed, is an imposing building, and not ill adapted simply for a Native Institution. It is however unfortunately situated far from the European station, and cannot without difficulty and expense be rendered suitable for the accommodation of the English Institution. It is of the greatest importance that the two should be brought together to the same place. Both will then be immediately and constantly under the eye of the Principal, and great facilities will thus be afforded for the acquisition of Oriental and English learning, which may be expected to exercise a

salutary influence over the former. The Executive Engineer is deliberating with the Principal on the best means of altering the building, so as to adapt it for the reception of the English Institution. If it ultimately prove that this cannot be done, I am of the opinion that it would be better to desert Ghazee-ood-deen's Madrassah.[61]

However, the Madrasa complex remained under the control of the College Principal, being used as a dispensary and also as a hostel from time to time (Ahmed 1919: 267).

The Oriental and English divisions of Delhi College, originally quite distinct in character and curriculum, were later organized as 'two strictly parallel sections'. 'In pursuance of this object, the students of the two departments were in 1843 examined, to a certain extent, in the same subjects and from the same Questions, and with a result not unfavourable, it was said, to the Oriental department.'[62] Delhi College had been established a decade before Macaulay, then heading the General Committee of Public Instruction, presented his infamous Minute on Education in 1835. The blueprint for a formal system of colonial education as state policy, it argued against government support for oriental institutions or for printing of oriental works. Government grants were to be exclusively employed for the promotion of English as the medium of instruction in a syllabus comprising only the European sciences and literature. Convinced of the innate superiority of western literature, Macaulay believed that both Persian and Sanskrit learning were of little intrinsic value 'because that literature inculcates the most serious errors which are hardly reconcilable with reason, with morality or even with that very neutrality which ought, as we all agree, to be sacredly preserved'. Macaulay's views were neither novel nor isolated in administrative or political circles at the time. In India, evangelical fervour found expression in a treatise, *Observations on the State of Society among the Asiatic Subjects of Great Britain* (1792), by a Company official, Charles Grant. He advocated diffusion of education in the English language to 'silently undermine, and at length subvert, the fabric of error' enveloping Indian society. While there is no direct evidence that Macaulay had read Grant's tract, the fact that his father was a prominent figure of an evangelical network which included Grant, and that Grant's son was one of Macaulay's closest political associates in the 1830s, makes it 'inconceivable that he had not studied *Observations* before penning his Minute' (Evans 2002: 263–64). Pointed reactions to the increasingly strident influence of the evangelists in Minutes penned at the time by prominent British administrators appear to strengthen this view. 'I am not actuated by any particular regard for Oriental literature. . . . But I am nevertheless very unwilling to join the ranks of those who are conducting a *crusade* against every Oriental feeling and institution' (W.H. Macnaghten, 25 March 1835; emphasis added).[63] 'It is the ignorant only that clamour against it (the literature of the East). . . . Shall this Government publish a *crusade* against both languages (Arabic and Sanscrit)?' (H.T. Prinsep, 20 May 1835; emphasis added).[64]

A Despatch of 29 September 1830 from the Company's Court of Directors already contained in entirety the policy advocated in Macaulay's Minute. Promotion of English as the principal medium of instruction was encouraged for creating 'an elite class of learned natives' trained in European science and literature, who were identified as 'fittest to communicate a portion of this improved learning to the Asiatic wider classes'. The government in India was instructed to use 'every assistance and encouragement, pecuniary or otherwise', including a declared preference in government employment, to further this goal. 'We wish you to consider this as our deliberate view of the scope and end to which all your endeavours with respect to the education of the Natives should refer' (quoted in Howell 1872: 20–21).

After Macaulay's departure from the Company's service and India, Lord Auckland attempted to defuse the controversy between the Orientalists and Anglicists in his Minute on Education, November 1839, by diagnosing the insufficiency of state funds as the cause of 'violent disputes which have taken place upon the education question'. He pacified the former group by agreeing to restore the funding which had been withdrawn for stipends, but only for the existing oriental institutions and for publication of selected works already in the process of being printed or translated into the vernacular. At the same time, promoting the official policy, he sided with the Anglicists in professing that he anticipated 'very impartial and imperfect results' from the earlier policy of engrafting European knowledge on the studies of the existing learned classes of maulvis and pandits, and announcing his 'principal aim to communicate through the means of the English language, a complete education in European literature, philosophy and science to the greatest number of students'.[65]

Delhi College belied the approach that now informed British educational policy. It provided an environment of constructive engagement between the oriental and western traditions. The sources of this engagement 'were more indigenous than imported' and 'it took place in the vernacular' (Minault 1986: 290). This has been cited as a reason for scholars either ignoring the Delhi renaissance altogether, or unfavourably comparing it with the Bengal renaissance, because it was a movement of preservation as well as renewal. The neglect has probably been influenced by what appeared to be a sustained official downgrading, at the time, of an institution that had formerly been well-regarded. In 1831, W.H. Macnaghten, desired by Lord Bentinck to examine the senior Arabic, Persian and Sanskrit classes, reportedly gave an unfavourable account to the General Committee of Public Instruction. The Secretary of the College, in his Annual Report of 1833, observed that a study of the Arabic language 'was only followed by an empty and unsubstantial celebrity'. In its general report on education for 1835, the Committee of Public Instruction reacted to the complaint of the local committee

> that high attainments in Persian and Arabic, the fruit of so much study, time,
> and expense, did not supply a certain means of livelihood. The General Com-

mittee expressed surprise at these complaints. As Persian was still the official language, it was to be expected that when, by the introduction of the vernacular in the Courts and offices of Government, all foreign languages were placed on a level, the system of education pursued in the Oriental department would be of still less practical use, than it had been hitherto.[66]

The neglect and denigration of classical oriental learning had become part of official policy, but the role of scholars trained in the vernacular at Delhi College in diffusing the 'new learning' in colleges and schools in the North-Western Provinces and beyond could not be ignored, and continued to be lauded. Reviewing the state of education a year after the annexation of the Punjab, the first Administrative Report of the Province in 1849–50 refers to a school 'established at Goojerat under competent teachers from the Delhi College' where European science was being taught.[67]

The difference in motivation between the intellectuals of the Delhi and Bengal movements has been seen not merely as the greatest point of contrast between them, but also as a basis for comprehending how 'the well springs of their thought insured that their work continued in Aligarh, Deoband, Lahore and in Delhi itself', even after the defeat of 1857 brought about a diaspora of Delhi's intellectuals.[68]

Delhi College was closed down after the defeat of the 1857 Revolt. Its library, located since 1842 at the Qutbkhana Dara Shikoh, was plundered by the rebels on 11 May 1857 because of its collection of books in English and because the College provided western education.[69] J.H. Taylor, who had become Principal in 1851, was killed in the uprising. Master Ramchandra managed to escape, but his colleague and fellow convert to Christianity, Dr Chimman Lal, was done to death.[70] The senior teacher Imam Baksh Sehbai met a tragic death after the reconquest of Delhi by the British in 1857. His family home was located in Kucha Chellan, an area southeast of the Jama Masjid, inhabited by the nobility and the learned elite. The British viewed it with suspicion as a centre of resistance. When a British soldier, apparently trying to enter a noblewoman's quarters, was wounded, the British retaliated by rounding up the male citizens of the quarter and shooting them on the banks of the Yamuna. Imam Baksh and his two sons were among the victims.[71] A detailed description of the incident, based on Zahir Dehlavi's *Dastan-i-Gadar*, is provided in Sen (1959: 116). It is said that about 1,400 persons were shot and their bodies thrown in the river. The women and children came out of their homes and killed themselves by jumping into the wells of Kucha Chellan, which were filled with dead bodies.

> When the raging lion-hearts set foot in the city, they held it lawful to slaughter the helpless and burn the houses, and indeed, in every territory taken by force of arms these are the sufferings that people must endure. At the naked spectacle of this vengeful wrath and malevolent hatred the colour fled from men's faces, and a vast concourse of men and women, past all computing, owning much or owning nothing, took to precipitate flight through these three gates (the

Ajmeri, the Turcoman and the Delhi gates which were still held by the rebels).[72]

The former capital of the Mughal empire was transformed by the traumatic aftermath of 1857. Thousands of its inhabitants were killed or exiled and
important areas of the city were razed to the ground. 'The old king and his wife
were exiled to Burma, the princes had been killed, and the court which till the
end had preserved vestiges of Mughal culture, was disbanded. . . . Delhi lost its
brilliant individuality and soon became indistinguishable from many other large
British stations' (Archer 1986: 277). Once the centre of a vibrant culture, in the
latter half of the nineteenth century Delhi became 'a quiet provincial town, governed from Lahore, dominated by traders' (Pernau 2003: lv). Madrasa Rahimiya
and the Khanqah of Mirza Mazhar Jan-e Janan[73] were disbanded, and Madrasa
Ghaziuddin was occupied by British forces, initially as an artillery barrack and
later as the police lines. The Anglo-Arabic School would be located there only in
1889.

The vindictive attitude of the British and the retaliatory hardening of
religious opposition to English education would take their toll of the fortunes of
the institution that had been the focus of the composite culture that thrived in the
city in the first half of the nineteenth century. C.F. Andrews cautioned that if the
Delhi renaissance appeared to be 'less enduring in character' than that of Bengal,
it was because 'no horrors of bloodshed and upheaval overtook Calcutta such as
those which happened in Delhi in 1857' (ibid.: 44). The decline in impact of the
once celebrated mathematician, Master Ramchandra, is illustrative. 'Ramchandra
never commanded the kind of influence he had previously' even when the situation stabilized. The 'closure of the Delhi College' and the shift of the 'epicentre of
intellectual ferment' to Calcutta, rather than the intrinsic limitations of his work,
are identified as probable reasons for his eclipsed reputation and influence (Raina
and Habib 2004: 37).

Recognition of the brutality of the rupture is crucial for an adequate
understanding of the deep impact it had. 'Everything was swept away at the
mutiny, all the masters and professors were I think murdered [sic] and the pupils
scattered, and the name of Delhi was at a discount, nor has the college ever since
recovered, the same footing that it had before.'[74] The traumatic personal experience of Master Ramchandra, not only during the Revolt but particularly after the
British re-established their authority, is recounted in a letter dated 27 November
1857, addressed to Col. H.P. Burn, Military Governor of Delhi. Ramchandra,
then employed at the Delhi Prize Agents, writes in detail of instances of harass-
ment, humiliation and even beatings at the hands of British officials while engaged in 'private and public business. . . . I found to my great grief that I was not
only in danger in deserted streets but in my very house also.' All appeals that he
was a government servant, and a Christian, were derisively rebuffed and only
invited further humiliation, even when he was accompanied by subordinate staff
of the Agency. An anguished Ramchandra concluded his appeal for protection as
follows:

Before the English camp was pitched in the Cantonments on the 8th of May [sic. June?] . . . and before I joined it on the 12th of the same month I lived in villages in greater danger of being cruelly and disgracefully treated and at last of being killed, but then . . . I thought that if the mutineers find me and kill me, they will do so merely on account of my having abjured the creed of my forefathers and embraced Christianity and that I will die a witness of the faith of the blessed Saviour, . . . but there is hardly any comfort remaining, when a Christian is in danger from Christian officers themselves merely because he was not born in England and had not a white skin. This was not the case even among the rebels in Delhie who were professors of false religion. A Mahommedan or Hindu was received as a brother among them.[75]

Ramchandra, who had refused the offer of the post of native headmaster at Thomason College, Roorkee, several months before the rebellion because of his precarious health, and a 'constant and sincere wish to remain in Delhie', now gratefully accepted the position as 'there is no power in Delhie and natives of every description in general are suffering and are in danger every moment'.[76] The atrocities imposed on the civilian population by British officers in the North-Western Provinces, which reportedly led to suicides in many instances, would become embarrassingly public in 1859 when the Lieutenant-Governor of the Province placed written reports by serving officers, without reprobation or rebuke either from him or their senior officers, before the Legislative Council. The officers declared that to govern the Indian people, 'they must not be treated as civilized or intelligent beings', and advocated 'the maintenance of a foreign mercenary army so that we may be in a position to pass what laws and impose what taxes we choose "without the slightest regard for the opinion of the whole native world".'[77]

When Delhi returned to civilian authority in 1859, the old Delhi College was initially replaced by a municipal school and subsequently by a district-level school. The expenses were borne by the Itmaduddaulah Fund. Master Ramchandra returned to Delhi as its first headmaster a few months before his death. In 1862 the institution sent up candidates for the entrance examination of Calcutta University for the first time, and intermediate classes were started once again in 1864 with twenty-five students. While sanctioning the collegiate section, the Viceroy observed that the old Delhi College 'had risen to a high order of excellence; not a few of our very best native officials were brought up there. Delhi's aristocracy and gentry will still supply a class of youths peculiarly well adapted for a high degree of mental training' (Gupta 1981: 104). However, English now replaced Urdu as the medium of instruction in the sciences, and alimentary stipends were stopped for students offering Persian, Arabic and Sanskrit in the Oriental section. The total number of scholarships available to students were also drastically reduced, which further affected the intake of scholars, particularly from the 'new poor' among Delhi's dispossessed Muslim population, many of whom had been forced to relocate their families in surrounding towns and rural areas. Some of Delhi's wealthy citizens instituted scholarships for the assistance of this section. However, the prospect remained bleak. At the close of the academic year 1870–71, of the 51 students enrolled in the collegiate classes, there was only one Muslim (Howell 1872: 191).

Although the College started B.A. classes in 1866 and M.A. classes in 1871, the decision to close down the institution and transfer its staff and library to Lahore was finally announced at the time of the Delhi Durbar held in 1877 to celebrate the proclamation of Queen Victoria as Empress of India. During the fourteen years of its collegiate existence, the institution usually maintained a high place in the results of the Calcutta University examinations – once having taken the highest position in the Master of Arts degree examination. It passed greater numbers than all the other colleges in the Punjab and the North-Western Provinces. Prior to the closure of classes, Delhi College had passed 61 candidates at the F.A., eighteen at the B.A. and four at the M.A. examinations. The average number of students on the rolls in its last year was thirty-seven.[78]

The Lieutenant-Governor of the North-Western Provinces, in his Resolution, remarked that it was with great reluctance that this decision had been arrived at. The grounds for the abolition were the inadequacy of the existing staff in the colleges of Lahore and Delhi, and the inability of the government to meet additional expenditure for supporting both colleges. However, the logic of abolishing this premier institution was questioned not only by the citizens of Delhi, but also by influential members of the British administration.

> I am perfectly certain that the removal of the Delhi College is felt severely by the people of Delhi themselves. I can say that I have for some twenty-five years known the people of Delhi well, . . . But I can say more than this, I believe that the feeling is far more widely spread. The allegation of the Punjab Government that Lahore is more literary than Delhi, simply is too astounding to be credited. . . . To the feeling of the people of Delhi and to some extent of the people of North-Western India generally, the abolition is very much that which would have been felt in England if Oxford or Cambridge had been abolished to assist in founding the University of London.[79]

Delhi already had 'a special name for educational progress' and there was 'abundant material to work upon and utilize', and it was recognized that without education, training for superior commercial or professional employment was impossible. Yet, students in the area from Agra to Lahore, 'a tract of country having a population of over forty millions', found that there was now 'not an institution which could educate to the highest standard'. Students 'of this part of the country and of the city cannot in any large numbers leave their home and go to the expense of staying five years at Lahore'. The abolition of the College was therefore 'a severe blow to higher Education in Delhi'.[80] The vacuum thus created facilitated the setting up of St. Stephen's College by the Cambridge Mission in 1881, with a generous grant-in-aid from the Punjab government.[81]

The culture of a people who had lost both political and economic status could not be regarded as a standard when a new culture had established itself along with a new administration, and qualities and accomplishments of a different kind were required for getting on in life. . . . A change similar to that of Bengal took place in North India also, but here it was more gradual, because the number of non-muslims who had imbibed the common culture was much larger than in Bengal, and (it) had been objectified in the form of a common language. (Mujeeb 1967: 521)

The tension had already been evident in a celebrated incident in 1842, when Delhi College had been reorganized on new principles. Thomason, then Secretary to the Government of India, was interviewing candidates invited for an appointment in Persian. On being informed that Ghalib had arrived, he sent for him immediately. But Ghalib waited outside in his palanquin for the customary welcome. Thomason personally came out to explain that as a candidate for employment he could not be given the formal welcome appropriate to the Governor's durbar. 'Ghalib replied, "I contemplated taking a government appointment in the expectation that this would bring me greater honours than I now receive, not a reduction in those already accorded me." The Secretary replied, "I am bound by regulations." "Then I hope that you will excuse me", Ghalib said and came away.'[82]

The abolition of Delhi College, which ceased to exist from 1 April 1877, was 'much regretted by the inhabitants [of Delhi], and attempts have been made, though as yet without success, to obtain funds for its re-establishment by private subscriptions'.[83] The arguments against the closure, suggested as early as 1868 and repeatedly deferred because of persistent opposition, had already been circulated in 1876 in the *Akbar-o-Anjuman* of Lahore, the *Delhi Gazette* of Agra and the *Times of India* of Bombay, as the Delhi College issue started to arouse interest outside the city. The *Oudh Akhbar*'s comment in an article entitled 'What is Civilization?' is revealing: 'Ask the Bengalis, and they will reply that the English are civilized; the Muslims at Lucknow . . . will say "Go to some Maulvi". In Delhi they pointed to the School' (quoted in Gupta 1981: 106). The Delhi Society,[84] many of whose members were alumni of the old College, were agitated, although loyalists among them joined the Municipality in objecting to College classes being engaged in the institute where their meetings were held. The matter was referred to a committee of Punjab College headed by C.W. Leitner, who had already recommended amalgamation in 1868 and had allied with Nawab Hamid Ali Khan in claiming that the Itmaduddaulah Fund was being illegitimately used by the College, thus denying Shia youth the full benefit of the Fund. In a memorial to the Viceroy, the Anjuman Islamia of Delhi would publicly deny this claim, identifying the 'special object of the founder being the promotion of high education amongst the people of Dehli, irrespective of colour and creed'.[85] Leitner continued to disparage the institution but could not convince the committee, which emphatically decided that the College should be retained.

Therefore the decision to abolish the College was perceived as both harsh and unexpected. The response was swift and often equally harsh. A memorial from 'the inhabitants of Delhi', while statistically countering the arguments given by the Lieutenant-Governor and others, asserted that their appeal was based 'not on the grounds of any statistics, [but] . . . . exclusively on the claims of our city, and on the history of our college'. They said what many others, officials and private individuals, were to say, that

> we feel the College to be one of our own institutions; reared and fostered by us, and not like most other institutions in the country, the gift of the British government; that in the circumstances, . . . if the college be abolished, we shall actually be left in a worse condition educationally, and with less means to help ourselves than we were when the institution was made over to the Government.[86]

A large meeting, at which alumni of the College were most vocal, was convened in support of the memorial 'because the Delhi College was not only of incalculable benefit to the people but shed a lustre upon the city'. Three 'large and influential meetings' were held: on 21 February 1877, 9 December 1877 and, finally, on 6 February 1880. At the last meeting, held at the Town Hall, 'the room was full to overflowing. It showed that the people were not indifferent to the cause of education.' When, despite this, the state refused to reverse its decision, it was disingenuously suggested that 'it behoves a grateful people to walk in the way shown by the Government and to work out the scheme of high class instruction itself'.[87] A memorial, drafted by a former student, Pandit Manphool, and backed by a hundred signatories from Lahore, stated 'that to abolish a well tried College . . . and deprive a populous and important city like Dehli of such a valuable and necessary blessing, is not only retrogressive but impolitic, when . . . . its absence will remove all counteracting influences over the conservative and bigoted element ever present at Dehli.'[88] Apart from the local press, newspapers at Meerut, Kanpur, Amritsar and Lahore echoed the protests. Yet, Governor-General Lytton backed the inflexible Lieutenant-Governor, offering the petitioning memorialists the specious plea that primary education had a greater claim on government funds than higher education.

At a meeting of Delhi citizens, now convened to revive the College through public efforts, Maulvi Syed Fariduddin Ahmad, a judge at Aligarh who had accompanied Sayyid Ahmed Khan to the meeting, 'lashed out at the policy of economizing on education and spending so lavishly on the police force'. Contributions were readily promised and the College Memorial Committee planned a sustained fund collection drive. Applauding the movement, Surendranath Banerjea castigated a government which 'could not spend Rs 12,000 a year for maintenance of an ancient and time-honoured seat of learning [when] the Delhi Assemblage cost 60 lacs'.[89] Supporting the efforts of the people of Delhi, he added that the city would have a college of its own, 'this time depending no longer on the generosity of the government'. For three years after the abolition of the College the possibility of revival seemed imminent. Sixty thousand rupees were collected by the Delhi College Committee to set up the College on a firm and independent footing, and the Municipality's report of 1879–80 spoke of increasing the sum for education 'when a college is re-established in Delhi'.[90] Lieutenant-Colonel W.R.M. Holroyd, Director of Public Instruction, who had initially supported the merger, now reasoned that given the strong demand for revival, the matter be reconsidered. The debate among British officials was often openly partisan. Senior officials tried to reopen the issue with the Lieutenant-Governor. 'During my long residence in Delhi,' wrote Rev. Smith of the Baptist Mission, 'I remember no subject on which the public mind has been so much excited, nor is there a boon the Local Government has in its power to grant which would be received with more joy and gratitude.' The Lieutenant-Governor, however, remained adamant. 'The almost universal belief is that the opportunity was designedly set aside in favour of a mission establishment' (quoted in Gupta 1981: 110). The effort to resuscitate the College as an aided institution was rejected as the Lieutenant-Governor regarded the sum of Rs 60,000 to be

> insufficient and was moreover unwilling to recognize annual subscriptions as a stable source of income. Under these circumstances the Cambridge Mission, which was already preparing to start a college class for students connected with the Mission, offered to establish an aided college for the benefit of the public at large. This offer was accepted by the Government and a grant-in-aid of Rs 5,400 with a special grant of Rs 2000 for scientific apparatus was sanctioned for the first year.[91]

There were ironic episodes in the dramatic events associated with the abolition of Delhi College. The bureaucratic ways of the colonial administration led to an entertaining exchange of files during May and June 1877, between the Government of Punjab, the Supreme Government and the Secretary of State in Britain. In 1876, Lord Northbrook had purchased promissory notes yielding Rs 160 per annum, and instructed the Mint Master to strike off two gold medals to be sent to the Director of Public Instruction, Punjab, for the best students of Delhi College and Mohender College, Patiala, respectively. In 1877, the Maharaja of Patiala suggested that a clasp be added to the medal so that the awardee could wear it on suitable occasions. Here the correspondence begins.

'Better ask the Mint Master if he can provide metal and clasp out of the money. But before this is done I think Lord Northbrook should be consulted whether he approves of *any* change in his donation.' (A.P.H., 11-5-77)

'Yes, particularly *in re* the abolition of the Delhi College when that matter is settled.' (E.C.B., 11-5-77)

'In this case it is presumed that the wishes of Lord Northbrook in regard to the clasp and as to the disposal of the medal intended for the Delhi College will be obtained through the Secretary of State for India. For orders.' (E.T., 16-5-77, J.A.S.)

'To Secretary – No, as I understand, the provision of a clasp is so trivial a matter that it is not thought necessary to refer to Lord Northbrook before we hear from the Mint Master. . . . It is when the matter of the abolition of the Delhi College is settled (and affirmatively) that we must refer to Lord Northbrook.' (L.N., 17-5-77)

'Better lay the whole matter before Lord Northbrook, at once and *direct*, both as to the clasp and as to the abolition (which will doubtless be final) of the Delhi College.' (A.P.H., 18-5-77)

Lord Northbrook, finally approached through the Government of India and His Majesty's Secretary of State, responded to the letter 'asking me 1st, if I have any objection to the addition to the medal . . . and 2ndly, what I wish done in regard to the medal which I presented to the Delhi College in the event of the College being abolished'. He had no objection to the addition of the clasp, but in the event of the latter, he requested that the promissory notes be returned to him![92]

The donation by the Nawab of Rampur for the resuscitation of Delhi College created its own problems when the scheme was finally abandoned. On the return of his donation, the Nawab informed the Commissioner, Delhi Division, that he would not receive any interest on the amount. 'What shall be done with it?' was the confused response from the Commissioner's office. 'Return to the bankers as requested by them', came the curt reply.[93]

In 1924, the Principal of the Anglo-Arabic School, Maulvi Fazluddin, finally obtained permission from the local government and the university to open an intermediate college in connection with the three schools under the Itmaduddaulah Trust administered by the Chief Commissioner of Delhi. Although almost fifty years had elapsed since the abolition of Delhi College, the event was perceived as 'only the revival of an old tradition' which answered the 'very definite loss to this city occasioned by the transfer of the Delhi Oriental College to Lahore in 1877'.[94] There were other reverberations from the past. From 1917 onwards, a series of grants were received from the Nizam of Hyderabad, including a building grant of Rs 17,000, which was used to construct a hall and classrooms at the site of the madrasa which housed the Anglo-Arabic School at the time. The additional accommodation allowed the resumption of collegiate classes, and affiliation to the University of Delhi in 1925. On 30 September 1945, the Rules and Regulations of the governing body of the Anglo-Arabic College were amended to formally include, alongside the nominee of the University of Delhi, '1 person to be nominated by the Government of His Exalted Highness the Nizam of Hyderabad'.

The revival was a modest beginning as the College was accommodated in two large classrooms and offered instruction in six Arts disciplines. In 1928 the science laboratories were set up. Degree classes commenced in 1929 and the College gained recognition as a constituent degree college of Delhi University. Over the next few years, construction of new classrooms was undertaken. Separate tutorial rooms for each tutor became the focus of interaction between faculty and students. A number of academic and co-curricular societies enthusiastically contributed to the rebuilding of the College. In 1932, the societies raised fifteen hundred rupees for developing tennis courts and lawns in the College campus. The following year, they contributed 326 volumes worth nine hundred rupees to the library, which, by 1935, contained 4500 volumes. Guided by faculty members, the student societies arranged academic lectures and discussions, and encouraged reading of papers by students and other scholars.

Sports activities and facilities rapidly developed with the College teams participating at the university level in football, hockey, cricket, athletics and volleyball. The football team, 'the heroes of the College', won the university tournament for the first time in 1935, a success frequently repeated in the years ahead. Even today, the College football team remains a firm favourite at the university's inter-college tournament, and the College hosts the Zakir Husain Memorial football tournament.

In February 1933, the Students' Union passed a comprehensive 'Arabic College Parliament Bill'. Obviously influenced by national events, the Bill drew a distinction between 'moderates', defined as 'persons not altogether disliking things as they are but rather desiring them to change slightly', and 'radicals', who were identified as 'persons advocating uncompromising and original reforms'.

The social service society, *Anjuman*, drew a number of students into its activities. A night school for illiterate and semi-literate workers from the city ran for several years. The January 1941 issue of the College magazine recounts how students would

> visit the various factories, knock from door to door in the streets, and explain their mission to anyone courteous enough to give them a hearing. They are ridiculed by the ignorant and actually pushed away by the unfortunate. Only a few accept their invitation. Out of these more than 50 per cent come to our centres only to inspect, as it were, and do not show their faces after their first visit. Others stay to read.

However, attendance averaged about 70 persons per night even after five years, justifying Dr Zakir Husain's remark that probably 'no other institution in Delhi is so efficiently and on such a large scale rendering services of this kind'.

The Anglo-Arabic School and College were faced with a severe financial crisis in 1937. Leading citizens of Delhi were invited to start an educational society to manage its affairs. Formed under the guidance of Dr Zakir Husain and Sir Maurice Gwyer, Vice-Chancellor of Delhi University, the society attracted 300 members who contributed a hundred rupees each. Anis Ahmed Rushdie, father of novelist Salman Rushdie, was elected secretary, and Nawabzada Liaquat Ali Khan, who would become Prime Minister of Pakistan, accepted the presidentship.

The partition of India in 1947, the communal riots and transfer of populations across the borders of the two newly formed states, struck a body blow to the College. It was attacked and set on fire by incendiary mobs. Courageous staff members, including Professors Mirza Mehmood Begg and Hari Shankar among others, managed to save the library and office records from being completely destroyed. But there were more intractable problems. The College had been closed as many of its trustees had fled to Pakistan, and the entire property of twelve acres at Ajmeri Gate was declared evacuee property. The indomitable Begg Saheb undertook a journey, fraught with danger, across the Wagah border. With great difficulty, he succeeded in contacting erstwhile members of the Trust and re-trieved the relevant papers. His efforts, and the support given by Dr Zakir Husain and Sir Maurice Gwyer, resulted in the revival of the modern Delhi College as a declared non-denominational institution in 1948. In a letter to the Governing Body, dated 28 October 1948, Sir Maurice wrote:

> I am extremely pleased to learn from your letter of the 27th that the Governing body of Delhi College has appointed Mirza Mehmood Begg as the Principal of the College. I cannot think of a more suitable appointment, and the events of the last twelve months have shown him to be a man of great character, courage and qualities of leadership. His purely academic qualifications have long been known, and I think that the College is much to be congratulated on its choice.

The problems faced by the College and the university were similar to those being encountered by people in other walks of life all over the country. Colleagues and friends were missing, and anxiety concerning their whereabouts compounded the tribulations of trying to get an institution, and its distressed students and teachers, back to the classroom.

> The Vice-Chancellor reported that the whereabouts of some of the absent servants of the university were known . . . but unhappily in some cases no information of any kind was available. The Vice-Chancellor said that in his opinion, disregard of a notice requiring University servants to return to their duty by a certain date [27 October 1947] could not itself put an end to the contract of service, if the servant was ready and willing to resume his duty but was unable to do so by reason of danger to life and limb.[95]

Resolution No. 194 of the University's Executive Council, passed on 29 January 1948, a day before Gandhiji's assassination, considered the report of the committee which had met on 5 January 1948, on the question of leave to Muslim staff. The committee, while recommending that posts be kept open till March 1948 for Muslim employees wishing to return to duty 'as soon as conditions permit', cautioned that 'members of the staff should, however, be informed that in case they decided to return, they would be well advised to secure residential accommodation in the [Walled] City, as it would perhaps be unwise to live in the Rajpur Road Quarters [near the University campus].' The warning would be issued twice more.

Gradually, the task of reconstruction began. On 19 October 1948, the Governing Body resolved that government 'be approached to give a special grant for Library, furniture, science equipment, etc.' which had been destroyed, and that the 'Custodian be consulted before payment of PF money to teachers who had left the service of the college'. In an ironic reflection of its past, the College requested the District Magistrate, Delhi, 'for reasonable rent for the building occupied by the 4th Madras regiment'. However, it would be some time before things settled. In December 1950, the Principal informed the Governing Body that an application had been sent to the Ministry of Rehabilitation through the Ministry of Education for a special grant of Rs 1 lakh to meet the deficit in the College budget, 'because this deficit was due to the money spent on rehabilitation and education of refugee students, about 90 per cent of the total strength, on the college rolls'. Dr Zakir Husain suggested that a 'special scholarships grant from the Government for refugee students' could be realized 'if efforts were made'.

The legendary Begg Saheb, whose name would become almost synonymous with the modern Delhi College, moulded the institution with a deep sense of its historical past, nurturing a culture that even today gives it a distinctive quality. In doing so, Begg Saheb was responding to a living tradition. An article on Ghaziuddin Khan reproduced in the March 1935 issue of the College magazine carried the following editorial comment by a student: 'The account of Firuz Jang's career which we are here privileged to reproduce from Dr Yusuf Hussain's article, is most illuminating, and will be read we are sure with deep interest by all members of the College which gratefully acknowledges its debt to Ghaziuddin Firuz Jang as its first founder.'

The College cultivated an intimate, almost familial atmosphere in which Begg Saheb knew each student by name, kept himself abreast of their successes and their limitations, and took upon himself, as the head of the institution, the responsibility of seeing that 'his' students were well set on their way in life. Leading by example, he gathered around him a dedicated faculty that he fiercely protected, and who only too frequently bypassed opportunities to further their personal careers either because they could not say no to him, or because they would not leave their college.

Every institution has its luminaries, teachers and students whose achievements reflect back on their alma mater. The modern Delhi College was no exception. The following names – renowned Urdu poets Ebadat Barelvi, Akhtarul Iman, Jameeluddin Aali, Ali Sardar Jafri; eminent Hindi writer Bhisham Sahni; Persian scholar and authority on Shahjehanabad, Dr Yunus Jaffery; J.N. Dixit – are barely illustrative, for an adequate listing, let alone a comprehensive one, would not be possible here.

The Evening College, now a postgraduate institution, was started in 1958. Delhi College was renamed Zakir Husain College in 1975, as the institution had been transferred to the Zakir Husain Memorial Trust a few years earlier. The academic and administrative sections of the College shifted to new premises in front of Turkman Gate in 1986.[96] However, the hostel continues to be housed in the rectangular complex facing the tomb of Ghaziuddin Khan and the adjacent mosque at Ajmeri Gate.

A number of new disciplines have been introduced in the curriculum over the years, but the College retains its traditional strength in mathematics and the sciences. It is also distinguished among Delhi University's many colleges for having the largest number of classical and modern Indian language departments. The links with its past remain a bond cherished by the college community.

MADHU PRASAD
Department of Philosophy
Zakir Husain College

Notes

1 Asher (1992: 274–75) notes that the mosque resembles the one of Zinat al-Nisa, second daughter of Emperor Aurangzeb, which was also built around the same time, that is, before 1700.

2 Carr Stephen ([1876] 2002: 264) notes that 'the Madrasah was closed for want of funds in 1793'. Interestingly, H.C. Fanshawe ([1902] 2002: 65) also records the closure of the building '80 years after the founder's death for want of funds'.

3 From the Report on the Madrasa Ghaziuddin, 1824, by J.H. Taylor, Secretary to the local Agents and to the Local Education Committee which was comprised of the principal officers of the Agency. Referred to in Dr Khwaja Ahmed Farooqui's Introduction to Kidwai (1971: 5), and in Syed Amjad Ali, 'The Three Hundred Years Past of Anglo-Arabic College and Schools of Delhi, Karachi and Rawalpindi', a publication marking the Golden Jubilee celebrations in Pakistan (1949–99) of the Old Boys Association of the Delhi Anglo-Arabic College and Schools, p. 10.

4 *Punjab Gazetteer, Delhi District 1883–84*, Chapter V, A. General and Military, p. 151.

5 T.G.P. Spear (1945: 11) notes that 'when the Marathas attacked Delhi in 1804 the fighting was on the south side, from the Delhi to the Ajmer Gate'.

6 F.N. 10, August 1883, Delhi College files (Delhi Archives).

7 Report based on the reply, dated January 1824, of the local Agents at Delhi to the General Committee of Public Instruction, 'Delhi College', Chapter IX, *Public Instruction in Bengal: A review of educational institutions of Bengal and the North Western Provinces (1835–51)*, Part II, p. 191. (The volume is available in the National Archives of India. Its title page is missing, and no details of publication are presently available in the archival records.)

8 See Kopf (1969).

9 J.H. Taylor, letter dated 3 February 1827, Delhi College Office, Home/Public/15th July 1840/Nos 8–14 (National Archives of India).

10 Reply of the local Agents at Delhi, January 1824, *Public Instruction in Bengal*, Part II, p. 192.

11 In 1837 the Local Committee recommended that Taylor be appointed Principal on an enhanced salary of Rs 800, but, as Secretary to the local Agents, he would continue to attend to other public duties and devote only a small portion of his time to the College. The government delayed action on this request; in 1839 it was decided to have a full-time Principal, and Felix Boutros was appointed.

12 Fisher's Memoirs – Delhi, Memoir dated 7 February 1827, Supplement added 1832, in *Selections from Educational Records, Part I* ([1920] 1965: 189). Walter Hamilton's account ([1820] 1971: 413) confirms Fisher's assessment. 'Within the city of Jehanabad, or new Delhi, are the remains of many splendid palaces, which formerly belonged to the great Omrahs of the empire. Among the largest are those of Kummer ud Deen Khan, Ali Mardan Khan, Ghazi ud Deen Khan, and Safdar Jung.'

13 Letter of A. Stirling, Persian Secretary to Government of India, dated 2 November 1827, Home/Public/15th July 1840/Nos 8–14 (National Archives of India).

14 This was a feature shared with indigenous madrasas which not only provided religious instruction, but also lessons in Persian literature and Oriental sciences. In some

cases, a pundit would take care of the religious training of the Hindu students. Thus the unrestricted admissions at Delhi College may have continued a practice prevalent in the once flourishing madrasa on which the College was engrafted. 'The Persian schools are the most genuine educational institutions in the country. They are attended largely by the Khatris, the Hindus forming a greater proportion than the Muhammadans.' W.D. Arnold's First Report, 1857, in *Selections from Educational Records, Part II* (1922: 290). The Commission on Education 1882 also reflects a similar understanding: 'The popularity of these Persian schools is attested by the fact that Hindus attend them in large numbers.' Quoting Sayyid Ahmed Khan, a member of the Commission, it refers to the intellectual and cultural significance of these schools. 'They have mainly contributed to the preservation of oriental literature and science in this country. Even those who have acquired any degree of fame for proficiency in oriental science and literature will be found to owe their celebrity to these schools.' *Report of the Education Commission, 1882,* Chapter III, p. 61.

[15] *Public Instruction in Bengal,* Part II, p. 192.

[16] *Report of the Education Commission, 1882,* Chapter II: 'Historical Review of Education in India', p. 18.

[17] *Public Instruction in Bengal,* Part II, p. 197.

[18] Fisher's Memoirs – Delhi, in *Selections from Educational Records, Part I* ([1920] 1965: 189).

[19] 'Religious elders, both Hindu and Muslim, felt that this would "corrupt the youth".' Haq (1989: 17). 'The traditional Hindus and Muslims of the walled city of Delhi, from the same platform, started clamouring against introduction of the English medium saying it was the first step for proselytizing and that such a thing was anti-Vedic and anti-Islamic.' Ahmed (1997).

[20] Fisher's Memoirs – Delhi, in *Selections from Educational Records, Part I* ([1920] 1965: 189).

[21] Pernau (2003: lxvii). Following 'trouble' in 1807, occasioned by the activities of the Baptist missionaries Dr Carey, Marshman and Ward in the little Danish colony of Serampore, the Court of Directors of the Company had issued a dispatch, in September 1808, declaring strict religious neutrality and refusing to lend authority to any attempt to propagate the Christian religion. However, Carey was appointed Professor of Sanskrit at Fort William College and Lord Moira visited the colony in 1815, indicating that the government did not exactly discourage their activities.

[22] Home/Education A/August 1877/Nos 27–34 (National Archives of India).

[23] *Monuments of Delhi* ([1919] 1997: 1). The link between the Madrasa complex and the Oudh Vazirs reportedly goes back to the deaths of Mir Manu and his wife. 'This practically extinguished the influence of Ghaziuddin's line and the Oudh Vazir obtained an ascendancy on account of his acting as plenipotentiary between the King and Ahmed Shah Abdali and the building passed into their hands.' Memorandum by the Hony. Secretary of the Managing Committee, Mir Mohd. Husain, in 'The Tombs in the College Grounds', *Arabic College Magazine,* Vol. VI, No. 3, March 1936. The Deputy Commissioner's Report on the petition requesting return of the building to the Anglo-Arabic School in 1883 further states that 'one Sayad Hussain Mirza who was the Agent at Delhi of the King of Oudh after the Mutinies, and who is also a descendent of Nawab Fazl Ali Khan, who founded the Itmaduddaulah Fund, states that when a lady of Nawab Ghaziuddin's family was married to Asafuddaula, the Nawab of Lucknow, the Mausoleum along with other buildings, was given in dowry to the bride, and passed into the hands of the King of Oudh. . . . After the Mutiny, enquiries were made regarding the properties of the Nawab of Oudh but there is no trace of any reference to the building in those enquiries, nor is the building to be found in any of the lists of the King of Oudh's property filed by Sayad Hussain Mirza.' F.N. 10/August 1883, Delhi College files (Delhi Archives).

[24] Quoted in Haq (1989: 20). Government of Punjab records (No. 2244, dated 23 May 1877, based on J.R. Colvin's *Note,* dated 22 June 1840), quote the Nawab's will as stating that the endowment was 'solely for the instruction and study of the sciences in Arabic and Persian, the sciences of my own religion', and expressing confidence that

it 'will always be appropriated to the expense of the children of respectable persons and of the professors of the College'. Home/Education A/August 1877/Nos 27–34 (National Archives of India).

[25] Deputy Commissioner's Office, Delhi Division, Education, F.N. 11, Delhi College files (Delhi Archives).

[26] Minute of 8 April 1841, Home/Public A/30th June 1841/No. 19 (National Archives of India).

[27] Although the notification was 'avowedly temporary and experimental', he would be reprimanded for having 'so far exceeded the clear limits of his powers and by acting instantly upon his own views, should have pledged the Government as well as himself, to the public in a manner which seriously embarrasses the superior authorities.' Letter from Secretary to the Government of India to Secretary to the General Committee of Public Instruction, Home/Public A/30th June 1841/No. 20 (National Archives of India).

[28] Thomason, Minute of 7 May 1841, in *Selections from Educational Records, Part II* (1922: 253–54).

[29] *Report of the Education Commission, 1882,* Chapter IV: 'Collegiate Education', p. 260.

[30] Although the representation of Hindus in such debates was asymmetrical and complex, and the religious establishments of the communities tended to maintain their distance, well-tried procedures of arbitration, joint representation and mutual consultation had evolved over time. The articulated structure of the Mughal state comprised a reliable and professional imperial elite at the centre, and cooperating regional aristocracies elsewhere. Consequently, there was a tradition of well-informed debate about non-Islamic religion and culture among the learned elite comprising Delhi's scholars and genteel citizens.

[31] Sirhindi (1564–1624) was a dominant and controversial figure of the orthodox Naqshbandi Sufi order. In what came perilously close to heresy, he claimed that, like the companions of the Prophet who shared in His prophetic qualities, he too had direct access to divine inspiration and could offer guidance for a revival of Islam and reversal of Akbar's non-discriminatory policies towards non-Muslims. Sirhindi wrote hundreds of letters – to his disciples, to the nobility and Emperor Jahangir. Dehlavi, one of the most respected scholars of his time, publicly challenged Sirhindi's views, disapproving his arrogance and disrespect to the Prophet. His studies covered the whole field of religious knowledge, including Sufism, and he was a prolific writer. Shah Walliullah (1702–1763) was one of the most significant religious thinkers after Dehlavi. Convinced of the completeness, consistency and perfect wisdom of universal order as conceived by Islam, he nevertheless stimulated thought by searching widely for evidence of divine wisdom, disparaging blind acceptance and using a historical approach to explain the development of Sufism. See Mujeeb (1967: 243–47 and 271–82).

[32] 'The most vital intellectual culture in both the Shia and the Sunni traditions, which had survived through wars and revolution, was the pursuit of the Islamic rational sciences.' Bayly (1999: 139).

[33] Ibid.: 190. The introduction of paper in the eleventh century and its subsequent widespread use not only made centralized administration easier for the Mughals as their empire expanded, it also allowed information flows to become more profuse and reliable. The diffusion of ideas was facilitated by the Muslim emphasis on the written text, a characteristic reflected in the developed aesthetic of calligraphy.

[34] Ibid.: 190–91. Apparently, the implementation of the 1829 regulation banning *sati* and making it punishable by criminal courts was not without its dilemmas. An 1814 despatch of the Company's Court of Directors made it clear that political considerations were from the outset the central feature of British cultural and educational policy. The 'peculiar circumstances of our political relation with India which, having necessarily transferred all power and pre-eminence from native to European agency, have rendered it incumbent upon us, from motives of policy as well as from principles of justice, to consult the feelings, and even yield to the prejudices, of the natives,

whenever it can be done with safety to our dominions.' Quoted in Zastoupil and Moir, eds (1999: 94).

[35] 'As in pre-colonial times, in modern India the dialects spoken at home are numerous, the line of demarcation between one language and another vague, and multi-lingualism widespread.' Talbot (2003: 101).

[36] Dr Feroze of the Urdu department, Zakir Husain College, provided this nugget of information.

[37] See Minnault (2005: 110–14). After the sepoys entered Delhi, Maulvi Baqir hid Taylor, the College principal, in his cellar for over twenty-four hours before word spread in the locality that a *gora* was being given shelter. Fearing for Taylor's safety, he dressed him in Indian clothes and helped him flee. Unfortunately, Taylor was recognized and killed. The British held Maulvi Baqir responsible for his death. Ram (1875: 57).

[38] Classmates in the English department in the late 1820s, they exemplified the new type of munshi, accomplished Persian speakers with an exposure to English education. Distanced from their traditional culture and dismissive of the 'superstitious' nature of popular forms of Hinduism and Islam, both were ostracized for their contact with the British. Although they were protégés of Charles Treveleyan, an influential aide of William Bentinck, they appear consistent in being equally critical of British conduct and policy. Bayly (1999: 232) even refers to Mohanlal as 'India's first modern anti-imperialist' for his 'sustained assault on Company policy in the northwest in concert with British opponents of the Afghan war'.

[39] Headmaster of the Gurgaon school, and then the Delhi Normal School, Munshi Pyare Lal eventually become Inspector of Schools in the Punjab. At his death, Ghalib wrote, 'I now know that I have no one in Delhi.'

[40] Andrews (2003: 43). In his Introduction, 'Sharif Culture and Colonial Rule: A "Maulvi"–Missionary Encounter', Mushirul Hasan states that Delhi College successfully 'mediated between eastern and western cultures and mentalities, and did so in the vernacular, contributing to an Urdu-speaking and reading public that belonged to different religious persuasions. . . . [It] embarked upon changes in the curriculum and created a climate for fostering liberal thought and the rational spirit.' Hasan (Introduction to Andrews 2003: xxiii).

[41] Minault (1986: 290–91). One possible reason for this response could be that 'knowing English was simply not necessary, at least as far as employment in the British administration was concerned. Urdu was still the language of administration in Northern India, and thus a traditional education, plus personal connections, were sufficient to gain access to jobs in the administrative hierarchy.' Ibid.: 288.

[42] The ambivalence discernible in Master Ramchandra's use of a phrase that obviously recalls Macaulay's dismissal of Oriental science as 'astronomy which would move laughter in girls at an English boarding school', in his Minute of 2 February 1835, cannot be overlooked.

[43] This tract is referred to in Salman Hashmi's notes. Unfortunately, I have been unable to locate it.

[44] Sender (1986: 322). Sender notes that the Mughals observed a 'ruling ethos' that was non-communal and led to the emergence of a cross-communal service class. Akbar's descendants continued with his legacy of drawing upon differentiated symbols of legitimacy. Standards were aristocratic rather than communal. The commitment to Persian and later to Urdu was an 'affective as well as material' bond. Among the elite, communalism was regarded as bad manners.

[45] Felix Boutros on Indian Education, in *Selections from Educational Records, Part II* (1922: 8).

[46] *Public Instruction in Bengal*, Part II, p. 199.

[47] Ibid., p. 206. The 'other systems' referred to primarily include the post-1835 policy of enforcing English as the principal medium of instruction in all government institutions of higher learning.

[48] 'One of the most prominent defects noticed by the Examiners, during the early years of the English Institution, was an imperfect knowledge of the language. It was

observed in 1836 that some of the pupils had commenced science too soon, before they were properly instructed in English. . . . Some years later Sir E. Ryan found that scarcely a boy in the whole Institution could read English correctly and with a good pronunciation, although some of them were studying Brinkley's Astronomy.' Ibid., p. 199.

49 *Selections from Educational Records, Part II* (1922: 256). Dr F.J. Mouat was First Physician of the Medical College at Calcutta and Secretary of the Council of Education at Bengal.

50 Thomason's reasons for deviating from the Bengal policy were based on the argument that 'much less encouragement exists here for the study of English than is the case in the Lower provinces and in the Presidencies of Madras and Bombay. . . . There is no wealthy body of European merchants transacting their business in English language and according to the English method. There is no supreme court where justice is administered in English, no English bar or attorneys, no European sea-borne commerce with its shipping and English sailors, and . . . even in the public service, the posts are very few in which a knowledge of the English language is necessary for the discharge of their functions.' Quoted in Srivastava (1955: 59).

51 Thomason to Wilson, 16 November 1847, quoted in Bayly (1999: 219). 'While it is true that the constructive orientalists' lessons failed to percolate downward quickly, new communities of knowledge did begin to form among Indians. . . . Cliques of this type broadened the range of the critical public and generated innovative responses amongst traditional scholars.' Ibid.: 226.

52 'They looked to what was practically useful, one main objective being to substitute the homely vernaculars for a foreign literature to which the more ambitious of the indigenous schools were so much addicted.' *Report of the Education Commission, 1882*, Chapter II: 'Historical Review of Education in India Prior to 1854', p. 18.

53 *Public Instruction in Bengal*, Part II, p. 197.

54 The range of subjects covered trignometry, analytical geometry, principles of arithmetic, differential and integral calculus; astronomy, physics, natural philosophy, refraction and polarization of light, magnetism, hydrostatics, mechanics and hydraulics; surgery; geography and travel; Utilitarianism, mental philosophy and morality; the history of education in British India, the histories of Greece, Rome, Mughal India, and British India; political economy and public revenue; laws of nations, civil law and principles of legislation.

55 J.R. Colvin's *Note*, in *Selections from Educational Records, Part I* ([1920] 1965).

56 *Public Instruction in Bengal*, Part II, p. 205. Figures available from 1835 to 1851 clearly show the proportionate strengths to be stable.

57 Official report submitted to the General Committee on Public Instruction, Calcutta; quoted in Ali (1999: 12).

58 Mamluk Ali, a distinguished scholar and adherent of the teachings of the Madrasa Rahimiya, was held in high esteem as a teacher. He constituted a bridge between traditions, counting among his pupils both Sayyid Ahmad Khan, founder of the Muhammedan Anglo Oriental College at Aligarh, apparently as a private student, and Maulana Muhammad Qasim Nanatawi, the founder of Deoband.

Imam Baksh 'Sehbai' was an outstanding linguist with publications on Urdu grammar and poetry to his credit. A well-known poet in Persian, he counted among his friends both Sadr us Sudur 'Azurda' and Ghalib. He assisted Sayyid Ahmad Khan in the exacting task of deciphering inscriptions and taking measurements of the monuments of Delhi for the latter's seminal work, *Asar us Sanadid*. Written in Urdu and first published in 1846 before the setting up of the Archeological Society of Delhi, it is 'probably the most complete and authoritative historical description of Delhi's main buildings and monuments, "the remains of former ages and the life and customs of the eminent personalities" associated, in one way or another, with Delhi'. Frykenberg (1986: xxx). Although a French translation followed almost immediately in 1852, an English version became available only in 1979.

59 Thomason's report on Agra College for the General Committee of Public Instruction. Home/Public A/30th June 1841/No. 19 (National Archives of India).

[60] The library of Prince Dara Shikoh at Kashmiri Gate became the Residency in 1803. Lord Metcalfe and Sir David Ochterlony lived there. The British added a verandah and colonnade to alter its appearance.

[61] Thomason's Minute dated 8 April 1841, Home/Public/30th June 1841/No. 19 (Consultations) (National Archives of India).

[62] *Public Instruction in Bengal*, Part II, p. 199.

[63] Home/Public A/22nd April 1835/10–10A and 11 (National Archives of India).

[64] Home/Public/3rd June 1835/6–8 (National Archives of India).

[65] Auckland, Minute on Education, in *Selections from Educational Records, Part I* ([1920] 1965: 157).

[66] *Public Instruction in Bengal*, Part II, pp. 194–95.

[67] *Selections from Educational Records,* Part II (1922: 282).

[68] Minault (1986: 292). Not only was Sir Sayyid Ahmed Khan 'an outstanding example of a Delhi Renaissance man . . . [but] students from Delhi made up the largest contingent at the college in its early years . . . and it is easy to see in the original plans of the college, which was to include both Oriental and English sections, the model of the old Delhi College.' A number of the founders of Deoband had attended Delhi College, and the links between it and the Delhi renaissance 'are quite clear'.
    The declared objectives of Lahore College, established in 1869, clearly bear the stamp of Delhi College: 'i) to promote the diffusion of European science, *as far as possible*, through the medium of the vernacular languages of the Punjab, and the improvement and extension of vernacular literature generally; ii) to afford encouragement to the enlightened study of Eastern classical languages and literature; iii) to associate the learned and the influential classes of the Province with the officers of Government in the promotion and supervision of popular education. The above are the special objects of the institution; but at the same time every encouragement will be afforded to the study of the English language and literature.' Quoted in Howell (1872: 194–95).

[69] Although the library and College had been completely sacked, it is significant that 'many of the Oriental works were recovered after the outbreak was quelled'. *Punjab Gazetteer, Delhi District*, 1884, Chapter V, A. General and Military, p. 152. An advertisement dated 29 July 1858, issued by the Delhi Prize Agents, announced the auction of a selection of '17,000 volumes in vernacular many of them illuminated. Comprising works on Theology, Medicine and General Literature'. Lieut. W.N. Lees, Secretary to the Board of Examiners at Calcutta, telegraphically urged the Governor-General to purchase 'the whole', if the government would not exempt collections of manuscripts from Prize property, because of 'the very great value set upon Oriental manuscripts by the European nations, England being the sole exception'. Home/Public – G.G's Progs/September 1858/Nos 211–25 (National Archives of India).

[70] The Delhi Civil Hospital where Dr Chimman Lal was sub-assistant surgeon was located to the north side of the fort. 'It contained indoor patients but very little is known about it, as the records were all destroyed on the fateful night of 10th May 1857, when . . . Chimman Lal, a Christian and a Delhi Kayath by caste, fell the very first victim, being pointed out to the mutineer sowars by one of his establishment.' *Punjab Gazetteer, Delhi District*, 1884, Chapter V, A. Medical, p. 155.

[71] Pernau (2003: lxxiv).

[72] Ghalib, quoted in Russell and Islam (1968: 67–68).

[73] Mirza Mazhar (1702–1781), renowned both for his scholarship and refined simplicity, advocated an ideological affinity between Hindus and Muslims, seeing Hinduism as one of the religions superseded by Islam. Hence he declared the Vedas to be revealed, and the great personalities mentioned in it to be Prophets.

[74] An official note of dissent, dated 7 July 1877, from 'E.C.B.' to the Governor-General, challenging the Punjab government's recommendation for the closure of Delhi College. Home/Education A/August 1877/Nos 27–34 (National Archives of India). The initials 'E.C.B.' stand for E.C. Bayley who, as Offg. Secretary to the Government of the North Western Provinces in 1858, was involved in matters relating to Delhi

College. In this note he refers to his twenty-five-year-old association with Delhi and its intellectual elite. The note is approvingly referred to in the Lahore citizens' Memorial opposing the closure of the College.

75 Letter no. 524, Foreign/Secret Consultation/29 January 1858/No. 17 (National Archives of India).

76 Letter to William Muir, 13 December 1858, Foreign/Secret Consultation/29th January 1858/No. 17 (National Archives of India).

77 Letter from the Secretary, Home Department, Government of India to Secretary to Government of the N.W. Provinces, Home/Public A/7th July 1860/No. 17 (National Archives of India).

78 *Report of the Educational Commission, 1882*, Chapter IV: 'Punjab', p. 264.

79 'Delhi College Classes', communication of E.C. Bayley to the Governor-General, Home/Education A/August 1877/Nos 27–34 (National Archives of India).

80 Deputy Commissioner's Office, Delhi Division, Education, F.N. 11, Delhi College files (Delhi Archives).

81 St. Stephen's School, supported by the Society for the Propagation of the Gospel (SPG), had been founded in 1853 at Kashmiri Gate, where James Skinner's church formed the focal point for the Anglican community. Although it was referred to as St. Stephen's 'College' by Rev. M. Jennings, who was killed in 1857, the school would be affiliated only in 1864 to Calcutta University. The affiliation 'was, however, practically in abeyance till 1881', as the institution failed to send up any candidates for the examination. *Punjab Gazetteer, Delhi District 1883–84*, Chapter III, p. 210. It was only after the SPG was supported in its resolve to establish an institution of higher learning by the Cambridge Brotherhood, that the College was established.

82 Hali, quoted in Kaul (1985: 123–24).

83 *Punjab Gazetteer, Delhi District 1983–84*, p. 151.

84 Set up in 1865 by Commissioner Hamilton with seventeen Englishmen and 76 Indians, the Society was intended to recreate the enlightened atmosphere of intercourse and debate that had characterized the 1840s and 50s. The proceedings were conducted and printed in Urdu, continuing to that extent the spirit of the modern Urdu renaissance that Delhi College had epitomized. However, the spirit of the Vernacular Translation Society could not be recovered. With the demise of the Court and the introduction of English, the prospects were discouraging.

85 Lahore Citizens Memorial, Home/Education A/August 1877/Nos 27–34 (National Archives of India).

86 Memorial, Home/Education A/August 1877/Nos 27–34 (National Archives of India).

87 Deputy Commissioner's Office, Delhi Division, Education, F.N. 11, Delhi College files (Delhi Archives).

88 Home/Education A/August 1877/Nos 27–34 (National Archives of India).

89 'Sixty-three ruling princes and three hundred other chiefs and rajahs [were summoned] to a Delhi Durbar. A vast tented city rose on the plain and thousands of British and Indian soldiers saluted the proclamation. Some dismissed the event as a costly extravaganza.' Tinker (1986: 351–52).

90 'The Commissioner Colonel Birch remarked that he had received assurances of the people's desire to help in establishing a College in Dehli but it had been represented to him that they hesitated in coming forward in-as-much-as they dreaded that by doing so they would incur the displeasure of the Government. He stated that . . . instead of opposing it the Government cordially desired that the people's efforts should prove successful.' Deputy Commissioner's Office, Delhi Division, Education, F.N. 11, Delhi College files (Delhi Archives).

91 *Report of the Education Commission, 1882*, Chapter IV, pp. 264–65. The institution continued to depend heavily on the government and the Delhi Municipality for funds, with nearly half its income coming from these sources even four decades later. By then, 'New Delhi was beginning to take on its Olympian bureaucratic character. . . . Increasingly, St. Stephen's catered for the sons of the administrative, professional and political elites of the capital.' Tinker (1986: 363).

[92] Home/Education A/August 1877/Nos 40–41 (National Archives of India).

[93] F.N. 9/12th August 1882/Delhi College files (Delhi Archives). Other prominent donors included Maharaja Holkar of Indore, the Begum of Bhopal, the Nawab of Basauda and Raja Pertab Singh of Tehri.

[94] Principal's report on College Day, 10 March 1935.

[95] Resolution No. 110 of the Executive Council of the Delhi University, 30 October 1947.

[96] In the early 1930s, it was proposed to make Delhi University a federal body with its colleges concentrated on the campus surrounding the old viceregal lodge. The existing colleges moved to the new premises. The then Anglo-Arabic College had several opportunities to do the same. The advantages of shifting were obvious, but so too were the disadvantages of relocating 'so far from the city'. The question of 'how the Delhi residents will receive this idea' was even raised in the June 1932 issue of the College magazine. After serious consideration, the College eventually decided on retaining its proximity to the walled city.

References

Ahmed, Firoz Bakht (1997), 'Witness to History', *Hindustan Times* (Delhi), 16 April.

Ahmed, Maulvi Basiruddin (1919), *Waqeyat-e-Darul Hukumat Delhi*, Vol. 2 (Delhi).

Ali, Syed Amjad (1999), 'Three Hundred Years Past of Anglo-Arabic College and Schools of Delhi, Karachi and Rawalpindi', publication marking Golden Jubilee celebrations in Pakistan (1949–1999) of Old Boys Association of the Delhi Anglo-Arabic College and School.

Andrews, C.F. (2003), *Zaka Ullah of Delhi* (New Delhi: Oxford University Press).

Archer, Mildred (1986), 'Artists and Patrons in "Residency" Delhi, 1803–1858', in Frykenberg, ed., *Delhi through the Ages*.

Asher, Catherine B. (1992), *Architecture of Mughal India* (Cambridge University Press).

Bayly, C.A. (1999), *Empire and Information: Intelligence gathering and social communication in India, 1780–1870*, Cambridge Studies in Indian History and Society (South Asian edition, New Delhi: Foundation Books).

Evans, Stephan (2002), 'Macaulay's Minute Revisited: Colonial Language Policy in Nineteenth-Century India', *Journal of Multilingual and Multicultural Development*, Vol. 23, No. 4.

Fanshawe, H.C. ([1902] 2002), *Delhi: Past and Present* ([London: John Murray] reprint, Aryan Books International).

Frykenberg, R.E. (1986), 'The Study of Delhi: An Analytical and Historiographic Introduction', in Frykenberg, ed., *Delhi through the Ages*.

Frykenberg, R.E., ed. (1986), *Delhi through the Ages: Essays in Urban History, Culture and Society* (New Delhi: Oxford University Press).

Gupta, Narayani (1981), *Delhi between Two Empires (1803–1931): Society, Government and Urban Growth* (New Delhi: Oxford University Press).

Hamilton, Walter ([1820] 1971), *Description of Hindoostan and the Adjacent Countries* (first Indian reprint, Delhi: Oriental Publishers).

Haq, Maulvi Abdul (1989), *Marhoom Dehli College* (Delhi: Anjuman Tarraqui Urdu [Hind]).

Hasan, Mushirul (2003), 'Sharif Culture and Colonial Rule: A "Maulvi"–Missionary Encounter', Introduction to Andrews, *Zaka Ullah of Delhi*.

———— (2005), *A Novel Reckoning: Muslim Intellectuals in Nineteenth Century Delhi* (New Delhi: Oxford University Press).

Howell, Arthur (1872), *Education in British India: Prior to 1854 and in 1870–71* (Calcutta: Superintendent of Government Printing).

Jafar, S.M. (1936), *Education in Muslim India* (published by Muhammad Sadiq Khan, Lahore: Ripon Printing Press).

Kaul, H.K. (1985), *Historic Delhi: An Anthology* (New Delhi: Oxford University Press).

Kidwai, S.R. (1971) *Master Ramchander: Kadeem Dilli College ki ek aham shaksiyat* (Bombay: Adabi Printing Press).

Kopf, D. (1969), *British Orientalism and the Bengal Renaissance* (Berkeley: University of California Press).

Metcalfe, Barbara (1978), 'The Madrasa at Deoband', *Modern Asian Studies,* XII, 1.

Minault, Gail (1986), 'Sayyid Ahmed Dehlavi and the Delhi Renaissance', in Frykenberg, ed., *Delhi through the Ages.*

——— (2005), 'From *Akhbar* to News', in *Wilderness of Possibilities: Urdu Studies in Transnational Perspective,* edited by Kathryn Hensen and David Lelyveld (Oxford University Press).

Monuments of Delhi: Lasting Splendour of the Great Moghuls and Others ([1919] 1997), compiled by Maulvi Zafar Hasan, edited by J.A. Page, Vol. II (reprint, Aryan Books International).

Mujeeb, M. (1967), *The Indian Muslims* (London: George Allen & Unwin).

Pernau, Margrit (2003), 'Preparing a Meeting-Ground: C.F. Andrews, St. Stephen's, and the Delhi College', Introduction to Andrews, *Zaka Ullah of Delhi.*

Raina, Dhruv and S. Irfan Habib (2004), *Domesticating Modern Science: A Social History of Science and Culture in Colonial India* (New Delhi: Tulika Books).

Ram, Malik (1875), *Qadeem Dilli College* (Maktaba Jamia Ltd.).

Richards, John F. (1993), *The Mughal Empire,* The New Cambridge History of India (Cambridge University Press).

Russell, Ralph and Khurshid ul Islam (1968), *Three Moghul Poets* (London: George Allen & Unwin).

Selections from Educational Records, Part 1, 1781–1839 [1920] 1965), edited by H. Sharp ([Calcutta: Bureau of Education] reprint, National Archives of India).

Selections from Educational Records, Part II, 1840–1851 (1922), edited by J.A. Richey (Calcutta: Superintendent Government Printing).

Sen, Surendra Nath (1959), *Eighteen Fifty-Seven* (New Delhi: Publications Division, Ministry of I&B, Government of India).

Sender, Henny (1986), 'Kashmiri Pandits and the Culture of Delhi', in Frykenberg, ed., *Delhi through the Ages.*

Sleeman, W.H. (1844), *Rambles and Recollections of an Indian Official,* 2 vols (London: J. Hatchard & Son).

Spear, T.G.P. (1945), *Delhi: Its Monuments and History* (reprint, Oxford University Press).

Srivastava, B.D. (1955), *The Development of Modern Indian Education* (Orient Longman).

Stephen, Carr ([1876] 2002), *The Archaeological and Monumental Remains of Delhi* ([Simla: Civil and Military Gazette and Station Press] reprint, Aryan Books International).

Talbot, Cynthia (2003), 'Inscribing the Other, Inscribing the Self', in Richard M. Eaton, ed., *India's Islamic Traditions: 711–1750* (Oxford University Press).

Tinker, Hugh (1986), 'C.F. Andrews and St. Stephen's', in Frykenberg, ed., *Delhi through the Ages.*

Zastoupil and Moir, eds (1999), *The Great Indian Education Debate: Documents relating to the Orientalist–Anglicist Debate, 1781–1843* (Richmond: Curzon Press).

Tomb of Ghaziuddin Khan   *Madrasa Ghaziuddin*

A view of the old college building

C. Eyre Walker, Principal of
Anglo-Arabic College, 1927–40

Mirza Mehmood Begg, first Principal of
Delhi College in the post-Partition period

Master Ramchandra (1821–1880),
student and teacher of mathematics,
Delhi College, and leading light of the
'Delhi renaissance'

Nazir Ahmed (1836–1912),
alumnus of Delhi College,
administrator and reputed author

College magazines, Delhi College, 1937 and 1938

Maulvi Zakaullah,
alumnus of Delhi College,
mathematician and social historian

Dr Zakir Husain

A view of the old college building

A view of the new college building

Introduction

It is said that the twentieth century closed with the 'end of history', the demise of ideology and many certainties. We are supposed to be living in an era of glorious uncertainties. However, a view has also emerged that the proclaimed demise of all certainties in itself has turned into a new orthodoxy, thereby necessitating the need to critically engage with all forms of received knowledge – old and new. The Zakir Husain Memorial Lectures seek to do precisely this, that is, interrogate a range of ideas that continue to inhabit and shape our contemporary intellectual space. These lectures grapple with critical issues that are at the heart of contemporary life: the nation-state, capitalism, modernity, globalization and a variety of representations – linguistic, cultural, pedagogical and historical. The themes may seem diverse and eclectic but they are held together by a quest for intellectual inquiry and debate. While they weave together larger issues, these essays also delve deep into their specific aspects, attempting an interface between the general and the particular. The writers are experts belonging to different disciplines; they are firmly rooted in their subjects but they possess the macro-vision to make connections with broader processes, especially globalization, identity formation and democratization.

The early 1990s witnessed the collapse of the second world and the spread of global capital that fuelled unprecedented consumerism and legitimized neoliberal market policies. These trends are analysed by P.C. Joshi and Prabhat Patnaik who reflect on the antecedents and current nature of capitalism, globalization and the nation-state. P.C. Joshi dwells on the resilience of capitalism and tries to excavate the causes for its continuing survival, seeking insights from Weber and Sombart. He demonstrates the influence of Sombart on Zakir Husain, especially on his understanding of 'late capitalism'. In the process, Zakir Sahib also reflected on the specific contours of 'Asian capitalism'. Joshi has no hesitation in acknowledging that no viable alternative to capitalism is in sight, and that the failure of bureaucratic state socialism and the second world has damaged the image of socialism. However, he adds a very important caveat: before the triumph of capitalism is celebrated unconditionally, the anti-labouring poor logic of capitalist development should be recognized. He underlines the highly destructive implications of the greed and covetousness of capitalism that has brought enormous harm to the environment and to a humanist social vision. He laments the marginalization of the labouring poor in recent years when public action and state intervention in favour of the disadvantaged in society have diminished. Joshi's prognostic reading of capitalism hinges on social conscience, which, in his view, has the capacity to subvert the basic economic tendency of capitalism, i.e. its anti-poor logic.

Prabhat Patnaik extends the argument further in an insightful essay on globalization and its impact on the nation-state. He argues that it is not just socialism that has collapsed but virtually all interventionist ideological trends that had any claim to improvement of the human condition. Hence social democracy, welfarism and planning have suffered ideological setbacks, leaving only the nation-state with a capacity for intervention. However, its capacity has been seriously undermined by the neoliberal policies of the era of globalization and the accompanying fluidity of finance. This era has produced 'secessionism of the rich' – of not just rich regions but also the global elite living in different nation-states. Simultaneously, globalization has produced poverty, unemployment, separatism, communalism, crime and violence on an unprecedented scale, despite a promise of higher growth. This has led to an 'emasculation of the nation-state everywhere', rendering the agenda of improvement of the living condition of people vacuous. Recent studies of nationalism and the nation-state have been heavily influenced by Benedict Anderson's seminal study, *Imagined Communities*, and have focused on nationalism's cultural underpinnings. What is significant about Patnaik's study is that he grounds his comprehension of the nation-state in political economy and revisits some older debates like the Kautsky–Lenin controversy. He ends with the suggestion to learn from East Asia in the sphere of positive state intervention while eschewing the East Asian neo-mercantilist development strategy and state authoritarianism.

A number of authors engage with aspects of civil society, law, the Indian Constitution and human rights. Veteran Marxist leader and parliamentarian Somnath Chatterjee assesses fifty years of India's constitutional history and raises two basic questions: first, whether there are any shortcomings in India's Constitution that inhibit the realization of people's aspirations; and second, whether those who have been in power have proved inadequate in discharging the constitutional mandate. Chatterjee singles out four major problems that are anathema to the letter and spirit of the Constitution: communalism, secessionism, corruption and divisiveness. Tracing the crucial ideas that have gone into the making of the Indian Constitution, he reiterates that there is no alternative to parliamentary democracy with adult franchise and a federal set-up. However, Upendra Baxi laments that the managers and agents of Indian globalization are now lawlessly liquidating the promise and aspiration of the Indian Constitution. He writes with anguish as a 'proud but wounded' citizen on the state of human rights in the era of globalization. He argues that even as the alleged 'end of ideology' is proclaimed, human rights discourse emerges as the only universal ideology-in-the-making. Baxi asserts that human rights are neither western nor non-western in their origins, and despite the vicissitudes of power and governance, people have a right to be human. Ours is an 'Age of Rights', he says, and warns that human rights are threatened by some key elements of globalization: the new division of labour, the digital revolution and biotechnology. These are deperson-alizing the means of violence, entrenching multinational marketplace ghettos and unleashing a process of cultural appropriation.

Sociologist André Béteille broadens this theoretical inquiry by focusing on the concept of civil society, which he distinguishes from a 'good society'. Béteille traces the historical roots of the concept of civil society and shows that various thinkers in the past distinguished it from military society or natural or industrial society. He notes that for many European thinkers, civil society was not possible in non-European contexts. This possibility was considered even more remote for a colonized society like India where the colonial state conferred subjecthood on Indians but not citizenship. Béteille argues that the Constitution of India conferred citizenship on its people, although ties of caste and commu-nity have continued to shape the dominant identity of Indians. Nevertheless, mediating institutions – schools, libraries, the press, hospitals, banks, political parties, etc. – have contributed to the emergence of a civil society in India. André Béteille also reflects on the non-government sector that has come to occupy an important place during the 1990s between the state, market and the people. He neither regards this sector as sacrosanct nor believes that non-government orga-nizations (NGOs) are compradors. However, he does raise questions about their accountability, unrepresentative character and the possibility of them 'getting tainted' with some Indian traits like casteism and nepotism. Béteille also pro-vokes the reader to ponder some larger questions: whether NGOs can be equated with civil society, and the nature of the 'public sphere' in contemporary Indian society. He adds the caveat that, of late, the Indian state has shown a tendency to withdraw from welfarism, and emphasizes the weak tradition of mutual aid and voluntary action in India except for religious purposes. Béteille concludes that the state and civil society are not necessarily antithetical, and that civil society cannot function under a totalitarian regime but only under a liberal, pluralist, accommodative and secular regime.

Two leading historians of our times, Irfan Habib and Romila Thapar, express similar concerns and make an appeal to approach history with reason so that we are liberated from the tyranny of labels. They question the prevalent monolithic and static representations of the past and make a strong case for diversity in historical interpretation. Both raise theoretical objections to the ho-mogenization that categories like 'Hindus' and 'Muslims' entail. They visit many old but nagging debates of Indian history that have generated questionable ste-reotypes and shibboleths, for example, the origins of Aryans, the so-called 'Muslim period', etc. Romila Thapar demonstrates that in the pre-Islamic past of India, the notion of a community defined by a single religion had no basis. Her evi-dence shows the differentiation that existed on the basis of caste and religion, and the same applies to the history of Islam in India which was not unilinear, homogeneous and classless. Irfan Habib questions the notion that 'Muslim rule' brought unqualified equality in an inegalitarian society and shows that hierarchy was central to it. He interrogates some of the new orthodoxies and assumptions about Indian society – that it is 'timeless' and 'exceptional' – although these tempting ideas enable us to invest Indian civilization with greatness. Habib points out that the seminal writings of Louis Dumont (*Homo Hierarchicus: The Caste System and its Implications*, 1970) and Edward Said (*Orientalism*, 1978) imply that Indian society should be studied on its own terms and not in terms of universal modern criteria. Habib and Thapar plead for a diverse and historical reading of the past, avoiding monolithic constructions, and suggest that identity formation is far more complex although contemporary politics tends to create the oppositional categories of 'we' and 'they'.

A number of essays explore claims of superiority on the basis of language that reflect the social and political hegemony of a particular community. In the case of India, this is particularly true of English as well as Hindi, though the former is spoken only by a few and the claims of Hindi often rest on numbers smacking of majoritarianism at times. Sisir Kumar Das delves into the archaeology of the hegemony of English and recognizes its modernizing power despite perpetuating colonial values. He concedes that it is virtually impossible to conceive of any society where languages are at par or treated equally. If a community is socially and culturally dominant, then its language almost inevitably is endowed with claims of superiority over its rivals. This is a worldwide phenomenon of modernity in which the process of standardization of any dominant language is invariably accompanied by a marginalization, appropriation and, at times, demise of dialects. Tracing the origins of the Indian literary tradition in the English language, Das underlines the tension its practitioners experience vis-à-vis their mother tongues. He insightfully constructs a trajectory of this experience in India where, earlier, Sanskrit and Persian posed a question of choice between the acquired language and mother tongue, but someone like Ghalib bridged the divide admirably. 'Indians were competent in an acquired tongue, in their mother tongue they were immortals.' The tension increased with the advent of Indian writing in English in the colonial period, when many writers probably found their mother tongues inadequate to capture their experiences. However, Das believes that this tension is far less true for post-independence writers as they are primarily monolingual and are not apologetic about writing in English. While not denying the literary merit of these new writers, Sisir Kumar Das asserts that their social base is narrow. Indian writers in English now have a global presence, which shows that the importance of a language does not depend on the number of its speakers alone or its territorial base or even the quality of literary works written in it, but on the hegemony derived from political and social power.

Literary critic Namwar Singh carries forward these linguistic reflections and passionately comments on the fate of Hindustani, the Hindi–Urdu divide and the enormous role of language in identity formation in modern India.

According to him, Hindustani was a late eighteenth-century colonial construct that was basically a new name given to the prevalent Urdu. However, over the next one hundred and fifty years or so, in the crucible of colonialism, through a complex interaction of sectarian politics, the advent of print culture and nationalist mobilization, Urdu and Hindi came to acquire separate identities that were oppositional at times. Namwar Singh discusses Premchand's views on linguistic identity and shows that by 1936, when Premchand died, Hindi and Urdu were no longer the same language with two scripts but two different languages with separate scripts. If Premchand was trying to bridge the gap between them, that was for the sake of communal harmony and for the unity of the communities for nationalist purposes. Namwar Singh laments the steady decline of Urdu in independent India. He vehemently dismisses the suggestion that in order to survive, Urdu should abandon its script and adopt Nagri for wider acceptance. He reiterates that the Urdu script is absolutely vital for its identity, and fears that the appropriation of Hindi by Hindu nationalists and their slogan of 'one nation, one national language' will lead to an undesirable hegemony of Hindi that is detrimental to the rich linguistic diversity of India.

Eminent scholar and Urdu historian Shams-ur-Rahman Faruqi reconstructs the fascinating world of the famous Urdu poet Akbar Ilahabadi (1846–1921). Faruqi tries to rescue the poet from the enormous condemnation and condescension that he faced from critics, especially Urdu critics who dubbed him anti-modern. He points out the contradictions in Akbar Ilahabadi's life: he held a government job, wrote an adulatory *qasida* on the golden jubilee of Queen Victoria (1887) and yet hated virtually all things that came with the British – the railways, piped water, newspapers, etc. Faruqi argues that Akbar's contradictions and paradoxes were of his age. Akbar distrusted the modernizing agenda of the Indian renaissance, including Sir Syed Ahmad Khan's reforms, much as he admired Sir Syed's sincerity and devotion to the cause of education of Indian Muslims. Faruqi pleads that a superficial reading of Akbar will easily lead one to dismiss him as being anti-science, anti-modern and anti-progress. A closer reading of Akbar's brilliant satirical compositions reveal the poignancy and subtle bitterness of defeat in him. When Akbar Ilahabadi writes sarcastic literary gems on the gifts of colonial modernity, he is in fact being critical of crass materialism, commercialism, the Hindu–Muslim divide, the Hindi–Urdu controversy, and the over-regulatory and interventionist presence of the colonial administration. Akbar's poetry is actually a lament for the loss of self-respect and dignity that accompanied the tools of colonial modernity, and the cultural hegemony inflicted by them. Through a nuanced reading of Akbar Ilahabadi, the author draws our attention to the dangers of blind and uncritical imitation of the west in the name of globalization, and cautions us against the rise of totalizing ideas on politics, culture and education in the name of nationalism.

Two eminent thinkers provide theoretical insights into education and learning and suggest pragmatic solutions for the specific pedagogical requirements of Indian society. M.S. Swaminathan coins a new term, 'techniracy', based on the idea of technical literacy, which he finds more relevant and meaningful than formal or functional literacy. He regrets that in India the obsession with university education has led to a woeful neglect of rural education. He emphasizes the need to make farm graduates computer, patent and trade-literate to compete in today's world. He goes on to link educational planning with larger changes in the global order that has now entered the information age. Swaminathan argues that education should seek to end gross economic inequity and ensure gender justice and equity. He expresses deep concern about feminization of poverty and stresses the need to look at individuals within households for poverty alleviation because women and children tend to receive unequal shares within families. He redefines the notion of food security and instead suggests livelihood security, which will be possible only by eliminating unsustainable lifestyles that deplete human and environmental resources.

Educationist Anil Sadgopal who combines years of activism with experience at the official level, examines the impact of globalization on education. He historicizes the evolution of basic education in modern India and shows that the nationalist pedagogical agenda was formulated in response to the *babu* manufacturing colonial education. He analyses Gandhi's approach to education which aimed at integration of the 'world of work' with the 'world of knowledge'. This was enunciated at the Wardha Education Conference in 1937 where Zakir Husain was asked to give concrete shape to the curriculum of basic education. Zakir Sahib's pedagogical ideas fructified as the concept of *Nai Talim*, but, unfortunately, in independent India, the colonial practice of delinking knowledge from productive work and social reality persisted. The very essence of *Nai Talim* was subverted when work was alienated from the mainstream school curriculum and marginalized in the form of 'vocational education'.

With the new economic policy and the structural adjustment of the 1990s, the Indian state has increasingly abdicated its educational responsibilities. There have been many commissions and committees to reform the education system, but the overall shift has been towards privatization and commercialization. Although the Ambani–Birla Report (2000) recommends that elementary education must be entirely the responsibility of the state, expenditure on education has remained low (below 4 per cent of GDP), proving the impact of the neoliberal policy shift. Sadgopal deconstructs policies that appear to be promising, for example, the one aiming to provide free and compulsory elementary education, and shows how such policies become tools to legitimize exclusion and inequality. He locates these trends in the fundamental conflict of an epistemological nature between globalization and social development. Globalization equates information with knowledge and promotes free market policies, but also has a 'hidden agenda' of minimizing cultural diversity across national boundaries. According to Sadgopal, the knowledge industry of globalization has increased educational inequalities, and, in the case of India, it has sharpened communal tensions and aided the undemocratic process by which textbooks are rewritten and curriculums changed. Educational institutions are being subverted by the twin assault of the market and a socially retrograde agenda that is insensitive to women, dalits and minorities.

These essays are tracts of our times and they express critical theoretical endeavours of some of the leading intellectuals of modern India. They have dissected contemporary issues with a sense of history and with the primary intention of generating debate, which is the essence of democracy. The passion and commitment to a liberal, just, humane and egalitarian society that permeates these essays will be more than apparent to all readers of this volume.

SANJAY SHARMA
Department of History
Zakir Husain College

Capitalism and the Labouring Poor

Some Reflections

P.C. Joshi

Remembering Zakir Sahib today is a very uplifting experience, uplifting both intellectually and morally. It is also a chastening experience. It reminds us of the disquieting contrast between the India of yesterday and the India of today, between the universities and colleges of yesterday and the universities and colleges of today. It makes us aware of the contrast between men like Zakir Sahib, who were growing all the time in stature while struggling for a better India and better life for its people, and men and women dominating the politics and academics of our time, who seem to have virtually given up the struggle for larger causes.

In order to understand the sweep and fullness of Dr Zakir Husain's personality, we have to appreciate that he belonged to the heroic age of Indian nationalism when men and women of great intellectual potentialities were drawn into the freedom struggle and into active public life. Zakir Husain had all the discipline and sophistication of an ivory tower intellectual but he did not spend his life in an ivory tower. He carried his intellectual temper into the sphere of social action and public service. He also carried a sense of social purpose and social urgency into the intellectual domain. He lived up to Mahatma Gandhi's ideal that intellectuals must come out of their ivory tower and serve the suffering people. He did not, however, share the anti-intellectualism of many conventional Gandhians who denigrated intellectuals and the intellectual dimension of the struggle for freedom. Zakir Sahib was not in the centre of the national struggle on the political plane. But he was, undoubtedly, in the centre of national struggle on the educational, social and cultural planes. He was one of those who served as a bridge between the world of politics and the world of education and culture, in the widest sense of the term. He served as a bridge between the world of thought and the world of public service. Men such as Zakir Sahib played a great role in the freedom struggle by nourishing the will to freedom at its roots, that is, in the sphere of educational social reform and cultural enlightenment. We must not forget that the conditions for India's continuing enslavement were first

Fifth Zakir Husain Memorial Lecture, 10 February 1992.

created in the realm of mind and consciousness through the colonial system of education and through colonial cultural domination. The key to liberation, thus, lay in the sphere of education and culture. Zakir Husain rendered the same service to the cause of India's liberation via his contribution to education as Radhakrishnan rendered via his contribution to philosophy. The following passage from S. Gopal's biography of Radhakrishnan can easily apply to Zakir Sahib, if we substitute the term 'education' for 'philosophy'.

To quote:

> The 'battle for consciousness' was part of the challenge to colonial domination. . . . Philosophy and politics are not separate ways of thinking in a colonial society; and in a suffocating intellectual climate it is difficult for the least sensitive to be indifferent. In India, from the second half of the nineteenth century, even a philosopher could not hope for an autonomous life of the mind, with no commitment to society. For a bruised community, conscious of its political impotence, a culture provides both a touch of healing and an element of defence. It plays an important political role, preserving, reforming and idealizing the vision of an independent homeland. . . . The power of ideas was an important lever for political mobilization. The pressures of colonialism demand a merger of the inner and outer landscapes.
>
> Such a merger had to be effected in the context of an educational system intended primarily to produce clerks for the lower levels of the administration but having also the wider effects of uprooting its products. (Gopal 1989: 6–8)

This is the historical context – that of the struggle to free the minds and souls of India's men and women, to end the alienation of the intelligentsia from the people, and to create human agents of freedom. It is this context that provides the key to the life and thought of educationists and enlighteners like Zakir Sahib.

Zakir Sahib's work as the Chairman of the Wardha Committee on Basic Education, his leadership of Aligarh Muslim University, his crusading zeal in the building up of Jamia Milia Islamia as the model of new education and his role as the creative expositor of a new approach to education, were all inspired by a vision of the transforming and regenerating role of education in India. The life of Zakir Sahib carries the message that it is the work of educationists and enlighteners to enable the people to get liberated from mental and spiritual captivity, and to become creative agents of historical change. It is they alone 'who can establish the status of a nation' and mould the world-view and character of the people. It also carries the message that the struggle in the sphere of politics cannot fulfil its aims if it is divorced from the struggle in the sphere of education and culture. As Zakir Sahib himself put it, 'national renaissance could not come through the narrow gates of politics.'

It is therefore as a bridge-builder between the national struggle and educational reform that the true significance of the life and thought of persons like Zakir Sahib can be understood. Why is it that the dream of Zakir Sahib and others of transforming education into a revitalizing force did not realize?

Considering the fact that some of the basic constraints on India's social transformation today arise from unfinished tasks in the realm of education, a reappraisal of the heritage of Zakir Sahib and other educationists is on the agenda today. This is an ideal theme for a memorial lecture. But my competence in this field is very limited. I have therefore chosen the theme of 'Capitalism and the Labouring Poor' for my lecture today. This is a theme that reflects my personal concerns as a sociologist, as a socialist, and as a person of an activist temper and orientation for more than four decades of my working life. But this theme was also of very deep concern to Zakir Sahib, both as a citizen and a scholar.

It is not known to many that Zakir Sahib's Ph.D. dissertation in economics at Berlin University, under the supervision of the famous economist and sociologist, Warner Sombart, was on 'The Agricultural Economy of India'. In this dissertation, the phenomenon of capitalism was explored by examining the Indian economy as an agrarian hinterland of the British empire. The work was completed in 1928. Much later, in 1944–45, Zakir Sahib had occasion again to reflect on the phenomenon of capitalism with all the analytical sophistication of a scholar in a series of ten lectures delivered as the Sir Kikabhai Premchand Readership Lectures. These lectures were published by Delhi University under the title *Capitalism: An Essay in Understanding* in 1948.

Zakir Sahib pursued his enquiry primarily with the aid of tools and insights provided by Sombart; he also incorporated some of the basic ideas and insights of Karl Marx and Max Weber. The questions he asked are of great historical as well as contemporary interest, even though the lectures were delivered more than fifty years back.

Considering the fact that capitalism, far from becoming obsolescent, is still alive and kicking, and that instead of vanishing from the world stage, it has returned to a central position again, the questions posed by Zakir Sahib about the inner resilience and prospects of capitalism, especially in the Asian countries, have acquired a new legitimacy and a new relevance. Considering also the fact that so much has been written on capitalism by thinkers, scholars and commentators over such a long period of time, it is a tribute to Zakir Sahib's mental calibre and powers of perception that his lectures still embody perceptions and insights that have proved to be of enduring value and that continue to have a refreshing quality.

As earlier stated, Zakir Sahib imaginatively applied the method of thought and basic insights of his illustrious teacher, Warner Sombart, for an understanding of capitalism. Central to Sombart's concept of capitalism is the spirit or the economic outlook of capitalism, which is the sum total of purposes, motives and principles determining men's behaviour in economic life during an entire epoch. The economic outlook of capitalism is dominated by three ideas: acquisition, competition and rationality. And it is these three mutually reinforcing instincts that generated the internal dynamism of capitalism as an economic system, as distinguished from previous economic systems which were characterized by slow growth of productive forces. In Sombart's view, as a result of the lack of understanding of the sources of resilience of capitalism, economic experiments for finding a substitute for capitalism either failed or did not achieve the desired results. This was because these experiments, while trying to remove the evils of capitalism, also damaged the basic motive forces of growth – viz. principles of acquisition, competition and rationality – which had accounted for the resilience of capitalism. In a very perceptive and, indeed, highly prophetic observation, Sombart remarked how 'the Russians grasped less than any other nation the peculiar character of the capitalist economy when they banished the capitalistic entrepreneur and thereby brought the mechanism to a standstill' (Sombart 1950: 205).

Sombart was fully aware that the economic success of capitalism as a productive agent has a sharply negative side. Under capitalism the *economic* side of human life grows and progresses at the cost of its moral and aesthetic side. According to Sombart, the very strength of capitalism becomes its weakness from the perspective of wholesome development of human life. He remarked:

> Whenever acquisition is absolute, the importance of everything else is predi-
> cated upon its serviceability to economic interests; a human being is regarded
> merely as a labour power, nature as an instrument of production, life as one
> grand commercial transaction, heaven and earth as a large business concern in
> which everything that lives and moves is registered in a gigantic ledger in terms
> of its money value. Ideals oriented upon the values of the human personality
> loosen their hold upon man's mind; efforts for the increase of human welfare
> cease to have any value. Perfection of the business mechanism appears as the
> only goal worth striving for, the means become an end. (Ibid.: 197)

Sombart's analysis is the precursor of Galbraith's more recent insight into the inherent and inexorable logic of the modern technostructure, which excludes all goals – educational, cultural, ethical and aesthetic – except the narrowly economic.

Equally fundamental is Sombart's insight into the contradictory nature of capitalism. He remarked that:

> while individual action under capitalism is informed by the ideal of the highest
> rationality, the capitalist system as a whole remains irrational. . . . From the
> coexistence of well-nigh perfect rationality and of the greatest irrationality origi-
> nate the numerous strains and stresses which are peculiarly characteristic of the
> economic system of capitalism. (Ibid.: 198)

Sombart treated capitalism as a dynamic system with new features of internal structure and forms of organization distinguishing different stages of capitalist evolution. Thus 'early capitalism', lasting from the thirteenth to the middle of the eighteenth century, is followed by 'full capitalism', which closed with the outbreak of the First World War, and this in turn is followed by 'late capitalism', which is still continuing. While the basic spirit of capitalism characterized all its phases and explained its essence as a distinctive social formation, the systems passed through internal structural changes from phase to phase.

It is important to note that Zakir Sahib's treatment of capitalism was not as cold and logical as Sombart's treatment. In Zakir Sahib's exposition, logical rigour and empirical support were blended with an emotive quality that was very marked throughout the exposition. Zakir Sahib's essay combined intellectual quality with a *moral passion* which he shared with all radical analysts of capitalism. But, unlike many radical thinkers whose moral passion colours their assessment of the working of capitalism as an economic system and makes them highly subjective in their prognosis, Zakir Sahib combined a high degree of objectivity about the growth potential of capitalism with a sharp perception of the destructive and brutal side of capitalist development.

Zakir Sahib's concept of understanding as a method of social science implied rigorous investigation and analysis, but it also transcended its narrow limits. Comprehending the totality of the system and its inner dynamics was as important as illumination of the specific aspects of dimensions of the working of the system. Understanding also implied encompassing the points of view, the feelings, the perceptions, the interests, and, indeed, the overall contradictory fortunes and destiny of the classes and masses that are caught in the vortex of epochal social transitions like the emergence and development of capitalism. Understanding meant not only deconstruction but also overall reconstruction, not only analysis but also synthesis, not only illumination but also overall judgement. It meant seeking truth not merely in abstract terms or statistical categories, but in terms of the sorrows and sufferings, torments, traumas and prospects of millions and millions of living and real human beings. Familiar economic categories and tools were not enough for understanding. A sense of history, imagination and empathy was as indispensable as analytical and logical rigour for real insight into historical processes and into the great human drama called 'capitalism'.

Why do we attach such great importance to the methodology of studying capitalism? This is because, in recent years, an 'ultra-academic view' of capitalism has become fashionable as opposed to the 'classical view'. This has amounted almost to a deliberate design to shut out from our view the vital dimensions of the social reality of capitalism as an enormously destructive and dehumanizing force, and to magnify its contribution to economic growth as reflected in quantitative categories. Such a tendency to shut out the *brutal* side of capitalism is highly fashionable in the current debate on 'socialism vs capitalism', 'planning vs the market'. In this debate, bureaucratic 'socialism' and statist 'planning' are rightly under attack for their evils, but 'capitalism' and 'the market' are mystified, and the darker side of capitalism and market failure in achieving social ends are ignored. Understanding of the past, therefore, is not only of historical interest. It is crucial for our present-day perception of policy alternatives, and for our choices and options in regard to systems, strategies and policies.

In support of my argument, I wish to draw upon the path-breaking work of E.P. Thompson, entitled *The Making of the English Working Class*. Sharply focusing on the tendency which I indicated above, Thompson wrote:

> To see (capitalism) and the working class in this way is to defend a 'classical' view of the period against the prevalent mood of contemporary schools of economic history and sociology. For the territory of Industrial Revolution, which was first staked out and surveyed by Marx, Arnold Toynbee, the Webbs and the Hammonds, now resembles an academic battlefield. At point after point, the familiar 'catastrophic' view of the period has been disputed. Where it was customary to see the period as one of economic disequilibrium, intense misery and exploitation, political repression and heroic popular agitation, attention is now directed to the rate of economic growth (and the difficulties of take-off into self-sustaining technological reproduction). The enclosure movement is now noted less for its harshness in displacing the village poor, than for its success in feeding a rapidly growing population. The hardships of the period are seen as being due to the dislocations consequent upon the wars, faulty communications, immature banking and exchange, uncertain markets and the trade cycle, rather than to exploitation or cut-throat competition. . . . Thus, Industrial Revolution, it is argued, was an age, not of catastrophe or acute class conflict and class oppression but of improvement. (Thompson 1980)

This dilution of the view of capitalism or the industrial revolution, to which Thompson drew attention about three decades back, has become the dominant trend in academic circles and in political debate in the present period. The 'anti-catastrophic' view, in fact, has emerged as a trend dominating social consciousness today. To allow this anti-catastrophic view to go unchallenged is to be a partner in the conspiracy against development in history and against those who continue to be victims of the inherent logic of capitalist development today. It is important to note that Zakir Sahib was fully aware of the anti-labouring poor logic of the process of capitalist development.

In this background, Zakir Sahib's exposition poses before scholars major questions relating to the destiny of capitalism. What explains the unprecedented resilience of capitalism as a historically conditioned but evolving form of economic organization? What explains the fact that capitalism has belied the predictions of its disintegration and collapse through the inexorable logic of its own insoluble internal contradictions?

We reproduce Zakir Sahib's own words below on these aspects which have represented a puzzle and a paradox of great complexity both for experts and for laymen:

> Does it not appear reasonable to suppose that some day capitalism will break its neck in a crash like this?' It has been the hope of great minds who have devoted themselves most diligently to the study of capitalism. It is, I am afraid, wishful thinking. . . .

The three pathological developments which were expected to hasten the end of capitalism – increasing misery of the labouring classes, ever-growing concentration, and (recurrent) crisis do not seem to justify the hope or the fear, as one's attitude of approval or disapproval of capitalism might lead one to say. . . .

Sombart had in a *place* recorded the conversation he had with Max Weber about the future of economic life. The question was when the witches sabbath of humanity in the capitalist countries will at last come to an end. Max Weber said, 'when the last ton of ore has been smelted with the last ton of coal.' This moment may not be very far off. . . . But if capitalism has managed to survive Marx's prophecy, it can also survive Max Weber's. Even the end of iron and coal will not find capitalism at the end of its resources. . . . No, Max Weber's prophecy can also come true.

From this perspective, Zakir Sahib posed the question of the future of capitalism as follows:

What, then, is the prognosis? Will this amazing work of human perversity continue unchallenged? That it is result of perversity we have come to know. The motive force – the greed, the covetousness, the urge to acquisition, to untrammelled and unlimited expansion, to unconditional and inconsiderate acquisition – is a perversity. The astonishing thing is that this motive which really has hardly anything to do with natural economic activity has applied itself to economic life and reshaped it from the very foundations. Under the urge of this profit motive an economic structure has come into being so big, so widespread, so mighty, that one stands and gapes and is inclined to mistake its bigness for greatness. Starting from almost a scratch an economic system has been built up under which population has increased by a few hundred million; the length of life has increased, exit permits are obtainable with increasing difficulty; the standard of living has been raised under which it has been possible to feed and clothe and house a much larger number of people than ever before in human history – and yes, to amuse them evening after evening; under which life has been changed beyond recognition; under which the wonders of technique have come to pass, empires have risen and fallen; under which men have toiled as never before and not known the joy of work; under which men have earned as never before and not known even to relate their earnings with their lives; under which means have become ends, and absolute aims and ends and values been forgotten.

In his prognosis for European capitalism in its phase of 'late capitalism' Zakir Sahib took note, as Sombart did, not only of the important changes concerning the internal structure of capitalism, but also of the changes imposed on capitalism by the growth of 'social conscience'. It is 'social conscience' that makes society assume the upper hand and forces capitalism to subordinate itself to social purpose; it is 'social conscience' that makes society take over very extensive and ever-growing fields of economic activity from the capitalist entrepreneur and organize them as a 'planned social economy' even in the strong-holds of capitalism.

Zakir Sahib, in this way, shows that the growth of 'social conscience', and of society's ever-growing capability to curb the 'overall irrationality' (à la Sombart) of capitalism and to make it conform to society's will, were major factors due to which Marx's prediction was proved wrong. This implies that it was not Marx the economist formulating the law of mass immiserization as a basic tendency of capitalism who was proved wrong. It was Marx the political scientist who was proved wrong by not fully appreciating the prospects of grow-ing 'social conscience', especially in a democracy, and its capacity to check if not subvert the basic economic tendency of capitalism.

But Zakir Sahib, as a discerning analyst, took full account of *the long interval* between the emergence of the trends of mass 'pauperism' and immiserization, and the growth of a 'social conscience' (or, to use Galbraith's phrase, countervailing power) capable of counteracting these trends. And it was this 'long interval' during which there was neither any remedy nor any social protest that was shut out from our view of apologists of capitalism. It was this long interval that was a matter of deep concern and reflection for Zakir Sahib. In other words, if the phenomenon of misery and exploitation emerged on the sur-face as a pervasive evil during 'early capitalism', the consciousness of it ap-peared only in the phase of 'full-grown capitalism' and the remedy for it emerged largely in the phase of 'late capitalism'. And, in some sense, misery and exploi-tation have not totally disappeared in the developed world even now.

If this was the way capitalism could escape Marx's prophecy of its down-fall, how did it escape Max Weber's prophecy? It can be said from hindsight that Max Weber, perhaps like Malthus in a different context, had a very static view of the resources required by capitalism, and he underestimated the possibilities of scientific progress and of the discovery of new resources and new sources of energy that gave capitalism a newer and newer lease of life.

Even in regard to resources, however, one must not ignore the highly destructive implications of the way the greed and covetousness of capitalism has led it to seek, exploit and overexploit the natural resources of the world; how the recklessness of capitalism has caused enormous damage to ecology and the envi-ronment, and, ultimately, to the inherent balance and harmony of the natural system. Above all, one must not overlook how, by creating an antagonistic rela-tionship between man and nature, capitalism damaged the original vision of harmony between man and nature without which there can be no long-term prospect of a viable and enduring human civilization. Did Marx not cherish the goal of a 'humanist socialist vision'? And, according to him, damaging the har-mony of man and nature was the major sin of which capitalism had to be re-garded as guilty.

Here again, between the growing phase of capitalism characterized by massive damage to nature and to the system of natural resources, and the period of late capitalism characterized by consciousness of this damage to ecology and the environment and of the need to restore the health of the natural system, there was a long historical interval, a period of darkness as it were, before a glimmer of light could be seen on the horizon.

One should be quick to point out, here, that it is not as if 'the social conscience', once aroused will always remain active and alert. Human beings, as Myrdal pointed out long back, have a tendency to relapse into a state of moral apathy or 'moral discord', and to rationalize their apathy on the basis of some ethical principle or the other. In recent years, there has again been a deadening of the 'social conscience' which has been aided by a new economic philosophy that deplores public action and government intervention in favour of the unfortunate and disadvantaged in society. Drawing attention to this, J.K. Galbraith remarked in a speech at the University of California in 1980:

> My first plea is for a strong revival of what anciently has been called the social ethic, what more simply is a good sense of the community. This is not a subtle or a sophisticated thing; it is the will, in an increasingly interdependent world, to be concerned with what one must do jointly with others, to have as much pride in this achievement, as one has in what one does for oneself.
>
> In the last few years we have witnessed the growth of a contrary mood, and nowhere more manifestly than here in California. This is the celebration, even the sanctification of self-concern. A person's highest duty, it is held, is to own his income, his own personal enjoyment; freedom is the freedom to get money with the minimum of constraint and to spend it with the smallest possible contribution to public purposes. So defined, freedom is purely a first-person affair. No attention may be given to public action that enhances the freedom of someone else. In accordance with first-person ethic, deduction from private income for public schools, hospitals, playgrounds, libraries or public assistance to the disadvantaged or the poor means a net loss of liberty. . . .
>
> Partly it is unwise to be too specific, the new concern for self regularly takes the form of an attack on government in the abstract. Government and the associated bureaucracy are proclaimed the great and faceless enemies of personal freedom. This avoids mention of the many good things that the government does for all, including the self-concerned. And there is a further advantage in so disguising things: those involved do not wish it thought that this new preoccupation with self is a revolt of the rich against the poor. When so identified, it loses some of its appeal. For some crusades there must be a decent camouflage.
>
> We should not be misled. . . . The everyday public services are most used by the poor. The affluent can have private education; the poor must have public schools. The very affluent, if they are indeed very affluent, can buy books; poorer children need a public library. It is the poor who frequent the public playgrounds and the public hospitals. Welfare payments have a particular beneficence for the man or woman or family who has no other income. Messers

Howard Jarvis and Milton Friedman heading this new crusade for the self do not, of course, present themselves as enemies of the poor. They are friends of freedom and enemies of government. But no one should be in doubt about the object of their crusade: it is against the least fortunate of our citizens.

Galbraith went further and remarked on the implications of this revolt against the poor for the viability of capitalism.

There are consequences of this revolt against the poor that should be of special concern to conservatives. Capitalism did not survive in the United States or in other industrial countries because of a rigid adherence to individualist precept – the sacrifice of those who could not make it in a stern, competitive struggle. It survived because of a continuing and generally a successful effort to soften its sharp edges – to minimize the suffering and discontent of those who fall in face of competition, economic power, ethnic disadvantage, or moral, mental or physical incapacity. It was this ability of modern industrial society to develop, and on occasions, to enforce a sense of community that Marx failed to foresee.

I have quoted these long passages from Galbraith with a twofold aim. First, I wish to reinforce the point I made earlier: that social forces have been activated within developed industrial societies which have somewhat curbed and softened the inhuman face of capitalism and made it compatible with a certain degree of concern for the welfare of the disadvantaged and the deprived. Second, Galbraith's remarks reveal how the fundamental spirit of capitalism is oriented primarily to concern for the self and disregard for the non-self, and this exclusive concern for the self has a tendency to assert itself into prominence again and again and to prevail over 'social conscience' or the regard for non-self.

A new philosophical wind which is blowing in the western world, favouring self at the expense of non-self, has begun to invade the non-western world. It must be recognized that the failure of non-capitalist economic models to serve as viable models of growth and as effective substitutes for capitalism have made Asian countries like India vulnerable to individualistic winds from the west. Socialists must recognize that celebration of the failure of the socialist model has also begun to mean celebration of a new future for capitalism in India, in one of the largest countries of the world.

It is in this background that one must take note of the prognosis regarding the strong possibilities of an Asian capitalism that Zakir Sahib made more than fifty years back. His words have proved to be as prophetic as they were perceptive. It is obvious now that radicals had not seriously reckoned with the potentialities of an Asian capitalism and of capitalism striking deeper roots in the Asian soil. From this angle, Zakir Sahib had a better appreciation of Indian realities than many others. It is also obvious that while Zakir Sahib found it very hard emotionally to reconcile himself to this prospect, he did not shrink intellectually from the logic of his enquiry into recognizing this strong tendency. To quote:

Since I have allowed myself to be drawn into the rather uncertain domain of prophecy I may as well say that the stage seems to be set for the growth of an Asiatic capitalism in which India appears marked for a big role – that this new capitalism, although it will have its distinct individuality, will not be very much different from its Western predecessor, can be easily assumed. The forces that can be expected to range themselves against its will, I feel, not be strong enough to stop the new growth. They themselves have not courage, the imagination, and the experience to put Indian economy on a higher level of efficiency. The capitalist seems to me to have more of these and he seems resolved to try himself. He is apparently ready to subject himself to state control and regulation; should we be surprised if he is also planning to control and regulate the state? No, I do not think the Asiatic and Indian capitalism will be much different from the Western.

Maybe that it has less of the conqueror in it to begin with, but oh, it will have an inexhaustible fund of what we called the civic virtues at its disposal, the clever calculator, the shrewd diplomat will compensate for the lack of bellicose bravado. If it is not given to him, for a while, to get the riches that come from power, he will exercise the power that comes from riches. *We seem fated to go through the whole gamut.* Capitalism will set up the machinery, the apparatus of our economic life for his gain, and when he has run the mad race, the social conscience will assert itself, but will do so successfully only when the chances of maintaining economic life at a high level are assured and change the private profit economy of capitalism into the planned social economy for satisfying needs. How long, oh, how long, and then to imagine what must fill the interval.

As raised by Zakir Sahib long back, the relevant question even today is: are we condemned to live with capitalism and with the harsh logic of all that early capitalism brings in its wake? There is no easy answer to this question because the answer does not lie entirely in the realm of economics but also in the realm of society's consciousness, perceptions and choices, and, above all, in the realm of the level of organization and consciousness of the labouring poor who will be called upon to pay the price for untrammelled capitalist growth.

In making his prognosis, Zakir Sahib mostly took economics into account and not emerging socio-political processes and forces. The source of the complexities in the social situation of latecomers and Asian countries like India is that here, a strong anti-capitalist consciousness had already taken deep root much, much before capitalism could complete the tasks of modern economic development. In other words, a 'social conscience' had already emerged as a factor to reckon with before capitalist economic transition had been effected. There is, therefore, no question of tolerating a long 'interval' between the completion of the economic transition and the rise of a 'social conscience', as in western economic history, which was noted by Zakir Sahib. The rise of a 'social conscience' preceded the capitalist breakthrough.

The fact that an awakening of the poor can block a smooth capitalist transition if the interests of the poor are disregarded, is a major factor to reckon with. But the fact that any viable alternative to capitalism is not in sight, and that the image of socialism has already been darkened by the collapse of the second world and the failure of bureaucratic state socialism within the country, can also not be disregarded. Does it then mean a social stalemate? I am not inclined to surrender my faith that the ultimate answer lies with the labouring poor.

References

Galbraith, J.K. (1980), *A View from the Sands: Of People, Politics, Military Power and Arts* (London: Hamish Hamilton).

Gopal, S. (1989), *Sarvapalli Radhakrishnan: A Biography* (New Delhi: Oxford University Press).

Seligman, A.R. (ed.) (1950), *Encyclopedia of Social Sciences,* Vols 3 and 4 (New York: Macmillan).

Sombart, Warner (1950), 'Capitalism', in Seligman, *Encyclopedia of Social Sciences.*

Thompson, E.P. (1980), *The Making of the English Working Class* (London: Penguin Books).

Reason and History

Irfan Habib

It was under Dr Zakir Husain that I received my first employment at the
Aligarh Muslim University, but that is a personal matter. What is important is
Dr Zakir Husain's commitment to a free and secular modern India, to which he
adhered throughout his life – a cause for which he left Mohammedan Anglo
Oriental (MAO) College, which was then just becoming a university, and helped
to establish the Jamia Milia Islamia as part of the national education programme
of the Non-Cooperation movement. Zakir Husain, as one of the authors of the
Wardha Scheme, sought to bring education to the masses, and all his life he gave
expression to the aspirations of the Indian people for establishing a secular, enlightened and equitable society.

Keeping in view this commitment of the great figure after whom this
lecture is named, I thought it might be best for me to speak on 'Reason and
History', making it clear at the very beginning that I have here mainly Indian
history in mind. I have chosen the subject because it seems to me that the entire
modern tradition of historiography in India, a tradition particularly developed
by the nationalist school of historians, aiming to base the study of Indian history
on the rational, scientific approach, is being brought into question in this country; therefore, given my own profession as a historian, the best I can do is to
discuss the major points targeted by the current assault on reason in the understanding of our past. I should like to explain in the beginning that by reason I
have no philosophical concept in mind such as Kant's concept of reason. I have
simply in mind the meaning given to reason in ordinary discourse. Reason is
thus, for me, the application of argument and logic, and the decision not to
proceed with *a priori* premises as far as possible. I assume that historians who
want to study the history of their country, or, in fact, of any country, cannot
accept premises laid down by any particular religion or national or racial doctrine, but must try to apply an approach that could be applied by a person
coming from any kind of background, any kind of religion, any country. In other
words, he must try to see his country's history in a universalist fashion: Indian

Sixth Zakir Husain Memorial Lecture, 28 February 1994.

history cannot be approached differently from the history of Afghanistan or of England. Similarly, the history of Islam cannot be approached differently from the history of Hinduism or of Christianity. Nobody can say as a historian that this particular religion is the only true one, or that the self-view of his country alone must be accepted. Serious historians must always remember that when World War I broke out, those with the greatest names among English historians said in a statement that the fault lay entirely with Germany and the German historians, including almost all the biggest names amongst them, and they were countered with the assertion that the blame rested entirely with France and England. This clearly shows how easy it is for us to slip into irrational chauvinism, where historians take sides in interpretation of events according to the countries they belong to. For us, in India, it should serve as a warning not to read into India's past what we think should be good for her public relations today. Heeding the warning, we should, perhaps, look into the concept of 'India' itself.

India is a country. It is also a nation; but all countries are not nations. In fact, all geographical territories are not countries either. There is a historical process by which geographical territories become countries, and there is a further historical process by which countries become nations. We know, for example, in the case of Britain, where there would not be any quarrel about it, that the British Isles are geographically separated from Europe. But England was not a country when the Romans occupied Britain. English historians, therefore, do not speak of Roman England; they speak of Roman Britain. England as a country took shape as Old English became its language, and this was no earlier than the ninth century. But it still did not become a nation until the sixteenth century, when, under Tudor monarchy, it came to possess a nation-state. In India, similarly, the first time that the concept of India as a country can be traced back to is no earlier than the sixth century BC, with the listing of the sixteen Mahajanapadas; and it is perhaps not older than the third century BC, when Ashokan Minor Rock Edicts speak of Jambudvipa as a single country. India as a nation, on the other hand, is very modern. From here one must go to the definition of 'nation', especially that by John Stuart Mill, who stressed that a country becomes a nation when its people think that they should be governed only by persons from amongst themselves. Where this consciousness of political unity is not present, a nation is not yet born. A country is thus different from a nation; and my favourite quotation is from Ram Mohan Roy who, in 1830, said that India 'cannot be a nation because it is divided into castes'. He did not add 'and communities', but he could well have done so. In 1870, Keshav Chandra Sen, in his lectures in England, spoke of India becoming a nation as it struggled against its ancient inequities and divisions, and as it was awakening through modern education to the need for social reform. He called upon Britain, rather ingenuously, to help India become a nation. So, clearly, the creation of the Indian nation is a fairly recent phenomenon. India has become a nation mainly by its rejection of much of the inequitous part of its past culture. It has also become a nation by developing pride in its previous achievements. These two processes, in which we have felt pride in what has been done by our civilization in the past and, at the same time, felt indignant about what has divided us, are inseparable elements in the transformation of India into a nation. I would like to argue that these two approaches are also very necessary when we wish to analyse our past on the basis of reason.

There are, undoubtedly, well-known historians who see history as a narrative and find no reason for causal analysis. History, therefore, has professedly no great message for them. Fisher, for example, claimed that he saw no large rhythms in history. But we must also remember what Marc Bloch, perhaps the greatest historian of this century, told us in his last book, *Historian's Craft*, before he was executed by the Germans: that history has no meaning unless it is seen to be of some use. Surely we go back to our history in order to find out what faults we have committed so that we may not commit them again, and to remember what we have been able to achieve in the past in order to have the confidence to face the future. History has had, therefore, a part to play in the creation of our nation, in so far as it has told us what the evils of our past culture were, how British imperialism had exploited India, and, therefore, why imperialism should be opposed and why we should unite into a nation. It is not surprising that among the early nationalists, there should have been so much interest in history. Romesh Chander Dutt wrote on the civilization of ancient India, and is perhaps the greatest writer yet on Indian economic history. Dadabhai Naoroji was not only an economist of calibre, but also proved to be an economic historian of calibre, as when he traced the development of the Drain and how British rule had intensified poverty in India, and how it was therefore preventing the development of India into a modern country.

This is surely the substance of a reasoned approach to our history. It means that we take our country as a product of a larger cultural tradition, and we also see it as a part of the world. India would not have become a nation if modern ideas had not arrived. Modern apologists from the side not only of Indian chauvinists or Islamic fundamentalists, but also others, insist on finding these ideas in earlier philosophies and in earlier cultures, in such attenuated forms as to be reduced to mere formalities, bereft of substance. But even the fact of formal antecedents is not often borne out by the scrutiny of the actual content and substance of the pre-modern ideologies. What at best was only casual, scattered or incidental in the ideological systems of earlier cultures, became in the modern west, from the French Revolution of 1789 to the Socialist movement of the nineteenth century, the central substance of culture. Given the presence of such an ideological powerhouse in the west, it is vain to argue that modern India could develop in isolation from its formative influences. It is often felt that to recognize western influence and to attribute any kind of 'regenerating' role to colonialism, after Marx, is humiliating for our national psyche and should be eschewed. But this is a mere ostrich-like closing of one's eyes.

We also tend to look for virtue and greatness only on this side of India's present political frontiers. Such, indeed, is the cult of the political borders that when, in 1992, the Indian Council of Historical Research, of which I was then

Chairman, decided to celebrate the four hundred-and-fiftieth birth anniversary of
Akbar, some of our BJP friends argued that Akbar was not an Indian because he
was born at Umarkot which belongs to Pakistan. This was by no means an
exceptional aberration. In our official archaeology, what is called 'Indus culture'
by the rest of the world, including the Pakistan Department of Archaeology,
becomes 'Harappan', as if it is a point of great political importance, although
Harappa too is in Pakistan! We are always anxious that somehow or the other
we should claim greater antiquity on our side of the 1947 frontier. Before 1947,
we had as much pride in the Indus culture as anyone else; now we are called
upon to concentrate especially on the Painted Gray Ware culture of west U.P. and
Haryana. When this goes on at the level of professional historians and archaeologists, we need not be surprised at repeatedly reading in textbooks that Indian
history has always been spoiled by foreigners. Muslims are foreigners: they have
been spoiling Indian history since AD 1200 and there have been arguments whether
India had been under foreign rule for 700 years or 200 years. Those who say 700
years treat the Delhi Sultans and Mughal emperors as foreigners. Professor Arjun
Dev once remarked in a note that when such statements about Muslims in textbooks were officially discouraged, textbook writers tended to attribute all the
faults in Indian culture, such as seclusion of women, *sati* and other evils, to the
depredations of the Huns, despite the fact that there is not a single Hun ruler who
can even be firmly identified as such. (Toramana and Mihirakula never described themselves as Huns in their inscriptions.)

The fact is that no country in the world has been free of foreign invasions, whether China, England, France or Russia. Before modern times, these
foreign invasions, with all their immediate destructive consequences, were one
set of means by which cultural cross-fertilization took place and technologies
diffused. The worldwide Mongol empire of the thirteenth century was one of the
greatest transmitters of technology, despite the horrors it caused. Gunpowder, the
magnetic compass, the printing press, the spinning wheel – all moved from China
and Central Asia into Europe through the routes opened by nomadic invasions,
and created the basis of the technological development that undermined the feudal system and sowed the seeds of modern Europe. How can one then say that
Indian culture did not at all benefit from foreign invasions (let us just remember
Gandhara art, Greek astronomy, Persian literature and painting), or that, left to
itself, India would have attained glories that now cannot be imagined of and
which only foreign conquests deprived us of?

We have also a view of pre-medieval India in which this irrational approach prevails. We are invited to trace back the Indian nation to antiquity,
almost to the Indus culture, and assume that Hinduism, in its basic essentials, has
not historically developed but has all its roots in the Indus culture and the Rigvedic
times; and that essentially the Indian culture had attained all possible pinnacles
(including 'Vedic mathematics'!) in that hoary past. This kind of parochial claim
is seldom so blatantly made but, unfortunately, it is often implicit in an increasingly large part of writing among Indian historians and archaeologists. One can

take as an illustration the preoccupation that has become very common among some Indian archaeologists and historians about 'the Aryan home in India'. When R.C. Majumdar was editing the Bharatiya Vidya Bhawan Series, *The History and Culture of the Indian People*, he was asked by K.M. Munshi, the patron saint of that series, to say that the Aryans had gone out from India. R.C. Majumdar had written much about the glories of ancient India, including its 'colonies', but he could not accept such a blatant myth. He had a very well-informed chapter written on the Aryans, but he was forced to include an appendix in which the claim of the indigenous origins of the Aryans was put forward. During that time, it was regarded as an idiosyncrasy. Today, I am afraid, the 'Indian home of the Aryans' is on its way to becoming a quasi-official doctrine. In 1979, when, in its second incarnation, the Jan Sangh had become very important in the Indian government and the second session of the Indian History and Culture Society created by the RSS was held, its president, Professor Khaliq Ahmad Nizami, called upon historians to watch 'what o'clock it is'. Apparently the hour had struck for an approach different from the earlier scientific one, and Professor B.B. Lal, responding to this change of time, and doubtlessly looking at the clock, wrote a paper which was published in 1981 in the same Society's volume, *Bias in Indian Historiography*, in which he put the foreign and Indian origins of the Indo-European languages at an equal level. So, what was an idiosyncrasy in the 1950s and totally unacceptable to R.C. Majumdar, was now put at par with the scientific approach to the diffusion of the Indo-European languages. Things have gone so far that Dr S.R. Rao, a well-known archaeologist, has propounded a reading of the Indus script on the basis of Vedic Sanskrit. Despite Mahadevan's criticisms and the refusal of serious linguists to accept Rao's decipherment, his readings appear as undisputed or unqueried in the official Archaeological Survey of India's pamphlet on Lothal. Although his decipherment would result in making Sanskrit a very primitive monosyllabic language, it says much for our culture that we are willing to sacrifice Sanskrit and its greatness if it could be proved that the people of the Indus culture were Aryans. In the same book, *Bias in Indian Historiography*, K.C. Verma had a long article saying that the Dravidians had no language of their own, and that Sanskrit has borrowed nothing from the Dravidian languages. So we are now actually initiating a divisive debate amongst ourselves by insisting that the Indo-Europeans or Aryans went from India, and that the Dravidians have no great past to which they can lay claim, except one which lay within the bosom of north Indian (Aryan) culture.

The 'neo-Aryans' among our academics tend to forget that there is no single race with which Indo-Europeans can be identified, and that most Indians and eastern Iranians are long-headed like Africans and Australasians and not broad-headed like Europeans, Slavs and west Iranians, with whom we wish to be associated as Aryans. It is therefore unlikely that there was an Indo-European race from which Slavs and Europeans have descended on the one side, and Indian Aryans, or those of us who think they are Indian Aryans, on the other. Nearly half of the Indus skeletons, as more than half of the people today in northern India, were classed as of the Mediterranean type dominant in north India, whose purest representatives, according to the physical anthropologists, were not found either in Europe or in the Garhwal Himalayas but in the Arabian peninsula which is the heartland of Semitic languages!

Moreover, linguistic history has made clear, ever since David Macalpin's discovery of links between Proto-Elamite and the Dravidian languages, that there once existed a long chain of Proto-Elamo-Dravidian languages right from western Iran to south India as early as late neolithic times. It is therefore much more likely that Indians or the people who lived in India spoke Proto-Elamite and Proto-Dravidian languages, or languages associated with them, rather than any Indo-European language, before 2000 BC. I would not like to go into further details, but on the basis of glotto-chronology, archaeological remains of the horse and the language relationships of Indo-Iranian dialects with Finno-Ugrian as worked out by Harmatta, the stagewise progress of Indo-European languages or vocabularies towards India around 2000 BC has been fairly well established. To insist, in the face of all this evidence, that it is to be put at par with the kind of theories that Rao and others put forward blithely, placing sometimes the *Rig Veda* and sometimes even the *Mahabharata* in the fourth millennium BC, is like putting the Darwinian theory of the evolution of species at par with the story of Adam being the first man. But the situation today is that if you open your newspaper, almost every week or fortnight some person who says that he has deciphered the Indus script and related it to the *Rig Veda*, or some person who says that a certain incident in the Indian epic happened in 3600 BC, is immediately reported as the brilliant discoverer of a new truth. And seminars and conferences to this effect are being held: we went to Mysore for the Indian History Congress in December 1993; immediately after the Congress a seminar was held to counter its profane influences and to urge that the Aryans had their original home in India. To my greatest surprise, many of the reputed names among historians and archaeologists of today were there. So something is clearly wrong with us, and that is why I think that the time has arrived to insist that things which may be populist in nature are yet very dangerous for this country. The preoccupation with the 'Indian home' of the 'Aryan' could well incite a disputation between the votaries of the 'Dravidian' and the 'Aryan' sources of our culture, a dispute which is largely irrelevant to a comprehension of the development of our civilization but which may lead to further ethnic bitterness, of which we have already a surfeit in our country.

Another important area in which unreason is becoming more and more manifest is the history of Indian society. For the last two hundred years we have accepted the fact that our society, especially the caste system, has been inequitous. From Ram Mohan Roy to Keshav Chandra Sen, from Gokhale to Gandhi, our national consciousness and the national movement spread by rejecting in varying degrees, this central institution of our past. But now, as we glorify our past culture without reservation, without limits, those criticisms of our past inequities are sought to be removed from our consciousness. It was seen in what was done with history textbooks in Madhya Pradesh, Rajasthan and Uttar Pradesh during the time that the electorates in these states chose particular governments which, though later dismissed, might yet return: criticisms of the caste system in history textbooks were either removed or strongly modified. The protest against these removals was unfortunately not as indignant, not as strong, as one might have expected. Somehow or the other, it is a popular position again to say that in our past culture there have been no or few inequities. This has also been helped by western scholarship which, for other reasons, has been arguing, as Louis Dumont does in *Homo Hierarchicus*, whose French edition came out in 1970, that to the Indian civilization, western approaches are not applicable. Louis Dumont has argued that economics is not applicable to the history of the caste system because economics as a science has developed recently and so Indians did not know economics. History is not applicable to the caste system because Indians did not care for history. As I have said elsewhere, if this were an acceptable argument, you cannot write the biography of a person who has not written his own autobiography, or talk about the economic factors of the decline of feudalism, because no economics existed in the fourteenth and fifteenth centuries in Europe. Dumont's claim that Indian culture must be understood on its own terms, that is, in terms of the ideology of hierarchy based on purity and pollution, is totally opposed to reason; and yet, because of its emphasis on an independent ideological framework for India, it seems so satisfying to our national pride. Moreover, however much we may talk about *swadeshi*, the moment a European scholar says something about our uniqueness, we seem to grasp it with particular enthusiasm. Yet, even Weber's argument that the caste system prevented mobility and therefore cultural development was based on a very one-sided interpretation of the caste system. In an important essay, 'Values as Obstacles to Economic Growth in South Asia', Morris D. Morris has rightly pointed out that the caste system is just a social institution subject to the same kind of economic influences as one would expect in other societies. The caste system was a particularly important element in our society for reinforcing class exploitation. I would repeat my argument made elsewhere, that the caste system has been of use to all ruling classes, whether of the Gupta empire or the Delhi Sultanate, the Mughals or the East India Company, in so far as it helped to increase the surplus which could be extracted out of the menial labourer, the outcaste and the low-caste peasants. It was not an institution which merely put the brahmans on the top of a purity-based hierarchy. It has been an institution which has benefited all the ruling classes, whether Vaishnavites or Saivites, Muslims or Christians (or Utilitarians). Therefore, to say, as one President of the Indian History Congress said in the 1960s, and what we used to read in our textbooks in the British days in the 1940s, that the caste system has both 'merits' and 'demerits', is absurd. It has merits only for the upper strata and it has nothing but demerits from the point of view of the lower classes and women. It poses essentially the question: with which side does the historian identify himself? Surely, in line with adult franchise, accepted as the national ideal since the Nehru Committee Report, 1928, and the Karachi resolution of the Congress, 1931, it is 'the greatest good of the greatest number' that the historian must consider and take his stand with regard to the caste system, as also all other institutions.

This makes me pass on to a third point where the opponents of reason are at work increasingly (and they have been at work for a long time). Religious people, including historians who are religious, have been saying that Marxists assign inadequate weight to the role of religion in history. Their criticism has gained weight now that Edward Said, in his *Orientalism*, has lumped the imperialists and the socialists together, putting William Jones and Karl Marx in one and the same basket. Since this book came out in 1978, very much as Dumont has become the prophet of Indian exceptionalism, Said has become the prophet of those who argue that Asian religions and cultures must be studied on their own terms, and not in terms of modern ideas or by modern criteria which have been nurtured in Europe. Said's book has become the new Bible to which the Islamic historians again and again appeal. You cannot study the history of Islam unless you are a Muslim, unless you accept the Revelation and Muslim law. My friend, Professor Athar Ali, has pertinently asked: how is one going to study the history of Jews and Christians in the time of the Prophet? Are there going to be three histories simultaneously, viz. the history of the Jews in seventh-century Hejaz, studied in terms of Judaism; the history of Christians in the same territory and the same period, studied according to Christianity; and Islamic history during the time, according to the terms supposedly laid down by Islam? A history of Hejaz, let alone Arabia, could then never be reconstructed, in the maze of contradictory quasi-histories. Not only, therefore, will I not accept the notion of history to be built up on someone's terms, but I will go further. If, as one must acknowledge, religion has been important in history, history has also been important for religion. Religions are established and develop as historical phenomena and processes; therefore, they too must be made subject to study by impartial and critical historical method. My experience with even university audiences tells me that the statement that all religions are subject to history is not usually well received. But the fact is that all religions evolve. The self-image of a religion is greatly influenced by the meaning assigned to scriptural words by the believers of that faith, the circumstances in which its believers find themselves at different times and places, and the images they develop (with varying degrees of accommodation or hostility) or religions with which they come into contact. One cannot write the history of the religions of India if one first accepts the Hindu tradition or the Islamic as the only valid one. If one accepts Hinduism as the only valid tradition, one would necessarily have a picture of Islam which is totally invalid according to the picture the Muslims have of their religion, and vice versa.

I would like to quote two passages here; the first from R.C. Majumdar, giving an allegedly Hindu view of Islam. 'The Hindus resented the Muslim conquest of India and wistfully looked forward to the day when the name Aryavarta, the land of the Aryans, would be once more justified by the extermination of the Mlecchas (Muslims).' Extermination of Muslims (the word in brackets in the quotation is put by Majumdar himself) is thus the only way to assuage

Hindu resentment. (By the way, this volume was supported by a grant from the Government of India in the early 1960s.) Then we have Ishtiaq Husain Qureshi from the other side, a leading intellectual of the University of Delhi before 1947: 'Hinduism is dangerous to Islam because it is instinctive, subtle and deep, but as efficacious in its result as the silent descending growth of root columns from the ever-spreading branches of an old banyan tree.' So the only thing you can do to protect Islam is to cut the banyan tree of Hinduism! Can one ask historians to look at Indian history by accepting either of these images of 'the other'?

It is not surprising that neither of the conflicting images, whether of *mlecchas* or *kafirs*, is historically accurate. R.C. Majumdar speaks of the democratic ideas of Muslims leading to a wonderful equality among the brothers in faith; and Ishtiaq Qureshi says much more in the same strain. But when one looks at the sources, especially the texts which Muslims wrote in the thirteenth and fourteenth centuries, the word 'equality' does not occur. Barani, the learned theologian and historian, is all for hierarchy of birth. Hierarchy is crucial to society, he says, and a society governed by Islamic law cannot flourish without hierarchy. If one looks at the criticisms of Hindus in Muslim texts, whether they are Sufic or orthodox, the caste system is not ever singled out for criticism. The main sins denounced are polytheism and image worship. In fact, Amir Khusrau even praises *sati*. In the eighth century, when Muhammad ibn Qasim occupied Sind, the brahmans went to him and said that the Jats of Sind, as pastoral nomads, were insufferable menials, and that the rule has been that they should wear no turbans nor shoes, and should be accompanied by dogs whenever they go out, and should not ride saddled horses, almost repeating the constraints prescribed for the chandalas in the *Manu Smriti*. Muhammad ibn Qasim approved of these rules and confirmed these disabilities. That there was no relaxation under Arab rule is shown by the fact that according to Balazuri, Amran, the Governor of Sind under Caliph Mu'tasim Billah, as late as the ninth century, ordered that Jats must go about only if they are accompanied by dogs. Any picture of Muslims as crusaders for equality is thus largely ahistorical. Both Muslims and Hindus were the subjects of Muslim rulers who never displayed any intention of touching the caste system, which, in fact, gave them access to an extra surplus that would not have been available had it not existed. Moreover, one should not forget that making slaves out of captives and thus combining war with slave-raiding was quite common. The slaves usually became Muslims and there were also converts to Islam among the subordinate ruling classes for both sincere and political motives. So, while Islam certainly grew by conversion, conversion itself was not an object of state policy under any Sultan. When a theologian suggested to Iltutmish, according to Barani, that Hindus should be given the option of either accepting Islam or facing the sword, and Iltutmish seemed carried away by enthusiasm, his vizier, Nizam-ul-Mulk Junaidi, took him aside to complain, 'What talk is this? If this is attempted, being just like salt in one's rice, we shall all be slaughtered.' So the Sultan was dissuaded from attempting a suicidal course.

We thus see that the actual facts of history are quite different from what the proponents of the two communal sides would like to imagine. This is a point long insisted upon by the nationalist school of historians. I think I need to quote only Professor Mohammad Habib, who, in his *Mahmud of Ghazni* (1924), said bluntly that 'Mahmud is still worshipped by such Musalmans as have cast off the teaching of Lord Krishna in their devotion to minor gods.' I think it would be very difficult for a historian of today to make a statement of such boldness. This could, of course, be said of the Hindu counterparts of such Muslims as well.

It is not my view that the conquests of the Arabs and the Sultans did not bring about any changes in economy and culture. I would rather recall what D.D. Kosambi, in his *Introduction to the Study of Indian History*, said in 1956, about 'Islamic raiders . . . breaking hidebound customs in the adoption and transmission of new techniques'. Perhaps in this statement he was influenced by the researches of P.K. Gode, the remarkable Sanskritist, who should be a model for an unbiased scientific approach to many of us today. We know now, after studies in the history of technology, that with the Muslims came right-angle gearing, very important for water-lift by the 'Persian wheel', as also the spinning wheel, the *charkha*, which became, with Gandhiji, the symbol of *swadeshi*. This latter device too was not present in ancient India. Its first description occurs in the metrical history of Islami, 1350. Previous to that, only the hand spindle was in use. As for liquor distillation, the Muslims made an important contribution by fashioning more efficient stills, and already in the late thirteenth century, liquor was being distilled not only in Delhi but also in Kol (Aligarh), my home town, the seat of the Aligarh Muslim University. The Muslims brought paper too, with all its cultural, political and financial consequences. Arcuate and brick construction by use of arch, dome, and cementing lime and gypsum were features of the Saracenic architecture, established in Delhi and then radiating from there. Pedals in the looms which increased the speed of weaving came in or before the fifteenth century. Sericulture was introduced in Bengal as well as in Kashmir. Professor R.S. Sharma has propounded an urban decline between AD 300 and AD 1000, and then an urban revival. But what happened in the thirteenth and fourteenth centuries was an immense expansion of towns, of which one can see an example in the Archaeological Survey of India's air photograph of the city of Tughlaqabad. The surface remains of other towns and the records and accounts of travellers give us an impression of the other great towns and cities of the Sultanate. At the level of ideology, we must remember that an extensive acquaintance with Greek rationalism and science came with Arabic and Persian. Of the scientific temper that Islam's Greek-learning gave rise to, we have a splendid product in Alberuni's famous *Kitab al-Hind*, *c.* 1035 – an unrivalled objective description of Indian philosophy and science. Rationalism had a notable revival at the court of Akbar. The last great product of medieval Graeco–Arab science was Jai Singh Sawai, the ruler of Jaipur and a great astronomer. Then we have contributions to art, especially Mughal painting and architecture, attributable largely to the Islamic contacts, and, finally, religious ideology. The presence of the two religions invited both confrontation and conciliation, producing some-thing that was quite unique in such challenge–response situations, namely, a rejection of both religions through an assertion of absolute monotheism by lower-class preachers like Namdev, Kabir, Sain and Rai Das, and by Nanak. The immense radicality of this ideological ferment in the sixteenth century is still not perhaps fully recognized. There is much wisdom in what a Muslim theologian of Akbar's and Jahangir's time, Abdul Haq Muhaddis Dehlavi, said, attributing the statement to his grandfather: There are Muslims and Kafirs or Hindus; but there is a third category, the *muwahhid* or monotheist, who is neither, and whose status or position cannot be understood unless one has grown up. And a recent President of the Indian History Congress rightly asked whether the Indian people have at last grown up enough to understand that Hinduism and Islam are not the end of everything!

Finally, I would urge a return to reason in looking at the history of colonialism and the national movement. The way these are being presented in researches emanating from western universities and western academics is, like Dumont's view of caste, fairly welcome to our own brand of national chauvin-ists, who have their own parochial view of our past. The new view of the sahibs marks a considerable departure from the earlier official view that Indian states were oriental despotisms, that the land revenue was equal to rent, and that, therefore, whoever governed, controlled Indian society. Such were the notions of James Mill and Macaulay. The corollary was the belief that the English, by stepping into the shoes of the Mughal emperors, were now controlling and moul-ding India in their own interest, and, perhaps secondarily, in the interest of the Indian people. This position was central to the official self-view of colonialism. If, on the other hand, one is to argue that the colonial conquest was not impor-tant, that the British conquest of India was a surface incident and therefore the national movement amounted really to tilting at windmills, then, one must also argue that no empire and no state of any power or position existed before the British conquest, and that when the English stepped into the shoes of such ephem-eral states, they really did not establish any truly colonial regime. Burton Stein opened the debate with his theory of a segmentary state in south India, in 1980. Fussman reinforced it by looking at the Mauryan empire in a paper in 1982 and questioning its credentials as a centralized state. C.A. Bayly, in his *Rulers, Townsmen and Bazars* in 1983, looked behind the bureaucracy of the Mughal empire to locate his 'corporate groups' who, when they shifted their loyalty to the British in their own interest, helped create the 'Indian empire'. The British conquest never really occurred, since British expansion was an Anglo-Indian enterprise, perhaps more Indian than English. Andre Wink argued in his *Sover-eignty in India*, 1986, that there was no state policy, there was only *fitna* or compromise (his peculiar meaning of the Arabic word) in Indian polities. Frank Perlin believes in another Arabic word, *watan*, representing local land-holding which, he believes, rather than the state, was central to Indian polities. The *New Cambridge History of India* in its scheme tells us that there was a colonial 'transition', so that Indians transited themselves into colonialism very much like feudal Europe developing into capitalist Europe; and then it also tells us that there was no British empire, only 'the Indian empire' (Vol. 2, *Transition to Colonialism* and Vol. 3, *Indian Empire*). And my friend, Professor Harbans Mukhia, tells us that colonial society in India is not really the creation of the colonial state. Apparently, it is the Indians' own creation! One might as well argue that the Aztecs and Incas created the Spanish conquest of the Americas.

Clearly, what we have here is a fairy tale, based on a total defiance of documentation and statistics. We are entertained increasingly to after-dinner stories, but not, alas, dinners in the form of proper substantiation. Amir Khusrau's tomb is situated by Bayly in Allahabad, although his first book being on Allahabad, he should have known better. Mukhia gets so carried away by this discovery that he thinks Khusrau Bagh of Allahabad must be a religious shrine, and since all Muslims go to a religious shrine, it must have become an intellectual centre of the Muslims of Allahabad! There are many similar captivating inaccuracies in the after-dinner stories, which there is no time to cite here. But one cannot pass by the lack of attention to statistics. These are essential. It is statistics that Dadabhai Naoroji and R.C. Dutt argued about; but it is characteristically economic statistics that appear nowhere in Anil Seal's well-known work on Indian nationalism. He can then easily say that India was a financial burden for Britain at the very time when the Drain was the heaviest, in the latter half of the nineteenth century. No economic statistics, only statistics about modern education and how dependent Dadabhai Naoroji was on money received from the lawyers and *banias* of Bombay! We must remember that according to the East India Company's official figures, the annual Drain in as early as the 1780s was nearly £5 million, or £0.9 million more than the annual revenues of Bengal! And then there was the process of deindustrialization in the nineteenth century, about which there has been much debate. These were the two central economic factors behind the creation of the Indian national movement, both of which are being brushed under the carpet by the new theology of the Cambridge School and its supporters, and, I am afraid, also by our 'Subaltern' friends (Professor Ranajit Guha and his followers) to whom the so-called autonomy of the Subaltern classes, which include zamindars, it seems to me, was more important than the major contradiction between British imperialism and the Indian nation, of which the rising bourgeoisie, the working class and the peasantry were the major components. The 'Subaltern' historians too seldom touch upon the aggregates in statistics, for example, those of national income and exports, the drain of wealth, taxation (indicating the exploitation of the Indian peasantry by indirect taxation), etc. But if we want to know what was happening to India, we must keep the national-level statistics in mind. Let us see what the Indian people in their majority were passing through, and then find out what colonialism meant and what the Indian national movement was about. Clearly, it is on these aggregates that, like those of Naoroji and Dutt, our judgements must rest.

I must conclude with an apology for such a long defence of reason in the study of Indian history. I have felt that if the profession of the Indian historian and archaeologist is to retain its reputation in the world, it is important that irrational approaches are confronted. Are we going to have a modern nation, a nation with social equity, for which the national movement fought? Or are we going to have a divided country, living in a manufactured, imagined past of the most parochial kind and, therefore, leading ourselves towards disaster? I am sure that duty calls to all of us, whether historians or citizens, who want to defend the Indian nation to close ranks in the battle of ideas that is now taking place: for this battle needs urgently to be joined with all earnestness.

The Nation-State in the Era of 'Globalization'

Prabhat Patnaik

Dr Zakir Husain was not only a great patriot and an outstanding statesman, but also an economist of repute. It is not generally known that A.V. Chayanov, the now well-known Russian populist writer who wrote on the 'peasant economy', was rescued from oblivion by none other than Dr Zakir Husain. Daniel Thorner, who introduced Chayanov to the western world, where his work received much adulation, by editing his *Theory of the Peasant Economy* and writing an introduction for it, recollects that he himself had never heard of Chayanov until his attention was drawn to him by Dr Zakir Husain. Dr Zakir Husain, in turn, had studied Chayanov's writings during his Heidelberg days, which gives an indication of the depth of his scholarship.

The subject which I have chosen to speak on today is one that is strictly outside of what most economists consider to be the province of their discipline. Nonetheless, I think that economics *does* have some light to throw on the vexed question of nationality and the nation-state. It is in this belief that I have chosen to venture into territory which people of my discipline normally never enter.

I

The development of nationalism in the third world countries, as is well known, followed a very different trajectory from that in the advanced capitalist countries. In the latter, it was a part of the process of the emergence of the bourgeois order in opposition to feudalism, while in the former, it was a part of the anti-colonial struggle. The impact of colonialism, though it differed across countries, had on the whole been in the direction of transcending localism and unifying supra-local economic structures through the introduction of market relations. The struggle against colonialism, consequently, took the form of a national struggle in each instance in which people belonging to different tribes or linguistic communities participated. And the colonial powers in each instance attempted to break this emerging national unity by splitting people along tribal, religious and other such lines.

Seventh Zakir Husain Memorial Lecture, 23 February 1995.

The *modus operandi* of this splitting was not just through political manipulation, as happened, for instance, in Angola, South Africa and a host of other countries; an important part of this *modus operandi* was through the nurturing of a historiography that just denied the existence of any overarching national consciousness. The *national* struggle, the *national* movement were given a tribal or religious character; they were portrayed as being no more than the movement of the dominant tribe or the dominant religious group, for the achievement of narrow, sectional ends. It was this kind of historiography that Thomas Hodgkin was attacking in his account of the emergence of nationalism in colonial Africa (Hodgkin 1956). But the important point is that while colonialism, on the one hand, objectively created the condition for the coming into being of a national consciousness at a supra-tribal, supra-local and supra-religious level, on the other hand, it sought deliberately to subvert this very consciousness by using the same forces which it had objectively undermined.

We in India are much too familiar with this dialectics for me to dwell upon it in any detail: if the development of a pan-Indian national consciousness concurrently with the provincial (or local 'nationality') consciousness among the existing regional–linguistic groups[1] was an objective contribution of colonialism, the fracturing of this national consciousness through the promotion of a religious divide was equally a contribution of colonialism. This is not to say that the soil for this divide did not exist, but then, as George Lukacs once remarked, even false consciousness must have an element of truth which does not in any way negate the fact of its being false consciousness (and hence capable of manipulation).

These national struggles brought into being a plethora of nation-states after decolonization. The success of these national struggles, however, owed not a little to another phenomenon that was occurring at the same time, namely, a deep disunity among the advanced capitalist countries, which were simultaneously the colonial powers – a disunity that Lenin had characterized as 'inter-imperialist rivalry' (Lenin 1963). Inter-imperialist rivalry provided the space within which the anti-colonial national struggles could emerge, develop and come to fruition. It not only prevented a coherent and coordinated response from the colonial powers acting in unison, but, by virtue of its eruption into wars among the major capitalist powers, weakened all of them for a considerable length of time, even while emboldening the national anti-colonial movements and widening their horizons. These movements, which often began as the feeble protests of a group of lawyers and other professionals for petitioning the colonial government for slight amelioration in the conditions of the colonized, developed into mass upsurges as the perception developed that the days of rule by colonial powers who were busy tearing each other's throats must be numbered.

But that was not all. Inter-imperialist rivalry underlay the profound and protracted economic crisis of the capitalist order during the inter-war years. The crisis was not *caused* by the fact of inter-imperialist rivalry. Different writers have emphasized different factors as being responsible for the crisis, and perhaps each of these factors had a contributory role.[2] But the fact remains that inter-imperialist rivalry played the role of accentuating the crisis. Capitalism requires an international leading power which can impose a degree of discipline among the capitalist countries. This was the role played by Britain, though with increasing difficulty, in what Hobsbawm calls the 'long nineteenth century', that is, until the First World War. The emergence of inter-imperialist rivalry not only undermined Britain's leadership, but, in fact, made any leadership impossible; at the same time, it also prevented any collusive action by the major capitalist countries acting in unison on the economic front. Capitalism, consequently, had no response to the crisis engulfing it; what is more, the disunity among the leading capitalist countries which made each one of them pursue a 'beggar-my-neighbour' policy to get out of the Depression, made the crisis much worse.

These economic developments had two very important implications for the third world. First, by pushing vast masses of the peasantry into debt and destitution, they contributed greatly to the widening of the sweep of the national movement, which in any case was gathering momentum taking advantage of the 'space' provided by the fact of inter-imperialist rivalry. Second, since they entailed a breakdown of the international economy (exemplified, for instance, by the drying up of capital exports and the formation of trade blocs in the 1930s), the economic programme of the anti-colonial national movement got firmly committed to *national* economic development through *planning*, that is, eschewed any strategy of getting tied to international market forces. To be sure, for countries which had experienced decades of colonial exploitation through *inter alia* the colonial powers' *use* of the market forces, a severance of links with the world market dominated by these powers would have seemed to be a natural accompaniment of decolonization. But the fact that this world market itself was disrupted must have provided an additional powerful reason. The third world nation-state with its *dirigiste* economic regime and its commitment to *planning* (of whatever description) was thus a natural outgrowth from the very same context that favoured the growth of third world nationalism.

To any dispassionate observer of the world scene, the period 1913–51 must have appeared as the last gasp of capitalism, and it is scarcely surprising that this perception constituted the cornerstone of the theory of the Leninist movement with its basic concept of the 'general crisis of capitalism'.[3] And it was this period that witnessed the Bolshevik Revolution, the beginning of the process of decolonization, the Chinese Revolution and, of course, the detachment of large parts of Europe from the capitalist orbit in the wake of the triumphant march of the Red Army to Berlin.

For my purposes, however, I would like to derive a general conclusion from the experience of this period, schematic though this may seem at first sight, namely, *disunity* in the first world promotes *unity* in the third world (unity in the sense of strengthening supra-local, supra-tribal, supra-regional, and supra-religious loyalties and commitments). I do not see this link between disunity in the first world and unity in the third world as a mere happenstance: it is not as if the period we are talking about merely *happened* to witness a coincidence of disunity in the first world with unity in the third world. I believe there is a causal connection between the two which I have been trying to underscore. And this causal connection also operates in the reverse, namely, *unity* in the first world promotes *disunity* in the third world, as indeed we have been witnessing in the more recent period. Let me turn to this period now.

II

The post-war stabilization and consolidation of capitalism has been a truly amazing phenomenon. Capitalism did not just climb out of the abyss into which it appeared to have sunk in the inter-war period; it experienced in its metropolitan base, the most pronounced boom ever experienced in its history. The collapse of the extant socialist challenge to it is hardly surprising under the circumstances. How could a movement which was premised upon the concept of a 'general crisis of capitalism' cope theoretically with a reality where capitalism *in its home base* was experiencing its most pronounced boom? The *old challenge,* in other words, simply could not be sustained. At first sight, in fact, it may appear intriguing that the battle in its *old form,* that is, based on the old theoretical perceptions, could be carried on for so long into the post-war period. A part of the explanation lies in the fact that Leninism was, and remains, to this date, the only *practical* theory of revolution, the only example, as Lukacs put it, of a theory which is so highly developed that it *bursts into praxis* (Lukacs 1970). But a part of the explanation lies elsewhere, and that is what concerns me here.

Within the post-war boom, there were different phases. Capitalism emerged from the war with, once again, an undisputed leader, the United States. The international monetary system was re-established under US leadership through the Bretton Woods agreement, which sanctified the dollar as being as good as gold. While an ordered international monetary system together with Keynesian demand management in the advanced capitalist economies provided the context of the post-war boom, the uneven development engendered by this boom, as manifested in the rapid growth of the shattered economies of Germany and Japan, progressively undermined US hegemony. When the Bretton Woods system collapsed in 1971 because the conflicts generated by this uneven development were accentuated greatly by the Vietnam war, it looked as if the capitalist world was once again moving into a phase of intensified inter-imperialist rivalry. In short, the idea of a 'general crisis of capitalism' unfolding itself along the lines of Lenin's prognostications still appeared valid, notwithstanding the pronounced boom of the 1950s and 1960s, even as late as the beginning of the 1980s, when the successive oil price hikes both confirmed the proposition about 'space' becoming available during periods of inter-imperialist rivalry and precipitated a massive slump.[4]

It was only in the 1980s that a new kind of unity appeared among the capitalist powers. This was not the unity imposed by one leader, the discipline brought about by a state of 'super-imperialism'; it was unity through agreement among the major powers. This is not to say that there are no major conflicts among these powers; there are, but on a number of issues, especially issues relating to the third world, they stand together. Even on matters affecting themselves, for example, on the agricultural policy of GATT, they strike compromises rather than pushing conflict too far. And, not surprisingly, despite the collapse of the Bretton Woods system, the international monetary system has continued to get along under the system of 'managed float' of currencies.

An associated development, together with this unity, has been a tremendous increase in the fluidity of finance across the frontiers of countries. These two developments, in my view, are related. Fluidity of finance overcomes all national boundaries, while disunity or rivalry among the capitalist powers entails rivalry among them along national lines. To say this is not to claim that rivalry among capitalist powers has disappeared or that conflicts among the national capitals of the metropolitan powers have become non-existent; but since no capitalist power can cordon itself off in a world in which finance is highly mobile, including its own nationals across its own frontiers, this fact imposes limits upon the extent of conflict among them. Together with the emergence of the phenomenon of highly mobile international finance, the advanced capitalist countries have reached a new level of unity. This unity does not preclude crises; in fact, a hallmark of the current situation is the exceedingly high levels of unemployment prevailing in the advanced capitalist world, which, in my view, is linked (for reasons we shall discuss later) to the emergence of highly mobile international finance. But this unity engendered by the internationalization of finance succeeds in breaking down the national reclusiveness of the third world economies and forcing their integration into global financial and commodity markets.

It is this integration that results in the *disunity* of third world societies, a retrogression into regionalism, separatism and even secessionism. Since such separatism requires for its sustenance an alternative identity, different from the old national identity, it tends to be accompanied by religious or ethnic conflicts. In short, I wish to argue that phenomena which usually have been investigated entirely in cultural terms, or in terms relating to the 'superstructure', have economic roots as well. To examine these, let us see what 'integration into the global economy' actually means.

The *justification* usually advanced for integration into the global economy is that *productive* capital has become internationally mobile at long last. As is well known, throughout the history of capitalism, the mobility of productive capital has remained confined to the advanced capitalist countries alone.[5] The phenomenon of underdevelopment has arisen precisely because of this: the underdeveloped countries saw the penetration of metropolitan goods into their markets precipitating deindustrialization in their own economies, but, despite their low wages, failed to attract productive capital from the metropolis to become manufacturing centres themselves. Had they done so, the gigantic unevenness or 'dualism' which we find in the world economy, the split between the advanced and backward economies, would have disappeared long ago. This, however, did not happen: productive capital from the metropolis went to the temperate regions of white settlement, such as the US, Australia and Canada, but never came to the backward economies of the tropics. And now it is being said in defence of globalization that things are changing, that if only the underdeveloped countries open their doors and create the appropriate climate of confidence, foreign capital would move in, not just to capture their domestic markets (which is of no benefit to them) but to locate its production facilities on their soil (owing to their low wages) for meeting *global* demand. It is on the basis of this promise (which, if it materialized, would indeed be conducive to their economic advance) that the underdeveloped countries are being asked to open up their economies, dismantle barriers to the free flow of capital into or out of their economies, and roll back the state as far as possible from the arena of production (since excessive state presence in the sphere of production is supposed to be inimical, for a variety of reasons, to the creation of business confidence).

As a matter of fact, however, what has become genuinely mobile across countries is not *productive* capital but short-term finance in the form of 'hot money' which moves around from country to country in search of quick profits, especially in the form of speculative gains. Now, this form of capital mobility does not induce any economic growth in the recipient country: the foreign creditors are not interested in undertaking any productive ventures, no genuine *entrepreneur* would undertake any productive venture financed by short-term speculative funds (since the sudden withdrawal of such funds would leave him bankrupt), and the state in any case is not allowed to undertake much productive investment. As a result, when 'hot money' flows in, it cannot be used for augmenting growth; and when it flows out, the strain of the balance of payments in any case prevents any growth. Of course, if the 'hot money' inflow has been used for stimulating imports of *consumption goods* for the elite, then its flowing out is accompanied by drastic squeezes on the living standards of the poor (for generating the requisite surplus for financing the outflow), by sharp cutbacks in whatever productive investment was occurring and by the transfer of national assets to foreign creditors 'for a song'. Mexico today provides a classic example of all this.

Thus globalization which is ushered in on the promise of higher growth, produces no such thing. On the other hand, the stagnation, the unemployment, the impoverishment which it produces, together with the consequent increase in crime and violence (which further snuffs out whatever prospects had remained of productive capital inflow), leads to a break-up of the nation for at least three reasons, which I discuss *seriatim*.

First, there is the 'secessionism of the rich'. If the growth prospects of the nation get tied to the degree of success in enticing direct foreign investment, then, the richer regions feel that they would be better placed in this regard if they acted on their own, unencumbered by the burden of belonging to the same country as the poor, violent, crime-infested regions. It is noteworthy in this context that the three Baltic states, Lithuania, Latvia and Estonia, which were the richest of the Yugoslav republics, were the first to secede from Yugoslavia. True, in all these cases, there were very strong undercurrents of nationality consciousness. But it can scarcely be denied that an important factor behind the surfacing of these undercurrents was the belief that more German investment would be forthcoming into these regions if they were on their own than if they were parts of larger wholes.

The 'secessionism of the rich' is not confined to rich regions alone. Within the bureaucracy, within the intelligentsia, among professionals, there is a division, a 'dualism', created between those who can 'network' successfully with the metropolis and the others. The very stagnation of the economy, the very squeeze on the population means that those who can 'network' with the metropolis become materially better placed as compared to their more 'unfortunate' counterparts. In other words, commitment to the nation is replaced, and perhaps perforce replaced, by a desire to ingratiate oneself to the dominant views, perceptions, opinions and orthodoxies prevalent in the metropolis. As a result, the rich (or at any rate the affluent), even when they do not physically escape, or 'secede', from the country, effectively undertake a mental 'secession'. And since no country can function without an effective intelligentsia, a cadre of bureaucrats, a group of teachers, scientists, etc., this 'secession of the mind' has a totally debilitating effect on the country. If the nation does not break up, it continues to exist through the courtesy of the metropolis.

Second, at the other end of the spectrum, that is, among the poor, too, there is a tendency for phenomena like separatism, secessionism, communalism, etc., to take root. Unemployment, deindustrialization and impoverishment, though their impact can be potentially radicalizing, are more often conducive to the growth of separatist, and even fascist, tendencies. The cause of the persisting misery of the local population is often located in the presence of 'outsiders', in which case there emerges a separatist tendency. Sometimes a particular religious group, or a particular linguistic community, which is alleged to be more prosperous than the others, is singled out as being responsible for the economic predicament of the rest of the population, and that provides the excuse for organizing pogroms against it. What is common to all such movements is the fact of a complete absence of any credible economic programme. Their blueprint for a better society starts and stops at organizing attacks on 'outsiders', or on members of particular religious or linguistic communities. Even when the movement is openly secessionist, it is totally bereft of any conception of how to organize an alternative economic order. Indeed, it often does not see the need for any such alternative conception, since the economic order is not even considered responsible for the economic plight of the people; it is only the 'outsiders', from other regions, religions or linguistic groups, who, with their malevolent designs, are supposed to be responsible for this economic plight.

The third tendency, which, notwithstanding superficial similarities, is quite distinct from this second one, is the emergence of religious fundamentalism. This has usually a populist, anti-consumerist and even anti-imperialist thrust which is completely lacking in communalism or regional chauvinism.

Fundamentalism of the kind I am talking about does represent a conscious reaction to the fall-out of globalization in the form of privileged islands, the consumerism of the elite and its subservience to the culture of the metropolis; but it represents a reactionary response. Its social and cultural programme is obscurantist, reactionary and invariably male-chauvinist (this last being a trait it shares with the second tendency); its economic programme is so patently absurd that in those exceptional situations where the fundamentalist forces become politically triumphant, this programme literally withers away: the initiative for organizing the economy fairly soon passes into the hands of a bunch of 'pragmatists', not as a sequel to any fierce ideological struggle but by virtue of the sheer vacuity of the original conceptions.

These tendencies are not watertight. All three in varying degrees appear in strength in a globalized economy. And, whether looked at singly or in terms of their conjoint outcome, their effect is to destroy the unity of the nation. They are the flip-side of the globalization coin, and they support the proposition which I advanced earlier, namely, that unity in the advanced capitalist world goes hand-in-hand with disunity in the backward capitalist world, in the sense of fracturing of the totalizing idea of a nation and the coming to the fore of divisive tendencies.

III

Let me now come to the nation-state, which is the topic of my lecture. Underlying this situation of unity in the advanced capitalist world and disunity in the backward capitalist world is an *emasculation of the nation-state everywhere*. The vortex of globalization, of which financial globalization is the most crucial aspect and which produces greater unity at one pole of the capitalist world, the metropolis, and greater divisions at the other pole, the outlying region, also entails an undermining of the nation-state as it has existed. And this has had very profound implications.

Much has been said about the collapse of socialism in recent years. As a matter of fact, however, it is not just socialism which has collapsed but literally every ideological–political tendency that emphasizes the necessity of some form of intervention by a conscious agency for the improvement of the human condition. Together with the collapse of socialism, there has been a collapse of social democracy, of Keynesianism, of welfarism and of third world 'planning'. And the reason for this collapse of *all* interventionist ideological trends lies in the fact that the scope for intervention today is so limited; the only agency capable of undertaking this intervention is the state, which necessarily means the nation-state, and this agency's capacity for intervention is greatly undermined by the fluidity of finance.

Let me elaborate. Any capacity to intervene presupposes that there must be a domain over which the intentions of the intervening agency, in this case the state, can be made to correspond approximately with the outcomes of its actions. I call this domain the 'control area' of the state, and my argument is that financial fluidity undermines this 'control area'. True, capitalism, even with state intervention, does not cease to be a spontaneous system, that is, the capacity of the capitalist state to bring about a correspondence between its intentions and the outcomes of its actions has severe absolute limits arising from the fact of social antagonisms underlying this system. But the point I am making is a different one. Financial fluidity undermines the capacity of the state to bring about an approximate correspondence between the intentions where social antagonisms do not stand in the way of this correspondence. If finance can move in or move out in unpredictable quantities at any time, then, whatever control the state has over the economy is clearly being undermined. It can try to achieve something but an entirely different *denouement* may come to pass because the caprices of the international speculators dictate otherwise.

I believe that this problem, of the 'control area' being undermined, affected the socialist countries as well. Unless an economy hermetically seals itself to the outside world, it is afflicted by this problem; even if all kinds of controls are placed upon foreign creditors and speculators, the nationals of the country itself would move funds around, and that too clandestinely, if necessary through the repatriation or non-repatriation of export earnings, to exploit possible gains in any society where such gains are not frowned upon. In the erstwhile socialist countries, the very process of reforms created the conditions for them to be caught in the vortex of financial fluidity with all its attendant implications. In the case of the Soviet Union, for example, the economic disruptions of the late Gorbachev period became a veritable crisis leading to a collapse of the system because of the non-repatriation of export earnings by Soviet firms.

For capitalist countries, the problem is self-evident. It is this undermining of the capacity of the state to intervene which has made all agenda based on the assumption of such intervention appear untenable. And this explains the collapse of all theoretical tendencies that give rise to such agenda.

If the fluidity of finance across countries undermines the possibility of an interventionist state, an important implication is virtual stagnation in the capitalist world and high levels of unemployment. No single country can expand the level of activity in its economy without giving rise to capital flight from it, which, of course, would make its exchange rate plunge and its rate of inflation accelerate. On the other hand, all the advanced capitalist countries cannot conjointly plan a simultaneous expansion in their levels of activity because, notwithstanding their unity, their circumstances are not identical; and any such joint thrust would push up raw material prices for speculative reasons and raise the rate of inflation, a phenomenon that is always opposed by financial (or rentier) interests.[6] Unemployment and recession, on the other hand, often suit their interests in so far as the balance of payments crises faced by third world countries in such periods enable them to acquire third world assets 'for a song'. A moneylender, after all, does not always worry if his borrower's income is not growing; in fact, often he may wish that it does not grow so that he can get hold of the borrower's assets! Exactly similar considerations hold at the international level.

To sum up, the current phase of capitalism is marked by the rise to dominance of financial or rentier interests, and the fluidity of finance across national boundaries. This has the effect of undermining the 'control area' of nation-states, of making all agendas of state intervention for improving the living conditions of the people appear vacuous, of precipitating stagnation and unemployment even in the metropolitan countries, and of prising open the third world economies for penetration not only of metropolitan goods but, even more importantly, of metropolitan finance. This economic milieu has the effect of producing greater unity in the advanced capitalist world (where there is talk even of supra-national states, as in Europe), and, as a dialectical counterpart of this, greater disunity in the third world, with tendencies towards separatism, divisiveness and disintegration acquiring prominence. The question which naturally arises is: are we now doomed to this fate for ever? Or can we overcome this fate?

The possibility of the 'joint exploitation of the world by internationally united finance capital' had been envisaged by Karl Kautsky, the eminent German theoretician of the Second International. Kautsky's position, however, had been attacked by Lenin, who had argued that the pervasiveness of uneven development under capitalism made any agreement among the capitalist powers temporary, to be followed by intensified inter-imperialist rivalry as the terms of the old 'truce' are rendered obsolete by new configurations of strength.[7]

In one sense, the present debate is reminiscent of the Kautsky–Lenin controversy, but in another very important sense, it is not. Both Kautsky and Lenin derived their concept of finance capital from the German context, and Lenin expressed this as representing a coalescence of banking and industrial capital. In other words, the concept encompassed nationally based, bank-controlled, industrially operated gigantic blocs of capital which were either in truce or in conflict. The finance whose fluidity was being talked of above, however, simply consists of enormous sums of money being pushed here and there by rentiers and speculators, big and small. This finance, therefore, is a somewhat different animal from the finance capital that both Lenin and Kautsky had in mind. About this finance, Hilferding's dictum that the nationalization of half a dozen banks would be the end of finance capital is even less appropriate than it was to the finance capital of his time. On the other hand, notwithstanding this difference, the two *general* perspectives articulated by Kautsky and Lenin continue to be of abiding interest.

The question raised at the end of the last section can be decomposed into two separate questions. First, can we think in terms of some agency transcending the nation-state that can be invoked as the agency for intervention in this new era? Second, if we cannot, and the nation-state still remains the only possible agency for intervention on behalf of the people, then, how can it ever revive, since, by our own argument, its capacity for intervention has got undermined?

The answers to these questions are difficult because they still remain hazy. They will emerge with clarity only in due course of time. Nonetheless, one can hazard some guesses. I believe that in the context of the third world, at any rate, the possibility of the emergence of an agency beyond the nation-state as an agency for intervention in the interests of the people remains remote. What is more, if the nation-state is incapable of intervention, then, any such agency too would be equally incapable of intervention. Enlarging merely the size of the agency would in no way contribute to the solution of the basic problem. On the other hand, I do believe that the nation-state can, and will, revive as an agency for intervention.

It is impossible to imagine that the levels of unemployment prevailing in the advanced capitalist world would become a perennial feature of metropolitan life without causing serious social disruptions. And any attempt, *no matter what its nature*, to reduce the levels of unemployment would necessitate a revival of the nation-state, and controls over the financial capitalist world could well come from the right rather than from any radical quarters, in which case such a revival would have a very different complexion, entailing chauvinism and jingoism, from the welfarist and social democratic conceptions of the post-war era; and the tremendous spread of racialism and neo-fascism all over Europe may be a pointer in this direction. But, no matter what the nature of revival of the nation-state in the advanced capitalist countries, any such revival would once again create the space required for a similar revival of the nation-state in the third world. This is not to say that one should welcome rightwing nationalism in the advanced capitalist world, or be indifferent between a radical revival of the nation-state and a chauvinistic revival; this is only to underscore the fact that it is impossible to visualize such a revival not occurring. If the world looks somewhat Kautskyite at the moment, that does not by any means signal the victory of the Kautskyite perspective in the debate between Lenin and Kautsky.

Besides, for us in the third world, it is not even the case that we have to sit quietly until the nation-state has been revived in the west. True, the scope for state intervention has been greatly reduced, but it has not disappeared altogether. What is required is that the state has to take *the constraints of living in a world with financial fluidity into account in planning its intervention*. While I consider any emulation of the East Asian model in the rest of the third world neither desirable (since this entails a neo-mercantilist development strategy that is necessarily accompanied by a degree of authoritarianism which is unwelcome) nor feasible (since it is the product of a very specific domestic class configuration as well as international correlation of forces), East Asia does demonstrate, in a way, the possibility of successful state intervention in a contemporary world marked by financial fluidity.

In contexts such as ours, if the nation is to remain united, then, the resuscitation of an agenda of development that entails conscious intervention by the nation-state in the interests of the people, as opposed to leaving economic development to be determined as a mere fall-out of the caprices of international speculators, is absolutely essential. This requires, however, an alternative class alliance underlying the state, one that would enforce accountability on the state, as well as provide it with sufficient sinews to face up to the challenge of international finance which is out to undermine its capacity for intervention. The forging of such a class alliance, which would necessarily be centered around the working people, including the peasantry, however, is a matter for political praxis.

Notes

[1] The existence of a dual national consciousness has been argued by Amalendu Guha in Guha (1982).

[2] Thus Alvin Hansen attributed the crisis to the closing of the frontier which resulted in the shrinking of investment opportunities; Schumpeter to the coincidence of the troughs of the three main cycles which characterize capitalism; and Paul Baran and Paul Sweezy, following Josef Steindl, to the emergence of under-consumptionism owing to the growth of monopolies.

[3] The concept of the 'general crisis of capitalism' was used in the programme of the Communist International. See Degras (1971).

[4] For an account along these lines of the development of the world economy in the post-war period, and also for an example of this particular kind of understanding, see 'On the Economic Crisis of World Capitalism' in Patnaik, ed. (1986).

[5] The classic discussion of this is in Nurkse (1954).

[6] The opposition of rentier interests to inflation was mentioned by M. Kalecki in 'Political Aspects of Full Employment'; see Kalecki (1971). For an interpretation of Reaganomics as pandering to rentier interests, and hence implicitly for a recognition of the important role of such interests in today's capitalism (which is the argument being advanced in the present paper), see Amit Bhaduri and Josef Steindl, 'The Rise of Monetarism as a Social Doctrine', cited in Bhaduri (1986).

[7] For Kautsky's views and for Lenin's critique of them, see Lenin (1963).

References

Bhaduri, Amit (1986), *Macroeconomics: The Dynamics of Commodity Production* (London: Macmillan).

Degras, Jane (1971), *Communist International 1919–43: Documents* (London).

Guha, Amalendu (1982), *The Indian National Question: A Conceptual Frame*.

Hodgkin, Thomas (1956), *Nationalism in Colonial Africa*.

Kalecki, M. (1971), 'Political Aspects of Full Employment', in *Selected Essays on the Dynamics of the Capitalist Economy* (Cambridge).

Lenin, V.I. (1963), *Imperialism the Highest Stage of Capitalism*, in *Selected Works*, Vol. I (Moscow).

Lukacs, George (1970), *Lenin: A Study on the Unity of His Thought* (London).

Nurkse, Ragnar (1954), 'International Investment Today in the Light of Nineteenth Century Experience', *Economic Journal*.

Patnaik, Prabhat, ed. (1986), *Lenin and Imperialism* (Delhi: Orient Longman).

Human Rights Education

The Promise of the Third Millennium

Upendra Baxi

Zakir Sahib was a master diagnostician of university education in India. In a historic aphorism, he summed up both the nature and the future of Indian education and Indian democracy. He said: 'There is too much politics in our education and too little education in our politics.' Politics is, of course, a complex term. What Zakir Sahib meant by 'too much politics' should not be a mystery to us in Delhi University. Indian campuses have become, by and large, playgrounds for party politics. At times, they also present themselves to the public view as political parties' battlefields. Universities are the only spaces in civil society which foster the life of the mind and help the cultivation of a mentality that enables us to combat the tyranny of political 'truths', the 'truths' of power. Pablo Picasso said, towards the end of his life, that for far too long he had been trying to convince the public of the truth of his lies. I believe he was wrong in describing aesthetic 'truth' thus. But he described presciently the nature of political 'truth'. Zakir Sahib's aphorism summons Indian universities, in our troubled times, to the true vocation of education, which is to construct people's 'truths' against the political production of 'truths'.

Not merely this. 'Too little' education in politics has also distorted and disfigured the landscape of liberal democracy in India. What Zakir Sahib meant, I believe, by 'education' in relation to politics, was not just formal education, critical though this is, but those processes whereby the managers of the Indian people learn from them the virtues of honest hard work, civility and rectitude in the exercise of power, and a fiduciary notion of political power. In a republican democracy, which India is, political power is to be regarded as public trust, not as private property. In today's India, citizens have become mere raw materials for practices of power, instead of being co-architects of a resurgent India.

The Indian state is becoming increasingly privatized through multinational capital. I will dwell on globalization and human rights in the course of this lecture. But one metaphoric way of capturing the Indian vicissitude is to recall the favourite song from an old Hindi movie called *Seema*, starring Balraj Sahani

Eighth Zakir Husain Memorial Lecture, 19 December 1995.

and Nutan, which begins thus: '*Manamohana, bade jhoothe . . .*'. Need I say anything more about the managers and agents of Indian globalization? Please note how the term '*jhootha*' captures the lie of the contemporary Indian production of its political 'truths'.

I said a moment ago that 'politics' is a complex terrain of discourse. Let me illustrate this by two random invocations. Michel Foucault, towards the end of his life, said that we are living in an era of the end of politics. This is so, he said, because if the 'other' of politics is signified by 'revolution', and when the conditions of revolution have ceased (or so it is widely rumoured), how then can 'politics' survive? Whatever we may say about Foucault's epistemology or sense of history, experientially we are, in India, witnessing the end of politics as an art and science, not just of governance but of governmentality, as that site of public or social consciousness/conscience which aspires to serve public interest or common good. And these are no empty phrases when we recall, as we must under Part IV-A of the Indian Constitution, enacting the fundamental duties of the Indian citizens, that the Indian Constitution defines only those development policies as just which disproportionately benefit the masses of the Indian impoverished. The managers and agents of Indian globalization are now lawlessly liquidating the promise and the aspiration of the Indian Constitution. That is where it hurts. Zakir Sahib, were he to be with us today, would have articulated this truth of the people. He would have said that constitutional illiteracy – too little education in politics – is the bane of Indian politics today.

I say all this as a proud but wounded Indian citizen. And I say this in the performance of my constitutional fundamental duties as a citizen to develop a 'scientific temper', a spirit of 'critical enquiry' and 'social reform'. It is scandalously superficial for me to add that I am not a politician.

The second observation that comes to mind is that of Albert Einstein who said, also towards the end of his life, that he now understood that politics was more difficult than physics. And I have the temerity to add a footnote: that politics which aims at promotion and protection of human rights is even harder than politics of possession, management and distribution of that form of political power which converts the power of the few into the destiny of hapless millions. I remain naive or vain enough to think that Zakir Sahib would have agreed with Einstein and my gloss on him.

I enunciate a few 'truths' concerning human rights and their relevance to human rights education. Incidentally, we live under the United Nations Decade for Human Rights Education (1995–2005) which, in its Plan of Action, urges governments and states, the international society of nations, social and human rights activists worldwide, to give primacy to the cause of human rights education.

Human rights education worldwide has to be based on the following premises.

First, human rights movements embody the truths of peoples' struggles everywhere. There existed no internationally recognized right of self-determination of peoples when Lokamanya Tilak proclaimed that '*Swaraj* is my birthright and I shall have it'; or there existed, full five decades before the United Nations proclaimed it, the truth of a Mohandas Gandhi (despite the political ambiguities in India of that last name) who began a renaissant struggle on what congealed in modern history as the formation of apartheid (long before United Nations treaties and declarations on outlawing, as a matter of discursivity of international human rights movements, all forms of racial discrimination).

Second, to the tasks of attainment of human rights all nations and societies come as equal strangers, as the United States' first ever report to the United Nations Human Rights Committee so overwhelmingly demonstrates.

Third, human rights are not, in their origins, western or non-western; human beings everywhere stand possessed, by virtue of their local struggles, in an ampitheatre of global struggles, of what I call the right to be human, despite the vicissitudes of power and governance. In other words, human rights as an ideology-in-the-making of human futures represent, and prefigure, the very future of human civilization in the next millennium; human rights struggles concretize the collective conscience of humankind.

Fourth, there is the phenomenon of appropriation or the theft of human rights gains – that is, the knowledge and literacy concerning international human rights codification is kept away from the people by states and governments which thrive, in their legitimation, on not just the rhetoric of human rights, but also on the legitimation of the power which it bestows on them.

Fifth, therefore, the human rights education movement is worldwide, a way of restoration of the estate of peoples everywhere in the world.

Sixth, the current phase of globalization ordains an end to the languages of human rights and human futures, especially through the paradigm of trade-related human rights which seek to subject the classical languages and aspirations of human rights.

An Age of Rights?

The better part of the twentieth century is characterized by a unique innovation: proliferation of the endless normativity of human rights' standards, especially in the discursive *praxis* of the United Nations. One may say, despite the reality of massive and monumental violations, that ours is an Age of Rights. No preceding century of human history has been privileged to witness such a range of rights enunciations as ours. Never thus far, too, have the languages of rights replaced all other moral languages. As the United Nations Secretary General observed at the Vienna Conference on Human Rights in June 1993, human rights constitute a 'common language of humanity'. Further, even as the alleged end of ideology is proclaimed worldwide, the human rights sociolect (discourse) emerges as the only universal ideology-in-the-making, enabling both legitimation and delegitimation of power, and critiques of anticipations of human futures.

All these critical developments have led to continuing confrontation between the emergent cultures of rights and the entrenched culture of power. Never has this dialectic between rights and power been so vividly persistent and poignant as in the last seven formative decades of the twentieth century.

Human rights cultures, however, have long been in the making by the praxis of victims of violations, regardless of the mode of formulation of human rights standards and instruments. The single most critical source of human rights is the consciousness of peoples of the world who have waged the most persistent struggles for decolonization and self-determination, and against racial discrimination, gender-based aggression and discrimination, denial of access to basic minimum needs, environmental degradation and destruction, systematic 'benign neglect' of the disarticulated, disadvantaged and dispossessed (including the indigenous peoples of the earth).

Clearly, human rights education must begin by a commission of a world history of people's struggles for rights and against injustice and tyranny. The emergence of more contemporary concerns with rights enunciations cannot be understood without a history of the everyday moral heroism of diverse peoples asserting the most basic of all basic rights, namely, the Right to be Human and to remain Human.[1]

Nor should the contemporary mode of formulation of human rights and fundamental freedoms be considered in isolation from the histories of these struggles. No doubt, the work of the United Nations in promotion and protection of human rights provides its own saga of the triumph of collective human/social imagination. But the practices of production of truths of human rights by governments, diplomats and statespersons have always been informed and formed by an ever-increasing and persistent human striving to make the state more ethical, governance more just and power more accountable.

In narrating histories of the Age of Rights, we have two vantage points of choice. First, we may narrate the histories of human rights movements from the perspective of myriad peoples' struggles, attending closely to a large number of narrative voices and to the micropolitics ultimately shaping the larger stories of politics of rights and liberation. The other vantage point is the one which allows appropriation of narrative voices by national actors (parties' leaders, constitution-makers, judicial actors) and the semi-autonomous fields of rights enunciation within the United Nations system and culture where enunciatory practices forever combine and recombine national interests with global considerations.

Though not mutually exclusive, the choice of narrative paths would offer very distinctive starting points for, and future impacts of, historiographies of human rights movements. More important, the choice of narrative paths may have an enduring influence on the movement of human rights education in terms of scope, objectives, principles, mission, pedagogies (styles of learning together), constitutional and management strategies. With the launching of the United Nations Human Rights Education Decade, serious engagement with historiographies of human rights movements may be deferred only at the cost of our common future.

We must also notice, in this perspective, that the received wisdom on human rights promotion and protection has been under the signature of crises for a considerable period and at least for the last two decades, from both the standpoints. Human rights discourse still remains legible as a site of an ever-potent regime of a corpus of restraints on the power of the postmodern Leviathan state. At the same time, increasingly, a great discovery of the Age of Rights is that civil society, the ensemble of relatively state-free spaces (actors, agencies and instructions), provides equally, and often enough, more pervasive fertile sites of human rights movements. On the one hand, the task of limiting the overweening power of state agents and hegemonies remains imperative. On the other hand, state action and intervention seem to offer the reassuring promise of providing chemotherapy to the cancerous growth of culturally rooted and economically 'derivable' forms of violation of human rights and fundamental freedoms. Thus arises the great dilemma of the Age of Human Rights. The rights discourse must, in a just and effective measure, simultaneously *disempower* as well as *empower* the state. An overwhelming liberalist focus on a minimal state is unlikely to foster the potential, in the short run, of human beings and groups to fight rights violations embedded in civil society formations: for example, gender-based aggression and inequalities, ethnic discrimination and prejudice, economic exploitation (including the new forms of neo-slavery), and violation of the vulnerable, especially children.

The new dialectic of simultaneous disempowerment and re-empowerment of the state (with postmodernist identity and even destiny) must be addressed seriously in fashioning programmes and strategies for human rights education.

Not to be ignored, even momentarily, are the aspects of technopolitics: the processes of production of politics by technologies of the present and future, based on an intertwining of the cybernetic and biotechnology revolutions. Technopolitics breeds technonarcissism;[2] both these tend to deconstruct and reconstruct human and cultural identities, primarily by breeding common cultures of desires which only serve the market and economy, power and profit.[3] Technopolitics also has the power of shaping images of human emancipation. For example, in a world where genetically mutated new forms of life are open to patenting (private corporate appropriation), or where species patenting is on the threshold of recognition as a private (corporate) right in a post-Dunkel world, notions of the autonomy, privacy and uniqueness of individual selfhood and group (collective) rights live (to invoke Soren Kirkegaard) in 'fear and trembling'. Similar crises are posed by the mass media, through satellite communication and cable diffusion, to the rights and freedoms of plurality and diversity. A new 'libidinal economy' (to borrow the title of a book by the postmodernist Jean-Francois Lyotard) is in the process of making in these halcyon days of 'globalization' of the world. New 'fundamentalisms'[4] emerge in this zodiac as last-ditch battles, as it were, against the homogenization of human futures. Neither, clearly, augurs well for human rights and fundamental freedoms.

The irony in this contemporary world formation of human rights education endeavours is ineluctable. *Globalization, which periclitates human rights and fundamental freedoms, is the crossroad on which human rights education is to have its birth and being.* Human rights education, in this conjuncture, has the mission of redemption of humane, self-forming (both individual and collective) *praxis* in a world which is supposed, and even required, to celebrate, with Francis Fukuyama, the 'end of history' and the advent of the 'Last Man' (Fukuyama 1992).

I revisit these themes towards conclusion, after a rapid *tour de horizon* of the United Nations biography of human rights education.

The Universal Declaration and Human Rights Education

The origins of notions of human rights education, even as itself constituting a human right, can be traced to the text of the Universal Declaration of Human Rights. The Preamble to the Declaration stresses the central importance of a 'common understanding' of human rights and fundamental freedoms to the achievement of 'freedom, justice and peace in the world'. In the operative part, it proclaims that a 'common standard of achievement' of these values nationally and globally requires, *inter alia*:

> That every individual and organ of society,
> Keeping this declaration constantly in mind,
> Shall try by teaching and education to promote
> Respect for these rights and freedoms.

'Education' in human rights is thus the individual and collective duty of all – nationally, regionally and globally.

Read in the context of the Preamble, Article 26 of the Declaration affirming everyone's right to education must, of course, include human rights education as a human right in itself. Article 26 postulates the following ends of education. Education 'shall be directed to':

- the 'full development of the human personality',
- the strengthening of 'respect for human rights and fundamental freedoms',
- the promotion of 'understanding, tolerance and friendship among all nations, racial or religious groups', and
- the furtherance of 'the activities of the United Nations for the maintenance of peace'.

'Education' here stands conceptualized not merely in terms of development of individual personality or even in terms of good citizenship of the nation-state. Education has a global orientation towards producing true citizens of the world, imbued with civic virtues of respect for pluralism, peace, dignity and rights. Nor is education, necessarily, all about *rights*. Article 29 of the Declaration categorically declares that 'free and full development' of human personality also entails fulfilment of *duties* to the community. Education, including human rights education, is a right indeed, but that right is not an end in itself. It is a means to other ends, enumerated above, pursuit of which in totality would contribute to the attainment of 'freedom, justice and peace in the world'.

In any progress towards human rights education, the Universal Declaration's understanding of the purposes of such education should, I believe, continue to guide us, even, and perhaps more so, on the eve of the third millennium.

This conclusion stands reinforced by the Preamble to the Declaration. The Preamble gives a conscientious *raison d'être* for human rights education, as well as a pragmatic justification. The former asserts that:

> Disregard and contempt for human rights have resulted in barbarous acts which have outraged the conscience of mankind, that the advent of a world in which human beings shall enjoy freedom of speech and belief, and freedom from fear and want, has been proclaimed as the highest aspiration of the common people.

The pragmatic justification for human rights education is that it is 'essential, if man is not to be compelled to have recourse, as a last resort, to rebellion against tyranny and oppression, that human rights should be protected by the rule of law.'

The reference to the 'highest aspiration of common people' and outraging of the 'conscience of the mankind' indicates that human rights and fundamental freedoms are common properties of human conscience and common moral sentiment. Barbarous practices of power are recognizable and recognized, regardless of *whether* and *how* politicians, statespersons, and jurists and international organizations have made human rights enunciations commensurate with the power of politics to produce a series of contingent, but monumental, evils. The experience of outrage and judgement on flagrant and massive violations of human rights *ante-dates* rights enunciations and survives their well-manicured formulations. The Declaration thus conceives human rights and fundamental freedoms as a domain of *collective conscience* (almost in the sense in which Emile Durkheim so imaginatively sculpted that notion to understand and analyse social solidarities). Human rights education strategies have to acknowledge, and build upon, this common human solidarity.

The pragmatic justification of the Declaration is no less striking. Tyranny is defined as an absence of human rights protection by the rule of law, institutions and structures, or, in other words, *absence or annihilation of human rights cultures, both in civil society and the state*. Such a situation leads to 'rebellion', a breakdown of social order, civil strife and repression, disrupting peace not just at a national level but also regionally or globally. Human rights education, as a strategic instrument for the protection of peace, in all dimensions and levels, was presciently recognized by the authors of the Universal Declaration.

As we move ahead in the imaginative reconstruction of human rights education, our effort will be enriched by recourse to this foundational enunciation in the Declaration. Any amnesia on this score will, I believe, impoverish our enterprise.

The 1974 UNESCO Recommendation Concerning Human Rights Education

The period after the Universal Declaration and the 1974 UNESCO Recommendation was marked by an endless proliferation of human rights enunciations. This tendency continued well into the 1993 Vienna Declaration; and anticipated even more profound discursive articulation of human rights and fundamental freedoms at the Copenhagen World Summit on Social Development. The Fourth World Conference on Women at Beijing seems to have been located on the same faultline.

The 1974 UNESCO Recommendation both enlarges and limits the notion of human rights education.[5] It enlarges the notion of education as implying: 'The entire process of social life by means of which individuals and social groups learn to develop consciously within, and for the benefit of, the national and international communities, the whole of their personal capacities, attitudes, aptitudes and knowledge. This process is not limited to any specific activity.' [Article 1(a)]. And the aims of human rights education are to promote 'international understanding', 'cooperation' and 'peace' considered as 'an indivisible whole', uniting concerns of 'friendly relations between peoples and states having different social and political systems', and of 'respect for human rights and fundamental freedoms'. This unity configures in the Recommendation as 'international education'.

This welcome expansion of 'education' is, however, marked by the construction of human rights education itself! Human rights and fundamental freedoms are only those defined in the United Nations Charter, the Universal Declaration, and the two International Covenants on Economic, Social and Cultural Rights, and Civil and Political Rights. Clearly, this limits the range of human rights normativity to the foundational texts; but human rights discursivity in the United Nations tradition extends much further.[6] And this contraction of the conception of human rights education sits strangely with the scope of human rights education as envisaged in Article 4 of the Recommendation. Of necessity, the present efforts at developing human rights education must include a larger number of related enunciations and instruments.

The aims or ends of human rights education in the Recommendation are multiple as well as diverse. Human rights education, or 'international education', should:

(1) promote both 'intellectual and emotional development'; the former developing 'critical understanding' of national and international problems, and the latter fostering 'a sense of responsibility and of solidarity with the less-privileged groups' such that it results in 'observance of principles of equality in everyday conduct' [Article 5];

(2) promote a culture of 'inadmissibility of recourse to war for purpose of expansion, aggression and domination or the use of force and violence

for the purposes of repression' and understanding of responsibility to
strengthen world peaces [Article 6];

(3) emphasize 'the rule interests of people and their incompatibility with the
interests of monopolistic groups holding economic and political power,
which practise exploitation and ferment wars' [Article 15];

(4) promote 'inter-cultural understanding' [Article 17];

(5) provide meaningful opportunities for 'active civic training' enabling learning of cooperative endeavour through 'the work of public institutions'
and thereby imparting competence to political participation [Article 13];
and

(6) create capabilities to eradicate 'conditions which perpetuate major problems affecting human survival and well-being' and which enhance
'international cooperation' to this end [Article 18].

In many respects, the Recommendation charts out the itinerary of
human rights education well beyond (excepting the commonality of the second
objective) the Universal Declaration. The differences may be highlighted as
follows:

• Whereas the Declaration addressed education, including human rights
education, as an aspect of 'intellectual development', the Recommendation also addresses 'appropriate . . . emotional development'.

• The Recommendation pursues militant egalitarianism, unlike the Declaration (see points 1 and 6 above).

• Whereas the Declaration speaks of 'tolerance', the Recommendation
invokes a discourse of 'inter-cultural understanding'.

• The Recommendation perceives education as a series of endowments of
competence, civic, political and international, in contrast to the Declaration which presumably subsumes all this under the rubric 'intellectual
development'.

These emphases, if not shifts, in the directions of human rights education
are of considerable pertinence to our re-imaging human rights education two
decades later. The clusters of concern and capabilities, purposes and promises
symbolized by the Recommendation stress on 'appropriate . . . emotional development' (without which solidarities remain incoherently emergent) and 'inter-
cultural understanding' (without which rights enunciations can be, and have
been, unfairly castigated as Eurocentric in their origins and functions), and a
radical quest for egalitarianism in everyday life, both nationally and globally,
ought not (in my belief) be overlooked in the future revitalization of notions of
human rights education.

Indeed, these motifs of human rights education assume even greater relevance in the post-cold war era, where (as noted earlier) the ideologies of human
rights and fundamental freedoms seem to emerge as the only authoritative ideology for world development.

The 1993 UNESCO Montreal Declaration on Human Rights Education

Building upon the 1974 Recommendation (and a subsequent set of associated enunciations since 1974[7]), the UNESCO World Plan of Action on Education for Human Rights and Democracy adopted by the International Congress (Montreal, Canada, 8–11 March 1993) unfolded, on the eve of the Vienna Conference on Human Rights, many an inaugural theme. Before commenting on the Montreal Declaration (which the Vienna Declaration explicitly invokes), some of its inaugural propositions may be noted.

First, the Montreal Plan explicitly addresses human rights education to the victims of human rights violations, as well as defenders of 'democracy'.

Second, while reiterating the notion of education as a lifelong process of learning, the Montreal Plan inaugurates the notion of human rights education 'in difficult situations'. Obviously, state failures (an amalgam always of national and global forces) present, increasingly, a testing time for run-of-the-mill notions of human rights education.

Third, the Montreal Plan anchors human rights education in the harbour of liberal democracy. It declares that all education, especially human rights education, should 'aim to nurture democratic values, sustain impulses for democratization and promote social transformation based upon human rights and democracy'.

Fourth, human rights education should itself be 'participatory and operational, creative, innovative and empowering at all levels of civil society'.

Fifth, human rights education has a prophylactic role and function; it must evolve 'special and anticipatory strategies aimed at preventing the outbreak of violent conflicts and related human rights violations'.

Sixth, the 'key challenge of the future' confronting human rights education is how to 'enhance the universality of human rights by rooting these rights in different cultural traditions'.

Seventh, this endeavour of cultural rooting (implantation) must recognize that 'effective exercise of human rights is also contingent upon the responsibility by individuals towards the community'.

Eighth, (without being exhaustive) the Montreal Plan offers at least three criteria by which the 'success' of any human rights education mission may be evaluated. It is successful when it:

- *changes* 'conduct leading to a denial of rights',
- *creates* a climate of 'respect' for 'all rights', and
- *transforms* the civil society in 'a peaceful manner and participatory model'.

The Montreal Plan is, of course, justified in strongly linking human rights and democracy. But without an acknowledgement of history, which has profound consequences for the future of human rights in the world as well of human rights education, this aggressive linkage may, in the short run, appear to the leaders, if not the peoples of the South, as aggressively Eurocentric.

The Montreal Plan text needs to be supplemented by notions of 'historic' time. The actually existing liberal democracies in the North emerged out of at least centuries of histories of peoples' struggles with the state and within civil societies. To imagine that human rights education strategies in themselves will *somehow* accelerate historic time for the rest of the world, is to arrest meaningful global movement towards the goals of human rights education.

It needs to be at least acknowledged that the erstwhile colonial powers aborted conditions of political development and maturation in most parts of the world. It also needs to be acknowledged that practices of power during the long dark night of the 'cold war' did not enable the former colonial powers and their allies to contribute to the decolonized nations' capabilities to 'nurture democratic values, sustain impulses for democratization', or promote 'peaceful' democratization of whole civil societies. Nor is the quest to locate, in the post-cold war era, the Other (the enemy) of a solitary superpower necessarily conducive to the rapid evolution of human rights and cultures across the world.

Democracies are processes, never fully formed historic *products*. Or, to put it in a language with which at least professional philosophers will feel at home, democracy is a process of Becoming, not of Being. And, from this standpoint, the dilemmas of *sustainable* democracy, while more acute in the South, are awesomely present in the North as well. Read thus, the Montreal Plan addresses human rights education, both in guiding principles and in strategies of action, to the critical tasks of democratizing and re-democratizing civil society and state formation *everywhere* in the world.

By the same token, the Montreal Plan, in conceptualizing human rights education strategies towards implantation (giving roots in 'different cultural traditions'), needlessly provokes suspicions of Eurocentrism (regardless of how diplomatic to the gallery of the South, in its reference to the responsibilities of individuals – see the seventh proposition above). Verily, concern for basic human rights is not unique to the cultures of the North; what is distinctive to these is a historic headstart which entailed extraordinary denial of human rights to a vast humanity. Once again, the Montreal formulations have to be considered as indicative of the need to make contemporary human rights enunciations, in their endless proliferation, a part of all the different culture traditions, whether of the North or of the South.

The Montreal Plan, however, moves close to the heart of contemporary darkness when it refocuses human rights education to its inaugural task of transforming civil society. This task is urgent and compelling, both for the South and the North; especially in the North where civil societies, while developing and nurturing impassioned cultures of human rights at home, are indifferent to how their elected representative may often play God abroad, especially in the South.

On this reading of it, one of the most precious objectives of the Montreal Plan is the articulation of the *non-negotiable need* for human rights education to address civil society in the North, in such ways that it is enabled to create a community of concern, an overarching unity, between and among human rights cultures both at home and abroad. It is only when human rights education missions succeed on this count that the prophylactic role of human rights education (and its mission 'in difficult situations') stands more historically addressed.

The Montreal Plan's reference to 'enhancing the universality' of human rights has a note of refreshing candour about it since it recognizes that while all human rights are potentially universal, not all are actually so. But this acknowledgement may have an unintended side-effect of nourishing the tendency to interrogate the 'universality' (and 'indivisibility') of all human rights, which the Vienna Declaration so emphatically now proclaims. Even those who resist or critique the 'universality' of human rights will, on deeper thought (*and* on reading the histories of peoples' struggles for rights), concede that some, if not most, human rights which now stand internationally enunciated are indeed *non-derogable*.

Finally, the Montreal Plan's teleology of human rights education raises an important question concerning human rights education. Human rights education is a means to an end (the end in the Plan being 'democracy'). The end to which human rights education might be a means could also be designated as 'peace', 'justice', development' and 'dignity'. The question is: should human rights education be regarded as an end in itself or as a means to some designated end? The question (not so unimportant as pragmatists might think it is) needs careful contemplation, for, on possible answers to it will depend the future of the legitimation, organization, accountability, autonomy, pedagogies, performance and implementation of human rights education.

The choice is between saying that we ought to pursue human rights education in itself as a human right to better achieve all other human rights and fundamental freedoms, or that we ought to promote human rights education for ends like 'good governance', 'sustainable development', 'economic progress', 'democracy' and 'transformation of civil societies'. And the choice is critical in the sense of the nature of national structuring of human rights education, including the very dispensability or expendability of human rights education. If we were to regard human rights education as a means for 'economic' development in societies exposed to structural adjustment programmes, for example, only market-friendly rights will be germane to the human rights education endeavour; similarly, cultures which regard patriarchy as 'divinely' ordained may not consider a regendering of human rights cultures as critical to many of the 'ends' described above.

The choice has to be clearly made. I believe human rights education is important because it is an end in itself. It is conceivable, and a matter of not just ethical but also political judgement, that as and when the human rights education mission succeeds, it may ill serve other postulated goals and ends. This is so because, as Roberto M. Unger has reminded us, 'rights typically have in history a destabilizing function, a "context smashing" tendency' (Unger 1983: 96). Neither of these features necessarily goes so far as to question the integrity or rationale of the nation-state itself, but both acutely interrogate all the processes of power and authority within the state and civil society. Human rights education as an end in itself seeks to reinforce the processes of empowerment of every human being in everyday life to experience freedom and solidarity, not fractured by grids of power and domination in civil society and the state. The ability to perceive such freedom as not threatening all that is good, true and beautiful in human achievement is, to my mind, the *summum bonum* that human rights education promises us. Mohandas Gandhi used to say that *swaraj* (independence that is just self-rule) brings exercise of freedom in non-threatening ways to the Other. That, I think, is the spirit of human rights cultures, too. Emmanuel Levians, in a different idiom, conveyed the same message to us when he evolved the notion of 'difficult freedoms'. Human rights education, in these terms, is a movement to achieve the most difficult of these 'difficult freedoms'.

Human Rights Education in the Vienna Declaration

Celebrating both 'the spirit of the age' and 'the realities of our time' in its germinal perambulatory formulation, the Vienna Declaration on Human Rights marks yet another milestone in the lexicon, theory and activism of human rights (Baxi 1994b: 1–17). Section D, Part II of the Declaration, and Paragraphs 33, 36, Part I, focus on human rights education. The Vienna Declaration, in brief:

- reiterates the expanded notion of 'education' first articulated in the 1974 UNESCO Recommendation;
- extends that Recommendation, making education and human rights education go beyond select bodies of human rights discourse to include 'peace, democracy, development and social justice';
- innovates human rights education as a gender-specific mission, stressing the 'human rights *needs* of women';
- reconstructs the enterprise of human rights education to make it inclusively communitarian; in other words, development of human rights cultures is an ongoing participatory endeavour of individuals, groups, associations and institutions in civil society, and of state actors and agencies, in a co-equal manner; and
- focuses human rights education programmes and strategies on special state agencies and agents 'such as military forces, law enforcement personnel, police and health professionals'.

The Vienna goals and strategies mark a culmination of thought and *praxis* on human rights education within the family of the United Nations. The most excitingly innovative dimension is, of course, the reference to the 'human rights needs of women'. Inaugurally, this formulation invites suspension of the dichotomy between 'needs' and 'rights' (with the associated perplexities of distinguishing between, in a hierarchy of needs, 'material' and 'non-material' needs).

The conception of 'human rights needs' enwombed in the motto 'Women's Rights are Human Rights', indicates the ongoing process, in contemporary rights discourse, of transmuting *needs* into *rights*. But, equally importantly, for human rights education pedagogies and strategies, identification of human rights needs must, minimally, include: access to information, access to opportunities for the exercise of rights, access to modalities and instrumentalities in the identification of violations of human rights, and access to public discourse which may contest state/society assertions that either no human right exists or, if it does, no violation can be said to have occurred.

This listing of human rights *needs* can, and must, be expanded with care, the implication being that human rights education can never be a static body of given knowledge of rights enunciations but must forever remain a dynamic engagement with these knowledges. In this sense, human rights education will be future oriented as well. Marshalling the tragic accumulation of experiences of victimage (rights violation), human rights education will provide a repertoire of resources for ongoing struggles to promote and protect human rights and fundamental freedoms. In this sense, the focus on human rights education will inhibit it from becoming an alienating/alienated tradition of knowledges. Perhaps the significance of the Vienna Declaration lies in inviting the attention of human rights education entrepreneurs to (what Paulo Friere so memorably called) 'the pedagogy of the oppressed'.

Like the 1974 UNESCO Recommendation, even the expanded range of human rights education in the Vienna Declaration is conspicuous by its lack of reference to some critical rights enunciations.[8] This lack is certainly remediable if we bear in mind the vision of human rights education animating the Vienna Declaration, which, in and through its own enunciations, does not merely consolidate existing the human rights juridical regime (*lex lata*) but is also commingled with human rights in the making (*de lege ferenda*).

Draft Plan of Action for the United Nations Decade for Human Rights Education: 1995–2005

The Draft Plan of Action (hereafter referred to as the Draft), naturally, builds upon the lineage of human rights education thus far canvassed. But it also marks advances, the most critical being the notion that human rights education is a unique strategy for the 'building of a universal culture of human rights' through the 'imparting of knowledges, skills and moulding of attitudes'. And the comprehensiveness of the conception of human rights education is welcomed as it goes beyond the 1974 Recommendation to include, besides the foundational texts, almost all major human rights enunciations.[9] The five normative bases of human rights education[10] continue to reflect the emergent consensus about its goals.

The notion of 'culture' in the Draft, however, seems to focus human rights education on intellectual development of knowledge (the absence of pluralization of knowledge is also discomforting[11]), skills and attitudes. 'Cultures' include these but of course encompass much more; 'values' constitute a salient part of cultures. But equally important are the sensibilities which make cultures possible and enduring. By 'sensibilities' I signify what Raymond Williams called 'structure of feeling' and what, in a different context, the 1974 Recommendation named 'appropriate . . . emotional development'. An overly rationalistic approach to human rights education may defeat, in the short and long run, the very objectives enshrined in the Draft.

The General Guiding Principles of the Draft (Part Two) are, indeed, noteworthy. *First*, human rights education should create the 'broadest possible awareness and understanding of all the norms, concepts and values' of the foundational texts, as well as all other relevant international human rights instruments. Put another way, human rights education is not directed merely to literacy concerning human rights texts; their *intertextuality* also has to be learned and imparted (that is, their cross-connections, reciprocal supplementation – their hermeneutical totality). The ideology-in-the-making of human rights ('all the norms, concepts and values') becomes, in the Draft, the repertoire of human rights education. This is further reinforced by the reference to 'universality' and 'interdependence of all rights'.

Second, human rights education has to move from the 'universal' to the 'particular', from 'abstract' to the 'concrete', from the 'global' to the 'local'. Effective human rights education for the decade

> shall be shaped in such a way as to be relevant to the daily lives of the learners, and shall seek to engage learners in a dialogue about the ways and means of transforming human rights from the expression of abstract norms to the reality of their social, economic, cultural and political conditions. [Paragraph 4]

This is a critical formulation. It summons human rights education *praxis* to tasks of everyday relevance in micropolitical, microsocial contexts. It formulates the imagination of human rights education as *dialogical. Dialogue,* by definition, *can occur only under conditions of discursive dignity and equality.* And dialogical human rights education strategies conflate, creatively, the distinction between the 'learner' and the 'learned'. Humility is, of course, the hallmark of learning. And dialogical human rights education interaction is, obviously, a confrontation between the 'pre-given' ('social, economic, cultural and political conditions') and future histories-in-the-making.

Third, the Guiding Principles envisage participatory human rights education *praxis* entailing 'equal participation of women and men of all age groups and all sectors of society, both in formal learning and non-formal learning through institutions of civil society, the family and the mass media' [Paragraph 3]. Human rights education, in this conception, aims to cut across hierarchies of formal/informal education systems, gender and age, and addresses itself, of necessity, to realms other than state power.

Fourth, the Draft marks a community of concern between 'democracy, development and human rights' (their 'mutually reinforcing nature'). Accordingly, it reiterates a prime function of human rights education, which shall 'seek to further effective democratic participation in the political, economic, social and cultural spheres and shall be utilized as a means of promoting economic, social progress and people-centered sustainable development'.

This remarkably imaginative formulation offers to human rights education missionaries an *embarras de richesses*. Human rights education strategies have to foster that order of participation which promotes both 'economic and social progress' and 'people-centred development'. In a sense, this formulation leads us back to an equally remarkable enunciation in Article 18 of the 1974 UNESCO Recommendation which rightly insists that all education, including human rights education, should address the major problems of mankind: 'Education should be directed *both* towards the eradication of conditions which perpetuate and aggravate major problems attacking human survival and well-being – inequality, injustice, international relations based on the use of force – and towards measures of international cooperation likely to help solve them.' Human rights education, like all education, must ineluctably be 'multi-disciplinary'. It should also be global, regional, national and local, all at the same time. And at all levels of learning.

Critiques of Human Rights as Sites of Resistance to Human Rights Education

Recognition of critiques of human rights enunciations is essential to the mission of developing a 'universal culture of human rights', especially through human rights education. There exists in the North a rights-weariness, and in the South, a rights-wariness. Neither can be wished away; each has to be grasped in its historicity and mutual lessons learnt through dialogical encounters. Knight-errantry of human rights and human rights education strategies can only lead to a quixotic enchantment, leaving the work untransformed at its core.

Rights-weariness is a kind of response to the explosion, in the recent decades, of human rights enunciations. Ethical theorists question the emergent hegemonies of rights languages, displacing all other moral languages (of virtue, of duty, of responsibility and of communitarianism). Pragmatists scoff at the quixotic character of many a human rights formulation, which seems to represent to them *not* a utopia but a dystopia. Rights-weariness is an ethical stance which doubts whether the liberal traditions of individual rights can be the privileged bearers of human transformation, especially when the ideality of rights stands squandered by an excess of rights talk.[12] Not only does rights-weariness produce such doubts and caveats; occasionally, it goes so far as to recall Bentham's dustbinning of all natural rights talk as 'nonsense or stills'.[13]

Rights-weariness provides a difficult genre of human rights critique. Critics in this genre do, in fact, regard it a duty to raise uncharitable questions concerning the career and future of human rights promotion and protection in the present mould. They perceive an immense duality, and even duplicity, in the endless propagation of human rights languages; even to the point of giving utterance to a phenomenon named as 'human rights colonialism' (see, for example, Shivji 1989: 42–68). Weariness about rights may best be captured by the following (perhaps too simplistic, oft-repeated, even well-worn) formulations:

(a) The discourse of human rights ought to be pluralistic, according equal dignity to all traditions of the world; by contrast, it is hegemonically 'western'.

(b) The classical liberal tradition of rights and justice carries the legacy of the original sin: these traditions are at their best and brightest in justifying/recycling colonialism/imperialism, both in 'classical' and 'contemporary' incarnations.

(c) The human rights agenda offers pathways, in different radical idioms, of the White Man's Burden; in other words, it masks the end of power and domination (political and economic) by the North.

(d) The North is unable, despite its proud boast, to make the world 'safe' for democracy and human rights, and unwilling to create conditions within its own jurisdiction to eliminate practices and circumstances which encourage massive and flagrant violation of human rights.

(e) This stands demonstrated (even outside the arena of foreign policy and the making of wars) in the North's pronounced inability and unwillingness to subject its own economic agents to a common human standard of regulation of risk and liability for injury (whether it is signified by Bhopal, or dumping of toxic wastes, or dumping in overseas markets of injurious drugs prescribed at home, or gender-aggressive contraceptive devices). Implicit in policies of export of hazardous processes and products is a double Racial Discrimination Convention.

(f) The North has betrayed commitments contained in salient United Nations declarations which provided for an authentic global structural adjustment programme for promotion and protection of human rights, especially for the South. Some of these declarations contained as well duties of *reparation* for massive and sustained violations of rights of colonized peoples and nations. One may refer, *inter alia*, to the following Declaration on:

- Social Progress and Development (1969), pledging 1 per cent of GNP of North as aid to the South, and *just*, non-discriminatory patterns of trade, commerce and intercourse between North and South;
- Eradication of Hunger and Malnutrition (1974);
- Use of Scientific and Technological Progress in the interest of Peace and Mankind (1975); and
- The Right to Development (1986).

(g) Human rights diplomacy of the North has been complicit, during and even after the 'cold war', with the worst violations of human rights in the nation-states of the South.

(h) The classical model of human rights spread an ideology of possessive market individualism where human beings are *homo economicus* or *homo consumeris* with rights devoid of any communitarian responsibilities and fidelity to the age-old spiritual heritage, transcending both the market and the state.

(i) The cosmologies of human rights discourse are based on variants of civic religion and secular nationalism, not cognizant at all of potential divergent, religious, cultural and inter-faith traditions for promotion of fraternity, solidarity, dignity, justice and rights.

In all these genres of critiques lies an impulse for rethinking human rights. They acknowledge, indeed, that some human rights and fundamental freedoms are universal and indivisible, but interrogate, for example, preferred hierarchies of rights, extolling civil and political rights, and economic, social and cultural rights.

Clearly, no amount of incantation of the *mantras* of 'human rights culture' is going to succeed in the face of these diverse critiques of human rights discourse. Nor would it do, even as a gesture, to deny elements of domination or hegemony, or to gainsay the ascendancy of one variant of liberal human rights formulations. It would also constitute a serious misrecognition of these genres of critiques to say that all these put together constitute merely self-serving resistance to human rights cultures.

The Tasks Ahead

Human rights education begins to gather global momentum precisely at a historical conjuncture when fantastically new forces of production (especially digitalization and biotechnology) have begun fostering new international division of labour through the rolled-up processes of globalization. If the ideological superstructures are varieties of a postmodernist ethic (including rights-weariness), the *realpolitik* of the emergent world is increasingly rights-wary. For once, the discourse is explicit: human rights are instrumentalities of social development which could best take place through 'free trade', and whose logic, in turn, is at odds with *so many* proclamations of human rights! The discursive twist explicitly since the United Nations summit on social development is clearly in the direction of a market-friendly (or specifically trade-related) human rights paradigm (Baxi 1995a).

To be sure, amidst all these transformations, the core objectives of human rights education remain more or less constant in the sense that:

- human rights education is, all said and done, *education*;
- as with other 'forms' of 'education', human rights education ought to contribute to the 'full development of human personality';
- human rights education contributes to this objective especially by strengthening respect for human rights and fundamental freedoms; and
- as 'education', human rights education must contextualize all learning by its focus on world peace, security and development in ways which nurture human rights cultures everywhere.

These objectives have to be attained in a world dizzy with the acceleration of history. The difficulties of human rights education are well worth pondering in this context, as a prelude to the identification of the tasks ahead.

No matter how 'education' is conceived (formal/informal/adult/continuing/extension education), human rights education has necessarily to relate to and deal with educational *formations* already in place everywhere. It has to engage itself with:

- educational systems as articulations of state policies and national objectives;
- educational systems as hierarchic grids of power within society;
- patterns of distribution of access to literacy, and to elementary, primary, secondary, tertiary education;
- patterns of relationships between educational apparatuses and the economy, national and global;
- ideologies, philosophies, epistemologies, technologies and pedagogies internal to the domain of education and cultivated by its practitioners;
- histories of education and of entrepreneurship; and
- traditions of academic freedom (as freedom to teach and as freedom to learn).

Human rights education conceived as 'education' needs to find an exponential entry point at each one of these, and related, levels. State constitutional policies, as in the Philippines, for example, can do a great deal to facilitate privileged space for human rights education.[14] But when these are unavailable, as is mostly the case (and poignantly, in the much-developed world, though clearly not only there), human rights education initiatives will have to emerge at the 'world systems' level. At this level, the required range of inter-agency collaboration within the United Nations system is simply incredible. Clearly, the Human Rights Commissioner and the Centre for Human Rights will need to interact in a sustained manner, for example, with the ILO, UNESCO, ICJ (the World Court whose jurisprudence is relevant to human rights education), UNEF, IAEC, UNFP, UNICEF, various treaty bodies (but especially CEDAW), the Committee on Crime Prevention and Treatment of Offenders, the Commission on Sustainable Development, and the World Intellectual Property Organization. With the best of political will, such inter-agency collaboration is hard to initiate or sustain. It is difficult to imagine that the Human Rights Commissioner or the Centre for Human Rights will engage in such an enterprise without the constant push and prod of human rights education NGOs and movements. In turn, human rights education groups will themselves need to activate and network educational NGOs. The tasks, overall, are indeed of a forbidding magnitude.[15] And if the history of human rights education initiatives in the UN system is any guide, it would be surprising if anyone attempted such a task.

Leaving the United Nations system in its own orbit to perform its wonders may be a comforting thought to many a human rights education activist, despite the fact that much of social and human rights activism is being heavily coopted for weal or woe by that very system. Activists thus inclined, for example, did not wait for the Jomyten Declaration and programme of Action on Education of All, or the Covenant of the Rights of the Child (see, for example, Baxi 1994c: 158–68), to embark on a whole range of literacy programmes, nor do they await significant state action to pursue their difficult tasks. Indeed, some activists go so far as to problematize the role of international policies and programmes, and are critical of their United Nations-struck sisters.

Regardless of all this, independent people's movements for literacy, numeracy and science education go beyond critiques of educational formations to an imagination of social struggles which would accomplish conquest of local spaces in ways which meaningfully empower human beings to delink their destiny from the state and the economy, and forces and relations of 'globalization'. On this vision, 'education' is such a full development of human personality as to endow human beings with the power to resist *colonization of the mind* by the state, civil society, inter-governmental regimes and multinationals. Education (to appropriate Giles Deleuze's thought in a different context) will signify those processes which prevent the state from thinking through our heads! In this image, human rights education will be a distinctly autonomous, decolonizing, deglobalizing, heretical project in which the very act of learning will be simultaneously an act of insurrection, aiming at the dissipation of imposed knowledges.[16]

Clearly, we arrive at radically different visions of education, but especially human rights education. Both are relevant, but each defines the movement for human rights education very differently, in its own image. In the dialectical development of projects thus envisioned lies, I believe, the redemptive potential of human rights education. At the same time, the challenges to both remain common, and to these I now turn.

Human Rights-Weariness and Human Rights-Wariness

Both these forms of thought, as action, challenge not merely the prospect of human rights education but the foundations of human rights notions as such, as a universal ideology-in-the-making. Clearly, a major task of human rights education, in either vision, is to show, as against prevalent moral philosophies, that:

- it is still possible, legitimate and valid to speak of a *subject* (despite the multifarious proclamations concerning the death of the subject), which designates a *human person,* who is the bearer of *rights*;
- human rights discourse is far from ethically nonsensical, and human rights are no mere 'moral fictions';
- the notions of 'humankind', 'humanity' still make logical and political sense;
- certain basic truths of human rights remain categorically moral imperatives and are *not* discursively negotiable (for example, prohibitions against genocide, ethnic cleansing, slavery, gender-based discrimination); and
- the languages of human rights are as, if not more, privileged (important) as all *other* moral languages.

Philosophic cottage industries, especially in the first world, have indeed made each one of these propositions deeply problematic.[17] Human rights education has to invade these comfortable discursive abodes which radiate an enormous amount of human rights cynicism, for good and bad reasons.

Similarly, human rights education ought to give salience to propositions

(d) to (g) of the rights-weariness critique. There is absolutely no question that the North's human rights diplomacy and advocacy are geared more to the exigencies of *realpoltik* than to coequal protection and promotion of human rights throughout the world, especially the South. But human rights education movements will need to contest some other parts of the critique and maintain that:

- authoritative human rights enunciations have occurred under the United Nations auspices through respect for difference amidst dialogue;
- in this discursive tradition, increasingly, non-governmental actors/agencies have acquired an increasing voice;
- it would be increasingly difficult, therefore, to maintain that all major human rights enunciations are hegemonically 'western';
- *read as a whole*, the corpus of human rights enunciations does not (nor can it be said to) spread the ideology of possessive market individualism, contrary to conceptions, just communitarianism; and
- preservation of plurality and multiplicity of ethical traditions, moral outlooks and systems of religion is *not* at odds with world human rights movements *unless* these traditions, outlooks and systems can be justifiably said to demand adherence to belief and practices which, for example, justify:
  - slavery (ownership of human beings as chattels)
  - genocide (including ethnocide or politicide, that is, 'ethnic cleansing' or killing of political dissenters)
  - any form of structural violence against women
  - denial of dignity and freedom to women in matters on which men already possess such dignity and freedom
  - denial of civilizational integrity to the indigenous people.

In other words, human rights enunciations and movements, in their totality, do not endanger 'just' communities. 'Such communities', by definition, 'achieve that level of just arrangements and distribution of goods (including dignity and esteem) as to comport with, or even exceed, the justice potential of human rights'. 'Just' communities do not allow some human beings to treat others as mere receptacles of domination or sites of subjection; that is precisely the ethics of human rights enunciations and movements. The latter, indeed, interrogate and endanger those societal and state practices which deny human dignity and autonomy. The first task of human rights education, therefore, is to articulate a vision of justice in a just civil society, a just state embedded in the totality of authoritative human rights-enunciations. Such an articulation will insist that the conditions and circumstances of pluralism and diversity in culture and religion may not be at odds with the notions of justice embedded in human rights.

The task of human rights education consists of addressing difficult dilemmas of communitarianism and libertarianism; excesses of either can make problematic the very notion of human rights in 'real' as well as 'imagined' communities around the world (see, for example, Sandel 1982; Mulhall and Swift 1992; Das 1995).

The Material Forces of Production

Science and technology, as Karl Marx reiterated long ago, can be constructed as material forces of production. The post-industrial mode of production rests upon fantastic development of new productive forces. Among these are technologies underlying weapons of mass destruction, space technologies, biotechnology, digitalization, 'civilian' nuclear power and biomedical technologies. Productive forces are inherently *amoral*. The overall impact of these developments is to make human rights paradigms problematic, and also, to some extent, obsolete. The following enables a glimpse into the emerging impact.

- The very notion of what it is to be *human* is being profoundly transformed by DNA research whose main premise is: 'all life is information', 'all life is a text', ready and ripe for interpretive appropriation,[18] thereby providing a future lack of foundation for the meaning of the human right to life.

- New forms of life (genetically engineered in corporate laboratories and universities/research institutions emerge as handmaidens of multinationals) are new forms of property: the herein of GATT/WTO 1994 trade-related intellectual property rights as *human rights* of biotech multinational corporations.

- 'Nature' is not pre-given but constructed by genetic engineering enterprise under the corporate carnal gaze; 'nature' is industrial raw material forever transformable into corporate lust for power and profit (see Shiva 1993 and Sand 1994: 0–13), a desire signifying a true Lacanian lack.[19]

- Biomedical industries engaged in germ-line therapeutics (as against somatic-cell therapeutics) legitimate 'positive' eugenics not just in relation to dreaded genetic diseases or disorders, but also in terms of human engineering of attributes (age, height, pigmentation and, in a not-too-distant human future, IQ). (Elias and Annas 1992: 142–56)

- While human rights promotion and protection has to be securely extended to practitioners of science/technology as essential components of freedom of speech and expression, actual practices of science/technology here-and-now escape accountability at the bar of human rights norms and standards (see, for example, Wright 1994).

- The digital 'revolution' initially, and in the short run, creates a 'global village'; only in terms of entrenching multinational marketplace ghettos to be commercially exploited, without a semblance of solicitude for plurality, diversity, identity and multiculturality (see, for example, Mander 1977).

- The digital revolution also makes possible depersonalization of means of violence, where violence becomes an end in itself, threatening in a very major respect the logic of human rights, however conceived.

- Digitalization also consummates the process of cultural appropriation worldwide, mocking at the very moment of their enunciation the human rights of indigenous people, especially in their folklore and their cultural rights to civilizational self-determination.

This list could be refined as well as expanded. But it should be sufficient to illustrate that science and technology, as forces of production, are human rights visually handicapped. In their relentless march, they acknowledge no obscenities of violation of human rights, the Bhopal catastrophe being an archetype. Forces of production can only cognize human rights appropriate to the mode of production and no other (Baxi 1993: 51–84). Thus, the only human rights which will, under this mode, be universally recognized are market-friendly human rights. The rest would sought to be consigned to the dust-heap of history. The struggle of human rights education would then be the struggle from this dust-heap!

The Social Relations of Production

'Globalization' is a complex phrase commonly used to summate the relations of production in a post-industrial mode. It is impossible, within the confines of this paper, to review the complexity and contradictions of various dimensions of globalization, even in relation to human rights visions and movements. But even a fleeting glance at some of the aspects of globalization is necessary if only to indicate the hard tasks awaiting human rights education.

First, globalization theorists posit, in different ways, the emergence of a new international division of labour. This division is marked by the impact of trade and investment patterns. Even while acknowledging some transformations in the 'developing' countries' economies,[20] it remains cruelly correct to say that these patterns have created and perpetuated an unprecedented and extreme gap between rich and poor societies (see Barraclough, ed. 1978: 294). The new division of labour is marked by a 'dematerialization' of production, in the sense that advanced industrial countries export labour-intensive production to impoverished countries; this enables flagrant violations of the human rights of workers, notoriously in the export-processing zones (see Adleman 1993: 195–218).

Second, despite the tendency towards slow transition of transnational corporations and 'alliances'[21] (or perhaps because of this), it remains true that multinational corporations dominate processes of globalization.[22] MNCs are new forms of sovereignty of late capitalism and resist with their might all claims to accountability and the rule of law, while claiming the fullest benefit of access to all basic human rights (including freedom of speech, the right to property and the right to legal personality consistent with corporate will and power).[23] In this sense, MNCs continue to reproduce the law's infamy (see Fitzpatrick 1993).

Third, with Ulrich Back we may reiterate that globalization creates a risk society (see Beck 1992). Globalization of risks entails '*new international inequalities*, firstly between the third world and industrial states themselves' (ibid.: 23) (Chernobyl and the current phenomenon of 'loose nukes' being the archetype). Although globalization posits the image of the 'whole world as a risk society', such that 'the life of a blade of grass in the Bavarian forest comes to depend on the making of and keeping of international agreements [given the "universality and supra-nationality of pollutants"]' (ibid.), millions of human victims of industrial mass disasters, especially in the third world, remain less fortunate than a 'blade of grass in the Bavarian forest' as MNCs continue to fail even generalized declarations of their human rights responsibilities.

Fourth, globalization produces its own epistemologies (for example, decision-making under conditions of uncertainty, cost–benefit analysis, risk analysis and management; in short, the 'globalization of doubt') consistent with their power and profit. Thus, the social relations of globalization increasingly create an impression of lack of agency (and therefore of human rights responsibilities), while 'the formation of a global stock market, of global commodity (even debt) future markets, of currency and interest rate swaps, together with an accelerated mobility of funds' signifies, inaugurally, 'the formation of a single world market for money and credit supply: 'the structure of this global financial system is now so complex that it surpasses most people's *understanding*' (Harvey 1989: 161).

Fifth, more recently, global business has sought and won increasing legitimation from the United Nations system (for example, the Business Council of the Commission of Sustainable Development). Many NGOs, including human rights education NGOs, are also on their way to mining their own business councils, in great expectations of ameliorating late capitalism.

Sixth, at the level of the symbolic, or in the political economy of signs (as narrated by Jean Baudrillard), globalization is a 'culture of excess' producing its own *hyper-realities* (see Baudrillard 1975; Kellner and Baudrillard 1989).

> Piles of images, heaps of information, flocks of desires, so multiplied, the images represent nothing but themselves, information does not inform, desires turn into their own objectives, the world is no longer a *scene* (place where the play is staged, when as we have the right to suspect, will be directed towards some concrete ending, even if we do not know in advance what is); instead, it is *obscene*: a lot of noise and bustle without a plot, scenario, director and directions. It is a *contactual*, not a *contractual*, world. (Bauman 1992: 151)

In an *obscene* world, human rights become tenuous of meaning. Rights enunciations fail to adjudicate the riot of multiplicity of meanings. They cannot perform the labours of a *social contract* in a *contractual world*. Where power, in Baudrillard's words, in its final form, becomes organization and manipulation of *death* (and death represents social, cultural, spiritual, civilizational cessation/cancellation of *being* human), human rights movements attain a monumental agenda under whose weight they also increasingly confront 'death'. Indeed, in a postmodern world or political economy of signs/simulations, the Prince of Denmark's prayer stands answered: the 'all-too-sullied word' melts into a dew in whose misty horizons images of human rights-oriented futures also flicker and fade.

Underlying all these and related features of globalization is the steady appropriation of human rights discourse by and for the multinationals.[24] For example:

- Despite its manifold horrors, the Green Revolution (first and second) is corporate servicing of the Human Right to Food!
- Despite devastation of pre-industrial lifestyles and cultures and of people's right to habitat, mega-irrigation projects signify corporate partnership to meet the basic human needs of the people.
- Despite extensive appropriation of biological diversity, the Dunkel–WTO aggressive protection of trade-related intellectual property rights is the MNC contribution to the human right to development!

It is needless to multiply instances, but it is clear that the MNC's image of human rights as market-friendly or trade-related human rights is already firmly entrenched, and will command increasing operational consensus of states and international agencies. Already, human rights discourse stands instrumentalized in terms of merely international public policy on *development* (meaning free trade, deregulation, liberalization, structural adjustment and allegiance to the hegemony of industrial countries – in the United Nations Summit on Social Development Declaration and Programme of Action).

Albert Camus foresaw and bemoaned the hypocrisy of such cooptation:

> But slave camps under the flag of freedom, massacres justified by philanthropy or by the taste of superhuman, in one sense cripple judgement. On the day when crime dons the apparel of innocence – through a curious transposition characteristic of our times – it is innocence that is called upon to justify itself. (Camus 1957: 4)

Forces and relations of globalization tend to 'cripple judgement' even among communities of human rights and human rights education practitioners. A utilitarian approach to science and technology, suggesting even 'gains' to human rights by some developments, does not fully address challenges to human rights inherent in the accelerated progress of globalization. The vicissitudes of a utilitarian approach are poignantly illustrated by biomedical advances facilitating reproductive rights, on the one hand, and on the other, by exploitation and expropriation of women's bodies by pharmaceutical multinationals.[26] There is much to be learnt, beyond mere utilitarian approaches, from the narratives of this conflicted discourse of women's rights as human rights and multinational appropriation – certainly, more than the recent, and somewhat juvenile, enthusiasm at building electronic solidarities through cyberspace (internet email) may suggest!

In many senses, the terrain of human rights and human rights education would seem to be moving in the direction of *deglobalization*, or at least deceleration of the pace of globalization. When labour is being 'dematerialized', consumption universalized and production localized, surely the site of human rights education must be the local as a ghetto of the global. It is on this terrain that the struggles of demystification of the operative and oppressive ideologies of globalization have to begin. Surely, the victims of globalization know its cruel truths, productive of their destinies, inscribed on their docile bodies and tormented souls. They certainly need to be 'empowered' by 'education'. But who would be these educators? How do we make ourselves wary of the real dangers of alienation from those whom we would help empower themselves? For how long shall we sleep with the enemy that forces and relations of globalization implant us with? How far can the jet-set, email, credit-card activist culture herald the struggles for deglobalization, for the conquest of local spaces, for the recovery of plurality, diversity, interculturality? How shall we chisel the image of authentic human rights educators? How shall we, in the words of Camus, be equipped to endure the burden of justification of our innocence?

Human rights education, howsoever conceived, has to simultaneously engage in *understanding* and *undermining* the new world in the process of becoming. It is on this perspective that the various formulations of the 'objectives' of human rights education in the United Nations discourses bare themselves to full view, and summon human rights education endeavours to beyond their *untruth*. The platitudinous-sounding conclusion of this essay has to be understood in this light.

The Way to Human Rights Education

The emergent discourse on human rights education has to be itself inherently dialogical. Its truth cannot be, by the very nature of the enterprise of human rights education, hegemonically legislated in advance, but has to emerge out of unrelenting praxis, just as some truths about human rights and fundamental freedoms have merged in contemporary times. The philosophical cottage industries of rights-weariness (mostly in the North) and rights-wariness (mostly in the South) have to be dissolved through dialogical enterprises.

This is perhaps easier said than done. Even eminent thinkers mix and merge both rights-weariness and rights-wariness. For example, one of this decade's most authoritative exponents of moral philosophy insists that human rights are no more than 'moral fictions', and the plain truth is that: 'there is no [human] right and belief in them is one with belief in witches and unicorns. . . . In the United Nations Declaration on human rights of 1949 what has since become the normal UN practice of not giving good reasons for any assertion whatsoever is followed with great rigour' (MacIntyre 1984: 69).

Many a political leader and regime, alas, will be tempted to agree. This is how practices of knowledge and practices of power often reinforce each other. Human rights education has to enable discourse which confers the status of 'truth' on human rights (which are no mere 'moral fictions'), and to enable people everywhere, including philosophers, to learn how belief in human rights is different from belief in 'witches' and 'unicorns'. Human rights education should develop the potential of the people to combat growing moral nihilism (a mark of postmodernism) and, in particular, of educating educators in the meanings of morality.

Discursive equality requires atonement for the past – the colonial/imperial past, the cold war past and the neo-cold war past in-the-making. Dialogical equality also requires construction of humiliation's Other – humility before history. Likewise, the silences in human rights education discourses (so far surveyed) have to be empowered to speak to us. Victims of human rights violations should be enabled to speak to us concerning conditions which make the gross and flagrant violations of human rights possible, including corruptibility of democratic regimes cultivated by transnational capital, traffic in armaments, state hospitality to 'mercenaries', spread of hazardous technologies worldwide, the arrogance of patriarchy (which denies dignity to women) and of the late twentieth-century forms of capital (which denies the dignity of labour, as if working-class struggles never took place in history).

The dialogism of human rights education must enable and empower the people of the world to pour content into 'abstract' conceptions such as 'progress', 'development', 'peace' and 'tolerance'. Dialogism has, by the same token, to create a fuller awareness concerning the attainment of international cooperation in these areas.

Dialogical human rights education, like all education, must begin with a sense of humility. To the tasks of human rights education, all nations come as more or less equal strangers, whereas all the people of the world come as cognoscenti who have experienced repression or struggle, and the knowledge which such experience brings concerning human rights and fundamental freedoms. Collective self-education (despite contingencies of headstarts privileged by history to some liberal democratic societies) is essential to build a true fellowship of learning, and indispensable to the emergence of human rights education.

This great human endeavour of human rights education has to modify Karl Marx's thesis on Feuerbach to say: 'The various Declarations on Human Rights Education have merely explained what human rights education might be; the task, however, is to change human rights education.' Like all authentic education, human rights education brings to shape its own destiny through its own daily *praxis*.

The tasks of human rights education are so historically imperative that with Schiller we must say:

> What is left undone one minute
> is restored by no eternity.

Notes

[1] For an elaboration of this notion, see Baxi (1986); for a revised version, see Baxi (1994a: 1–17).

[2] See 'Politics of Memory in an Era of Technonarcissism', Chapter Two, in Baxi (1994a: 18–27).

[3] Mary Daly insightfully defines 'consumer society' as Patriarchy, the 'State of Annihilation, the State of Reversal', in which the 'consumed' are misnamed as the 'consumers' and the 'true consumers' are honoured as 'prolific producers/creators'. See Daly (1985, 1987: 192).

4 See, for a most recent survey, Jurgensmeyer (1993).

5 As regards the social summit at Copenhagen, this expectation is fully borne out! On one reading of the text of its Declaration, all that the summit achieves is an articulation of what I have called 'trade-related human rights'. See Baxi (1995a).

6 As is now self-evident from the two volumes of United Nations Blue Books, *Human Rights: A Compilation of International Instruments*.

7 In particular, the Recommendations of the UNESCO International Congress on the Teaching of Human Rights (Vienna, 1978), the UNESCO International Congress on Human Rights Teaching Information and Documentation (Malta, 1987) and the International Forum on Education for Democracy (Tunis, 1992).

8 For example, Section 3, Part II of the Vienna Declaration on Equal Status of Human Rights of Women avoids references to the important 1962 Convention on Consent to Marriage, Minimum Age for Marriage, the Registration of Marriages, and on the 1976 Declaration on Protecting of Women and Children in Emergency and Armed Conflicts.

9 The Decade shall be, as per Article 1 of the Draft, based upon 'the provisions of human rights instruments, with particular reference to those provisions addressing human rights education'.

10 The normative bases, according to Article 2 of the Draft, are:
   (a) the strengthening of respect for human rights and fundamental freedoms,
   (b) the full development of the human personality and the sense of its dignity,
   (c) the formation of understanding, tolerance, gender equality, and friendship among all nations, indigenous peoples, racial, religious and linguistic groups,
   (d) the enabling of all persons to participate effectively in a free society, and
   (e) the furtherance of the activities of the United Nations for the maintenance of peace.

11 Pluralization of knowledge must be an important aspect of human rights education culture and pedagogy. The important distinction between 'organic' and 'crudite' knowledges (initiated by Antonio Gramsci and enriched by Michel Foucault) suggests that human rights education should be so designed as to allow experiential knowledges of peoples about rights and violations to emerge; from the cumulation of such organic knowledges it should also become clear (than is the case today) that most of contemporary human rights enunciations are refined articulations or echoes of authentic human experiences.

   If we conceive knowledge in the singular (as does the Draft), human rights education will only privilege crudite knowledge about the human rights standards which is to be transmitted. And the emphasis on 'participatory' pedagogy would be confined to rituals of confirmation about acts of reception of information.

   Human rights education, in the present opinion, has to avail interaction of both forms of knowledges (organic as well crudite) in order to be empowering.

12 For example, Maurice Cranston says, 'once a right is conceived as an ideal, you acknowledge its impracticality; it becomes easier to dismiss it as a right'; see Cranston (1983: 1–17). The writings of political philosopher Allan Buchanan consistently interrogate the claims of human rights languages to any unique or distinctive state. Invoking the notion of Age of Rights, he puts it to severe and sustained interrogation, but only at the level of the jurisprudence of national legal orders. See Buchanan (1992).

13 See also note 7 and the text accompanying it.

14 See Claude (1991) for a lucid overview of the evolution of human rights education as state policy and the activist response. Memorandum Order No. 20 (human rights education for arresting and investigating officers), Executive Order No. 27 (government departmental responsibilities for human rights education) and Executive Order No. 163 (mandating human rights education as an aspect of the Human Rights Commission) are important devices of state policy emergent during Corazon Aquino's regime. The interim Construction of South Africa under Article 116 also contains an incipient human rights education mandate for the Human Rights Commission.

[15] It is in this context that one welcomes the prospect of a World Report on Human Rights Education proposed recently by the People's Decade on Human Rights Education and the nascent Independence Commission on Human Rights.

[16] I have evocatively sketched the notion of human rights education as liberational education in the lineage of Paulo Friere and the notable work by Hernando de Soto. See de Soto (1989). Undoubtedly, this tradition has charismatic exponents and innovators worldwide. Human rights education in this tradition is well summed up by Sulamalth Koening (whose pioneering work in gestating the Human Rights Education Decade is well known) as 'education for social transformation'.

[17] See, for example, the provocative analysis in Bauman (1992: 1–26).

[18] See, for example, the US Biotech Corporation Genex 1982 Annual Report: 'DNA can be thought of as a language, the language in which all genetic information is written. As with any language, it is desirable to be able to read, write and edit the language of DNA. . . . It is by this editing process that the naturally occurring text can be rearranged for the benefit of the experimenter.' Quoted in Hobbelink (1991: 23). See also Shiva (1993).

[19] The most profound thinker of 'desire', after Freud, is Jacques Lacan, who has further mystified the 'enigma of desire'. 'Desire' for Lacan is an endless eternal 'stretching forward, towards the desire for something else'. Lacan (1977: 166–67).

[20] The most frequently mentioned are: the transition of some less developed countries (LDCs) into new industrial countries (NICs); 'cartelization' of manufacture by some developed countries (for example, OPEC) and the emerging presence of developing societies' multinational enterprises.

[21] Gilpin refers to a vast array of 'negotiated arrangements' which now obtain: 'cross-licensing of technology among corporations of different nationalities, joint ventures' orderly marketing arrangements, secondary sourcing offshore production of component and cross-cutting equity ownership'. Gilpin (1987: 256).

[22] About 300 MNCs account for 70 per cent of direct foreign investment and 25 per cent of world capital. About 20,000 MNCs commanded, in 1988, assets over $4 trillion; they appropriated 25–30 per cent of the aggregate GDP in all market economies, 75 per cent of international commodity trade and 80 per cent of world traffic in technology and management competencies. See Dunning (1993).

[23] See, for a draft declaration of a Bill of Rights for Multinationals, Baxi (1995a).

[24] See, for example, 'Our Global Neighbourhood: The Report of the Commission of Global Governance'; and, for a critique, Baxi (1995b).

[25] Justifiably, Camus inaugurates the end of his discourse in *The Rebel* by reaffirming: 'I rebel: therefore, we are'.

[26] Whether this be through carcinogenic intrauterine devices or contraceptives, Norplant or amniocentesis.

References

Adleman, Sammy (1993), 'The International Labour Code and Exploitation of Female Workers in Export-Processing Zones', in Adleman and Paliwala, eds (1993).

Adleman, Sammy and Abdul Paliwala, eds (1993), *Law and Crisis in the Third World* (London: Han Zell Publishers).

Barraclough, G., ed. (1978), *The Times Atlas of World History* (London: Times).

Baudrillard, Jean (1975), *The Mirror of Production* (St. Louis: Telos).

Baxi, U. (1986), 'From Human Rights to the Human', *India International Quarterly*, 13.

—— (1993), *Marx, Law and Justice: Indian Perspective* (Bombay: N.M. Tripathi).

—— (1994a), *Inhuman Wrongs and Human Rights: Unconventional Essays* (Delhi: Har Anand Publications).

—— (1994b), *Mambrino's Helmet?: Human Rights for a Changing World* (Delhi: Har Anand Publications).

—— (1994c), 'The Right to be Loved and to Learn' in Baxi, *Inhuman Wrongs and Human Rights*.

—— (1995a), '*Summit of Hope' in the Depths of Despair?: Social Development as Realization of Human Rights*, mimeo, March.

—— (1995b), *Global Neighbourhood and the Universal Otherhood': Notes on the Report of the Commission on Global Governance*, mimeo, June.

Bauman, Zygmut (1992), *Intimations of Postmodernity* (London: Routledge).

Beck, U. (1992), translated by Mark Ritter, *Risk Society: Towards a New Modernity* (London: Sage).

Buchanan, Allan (1992), *Marx and Justice* (Totowa, N.J.: Rowman and Littlefield).

Camus, Albert (1957), translated by Anthony Bower, *The Rebel* (New York: Alfred Knopf).

Claude, Richard Pierre (1991), *Human Rights Education in the Philippines* (Manila: Kalikasan Press).

Cranston, Maurice (1983), 'Are There Any Human Rights?', *Daedalus*, 112, Fall.

Das, Veena (1995), *Critical Events* (New Delhi: Oxford University Press).

Daly, Mary (with Jane Caputi) (1985, 1987), *Websters' First New Intergalactic Wickedary of the English Language* (Boston: Beacon Press).

de Soto, Hernando (1989), *The Other Path: The Invisible Revolution in the Third World* (New York: Harper and Row).

Dunning, J., (1993), *Multinational Enterprises in Global Economy* (Workingham: Addison-Wesley).

Elias, S. and G.J. Annas (1992), 'Somatic and Germline Therapy', in *Gene Mapping: Using Law and Ethics as a Guide.*

Fitzpatrick, Peter (1993), 'Law's Infamy', in Adleman and Paliwala, eds, *Law and Crisis in the Third World.*

Fukuyama, F. (1992), *The End of History and the Last Man* (New York: Free Press).

Gilpin, R. (1987), *The Political Economy of International Relations* (Princeton: Princeton University Press).

Harvey, David (1989), *The Condition of Postmodernity* (Oxford: Blackwell).

Hobbelink, Henk (1991), *Biotechnology and the Future of World Agriculture* (London: Zed Books).

Human Rights: A Compilation of International Instruments (1996), Sales No. E. 94, Vol. XIV, No. 1.

Jurgensmeyer, Mark (1993), *The New Cold War?: Religious Nationalism Confront the Secular State* (Berkeley: University of California Press).

Kellner, Douglas and Jean Baudrillard (1989), *From Marxism to Postmodernism and Beyond* (Cambridge: Polity Press).

Lacan, J. (1977), *Ecrits,* translated by Alan Sheridan (New York: Norton).

MacIntyre, Alasdir (1984), *After Virtue* (Indiana: University of Notredame Press).

Mander, Jerry (1977), *Four Arguments for the Elimination of Television* (New York: William Marrow/Quill).

Mulhall, Stephan and Adam Swift (1992), *Liberals and Communitarians* (Oxford: Blackwell).

Sand, Hope (1994), 'Biopiracy: Patenting the Planet', *Multinational Monitor*, June.

Sandel, Michel (1982), *Liberalism and the Limits of Justice* (Cambridge: Cambridge University Press).

Shiva, Vandana (1993), *The Monocultures of Mind* (Delhi: Natraj Publications).

Shiviji, Issa G. (1989), *The Concept of Human Rights in Africa* (London: CODESRIA Book Series).

Unger, Roberto M. (1983), 'The Critical Legal Studies Movement', *Harvard Law Review*, 561.

Wright, Susan (1994), *Molecular Politics: Developing American and British Regulatory Policy for Genetic Engineering 1972–82* (Chicago: University of Chicago Press).

The Tyranny of Labels

Romila Thapar

In the writing of Indian history, we have become accustomed to packaging our past and identifying it with labels. Such labels, even where they may include a variety of activity and experience, tend to force interpretations into a single category so that the infinite shades of difference within them disappear. When this happens, the historical perspective comes to be governed by the tyranny of labels: a condition which requires the historical unpacking of the categories and a redefining of the contents.

I would like, here, to explore two of these labels: the Hindu community and the Muslim community, with particular reference to the way they are used in the writing of pre-colonial history. My intention, in this exploration, is both to question the validity of these as all-inclusive categories in historical analysis, and to suggest the need to analyse afresh our historical understanding of what we are referring to when we speak of Hindu and Muslim communities in history. Such labels draw on conventional religious identities, but the form so demarcated is sought to be applied to every other aspect of life, whether applicable or not. It is also used to include a vast spectrum of social groups under the single label.

The viewing of Indian history in terms of these two monolithic religious communities has its origins in nineteenth-century interpretations of Indian history, where not only were the two communities described as monolithic, but they were also projected as static over many centuries. This is, of course, not to deny that the labels were used earlier, but to argue that they were used in a different sense, and their use has its own history which is yet to be investigated. A small part of this investigation is attempted here. My intention is to observe how those to whom we give a primary association with Islam, when they first arrived in India, were initially perceived in northern India, and the way in which such groups were represented as part of this perception. This was far more nuanced than is allowed for in the concept of monolithic communities, and these nuances require further exploration. The representation, in turn, had an impact on what

Ninth Zakir Husain Memorial Lecture, 9 December 1996.

have been described as the multiple new communities which came to be established. The newness was not because they were invariably alien but because there was a departure from the existing pattern of communities. The newness of these communities requires investigation and this links the study of the first millennium AD with that of the second. The continuities did not have to be literal but could have been conceptual, and while the nature of change in some situations was new, in others it could well have followed earlier patterns.

The definition of the Muslim community extends to all those who claim adherence to Islam, and the adherence is said to be demonstrated by a clearly stated belief and form of worship which, through conversion, confers membership in a large body of believers, a membership which also assumes the egalitarian basis of the association. The perspective of the court chronicles of the Sultans and the Mughals was that of the ruling class, and this perspective is not seen as broadly endorsing the above definition and reinforcing the projection of a Muslim community, a perspective in which the Hindu – as defined by such literature – was seen as the counterpart. It is as well to keep in mind that this is the current interpretation of these texts, and although some may conform to the view from the windows of power, not all do so. Although sometimes carrying some political and even theological weight, this view was nevertheless limited. As the articulation of a powerful but small section of society, it needs to be juxtaposed with other indicators.

The notion of a Hindu community evolves from a geographic and ethnic description gradually giving way to religious association. The Hindu community is more difficult to define, given the diverse nature of belief and worship, making it the amorphous 'Other' of the Muslim community in some of the court chronicles. The crystallization of this perception occurs when erstwhile Vaiṣṇavas, Śaivas, Liṅgāyats and others begin to refer to themselves as Hindus. Communities of the subcontinent have, in the past, been diverse, with multiple identities, and the attempt to force them into unchanging, static entities would seem to contradict the historical evidence. With the modern connotation of a religious community, both terms have come to include, even in the interpretation of the historical past, all manner of diverse societies across the subcontinent, for some of whom convergence with the formal religion is of recent origin, if at all.

The idea of two distinctive, segregated civilizations, the Hindu and the Muslim, in conflict with each other, was assumed in colonial scholarship. Thus James Mill differentiated the Hindu civilization from the Muslim, which gave rise to the periodization of Indian history, as that of the Hindu, Muslim and British periods. It crystallized the concept of a uniform, monolithic Hindu community dominating early history, as did the Muslim equivalent in the subsequent period, with relations between the two becoming conflictual. These notions were, in a sense, summarized by Christian Lassen who, in the mid-nineteenth century, attempting to apply a Hegelian dialectic, wrote of the Hindu civilization as the thesis, the Muslim civilization as the anti-thesis and the British as the synthesis (*Indische Alterthumskunde* 1847–62)!

Part of the insistence on the separateness of the two civilizations was the assumption that those who came with Islam had been regarded even by earlier Indians as alien, in fact, as alien as the Europeans. This, however, was an erroneous perception of earlier historical relationships. Those associated with Islam had come through various avenues, as traders, as Sufis and as attachments to conquerors. Their own self-perceptions differed, as also did the way in which they were perceived by the people of the land where they settled. For a long while, in India, they were referred to by the same terms as were used in earlier times for people from West and Central Asia, suggesting that their coming was viewed in part as a historical continuity. And there are good historical grounds to explain such a continuity.

The Arabs, Turks, Afghans and Persians were familiar to northern and western India, since they had not only been contiguous peoples but had been linked by trade, settlement and conquest – links which went back, virtually unbroken, to many centuries. Central Asia was the homeland of the Śaka and Kuṣāṇa dynasties which ruled in northern India at the turn of the Christian era, and later of the Hūṇas who came as conquerors and became a caste. In Iran, the genesis of the languages spoken there and in northern India were Old Iranian and Indo-Aryan, which were closely related languages as is evident from examples of common usage in the *Avesta* and the *Ṛgveda*. Persian contacts with India were initially through the Achaemenids who were contemporaries of the Mauryas, and later through the Sassanids, contemporaries of the Kuṣāṇas and Guptas. Territories in Afghanistan and the northwest were alternately controlled by rulers from both sides. Aśokan inscriptions in Greek and Aramaic in Afghanistan attest to Mauryan rule, and later dynasties with bases in the Oxus region and Iran brought northwestern India into their orbit. Trading links were tied to political alliances. Close maritime contacts between the subcontinent and the Arabian peninsula go back to the time of the Indus civilization, and have continued to the present.

There is, therefore, an immense history of interaction and exchange between the subcontinent and Central and Western Asia. The change of religion to Islam in the latter areas does not annul the earlier closeness. Interestingly, even the Islam of these areas was not uniform, for there were, and are, strong cultural and sectarian differences among the Muslims of Central Asia, Persia and the Arab world: differences which can, in some cases, be traced to their varying pre-Islamic past, and which are likely to have influenced the nature of their interaction with the subcontinent.

These were contiguous people whose commercial and political relations with India over a long past were sometimes competitive and hostile and at other times friendly, but were well-recognized. Battles were fought, campaigns were conducted, commercial exchange was encouraged and migrants moved across borders in various directions. Many had settled in India and married locally. One of the clauses of the treaty between Chandragupta Maurya and Seleukus Nikator has been interpreted as a *jus conubii*, freedom for the Greeks and Indians to intermarry. Such marriages, doubtlessly, gave rise to mixed communities of new castes and practices, a process that did not cease with the arrival of Muslim Arabs and others. Similarly, Indian traders and Indian Buddhist monks who lived in the oasis towns of Central Asia and in China were also to be found in ports and markets in West Asia, and were agencies of cross-cultural fertilization. Manichaeism, for example, became a major religion in the early Christian era largely because it drew on Mahāyāna Buddhism, Zorastrianism, Nestorian Christianity and elements of Central Asian animism. The dialogue between Indians, Central Asian Turks, Persians and Arabs was a continuing one, irrespective of changes of dynasties and religions, or of trade fluctuations. This dialogue is reflected, for example, in Sanskrit, Greek and Arabic texts relating to astronomy, medicine and philosophy, and in what is said of Indian scholars resident at the court of Harun al' Rashid.

The coming of the Europeans and the colonization of India by Britain was an altogether different experience. They came from distant lands, were physically different, spoke languages which were entirely alien and in which there had been no prior communication; their rituals, religion and customs were alien; their exploitation of land and labour exceeded that of the previous period; and, above all, they did not settle in India. The assumption that the West Asian and Central Asian interventions after the eighth century AD and that of the British were equally foreign to India, in origin and intent, would, from the historical perspective, be difficult to defend.

Colonial interpretations of the Indian past were often contested by Indian historians, but the periodization was accepted in essentials. This was implicitly the acceptance of the idea that the units of Indian society were communities defined by single religions, requiring, therefore, that monolithic religious identities be sought and established in history. This view coincided with the incubation of the nation-state. All nationalisms use history, some more evidently than the other. Essential to nationalist ideology was also the attempt to locate and define a national culture, often equated with that of the dominant group. Inevitably, other cultures get excluded in this process. But the historian also acts as a remembrancer, reminding society of the histories that are not always apparent up front.

When communalisms become visible on the political stage, as they did from the early years of this century, there is not only a contestation between them on the question of identity, but also a conflict with the earlier anti-colonial nationalism. The separation of the indigenous and the foreign emerges as a contentious issue and is taken back to the beginning of Indian history. Communal historiographies attempt to construct a religious majority into a monolithic community, claiming that their interpretations of the past which support such a monolith are the only valid ones. Religion is sought to be restructured in order that it can be used for political mobilization (Thapar 1985). There is inevitably a confrontation between historical evidence and its logic, counterposed with resort to a fantasized past, in what are projected as conflicting histories.[1]

I would like to illustrate this by taking up one central issue, now contested, of the period prior to the modern in South Asian history. The question of identities has hinged on the definition of communities as solely religious communities, Hindu and Muslim in the main, the former being indigenous and the latter foreign, and projected as generally hostile to each other. The assumptions have been that the Hindus and the Muslims, each constituted a unified, monolithic community, and were, therefore, separate nations from the start, and that religious difference provides a complete, even though mono-causal explanation for historical events and activities in the second millennium AD. The reconstruction of this history is largely based on particular readings of court chronicles and texts where political contestation is sometimes projected in religious terms, to the exclusion of other categories of texts which allow a different reconstruction.

My objection to the use of blanket terms such as 'the Hindus' and 'the Muslims' in historical readings is that it erases precision with reference to social groups, and is, therefore, methodologically invalid and historically inaccurate. It fails to differentiate between that which is more pertinent to religious history and that which relates to other aspects of life, even if there had been an overlapping in some situations. To explain the events of the time in terms of only an interaction between groups identified either as Hindus or as Muslims, is simplistic as a historical explanation. Some continuities in historical processes are arbitrarily broken by this usage, and, at the same time, it is difficult to observe historical changes. Questioning the existence of such monolithic, religious communities, therefore, has extensive historiographical implications.

The argument that the notion of community was always defined by a single religion, even in the pre-Islamic past, has been countered by the evidence of sources other than brahmanical normative texts. Such sources relate to diverse social groups and depict a different social scene. Theoretical interpretations emphasizing the nature of relationships between socially diverse groups and focus on access to power, whether through economic or other disparities, have also changed the contours of pre-modern history. The many studies of caste, clan, village, town, language and region have encouraged a diversified view of past identities. Caste as *varṇa*, earlier thought to be a definitive identity, is now being recognized as intersected by identities of language, sect and occupation. Each individual, therefore, had varied identities, of which some might overlap, but which interfered with the consolidation of a single, monolithic, religious identity, even in societies prior to the coming of Islam (Thapar 1992).

For Orientalist scholarship, the construction of what came to be called Hinduism was a challenge, being different from the familiar perspective of religions such as Judaism, Christianity and Islam. The latter were founded on the teachings of historically recognized prophets or of a messiah, with a theology and dogma, a sacred book and some ensuing deviations which took the form of variant sects. Yet the religious articulation which we recognize as constituting the religions which came to be called Hinduism did not subscribe to these features. Of its many variant forms, some were deviations from earlier belief and practice but others had an independent genesis. The juxtaposition of religious sects did result, almost through osmosis, in similarities which introduced some common features, but the diversities remained. Hence the preference in some recent scholarship for the phrase 'Hindu regions', rather than Hinduism.[2] Because of this flexibility and decentralization, the religious identity was frequently closely allied to caste identities, and since these incorporated occupation and access to resources, there were factors other than belief alone which governed religious identities. This is equally true of other religions in the subcontinent.

The term 'Hindu' as referring to a religion is initially absent in the vocabulary of Indian languages, and only slowly gains currency. This is quite logical given that earlier religious identities were tied to sect and caste. Membership was not of a specific religion, binding groups across a social spectrum and a geographical space, as was the case, for example, with Buddhism. The use of a single term to include the diversity would have been bewildering, and adjustment to this usage would have required a long period. When and why it came to be a part of the self-perception of what we today call the Hindus, would make a worthwhile historical enquiry. Terms such as 'Muslims' or 'Mussulman' are also not immediate entrants into the vocabulary of Indian languages after the arrival of Islam, although these terms occur in the texts of what were initially non-Indian languages. Prior to that, a variety of other terms are preferred and these have their own history. The Arabs, Turks, Afghans and others are referred to variously, such as Tājika, Yavana, Śaka, Turuṣka and *mleccha*. There is, therefore, an attempt to associate the new entrants with existing categories which are hence expressive of more subtle relationships than we have assumed. The categories gave them an identity which was familiar and, interestingly, provided them with historical links, emanating from India's connections with Western and Central Asia in the past. The use of these terms was, at one level, a continuation from the earlier past. What is striking is that initially none of these terms had a religious connotation. It would again be worthwhile to locate the point in time when this connotation was acquired, in cases such as Turuṣka and its variants, which later included a religious identity.

Inscriptions from the eighth century AD refer to Arab incursions coming from Sind and Gujarat into the Narmada delta (Avasthy and Ghosh 1935). The Arabs are referred to as Tājikas, which suggest some complex link to an Arab identity, in addition to their being maritime traders. The Rāṣṭrakūṭa kings of the ninth–tenth centuries had appointed a Tājika as governor of the Sanjan area of Thane district on the west coast, whose name is rendered as Madhumati, also thought to be the Sanskrit for Mohammed since it also rendered sometimes as Madhumada (*Epigraphia Indica*, 32: 47 ff., 64 ff.). He conquered the chiefs of the neighbouring harbours for the Rāṣṭrakūṭas and placed his officers in charge. As governor, he granted a village to finance the building of a temple and the installation of an icon. Arab writers of this period refer to Arab officers employed by the *rājās* and settlements of Arab traders, and in both cases they had to work closely with the existing administration (Athar Ali 1989).

The term Yavana was originally used for Greeks and later for those coming from West Asia or the west generally (Thapar 1978). The Sanskrit word *yavana* is a black formation from the Prākrit *yona*, derived from the West Asian *yauna*, referring to the Ionian Greeks. It was used in an ethnic and geographical sense. Buddhist texts speak approvingly of the Yavanas. Some became Buddhists or were patrons of Buddhism. There was also a curiosity about Yavana society, which, it was said, had no castes but had a dual division of master and slave (*Majjhima Nikāya*, 2: 149–92). The Greek-speaking population of the Indo-Iranian borderlands is familiar from the Mauryan period.

For most people the Yavanas were just another people, but the *brāhmaṇas* were initially antagonistic. A text of the early centuries AD, the *Yuga Purāṇa* of the *Gārgi Saṃhitā*, depicts them as unfriendly[3] even though some Yavanas declared themselves to be Vaiṣṇavas. Perhaps this hostility grew out of the memory of Alexander's brutal attack on the Malloi (Arrian 6.6 ff.; Plutarch 69) and the later resentment against Indo-Greek rulers in India patronizing what the *brāhmaṇas* regarded as heretical sects. The negative image of the Kālayavana reflects a dislike of the Yavanas in another source, the *Harivaṃśa* (Hein 1989) in spite of the original Kālayavana being of Indian parentage. Nevertheless, Yavanas were not only accommodated but accepted as rulers. They were, however, given the status of *vrātya kṣatriyas* or degenerate *kṣatriya* status, or those who, although born of *kṣatriyas*, had not married women of an equal caste (Manu X: 20). This was an example of providing a caste ranking for what was originally a ruling class which came from outside caste society. Much of the brahmanical hostility was because the Yavanas were seen as upsetting the norms of brahmanical society and not performing the rituals approved of by brahmanical orthopraxy (Manu X: 43–44). The didactic section of the *Mahābhārata*, thought to be an interpolation, mentions that the Yavanas fell from status because they disregarded the *brāhmaṇas* (*Mahābhārata*, 13, 35: 17–18), and the revenge of the latter led to their calling them *vratyas*. This hostility was limited to the *brāhmaṇas* for, in the narrative section of the *Mahābhārata*, thought to be less tampered with, the Yavanas are given a high status in that they are said to be descended from Turvaśa, one of the five sons of the ancestral hero, Yadu (*Mahābhārata*, 1.80.26).

Turks and Afghans are referred to as Yavanas in multiple inscriptions (Avasthy and Ghosh 1935, 1936). This was an indication of their being from the west and therefore alien, but also of not being all that alien since there was already a status and an identity for them in the existing system. It enabled them to be included later in the scheme of how the past was conceptualized, as for example in one eighteenth-century Marathi chronicle.[4] Such texts were partial imitations of the earlier tradition of maintaining king-lists, as in the Purāṇas and the *vaṃśāvalīs* or chronicles. With the establishment of Maratha power, there was the need for writing 'histories' to legitimize this power. As has been pointed out, the legitimizing of Maratha rule also required legitimizing the preceding Mughal and Turkish rule, which these texts refer to as the rule of the Yavanas.

But this was not a simple matter, for it had to conform to the *vaṃśāvalī* tradition. The earlier *vaṃśāvalī* had linked contemporary rulers genealogically to the ancient heroes of the Purāṇas. Something similar would have to be done for these more recent Yavanas. It was therefore stated that a certain text, called the *Ramala-śāstra*, contained the history of the Yavanas. We are told, in true Puranic style, that this text was first recited by Śiva to Pārvatī, and then through Skanda, Nārada and Bhṛgu to Śurka, the last of whom told it to the Yavanas. It is Śiva who sent *Paigambar* to earth and there were seven *paigambars* or wise men, starting with Adam. This is, of course, reminiscent of the seven Manus with which Puranic chronology begins. The *paigambars* came to earth during the Kali Yuga. They started their own era based on the *Hijri* era, different from the earlier Indian *samvat* era. They renamed Hastinapur as Dilli and initiated Yavana rule. They are thus located in time and space and provided with links to the past in accordance with the earlier and established *vaṃśāvalī* tradition.

The prime mover in this history is the deity of Śiva and this makes any other legitimation unnecessary. Since the Yavanas had the blessing of Śiva, Pithor Rājā Chauhana could not hold them back. The establishment of the Maratha kingdom also took place at the intervention of the deity. This kind of adjustment which emerges out of upper-caste interests may also have been in part a response to the necessary change in the role model. Those claiming to be *kṣatriyas* were now not approximating the lifestyle of their ancestors to the same degree as before, but were increasingly imitating the appearance, dress, language and lifestyle of the Mughal courts, as is evident from painting and literature. The culture of the elite had changed and there was a noticeable degree of accommodating the new. The importance of such accounts lies not in their fantasy of what actually happened, but in that they provide us with a glimpse of how a historical situation was being manipulated, in order to correlate a view of tradition with the problems of contemporary change. This might enable us to assess the nature of the ideological negotiation which conditioned such perceptions.

The term Śaka was the Sanskrit term for the Scythians, people from Central Asia who had ruled in parts of northern and western Indian around the Christian era. The reference to Turkish and Afghan dynasties as Śakas suggests a historical perception of place and people, a perception both of who the rulers were and how they might be fitted into the history of the ruled. A Sanskrit inscription of AD 1276 may illustrate this.[5] It records the building of a *baoli* and a *dharmaśālā* in Palam (just outside Delhi) by Uḍḍhara from Ucca in the Multan district. The inscription, composed by Pandit Yogeśvara, dated in the *vikrama samvat* 1333, begins with a salutation to Śiva and Ganapati. It then refers to the rulers of Delhi and Haryana as the Tomaras, Chauhānas and Śakas, the earlier two having been recognized as Rajput dynasties and the last being a reference to the Sultans.[6] This is made clear by the detailed list of Śakas, that is, the Sultans of Delhi up to the current ruler Balban, referred to as *nāyaka śri hammīra Gayāsdīna nṛpati samrāṭa*, and whose conquests are described with extravagant praise. His titles mix the old with the new. *Nāyaka* was an earlier title and *hammīra* is thought to be the sanskritized form of Amir. In the eulogistic style of the earlier *praśasti* tradition, Balban's realm is said to be virtually subcontinental – an obvious exaggeration. This is followed by a fairly detailed family history of the merchant in the traditional *vamśāvalī* style. He was clearly a man of considerable wealth. Other sources inform us that Hindu merchants from Multan gave loans to Balban's nobles when the latter faced a shortfall in collecting revenue (Habib 1978: 291, 295). The identity of the Sultan is perceived as a continuity from earlier times, and the identity of the merchant is in relation to his own history and occupation, and perhaps the unstated patronage of the Sultan. The sole reference to religion is oblique, in the statement that even Viṣṇu now sleeps peacefully, presumably because of the reign of Balban.

A Sanskrit inscription from Naraina (also in the vicinity of Delhi), dated *samvat* 1384 or AD 1327, follows the same format.[7] We are told that in the town of Dilli, sin is expelled by the chanting of the Vedas. The city is ruled by Mahamūda Sāhi who is the *cūḍāmaṇi*, the crest-jewel, of the rulers of the earth (a phrase used frequently in Sanskrit to describe a king), and is a *śakendra*, the lord/Indra of the Śakas. This may well be the rhetoric of sycophancy; nevertheless, the juxtaposing of Vedic recitations to the rule of Mohammad bin Tughlaq carries its own message. The identification with the Śakas is complimentary since the earlier Śakas were associated with the important calendrical era of AD 78, still in official use.

Another term is Turuṣka, and was originally a geographical and ethnic name. An interesting link is made with earlier Indian historical perceptions of Central Asia, when Kalhaṇa in his twelfth-century history of Kashmir, the *Rājataraṅginī*, used the term retrospectively. He refers to the Kuṣāṇas of the early centuries AD as Turuṣkas, and adds, ironically, that even though they were Turuṣkas, these earlier kings were given to piety (*Rājataraṅginī*, I, 170; VIII, 3412). Here, perhaps, the points of contrast are the references in two twelfth-century inscriptions to the Turuṣkas as evil, *duṣṭātturuṣka*, or to a woman installing an image in place of one broken by the Turuṣkas (Avasthy and Ghosh 1935, 1936). Familiarity with the Turks was also because they competed with Indian and other traders in controlling the Central Asian trade, especially the lucrative trade along the silk route between China and Byzantium, and because Buddhism, known to these areas prior to Islam, had been reinforced by missions from north India. The initial attacks of the Turks and Afghans were tied into local politics, what Kalhaṇa refers to as the coalition of the Kashmiri, Khasa and *mleccha* (*Rājataraṅginī*, VIII, 887) . The entry of the Turuṣkas on the north Indian scene is in many ways a continuation of the relations which had existed between the states of northwestern India and those across the borders.

Kalhaṇa writes disparagingly of the Kashmiri king Harṣadeva ruling in the eleventh century who employed Turuṣka mercenaries – horsemen in the main – in his campaigns against local rulers, even though the Turuṣkas were then invading the Punjab. The activities of Harṣadeva, demolishing and looting temples when there was a fiscal crisis, leads to Kalhaṇa calling him a Turuṣka (*Rājataraṅginī*, VII, 1095, 1149; VIII, 3346). But he adds that such activities have been familiar even from earlier times. However, the looting of temples by Harṣadeva was more systematic, for he appointed Udayarāja as a special officer to carry out the activities, with the designation of *devotpāṭana-nāyaka*, the officer for the uprooting of deities (*Rājataraṅgiṇī*, VII, 1091).

Alberuni, writing soon after the raids of Mahmud of Ghazni, states that Mahmud destroyed the economy of the areas where he looted, and this accounts for the antagonism of the local people towards the Muslim (Sachau 1910: 22). This is as much a commentary on Mahmud as a statement of what he perceived. The historical question would enquire into the degree of devastation, the areas referred to and the memory of the disruption. An interesting case is that of Somanātha, particularly associated with Mahmud's destruction of the Śiva temple in the early eleventh century.

Curiously, Bilhana, referring to his visit to Somanātha later in the same century, makes no mention of Mahmud's raid (*Vikramāṅkadeva carita*, XVIII, 97). An inscription from Veraval in the vicinity of Somanātha, and dating back to AD 1216, is a eulogy on the town and its temples, the Chalukya dynasty, the local governor Śrīdhara and the Śaiva priest of the temple, and speaks of the heroic Hammīra who was subdued by Śrīdhara; yet, there is no mention of the destruction of the temple or of its restoration (*Epigraphia Indica*, 2: 437 ff.). Here the Turuṣkas are a political enemy similar to others against whom the Chalukyas fought. Even more curious is the evidence of another inscription from Veraval, also in Sanskrit. It records that a Chalukya–Vaghela king gave a substantial grant of land in Somanātha for the construction of a mosque in AD 1264 to the owner of a shipping company called Noradina Piroja/Nur-ud-din Firuz (*Epigraphia Indica*, 34: 141–52), the son of Khoja Nau Abu Brahima of Hormuja-*deśa* or Ormuz. The mosque is described as a place for the worship of *rasūla*. It is said that Nur-ud-din had the cooperation of the local *paññca-kula* apart from the king. Among the members of the *paññca-kula* were Śaiva priests (perhaps of the Somanātha temple), merchants and administrators. Were memories surprisingly short, or was the destruction of the temple by Mahmud highly exaggerated, or were the profits of trade a surmounting concern on the part of the authorities at Somanātha? Or were the Turuṣkas seen as different from the Muslim traders from the Gulf since the former were political enemies, whereas the latter were contributing to local prosperity.

Finally, we come to *mleccha*, the most contentious among the words used. It has a history going back to around 800 BC (Thapar 1978; Parasher 1991), occurs originally in a Vedic text, and is used for those who could not speak Sanskrit correctly. Language was frequently a social marker in many early societies. The use of Sanskrit was largely confined to the upper castes, and gradually the word *mleccha* also came to have a social connotation and referred to those outside the pale of *varṇa* society – those who did not observe the rules of caste as described in the *Dharmaśāstras*, or those who belonged to certain categories of lower castes. When used in a pejorative sense, it included a difference of language and ritual impurity. The category of *mleccha* was again a well-established category, but used more frequently by upper castes to refer to those from whom they wished to maintain a caste distance.

It has been argued that *mleccha* was essentially a term of contempt for the Muslim, or, more recently, that the demonization of the Muslim invaders in using the term *rākṣasas* for them and invoking the parallel with Rāma as the protector was part of the Indian political imagination of the twelfth century (Pollock 1993). But the *rākṣas*ization of the enemy, irrespective of who the enemy was, has been a constant factor with reference to many pre-Islamic enemies and going back to earliest times. Sāyaṇa's commentary of the fourteenth century AD on the *Ṛgveda* refers to the *dāsas* as *rākṣasas* and *asuras*. An inscription from Gujarat dating back to AD 1253 states that Arṇorāja killed Raṇasimha in battle, and the latter was like Rāvaṇa-*rāvaṇamiva* and the Gurjarra *rājyam* is said to be greater than that of Rama (*Epigraphia Indica*, 1: 26 ff.). The inscription proceeds to mention the attack on the Turuṣka-*rājā* who is described as the lord of the *mlecchas*, but interestingly not as Rāvaṇa. The powerful *gaṇa-saṅgha* or chiefdom of the Yaudheyas issued coins in the early centuries AD, a few of which carry the name Rāvaṇa (Sharan 1972: 122, 127).

In later centuries, the reference to some Muslims *mlecchas* was an extension of the term to include them among the many others who were denied *varṇa* status. This usage is more common in sources which come from the upper castes, such as Sanskrit texts and inscriptions, and was more easily used for the lower castes who were, even without being Muslim, marginalized and moved to the fringes of society. The term itself included a multiplicity of peoples and *jātis*, but generally it referred to those who were not members of a *varṇa*.

There is, however, a marked ambivalence in the use of the term. In another Sanskrit inscription of AD 1328 from the Raisina area of Delhi, reference is made to the *mleccha* Sahāvadīna seizing Delhi. But he is praised for his great valour, in what is described as his burning down the forest of enemies who surrounded him.[8] If, in this context, *mleccha* had a contemptuous meaning, it is unlikely that a local merchant would dare to use it for a Sultan.

The same ambiguity occurs in earlier texts. It is in this sense that *mleccha* is mentioned in the narrative sections of the *Mahābhārata* (1.62.5). This is emphasized in the passage which relates that Vidura, the uncle of the Pāṇḍavas, spoke in the language of the *mleccha* – *mlecchavāca* – to a messenger (1.135.6). Vidura was the son whom Vyasa fathered on a slave woman, and was conversant, therefore, with both Sanskrit and the language of the *mlecchas*. The sixth-century astronomer Varāmihira states that among the Yavanas (referring to the Hellenistic Greeks), knowledge in astronomy had stabilized, and therefore they were revered as *ṛṣis* even though they were *mlecchas* (*Bṛhatsaṁhitā*, edited by M.R. Bhatt, II, 32); and a seventh-century inscription from Assam refers to one of the rulers, Śalastambha, as the *mlecchādhinātha*.[9] Thus the context of this term varied, but it was generally a social marker. The identification of what was regarded as *mleccha* lands and people could also change over time.

Social markers are frequently forged by those who demarcate themselves sharply from others, and this tends to be characteristic of the upper levels of society. The usage of *mleccha* is no exception. Among castes, *brāhmaṇa* identity was created in part out of an opposition initially to the *kṣatriyas*, as is evident in the Vedic corpus, an opposition which was extended to the heterodox teachings of the *kṣatriyas* in the Śramanic sects, and then to the non-*brāhmaṇa* in general. The dichotomy of the *brāhmaṇa* and the *śūdra* became common to virtually every part of the subcontinent. References to the rise of the *mlecchas* creating a social catastrophe of a kind expected of the Kali Age, as described in the Purāṇas, were frequently invoked when there was a political crisis (Talbot 1987). The insistence that the brahmanical ordering of the world had been turned upside down on such occasions was repeated in brahmanical texts each time this ordering was challenged. In the Kali Age, which was not a specific historical period but was symbolic of a time when the brahmanical normative order was reversed in practice, *mleccha* rulers were frequent. Alternatively, the existence of *mleccha* rulers in itself endorsed the characteristics of the Kali Age and required that their rule be described as such.

The social distinctions implicit in these terms applied to people of various religions. The connotation of these terms used in the last thousand years changed with time, application and context, and the mutation of meaning required analysis. The less frequent use of Yavana and *mleccha* for Europeans had been pared down in meaning by the nineteenth century. Some uses of these terms were mechanisms for reducing social distance, others for enhancing it. A major indicator of social distance was caste. Among castes which we now identify as Hindu, there was the separation of the *dvija*, or twice-born, from the *śūdra*, and even more sharply from the untouchable. Muslim society segregated the Muslim from Central and Western Asia and the indigenous convert. Even if this was not a ritual segregation, it was an effective barrier, and possibly encouraged the local convert to maintain certain earlier caste practices and kinship rules. At the level of the ruling class, the culture of the court influenced all those who had pretensions to power, irrespective of their religion. Further down the social scale, caste identities often controlled appearance and daily routine. Caste identity, because it derived so heavily from occupation and control over economic resources, was not restricted only to kinship systems and religious practices. The perception of difference, therefore, was more fragmented among the various communities than is projected in the image of the monolithic two.

Those from across the Arabian Sea who settled as traders along the west coast and married into existing local communities, the Khojas and Bohras of western India, the Navayatas in the Konkan, the Mapillahs of Malabar, assumed many of the customary practices of these communities, and sometimes even contradicting the social norms of Islam. This was also the case with some communities who had converted to Islam. Because of this, their beliefs and practices were distinct even from each other, influenced as they were by those of the host community. Today there may be a process of Islamization among such communities, encouraged by the politics of communalism which is ironing out these contradictions, but in the past there has been some uncertainty as to whether some of these practices could be viewed as strictly Islamic.[10] There have been marked variations in the structures and rules governing family, kinship and marriage among communities listed as Muslim in the subcontinent. These have quite often tended to be closer to the rules associated with the Hindu castes in the region (Ahmed 1976).

The process of marrying into the local community is unlikely to have been free of tension and confrontation in the initial stages. The orthodox among both the visitors and the hosts would doubtlessly have found the need to adapt to custom and practice on both sides not so palatable, but the presence today of these well-articulated communities speaks of the prevalence of professional and economic concerns over questions of religion. Their continuing historical existence points to the eventual adjustments of both the host and the settlers.

Even on conversion, the link with caste was frequently inherent. A multiplicity of identities remained, although their function and need may have changed. Not only was the concept of conversion alien to Indian society but conversion to Islam remained limited. Possibly one reason for this was that those who introduced Islam could not break through caste stratification. If conversion was motivated by the wish for upward mobility, then even this did not necessarily follow. Conversion, in itself, does not change the status of the converted group in the caste hierarchy. Even converts have to negotiate a change, and the potentiality for such negotiation would depend on their original status, or else a religious sect would have to evolve into a new caste; a process which has been observed for the history of caste society over many centuries. At the same time, conversion does not eliminate diversities and there would be a carry-over of earlier practices and beliefs. Caste ranking continued to be important to marriage and occupation, for a radical change in ranking would have involved confronting the very basis on which Indian society was organized.

Reports as recent as a century ago point to the continuing role of caste even after conversion. The Gazetteer of Bijapur district in 1884 is an example.[11] The Muslim population was listed as consisting of three categories: Muslims who claimed to be foreign, indigenous Muslims who descended from migrants from north India, and the local Muslims. Those claiming foreign descent listed their names as is usual, as Saiyid, Shaikh, Mughal, Pathan; insisted that they are Urdu-speaking and strictly Sunni; and many of them held office in the local administration. Like the scribes of earlier times, some sought administrative positions in the emerging kingdoms. The second group, working in a different capacity, claimed to have come from north Indian communities such as Jat cultivators, or from the trading communities of the west coast, and identified themselves by their earlier caste names. They too maintained that they were Sunnis. Their languages varied with some using Urdu, and others Marathi and Kannada, with some even preferring Tamil or Arabic.

The third group, with the maximum number in the district, was in many ways dissimilar. They were local converts, some of whom took on *jāti* names that had come to have a subcontinental status and connotation, such as Momin and Kasab, but many retained their original *jāti* names such as Gaundi, Pinjara, Pakhali and so on, and identified themselves by the same name which they had used prior to conversion. The *jāti* name was associated with the occupation as had often been so from earlier times. Their occupations ranked them at the lower levels of society as the poorer artisans and cultivators, and tended to conform to those which they had performed as members of Hindu castes. Their Urdu was minimal because they used Kannada and Marathi. Most of them are described as lax Sunnis, not frequenting the mosque, and instead declaring that they worship Hindu deities, observe Hindu festivals and avoid eating beef. The avoidance of beef may have been to distinguish themselves from untouchables who were not restricted from eating beef. The social and religious identity of this third group would seem to be closer to that of their Hindu caste counterparts than to that of Muslims of higher castes. From the thirteenth century, there was intense Sufi activity in the area; nevertheless, or possibly because of the openness of certain schools of Sufi teaching, groups such as these could keep a distance from formal Islam. This was the larger majority of those technically listed as Muslims, who, perhaps because of their lower social status and therefore distance from formal religion, are likely to have been untouched by *fatwas*.

This picture was not unique to Bijapur and can be replicated for other parts of the subcontinent. Such groups can perhaps be better described as being on the intersection of the Islam and Hindu religions. This gives them an ambiguous religious identity in terms of an either–or situation. Were they Hindus picking up some aspects of Islam, or were they Muslims practising a Hinduized Islam? Did caste identity have priority in determining the nature of the religious identity, and did these priorities differ from one social group to another?

Groups such as the third category mentioned above receive little attention from historians of religion since they cannot be neatly indexed. The same was true of their status in the historical treatment of Hinduism. The study of groups which reflect liminal spaces is recent, and here too, there is frequently a focus on the curious religious admixtures rather than the social and economic compulsions which encourage such admixtures. But in terms of the history of religion in the subcontinent, such groups have been the majority since earliest times, and have lent their own distinctiveness to belief and to the practice of religion. On occasions when they played a significant historical role, attempts would be made to imprint facets of the formal religion on to their beliefs and practices. History is rich in demonstrating the mutation of folk cults into Puranic Hinduism. For example, the hero who saves cattle from raiders was worshipped by the pastoralists of Maharashtra, but eventually emerges at Pandharpur under the patronage of the Yādava dynasty as the god Viṭṭhal, associated with Viṣṇu (Dandekar 1991). This was also one reason why belief and worship across the subcontinent, even when focusing on a single deity, was often formulated differently, except at the level of the elite who differentiated themselves by claiming adherence to forms approved of by brahmanical orthodoxy.

The evolving of Hindu religions with specific rituals and practices, often emerging from particular castes or regions, was a process which did not terminate with the arrival of Islam; nor did it turn away from Islam. The dialogue between Islam and earlier indigenous religions is reflected in various Bhakti and Sufi traditions which have been extensively studied in recent years. Since the indigenous religions did not constitute a monolith and registered a range of variations, there were a range of dialogues. These were partly the result of such movements having a middle caste and *śūdra* following, even if some of those who led them were *brāhmaṇas*. Formal religious requirements were often rejected in such groups. But not in their entirety. Where a few showed familiarity with philosophic doctrine (Lorenzen 1987), others broke away from such a dialogue. The attempt to sanskritize the Bhakti tradition, both in texts recounting the activities of the *sants* and in modern studies, has been cautioned against.

The famous *Hindu–Turk Samvād* of Eknāth written in Maharashtra in the sixteenth century is the imagined dialogue between a *brāhmaṇa* and a Muslim who seems to have been a *maulāna*, and there is an undercurrent of satire in the treatment of both (Zelliot 1982). The language used by each for the other would, today, probably cause a riot! The crux of the debate states, 'You and I are alike, the confrontation is over *jāti* and *dharma*' (v. 60). The attempt is at pointing out the differences between facets of what were seen as Hindu and Muslim belief and worship, but arguing for an adjustment. Kṛṣṇadāsa's *Caitanya-carita-amṛta* reflects similar concerns in eastern India, a different part of the subcontinent (O'Connell 1983). The pre-Islamic interweaving of religion and social organization was not broken, and the process of using new religious ideas to negotiate a social space continued. At a different level but at about the same time, in the seventeenth century, Shivaji was writing in a political vein to Jai Singh about the grave dangers Hindus were facing, chiding him for his support to the Mughals and offering him an alliance instead. This would be an indication of the perception at elite levels being different from those at other levels, and largely conditioned by factors of statecraft and political policy. Eknāth's reading of the situation stands in strong contrast to this.

This also becomes apparent in common cultural codes symbolizing an altogether different level of communication. For example, the imagery and meaning encapsulated in the depiction of riding a tiger and who rides a tiger becomes a powerful symbol. For those who live in the forests, the tiger is the mount of the forest deity, such as Dakhin Rai in the Sundarbans.[12] For Hindus, Goddess Durgā rides a tiger. Among Nāthapanthis, the *nātha* was depicted as riding a tiger and using a live cobra for a whip. In Sufi hagiography, the Sufi often rides a tiger and sometimes meets another Sufi riding a wall. At the shrine of Sabarimala in Kerala, the deity Ayyappan rides a tiger. In many rural areas, there is, to this day, an all-purpose holy man who rides a tiger and is variously called Barekhan Ghazi or Satya-pir, and is worshipped by all, irrespective of formal religious affiliations. This bond, or even the subconscious memory of a bond binding a range of peoples, had no formal definition. These were not individual deviants from conventional religions. This was the religious articulation of the majority of the people in such areas. When we arbitrarily attach such religious expression to either Islam or Hinduism, we perhaps misrepresent the nature of these beliefs.

The existence of parallel religious forms, some conflicting and other cohering, had characterized Indian society. Some of these distanced themselves from all orthodoxies and attracted those who participated in what might be called forms of counterculture(s), preferring the openness of the heterodox. Their ancestry can perhaps be traced through a lineage of thought and behaviour going back to the wandering *vrāyas*, the rogues with matted hair and the mendicants of the Upaniṣads (*Maitri Upaniṣad*, 7, 8), the *siddhas* claiming extrasensory powers, the Nātha *yogis*, and some among the *gurus*, the *pirs* and *faqirs*. This was not invariably a confrontation with those in authority, but a statement of social distancing. The power of deliberate social distancing could sometimes help in mobilizing popular support, the potential for which was recognized by those in authority. Hence the depiction of ruler paying homage to ascetics in myth, in history and in art. The absence of sharply etched religious identities among such groups gave them a universality, but was also responsible for history neglecting to recognize their significance. This, in turn, relates directly to the question of whose history are we writing.

Religious expression, if treated only in formal terms and indexed according to established religions, leaves us with a poverty of understanding. For, together with the formal, there is the constant presence of the informal, and of beliefs unconstrained by texts. These were often forms of legitimizing widespread popular practice which adhered neither to the formal requirements of Islam nor of Brahmanic or Puranic Hinduism. They could be, but were not invariably, manifestations of peaceful coexistence or even attempts at syncretism.

It has been suggested that it might be useful to investigate the dichotomy between conversion and syncretism. The question of what historical situations result in one or the other, needs exploration (Lorenzen 1981). Syncretism is often a transitory phase for what might, in the end, become the continuation of two traditions in an unequal relationship, although sometimes it may locate the new religion within the existing range. The locating can be based on metaphor which weaves complexities into the manifestation of religion. Perhaps a new description should be sought for.[13] The degree of institutional support or its curtailment in relation to religious practice and belief would result in varying patterns in the political impact of a particular religion. These variations become significant to questions of conversion and syncretism.

Concepts such as those of composite culture or syncretism are only partial explanations and refer to particular situations. Syncretism would apply, for example, to Akbar's attempts at combining variant religious activities and beliefs by propagating a religion of his own making, or to Eknāth in his formulation of a dialogue between the Hindu and the Muslim, the two remaining distinct. Akbar's efforts were, in part, a crystallization of the earlier Indian tradition where royalty bestowed patronage on a variety of religious sects, some even hostile to each other. Akbar's acceptance of a religious pluralism, irrespective of how he formulated it, was significant even to the subsequent interweaving of religion and political policy, although this was not characteristic of every aspect of religion during this period.

There were aspects of life in which religion was an identifier, but there were also many other aspects in which more broad-based cultural expressions, evolving over time and through an admixture of various elements, gave an identity to a social group. It is these which need to be investigated. Associated with this is the exploration of a multiplicity of causes for particular historical events, causes which include or emphasize aspects of political expediency, economic control, ideological support, social associations, religious practices and custom; the exploration of which provides variations in the ordering of priorities among causal connections and historical explanations.

Composite culture also presupposes self-contained units in combination or in juxtaposition. In the history of Indian society, such units would be *jātis*, sects, language groups and groups with a local identity, and would have a history in many cases going back to pre-Islamic times. The juxtaposition would not have been invariably between formal religions, Hinduism and Islam, as is often argued, since this again presupposes the notion of the monolithic community, but more often between variant articulations among the many constituent units of society. These units would have to be historically identified, an exercise which requires a sensitivity to the problems of writing the history of those on the intersections of varied religious expressions.

The concern would be with both social dissonances and social harmonies, and a need for adjustment. Occurrences of religious conflict were not unknown, but were more frequently associated with the attitudes of formal religions for whom the conflict was rarely confined to religious factors. It arose more frequently from competing claims to patronage and resources. Perhaps the existence of the parallel, informal religions played a role, not in preventing conflict, but in ensuring that intolerance was contained and remained at the local level, as it had done even in earlier times (Thapar 1987).

The relationship between segments of society, even those identified as Hindu or Muslim, would take the normal course of jousting for social space and social advancement. This would have involved diplomacy and management, or, on occasion, conflict of a violent kind, particularly where established statuses were being challenged by newly evolved ones, using the patronage of authority. But the conflict at levels other than those of the ruling class was localized. Friends and enemies were demarcated less by religion and more by the concerns of social and economic realities. Cultural transactions and social negotiations were common, but were bounded by the degree of proximity to the structure of power.

To unravel the creating and modulating of religious identities is a far more complex process than the chronicling of religious activities. I have tried to argue that it is linked to social identities and historical perceptions, which, in turn, hinge on access to resources and power, or, alternatively, to a deliberate distancing from these. I have also tried to suggest that if we move away from the notion of monolithic communities, we begin to see the historical potential of understanding how identities may actually have been perceived at points in time, and their multiple manifestations and functions. Exploring the perceptions which people had of each other in the past is not merely a matter of historical curiosity, for it impinges on the way in which current identities are being constructed. An insistence on seeing society as having consisted, for all times, of monolithic religious communities derives from the contemporary conflict over identities. Yet historically, identities are neither stable nor permanent. Inherent in the process of historical change is the invention and mutation of identities. And the identities of the pre-colonial period would seem to have been very different from the way in which they have been projected in our times.

Notes

[1] This was demonstrated in the debate over the history of the Ramjanmabhoomi at Ayodhya; Gopal (1990). See, especially, K.N. Panikkar, 'An Historical Overview', in Gopal (1990: 22–37). The pamphlet published by some JNU historians entitled *The Political Abuse of History*, is concerned with the same issue.

[2] As, for example, in some of the papers included in Sontheimer and Kulke, eds (1989) and Dalmia and von Steitencron, eds (1995).

[3] Sircar (1974), Mankad (1951); Mitchner (1986) gives a different reading.

[4] The *Cāryugāci-bākhar*, discussed in Wagle (1989).

[5] Palam Baoli Inscription in Prasad (1990: 3 ff.).

[6] Such a recounting of the rulers of Delhi occurs in inscriptions from elsewhere in northern India as well. Avasthy and Ghosh (1935, 1936).

[7] Naraina Stone Inscription in Prasad (1990: 22).

[8] Sarban Stone Inscription in Prasad (1990: 29).

[9] Bargaon Copper-Plate Inscription of Ratnapāladeva, quoted in Bahadur (1966: 66–67).

[10] For example, D'Souza (1955).

[11] Summarized in Eaton (1978: 310 ff.).

[12] In the Sundarbans, the tiger and its manifestations such as Dakhin Rai, the tiger-god, Bonobibi, the goddess of the forest, or Ghazi Sahib, are universally worshipped by Hindu and Muslim alike, and the mythologies which accompany this worship have diverse Hindu and Muslim sources, as also does the chanting at the *pūja*. For an account of the continuity of this worship to this day, see Montgomery (1995).

[13] McLeod (1969), quoted in Lorenzen (1981).

References

Ahmed, I., ed. (1976), *Family, Kinship and Marriage among Muslims in India* (Delhi).

Athar Ali, M. (1989), 'Encounter and Efflorescence. . .', *Proceedings of the Indian History Congress* (Gorakhpur).

Avasthy, R.S. and A. Ghosh (1935), 'References to Muhammadans in Sanskrit Inscriptions in Northern India, 730–1200 AD', *Journal of Indian History*, 15, pp. 161–84.

——— (1936), 'References to Muhammadans in Sanskrit Inscriptions in Northern Indian, 730–1200 AD', *Journal of Indian History*, 16, pp. 24–26.

Barua Bahadur, K.L. (1966), *Early History of Kamarupa* (Gauhati).

Dalmia, V. and H. von Steitencron, eds (1995), *Representing Hinduism* (New Delhi).

Dandekar, A. (1991), 'Landscapes in Conflict: Flocks, Hero-stones and Cult in Early Medieval Maharashtra', *Studies in History*, VII, 2, pp. 301–24.

D'Souza, V.S. (1955), *The Narratives of Kannara* (Dharwar).

Eaton, R.M. (1978), *Sufis of Bijapur* (New Jersey).

Gopal, S., ed. (1990), *Anatomy of a Confrontation* (Delhi).

Habib, I. (1978), 'Economic History of Delhi Sultanate', *Indian Historical Review*, 4, 2.

Hein, N. (1989), 'Kālayavana, A Key to Mathura's Cultural Self-Perception', in D.M. Srinivasan, ed., *Mathura* (New Delhi).

Indische Alterthumskunde (1847–62), Vol. 1 (Leipzig).

Lorenzen, D.N. (1987), 'Social Ideologies of Hagiography', in M. Israel and N.K. Wagle, eds, *Religion and Society in Maharashtra* (Toronto), pp. 92–114.

Lorenzen D.N. (1981), 'Introduction', in D.N. Lorenzen, ed., *Religious Change and Cultural Domination* (Mexico), pp. 3–18.

Mankad, D.R. (1951), *Yugapurāṇam* (Vallabhvidyanagar).

Mitchner, J.E. (1986), *Yuga Purāṇa* (Calcutta).

Montgomery, S. (1995), *Spell of the Tiger* (New York).

McLeod, W.H. (1969), 'The Problem of Syncretism', in S.S. Hartman, ed., *Syncretism* (Stockolm).

O'Connell, J.T. (1983), 'Vaiṣṇava Perceptions of Muslims in Sixteenth Century Bengal', in M. Israel and N.K. Wagle, eds, *Islamic Society and Culture* (New Delhi).

Prasad, P. (1990), *Sanskrit Inscriptions of the Delhi Sultanate 1191–1526* (Delhi).

Parasher, A. (1991), *Mlecchas in Early India* (Delhi).

Pollock, S. (1993), '*Rāmāyana* and Political Imagination in India', *Journal of Asian Studies*, 52,

Sircar, D.C. (1974), *Studies in the Yuga Purāṇa and Other Texts* (Delhi).

Sontheimer, G.D. and H. Kulke, eds (1989), *Hinduism Reconsidered* (Delhi).

Sachau, E. (1910), *Alberuni's India* (London).

Sharan, M.K. (1972), *Tribal Coins* (New Delhi).

Thapar, R. (1978), 'The Image of the Barbarian in Early India', in R. Thapar, *Ancient Indian Social History: Some Interpretations* (New Delhi), pp. 152–92.

Thapar, R. (1985), 'Syndicated Mokṣa'), *Seminar*, September.

Thapar, R. (1992), 'Imagined Religious Communities? Ancient History and the Modern Search for a Hindu Identity', in R. Thapar, *Interpreting Early India* (Delhi).

Talbot, C. (1987), 'Inscribing the Other, Inscribing the Self: Hindu–Muslim Identities in Pre-Colonial India', in M. Israel and N.K. Wagle. eds, *Religion and Society in Maharashtra* (Toronto), pp. 131–44.

Thapar, R. (1987), *Cultural Transactions and Early India* (Delhi).

Wagle, N.G. (1989), 'Hindu–Muslim Interactions in Medieval Maharashtra', in Sontheimer and Kulke, eds, *Hinduism Reconsidered*, pp. 51–66.

Zelliot, E. (1982), 'A Medieval Encounter between Hindus and Muslims: Eknath's Drama-Poem "Hindu–Turk Samvad"', in F.W. Clothey, ed., *Images of Man: Religion and Historical Process in South Asia* (Madras).

Uncommon Opportunities for a
Learning Revolution

M.S. *Swaminathan*

I learnt at a young age, many lessons from Dr Zakir Husain's speeches and lectures. The one I have often recalled is the following statement contained in his Sardar Patel Memorial Lectures of the All India Radio, delivered in 1958.

> We have turned the so-called intellectual book-school into a mechanical memory training school and succeeded in making our Work School, the Basic School, a place of mechanical work. The work is extraneously and uniformly prescribed; there is no semblance of a spontaneous motivation in the child, and he is supremely ignorant of any personal or social purpose behind his work. Work which is mechanical, work in which no mental exertion is involved, work in which one is satisfied with just any result and there is no constantly prodding urge to aim at its possible perfection, work in which there is no self-criticism and so no real progress, is in no sense educative. Schools that have such work are not Work Schools in any sense.

It is useful to remember this warning since there is once again interest in the vocationalization of education.

In 1970, I pointed out that the only feasible way of marrying intellect and labour was to take advantage of the new opportunities which recent agricultural progress has provided for bringing about a 'learning revolution', and I pleaded for the involvement of all university students in developmental and rural educational projects for at least two months in a year through a suitable built-in provision in Plan projects. With an understanding of the basic principles of biological productivity, a whole new world can be opened up, both for schoolchildren and adults in villages. Appropriate projects involving the study of birds, the identification and eradication of weeds, the detection of acidity, salinity and alkalinity, the harvesting of water, the prevention of damage by rats and pests both in the field and in the storerooms, the more efficient use of solar energy, organic recycling, social and man-made forestry, crop–livestock integration, and coastal and inland aquaculture, all would have immense educational and practical value.

Tenth Zakir Husain Memorial Lecture, 12 November 1997.

The equipment needed for such studies is simple and inexpensive, and mostly requires only a well-informed teacher who does not curb the questioning mind and is not afraid of long walks. With a little training, this is one field where all university students of agriculture and science can render great service.

'Techniracy'

Agricultural technology is rapidly becoming a sophisticated skill. Ecological agriculture involves the use of precision farming methods in activities like soil health care, irrigation water management, pest control and post-harvest technology. To successfully harness the full genetic potential for yield in a crop variety, an integrated application of intellect, physical inputs and managerial talent is necessary. Where the technology is characterized by ease of adoption without involving cooperative action on the part of an entire village or watershed community, the impact of the technology can be immediate, as was witnessed in the case of wheat in our country. The scientific advance in extending the yield frontiers has been equally great in rice, maize, jawar and bajra, but in these crops the scientific advance took time to get converted into production advance.

How are we going to extend the results of recent research to nearly 100 million farm families, a fair percentage of whom tend to be illiterate? In our obsession with university education, we have not given enough thought to the structural changes necessary in our rural educational system. A scrutiny of both our school education and technical literacy will be instructive since our success in eradicating poverty will be directly proportional to the effort we are willing to generate in these areas.

With the spread of new technology and the dramatic transformation of agriculture in certain areas, new dimensions of adult education also appear. There are new needs for education among farming communities. There is a great hunger not only for new knowledge related to agriculture, but also for new skills, particularly technical skills connected with it. The demand for 'techniracy', if one may coin a term based on the idea of technical literacy, is likely to be much stronger and deeper and also more widespread than that of formal literacy, or even of functional literacy. New approaches to adult education must capitalize on this new demand and need for 'techniracy'.

In 1994, I presented the report of the International Commission on Peace and Food, which I had the privilege to chair. In this report (Swaminathan 1994), titled *Uncommon Opportunities: An Agenda for Peace and Equitable Development*, we recommended six goals in education. I am repeating them here since I consider them important for a learning revolution.

Education is the greatest known civilizing force and the single most powerful lever for human development. Training imparts skills but education increases the capacity of the individual at a more basic level, making the mind more active and alert, converting physical energy into mental energy, training us to see things from a wider perspective, to question and challenge the *status quo*, to think and imagine, to innovate and invent, to make decisions for ourselves, and to act on our own initiative. *Education is the process by which society passes on the accumulated knowledge and experience of countless centuries to new generations in a systematic, concentrated and abridged form, so that today's young people can start their lives at the high point of knowledge and wisdom attained by preceding generations.* Education replaces the slow, subconscious process of trial-and-error learning with a swift, conscious process. This accumulated knowledge is a great power that can be utilized to accelerate human development and abridge the time needed for society to arrive at progressively higher levels of material, social and psychological fulfilment.

Despite the efforts of visionaries like Dr Zakir Husain to create awareness of the vital role of education in peace, democracy, economic development and environmental protection, progress on achieving UNESCO's goal of 'literacy for all by the year 2000' is still grossly inadequate. In 1990, 948 million people or about 20 per cent of the entire world population lacked even basic literacy skills. Adult literacy rates in the least developed nations still average less than 50 per cent and are less than half in a number of countries. Unless more intensive efforts are made worldwide, the absolute number of the illiterate will decline only marginally by the year 2000. Illiteracy is likely to increase by 10 per cent in South Asia – home to more than 40 per cent of the world's illiterate – and by nearly 7 per cent in Sub-Saharan Africa.

Although universal primary education has been a goal for decades and primary education has been made compulsory in most countries, globally, 128 million children living in remote rural areas, urban slums and refugee camps, representing 20 per cent of the total school-age population, are still excluded from primary education. Unless greater measures are introduced, this number may rise to more than 160 million by the turn of the century. Achieving true universality of primary education by the year 2000 will require a massive investment in school buildings, teachers and instructional materials for an additional 230 million school-age children. An additional four million teachers will be required, 20 per cent more than in 1990.

In addition to the quantitative deficiency in educational enrolment and achievements, the quality of teaching facilities, materials and staff is severely deficient in many countries. Most developing countries hire teachers with only a secondary school certificate and a minimum of teachers' training. This contributes to the high rate of primary school dropouts and grade repetition. Only 71 per cent of first-grade entrants complete primary school in developing countries.

Addressing these challenges will require a substantial increase in the financial resources devoted to education. In most regions, public expenditure on education has risen in recent years. In 1990, the world average was 13.5 per cent of total government expenditure, or 4.8 per cent of GNP. More than one-third of the countries in the world still spend more on the military than on education. Efforts to improve education must go hand-in-hand with efforts to promote peace and disarmament, and drastically curtailed military spending mechanisms should be put in place to ensure that a significant portion of reduced military spending is invested in education and training.

Six Goals in Educational Policy

First, the highest social priority should be given to six educational goals, in both developing and developed countries. There must be redoubled effort to achieve UNESCO's goal of *eradicating illiteracy* worldwide by the year 2000. Illiteracy can only be banished by an all-out commitment of every national government to eliminate the huge backlog of illiteracy, while, at the same time, ensuring that every child is taught to read and write.

Second, every possible step must be taken to provide education for female children, an essential requirement for social equity and quality of life improvement. Nearly two-thirds of the world's illiterate are women. In the poorest developing countries, literacy rates among females are 40 per cent below rates for males, and the average number of years of schooling for females is 60 per cent lower. But perceptible progress has been made. Between 1980 and 1990, female primary school enrolment rose from 44 per cent to 47 per cent of total enrolment, although it remained virtually unchanged in South Asia. Uneducated females represent a huge reservoir of untapped human potential that must be given every opportunity and full assistance to develop their innate capacities. This will call for accelerated efforts to establish creches and child-care facilities, abolish child labour, and remove gender bias from textbooks and educational institutions. The cost of raising female educational levels up to that of males worldwide has been estimated at $2.5 billion, a small amount for an initiative that could have such wide-ranging benefits.

Third, literacy must be complemented by *techniracy*, education that imparts basic technical information and skills to the population through a variety of teaching methods suited to the educational level of the recipients. Comparable efforts must be made to raise scientific literacy, which is essential for the continued growth of technology, productivity and employment in modern society. The pervasive influence of science in society requires that we bridge the gap that presently divides the sciences and the humanities, and evolve an educational system in which science is no longer regarded as a specialized field of study.

Fourth, radical changes are needed in the content of school curricula at all levels to make education relevant to the real needs of the students and the development of the country. A society whose system of education is integrated with the social aspirations of the country will develop most rapidly. The system of education prevalent in most developing countries is oriented towards the outer form – acquiring a degree or qualifying certificate – rather than the inner content of knowledge. Educated unemployment is a direct result of a system that fosters conformity rather than questioning and creative thinking. A new system of *development education* needs to be introduced at all levels to equip the student with an understanding of his/her society, its achievements and potentials, and the opportunities open to each individual to participate in its future growth. An index of its success will be the extent to which students of this curriculum seek self-employment rather than salaried jobs.

Fifth, the minimum and average educational levels should be raised in all countries. Two centuries ago, education was a luxury of the rich and it was simply inconceivable that every member of the population could receive even a minimum level of education. Raising the minimum levels of achievement further in all countries may be the most important initiative that governments can render to prepare their citizens for a more productive and purposeful future.

Sixth, new educational systems must be evolved to prepare people for life in the twenty-first century. Education imparts knowledge of the past and the general ability to deal with the future, but this ability is only in potential. It is not fully developed in the form of practically useful knowledge. An educational system that endows the individual with the capacity for physical accomplishment, psychological fulfilment and original thinking would enable society consciously to abridge the development process and accomplish goals within one or a few decades that would otherwise take place over the span of a century or more. A Committee on education for agriculture, which I chaired recently, has recommended that hereafter all farm graduates must be computer, patent and trade literate.

We believe that it is possible to fashion a system that directly prepares students for life in the twenty-first century because the necessary knowledge already exists subconsciously in society, and consciously in a few stray individuals or social groups. Materially, the world already possesses the knowledge needed to produce sufficient food and other necessities to eradicate poverty from the earth, but this knowledge is not yet a conscious possession of humanity as a whole that is passed on to every individual, even in the most advanced nations. Socially, every culture possesses the knowledge of the essential qualities necessary for lasting success. This knowledge, if consciously formulated, can be systematically imparted to the entire population through formal education. Psychologically, the right attitudes, values and motives enable the individual to attain a self-existent happiness and inner harmony which nothing can disturb. This knowledge, too, can be consciously formulated and communicated through the educational system of the twenty-first century. Mentally, our knowledge is partial, biased and largely dependent on social status and opinion, rather than purely rational criteria. True mental objectivity can be taught. Human fulfilment in the twenty-first century depends on our ability to provide an education that imparts not only material facts, but also the mental perspectives, psychological attitudes, personal values, individual skills and organizational abilities needed for the full blossoming of human resourcefulness and accomplishment.

Information Age

We have now entered an information age where it is possible to attain the latest information on any subject anywhere in the world. Past experience, particularly in our country, has shown that the trickle-down hypothesis does not work either in economics or in ecology or in education. Gandhiji's concept of *antyodaya*, focusing attention on the poorest and the most underprivileged sections of society, assumes importance in this context. This is where an information empowerment involving computer-aided education can help us reach the unreached. We must capitalize on modern information technology for achieving knowledge and skilled empowerment of the socially and economically underprivileged sections of our society. Even knowledge of numerous government programmes which are designed to help the poor does not reach them. Professor Mohammad Yunus rightly pointed out in a recent lecture that:

> Poverty is not created by the poor. It is created by the institutions we have built and the policies that we pursue. We cannot solve the problem of poverty with the same concepts and tools which created it in the first place. To create a poverty-free world, we need new conceptualization, and new analytical framework which takes ensuring human dignity to every human being as its central task.

How do we generate such a change in mindset and shift in strategies? Since we are celebrating fifty years of independence, it might be useful to reflect on the challenges ahead. If the past fifty years led to a green revolution in agriculture and impressive progress in industry and commerce, the next fifty years should witness the emergence of a nation known for tolerance, love of diversity and pluralism, in terms of religion, caste, gender, language, ethnicity and political belief, and for achieving an evergreen revolution in agriculture and industry. That these two goals are inter-related was pointed out by Mahatma Gandhi when he said, over sixty years ago, 'How can we be non-violent to nature, if we are going to be violent to each other?'

How do we achieve the twin goals of 'unity in diversity' in day-to-day life and 'green productivity' in every area of economic activity? In my view, the following seven steps are necessary to arrest the current trend towards social, political and economic disintegration, and help the nation become one where children are born for happiness and not for mere existence.

Demographic Transition

A demographic transition to low birth and death rates is vital for achieving the goals of food, drinking water, health, literacy and jobs for all. Such a transition can be achieved only if there is a paradigm shift from a technology and target-driven approach to a human and social development-centred one. The Expert Committee constituted under my chairmanship in 1994 to draft a national population policy statement recommended that population policies should be based on the principle 'think, plan and act locally, and support nationally'. Population stabilization should be a shared concern and responsibility of both men and women. With over a million women in elected panchayats, it should now be possible for the elected members of panchayats and municipal councils to draw up socio-demographic charters for their respective villages/towns, which can lead to achieving a balance between human numbers and the population-supporting capacity of the ecosystem.

Ending Gross Economic Inequity

Globally and nationally, the rich–poor divide is growing. Today, we have as many people below the poverty line as the entire population of India at the time of our independence in 1947. Globally, 358 billionaires have more income than 2.5 billion of the world's poor. Unsustainable lifestyles and unacceptable poverty coexist in every city, town and village. This situation must change if a Sarvodaya society is to emerge. The transition from destitution to secure livelihoods can happen fast if the rich consider themselves trustees of their surplus wealth, and adopt a caring and sharing ethic. It will be in their own self-interest to do so. Gandhiji's concept of *antyodaya* as the pathway to Sarvodaya must become the guiding spirit in developmental planning.

Gender Justice and Equity

India is one of the least gender-sensitive nations in the world. The sex ratio is very adverse to women. A beginning has been made to reverse this trend through the socio-political empowerment of women at the level of grassroot democratic institutions. This process should extend to Parliament, and must be coupled with the technological and skill empowerment of women. A gender code must guide all developmental, socio-economic and socio-political activities.

Job-led Economic Growth

We should refrain from taking to the jobless growth path of today's industrialized and rich nations. We should, instead, promote a job-led economic growth strategy based on a pro-nature, pro-poor and pro-women orientation to technology development and dissemination. This will call for a movement to spread market-driven micro-enterprises supported by micro-credit. Public policies which will safeguard the interests of micro-enterprises will be needed.

Structural Adjustment to Sustainable Lifestyles

Our population is predominantly young. We should actively promote teaching happiness in schools. Teaching happiness involves inculcating love of nature, flora, fauna, rivers, oceans, forests and mountains. The youth should know that it takes over a century in nature to make one centimetre of topsoil, and that we destroy several metres of topsoil within a few days in brick kilns. Again, Gandhiji's dictum that 'nature provides for everyone's needs but not for everybody's greed' should get internalized in the day-to-day behaviour of every citizen. At the same time, it must be realized that it is not adequate if we oppose unsustainable development. It is equally important to propose sustainable options. We need an ecology of hope and action.

Today, structural adjustment is being discussed and introduced only in monetary terms. This will not help achieve the desired social goals. What we need is adjustment to sustainable lifestyles. It is equally important to avoid ostentation and waste, and to adopt sustainable lifestyles. The tools of the information age, if deployed effectively, can contribute to bringing about the needed change in mindset.

Promoting an Evergreen Revolution in Agriculture and Industry
Industry should move towards adopting ISO 14000 standards in relation to environmental management. In agriculture, more food and other agricultural commodities will have to be produced without ecological harm from less per capita arable land, irrigation water and fossil fuel-based energy sources. This will call for a massive effort to develop and disseminate ecotechnologies based on a blend of frontier technologies, such as biotechnology and space, information and renewable energy technologies, and the best in traditional wisdom and ecological prudence. Water harvesting and equitable sharing must receive high priority.

Rural Regeneration
The growing marginalization of rural economies is leading to unplanned migration of the rural poor to urban areas, thus leading to the proliferation of urban slums. Strengthening rural livelihoods through the effective use of panchayats in the technological empowerment of socially and economically underprivileged families should receive attention. Innovative approaches are needed to create more wealth and jobs in rural areas. For example, all along our vast coastline, green health tourism can be promoted, because of our traditions in Ayurvedic and herbal systems of health management.

On the basis of a recent study, the International Food Policy Research Institute (IFPRI) located in Washington DC, USA, believes that by the year 2020 significant reductions can be made in poverty, food insecurity, malnutrition and micronutrient deficiencies, and significant advances can be made towards efficient, effective and low-cost food and agricultural systems that are in harmony with the natural resource base. The fact remains that although today the world produces enough food to feed each and every person, nearly 800 million children, women and men remain food-insecure. The reasons for this tragic irony are to be found in the non-food sector, such as lack of purchasing power and entitlements, poor sanitation and health care, and non-availability of clean drinking water. It is therefore time that we redefine our concept of food security as '*livelihood security for the households and all members within, which ensures physical and economic access to balanced diets including the needed micronutrients, safe drinking water, environmental sanitation, basic health care and primary education*'. Such a redefinition will help to articulate the public policy package needed to ensure food security at the level of each individual in a household. Emphasis on individuals rather than on families is important since, in many societies, women and girl children tend to suffer more from under- and malnutrition, and there is a trend towards increasing feminization of poverty.

In view of the globalization of economies, we also need action at the international level. I would like to refer to a few of these.

1. Implement both in letter and spirit, the plans of action agreed to at recent UN conferences, particularly at Rio, Cairo, Copenhagen and Beijing, and take speedy action to implement the provisions of the Desertification Convention.

2. Ensure adequate support for research and development efforts designed to promote national and international public good, since the fast-spreading intellectual property rights (IPR) environment is likely to promote greater investment only in a short gestation period and profit-driven research. Integrating the dimension of sustainability in research objectives, however, involves location-specific and participatory research with rural families. This kind of research is unlikely to attract adequate investment from the corporate sector.

3. Ensure the rapid dissemination of environmentally sound agricultural technologies, particularly among resource-poor farm families who may have difficulties in gaining access to green technologies as a result of the provisions of the Trade-Related Intellectual Property Rights (TRIPS) of the World Trade Agreement.

4. Promote increased trade in value-added agricultural commodities produced in developing countries by assisting them in improving post-harvest technology, and sanitary and phytosanitary measures.

5. Contribute generously to global emergency food security reserves and to food for livelihood security programmes, through the World Food Programme and other appropriate global, regional and national social security programmes, and organize a Global Coalition for the Sustainable End of Hunger so that every child, woman and man has the requisite entitlements for a healthy and productive life.

6. Mobilize the power of the information age to spread timely information among farming communities on meteorological, management (land, water, pests and post-harvest technology) and marketing factors.

No Time to Lose

We are facing a battle against time in safeguarding our natural resources. In his book *The Diversity of Life*, E.O. Wilson has warned that *Homo sapiens* is in imminent danger of precipitating a biological disaster of a greater magnitude than anything we have so far witnessed in our evolutionary history. There is, hence, no time to relax if we are to ensure that the Malthusian prophecy of famine and pestilence does not come true in the coming millennium. Legal, educational and participatory measures of programme implementation and benefit sharing, all will be needed for promoting a people's movement for conservation.

From the foregoing, it will be clear that the concept of sustainable development should be broad-based so as to incorporate considerations of ecology, equity, employment and energy, in addition to those of economics. This will call for a system's approach in project design and implementation. Both unsustainable lifestyles and unacceptable poverty have to be eliminated. Factors which influence climate and sea level have to be addressed with the seriousness they deserve and need. Sustainable development will become a reality if we keep in mind that the greatest responsibility of our generation, to quote Dr Jonas Salk, is 'to be good ancestors'.

It will be appropriate to quote here a statement from the US President's Council on Sustainable Development on 'Sustainable America: A New Consensus': 'Prosperity, fairness and a healthy environment are interrelated elements of the human dream of a better future. Sustainable development is a way to pursue that dream through choice and policy.'

Green Audit

In a recent article in *Science and Public Affairs*, published by the Royal Society of London, Julian Rose (1997) draws attention to the following facts.

1. The single most important factor in levelling the economic playing field surrounds the question of accounting. When a clear green audit emerges of the environmental, social, health and welfare costs attributable to current agricultural food production, processing, packaging and distribution systems, it will become abundantly clear that cheap food comes at an unacceptably high cost.

2. Work undertaken by the Soil Association has revealed that the need to extract nitrates and pesticides from drinking water is currently costing the taxpayer and industry approximately £145 million annually. Prior investment in water treatment equipment and control measures amount to a further £1,275 million. Annual losses of soil through erosion cost the equivalent of about £680 million per year in lost crop production (Rose 1997).

In our country there are many organizations which, rightly, oppose unsustainable development. What we lack is a similar capacity to propose sustainable options. As Ramalingaswamy, Jonsson and Rohde (1996) have pointed out, 'the time has come when countries in South Asia must face up to the fact that they have the lowest nutritional levels in the world. The consensus is that the high rates of malnutrition in South Asia are rooted deeply in the inequality between men and women.' We, therefore, need an Ecology of Hope, rooted in the principles of gender and social equity, employment generation, economic viability and environmental sustainability.

Today, India has nearly 15 per cent of the world's human and farm animal population, 2 per cent of its arable land, 1 per cent of rainwater, and 0.5 per cent each of forests and pasture lands. Undernutrition, caused by a lack of purchasing power, and hidden hunger, caused by deficiency of micronutrients, are widespread. How are we going to face these challenges in the coming millennium?

In my view, we need more science and not less. We need efficiency and innovations in all areas of human endeavour. I would like to conclude with a recent example of a socially relevant initiative to link science and society.

Women's Biotechnology Park

The Department of Biotechnology of the Government of India and the Government of Tamil Nadu have initiated a well-planned move to provide educated women with opportunities for remunerative self-employment in the field of biotechnology. The Women's Biotechnology Park, to be established near Chennai, will be based on the following principles:

- stakeholder management;
- market-driven enterprises;
- efficient use of credit and government programmes;
- information empowerment of entrepreneurs through an Information Centre; and
- adoption of ISO 14000 standards of environmental management and audit.

We need a New Deal for the self-employed on the lines of the Women's Biotechnology Park initiative. Jobless economic growth will be joyless growth. We should harness the tools of the information age to foster a learning revolution, if we are to achieve economically, ecologically and socially sustainable development.

Monsoon Management in India

We have more than a century of experience in managing the impact of the southwest and northeast monsoons on agriculture and human livelihoods. During the British rule, detailed Famine Codes and Scarcity Manuals were prepared for several parts of the country. The *annawari* system of estimating the impact of weather on crop yield was developed, for deciding on tax remissions and relief measures.

Thanks to the work of the scientists of the Indian Meteorological Department and of the meteorological scientists of our universities, we now have the capacity to insulate our agriculture very considerably from abnormal monsoon behaviour. Contingency plans involving alternate cropping strategies can be prepared to suit different rainfall patterns. Monsoon forecasting is getting increasingly perfected. Crop life-saving techniques are also getting increasingly perfected, and are becoming available. Using computer simulation models, we can be prepared both to take advantage of good monsoons and to minimize crop damage and human hardship during adverse monsoons.

During the 1979 drought, I had requested state governments, in my capacity as Union Agriculture Secretary, to establish crop Weather Watch groups at the district and state levels for taking concerted action in areas such as the following:

- Saving the crops already sown, through crop life-saving techniques.
- Preparing alternative cropping strategies and building up appropriate seed reserves.
- Setting up cattle camps near sources of water for saving animals.
- Dividing the state into *most seriously affected* (MSA) and *most favourable areas* (MFA). The aim is to give priority to relief and rehabilitation measures in MSA areas, both for the human and animal populations, and to enhanced crop production in MFA areas. MFA areas are

characterized by either assured irrigation facilities or by untapped ground water availability.

An end-to-end approach will have to be adopted in climate research if the knowledge and information gained from climate research are to be used in strengthening food and livelihood security.

Fortunately, modern information and telecommunication technologies can help our rural families derive maximum benefit from meteorological data. Macro-level information has to be converted into micro-level action plans. What farmers need is location-specific information and advice. For converting generic information into a location-specific one, we need a cadre of workers at the village level who can add value to climate information and help convert the know-how of meteorologists into field-level do-how. Helping to train and create a cadre of panchayat-level climate managers is the best tribute we can pay to the life and work of Professor Koteswaram. We can then replace the old saying, 'Indian agriculture is a gamble in the monsoon', with 'India's agricultural strength lies in its capacity to manage the monsoons.'

While charity begins at home, we also have a global responsibility in preventing adverse changes in climate. A workshop organized by the M.S. Swaminathan Research Foundation and the Climate Institute of Washington, USA, at Chennai in December 1995, has made valuable recommendations regarding the contributions we can make (*Impact of Climate Change* 1997). I hope we will soon have a *National Policy Statement* on climate and monsoon management policies and strategies adopted by the National Development Council.

References

Biswas, Asit K., ed. (1984), *Climate and Development* (Dublin: Tycooly International Publishing Company).

Inwing, Montzer M., ed. (1992), *Confronting Climate Changes: Risks, Implications and Responses* (Cambridge: Cambridge University Press).

Mohammad, Yunus (1997), *Towards Creating a Poverty-free World*, The Third D.T. Lakdawala Memorial Lecture (New Delhi: Indian Institute of Social Sciences).

Parry, Martin L. and M.S. Swaminathan (1992), 'Effects of Climate Change on Food Production', in Inwing, ed., *Confronting Climate Changes*.

Impact of Climate Change on Food and Livelihood Security: An Agenda for Action (1997), Proceedings of a Workshop, M.S. Swaminathan Research Foundation, India, and Climate Institute, USA.

Ramalingaswami, V., U. Jonsson and J. Rohde (1996), *The Asian Enigma: The Progress of Nations* (UNICEF).

Rose, Julian (1997), 'The Key to Organic Growth Science and Public Affairs', *The Royal Society and the British Association for the Advancement of Science*, Autumn.

Sustainable America: A New Consensus for Prosperity, Opportunity, and a Healthy Environment for the Future (1996) (Washington DC: The President's Council on Sustainable Development).

Swaminathan, M.S. (1984), 'Climate and Agriculture', ed., *Climate and Development*.

———— (1991), *Science and Integrated Rural Development* (New Delhi: Concept Publishing Company).

Uncommon Opportunities: An Agenda for Peace and Equitable Development (1994), Report of the International Commission on Peace and Food (Chairman: M.S. Swaminathan) (London, New Jersey: Zed Books).

The Constitution and the People

Somnath Chatterjee

When I was asked to deliver this lecture, I felt that in the situation in which the nation finds itself today almost after fifty years of independence, it would be apposite to have a general review of the functioning of our organic law, which is the Constitution of India, to ascertain whether the same has served the objectives for which the people fought for freedom, and to identify imperfections and shortcomings, if any.

The constitution of any country not only has to provide for the structure of the state and the mode of its governance, but is also expected to articulate the urges and aspirations of the people and contain provisions for achieving national goals. A constitution should emphasize national priorities, and lay down the methods to meet the needs of all sections of the people, and particularly the vulnerable sections of the community, by taking suitable legislative and executive measures.

Our freedom came after centuries of foreign domination. The British rulers had their own agenda to implement for the sustenance and strengthening of their imperialist stranglehold. Our freedom was not earned through a revolution or a war of independence, but through the heroic efforts and struggles of freedom fighters who suffered almost inhuman torture, and movements of the common people under the leadership of Mahatma Gandhi and revolutionaries who made great sacrifices. The downfall of the British empire was expedited by what is called the Naval Mutiny and the glorious achievements of the Indian National Army under the inspiring guidance of Netaji Subhash Chandra Bose.

Although we won a truncated freedom, there was great jubilation amongst the people which was naturally spontaneous, as with freedom came the opportunity to decide our own future, to prepare our own charter of development, to decide our own economic policies, to remove discrimination and disparity amongst the people, and to provide opportunities so that the citizens can live with dignity as human beings in a free country. To wipe every tear from every eye became the national commitment.

Eleventh Zakir Husain Memorial Lecture, 26 February 1999.

The Cabinet Mission recommended the setting up of a Constituent Assembly for drawing up the Constitution of the country, to come into force following the grant of freedom. Its composition was decided by the British government, with the ultimate concurrence of the Indian political leaders.

The Assembly came to be comprised of members who were indirectly elected by the Provincial Legislative Assemblies, which, in their turn, had come into existence by elections held on limited franchise under the Government of India Act, 1935. Important leaders of the Congress and Muslim League (they did not participate and ultimately rejected the plan) were elected to the Constituent Assembly, but the common people of this country neither had a role to play nor had an opportunity to elect those who would draw up the Constitution of free India. No doubt, several well-known non-political people, amongst whom were jurists and intellectuals, were also elected as members of the Constituent Assembly; but there was inadequate representation of women and the youth, and of the working class. The composition of the Constituent Assembly exhibited the limitations of a class-ridden society, segments of which were nurtured by the foreign rulers.

Probably that is why one finds, while going through the deliberations of the Constituent Assembly, that its members were somewhat groping for the direction that a free nation should take, what would be the priorities and who should be the target groups. Many wonder about the ideology of our Constitution, since the model was the Government of India Act, 1935. Significantly, the right to work and the right to have free education at least up to the primary level were not made Fundamental Rights, but the right to property was. Privy purses were protected, but even the expression 'socialism' did not find mention in the Preamble as originally adopted.

Obviously, the priority before the Constitution-makers was to evolve a structure which would be most suited for our development and speedy progress, particularly for the removal of poverty, for universal education, for an effective health-care system, jobs for all and other priorities which would transform our nation into a resurgent and dynamic one, and able to play its due role in the comity of nations.

Our Constitution-makers, after long deliberation, decided upon the system of parliamentary democracy with universal adult franchise as the most suitable one for our country. India has been declared to be a Union of States, providing for division of powers between the Centre and the states, as contained in the Seventh Schedule to the Constitution.

The Preamble to the Constitution resolves to constitute India into a sovereign secular democratic republic with the object of securing, amongst others, justice and equality, and particularly, assuring the dignity of the individual and the unity and integrity of the nation. The Supreme Court has now ruled that the objectives specified in the Preamble contain the basic structure of our Constitution.

Secularism is part of the basic structure of the Constitution, and the state is enjoined to accord equal treatment to all religions, religious sects and denominations, as has been observed by the Supreme Court in the Bommai case in 1994, wherein the Court also observed that 'secularism is more than a passive attitude of religions. So far as the State is concerned, the religion, faith or belief of a person is immaterial. In the affairs of the State, (in its widest connotation) religion is irrelevant; it is strictly a personal affair.'

The Constitution in Part IV elaborately indicates what should be the Directive Principles of State Policy, which, though not directly enforceable by the courts, lay down the principles fundamental in the governance of the country which every state should endeavour to apply by enacting suitable laws.

The Directive Principles stress on the state securing a social order for the promotion of the welfare of the people. The provisions of Article 39 (though not enforceable) indicate what should permeate every governmental function; that all citizens, men and women, should have the right to an adequate means of livelihood; that the material ownership and control of the resources of the community should be so distributed as to serve the common good; and that the operation of the economic system does not result in the concentration of wealth and means of production to the common detriment. Other provisions of Part IV deal with, *inter alia*, equal justice, right to work and education, living wages for workers, participation of workers in management, and free and compulsory education for children until they are fourteen.

Certain rights, which are treated as inalienable and fundamental rights of all citizens, are protected against state infringement by the provisions contained in Part III of the Constitution. Right to Equality is one of the important fundamental rights of the people enshrined in the Constitution, which covers within its ambit prohibition of discrimination on grounds of religion, race, caste, sex or place of birth, and also enjoins equality of opportunity in matters of public employment. The basic freedoms which every citizen enjoys in our country are contained in Article 19 of the Constitution, namely, freedom of speech and expression, freedom to assemble peaceably and without arms, to form associations or unions, to move freely throughout the territory of India, to reside and settle in any part of the territory of India, and to practise any profession or carry on any occupation, trade and business, though the Article itself contemplates imposition of reasonable restrictions in public interest on the exercise of one or other of the fundamental rights.

Articles 25 and 26 ensure to all persons the right to freedom of religion, that is, the right to freely profess, practise and propagate religion and freedom, to manage religious affairs, and protection of the cultural and educational rights of the minorities.

The Supreme Court observed in the Kesavananda Bharati case in 1973 that:

> the Fundamental Rights and the Directive Principles constitute the 'conscience' of our Constitution. The purpose of the Fundamental Rights is to create an egalitarian society, to free all citizens from coercion or restriction by society and

to make liberty available for all. The purpose of the Directive Principles is to fix certain social and economic goals for immediate attainment by bringing about a non-violent social revolution. Through such a social revolution, the Constitution seeks to fulfil the basic needs of the common man and to change the structure of our society. It aims at making the Indian masses free in the positive sense. Without faithfully implementing the Directive Principles, it is not possible to achieve the Welfare State contemplated by the Constitution.

But what we find today is that, in many ways, there has been negation of most of the important constitutional mandates, and the scantest regard has been paid over the years in applying the Directive Principles of State Policy. After fifty years of independence, almost in every sphere of national activity, aberrations and distortions have nearly taken over the functioning not only of the state, but also of the political and administrative systems, as a result of which large sections of the people are unable to enjoy even the minimum rights which the Constitution contemplates for them. Abysmal poverty, illiteracy, child mortality, lack of job opportunities for young people, unavailability of pure drinking water in many areas and lack of health care have resulted in the effective denial of basic human rights to them.

We have recently celebrated fifty years of our independence and several assessments have been made about the country's achievements, about whether the common people of the country, particularly the toiling sections, the workers, peasants and farmers, scheduled castes and tribes, and the minorities, have been able to fulfil their basic needs or not. To mark the occasion, the Parliament of India held special sessions to debate and discuss, not on party lines perhaps for the first time, the country's successes and failures, and unanimously passed a resolution containing an 'Agenda for India', pledging, *inter alia*:

(i) to free the political life and processes of the adverse impact on governance of undesirable extraneous factors including criminalization;

(ii) to launch continuous and proactive efforts for securing greater transparency, probity and accountability in public life;

(iii) to preserve and enhance the prestige of the Parliament;

(iv) to launch a vigorous national campaign to combat unsustainable growth of population;

(v) to achieve the constitutional mandate of universalization of elementary education by 2005, and to make education at all levels employment-relevant;

(vi) to manage the national economy prudently with emphasis on achieving full employment, eliminating poverty, securing equity and social justice and balanced regional development;

(vii) to achieve, in a time-bound manner, marked improvement in the quality of life of all citizens with special emphasis on provision of minimum needs for food, nutrition, health, security, potable water, sanitation and shelter; and

(viii) to establish gender justice, with particular emphasis on education of the girl child.

I have taken the liberty of mentioning the basic issues referred to in the resolution as they indicate the unfulfilled commitments and challenges which we still face, and the need for urgent attention and solution.

After almost half a century of independence, the problems of the common people have remained acute. With a greater chasm among the people, and nearly half of our people living in grinding poverty and over 60 per cent of the people remaining illiterate, the question is being and should be asked: is there any deficiency in the constitutional provisions which inhibit fulfilment of the people's needs? And have those who have been in power failed to discharge the constitutional mandate?

For five decades since independence, there has been an almost unchecked growth of population, which has proliferated from 36 crores in 1951 to over 93 crores in 1991, and is likely to reach 100 crores by the turn of the century, while the names of 4 crores of job seekers were registered with employment exchanges at the end of 1997. At the same time, we find the rate of infant mortality to be 72 per 1,000 in the year 1996; 64.13 per cent male literacy and 39.29 per cent female literacy (only 52.21 per cent were literate among the entire population as per the census of 1991); the drop-out figure in Classes I to V during 1996–97 was 38.95 per cent of the students, in Classes I to VIII for the same year it was 52.26 per cent, and in Classes I to X, 62.02 per cent; the per capita annual income of the people as measured by per capita net state domestic product at constant prices along with all India per capita net national product and per capita national domestic product at factor cost at constant prices was Rs 2,573 in 1995–96. The common people find the prices of essential commodities almost beyond their reach. The country has a very powerful parallel economy, with the amount of black money in circulation calculated to be approximately over Rs 36,000 crore in 1983–84, which, by common understanding, has multiplied at least by three times since then. Further, atrocities against women and the minorities have reached alarming proportions. There is a relentlessly soaring rate of crimes against women, with more and more women falling victim to crimes at home, at workplaces and in the community. In 1996, there were 1,06,723 incidents of crime against women, a 56.2 per cent increase from the incidents in 1990. There were 5,250 reported cases of dowry death in 1996, an 8.6 per cent increase from the figures for 1990. The fate of the girl child is miserable in many areas. We still have temples in our country to worship '*sati*'. The recent spate of attacks and atrocities on the Christian minorities, including the ghastly, inhuman and brutal killing of Dr Graham Staines and his two sons, has exposed the so-called secular tradition of some organizations and sections of the people; the nation hangs its head in shame today.

The condition of the working class in the country is becoming more and more precarious, with a large incidence of industrial sickness, widespread retrenchment and closure of public sector undertakings, including a large number of coal mines operating under the public sector company, Coal India Limited. Even Steel Authority of India Limited (SAIL) has become a sick undertaking. Indian industry today is in doldrums, mainly because of what many perceive as senseless globalization and liberalization without any attempt to meet the needs and demands of indigenous industries; in the name of competition, Indian industrial units are becoming non-competitive and going out of existence. Loss of employment in the industrial sector has reached alarming proportions.

The country is further facing serious problems because of insurgency, secessionist movements and militant activities in different regions, including Kashmir. In the north-eastern states, the tribal population feels alienated from the mainstream because of lack of development, lack of opportunities for earning a livelihood and threatened loss of identity.

Over and above all this, recent incidents of attacks on religious minorities are almost tearing the country apart. Communal and fundamentalist organizations, through misuse, in some places, of the administrative machinery, are utilizing religion for narrow political purposes. Religious fanaticism is replacing sane and responsible behaviour, and people are being divided on the basis of the God they worship.

The nation is under a state of near-siege by communal elements. Corruption and criminalization of politics are eating at the vitals of our body-politic; money power and muscle power are being used for political purposes. Corruption and violence have become all-pervading. In October 1993, N.N. Vohra, the then Union Home Secretary, submitted a confidential report to the Minister of Home Affairs, about the nexus between crime, politics and administration in the country. The report was leaked, and it became the subject matter of an intense debate in the Lok Sabha. Vohra, in his report, referred to the views of the then Director of the Central Bureau of Investigation, that the money power acquired by crime syndicates/the mafia 'is used for building up contacts with bureaucrats and politicians and expansion of activities with impunity'. Money power is used to develop a network of muscle power, which is also used by politicians during elections. The report further stated that 'the nexus between criminal gangs, police, bureaucrats and politicians has come out clearly in various parts of the country'. It records the views of the Director, Intelligence Bureau, that

> there has been a rapid spread and growth of criminal gangs, armed senas, drug
> mafias, smuggling gangs, drug peddlers and economic lobbies in the country,
> which have, over the years, developed an extensive network of contacts with the
> bureaucrats/government functionaries at the local levels, politicians, media per-
> sons and strategically located individuals in the non-state sector

and that, 'some political leaders become the leaders of these gangs/armed senas and, over the years, get themselves elected to the local bodies, State Assemblies and the national Parliament'. Vohra's conclusions, *inter alia*, were as follows:

(i) On the basis of the extensive experience gained by our various concer-
    ned intelligence, investigative and enforcement agencies, it is apparent

that crime syndicates and mafia organizations have established themselves in various parts of the country.

(ii) The various crime syndicates/mafia organizations have developed significant muscle and money power and established linkages with governmental functionaries, political leaders and others, to be able to operate
with impunity.

In spite of a lengthy debate in the Parliament and assurances given by
the Home Minister of the then government, no visible action was taken or is
being taken, to deal with the alarming situation mentioned in Vohra's report,
which has also resulted in the pollution of the political system in this country.
The identity of the people and of the organizations was, significantly, not di-
vulged in the report, nor has the government at the centre taken effective and
bonafide actions to identify and apprehend them.

This country has immense possibilities and potential, but its natural
development cannot take place until its political and administrative structure is
cleansed and the country is governed with commitment to the ideas and objectives that are enshrined in the Preamble, and Parts III and IV, of the Constitution.

It is a matter of the gravest concern that in India, politics has, to a large
extent, become criminalized, and that crime has become politicized. Politics has
almost become a game played by economic offenders, mafias, religious fanatics
and fundamentalists. Our temple of democracy is being desecrated by divisive
and obscurantist forces.

The country's strength lies in unity in diversity. Secularism cannot be a
mere jargon or a paper provision of the Constitution. Mixing of religion with
politics is playing havoc on our secular structure, as has been exemplified recently by the series of attacks perpetrated on the Christian minorities of this
country. It is, of course, part of the pattern of fundamentalist activities, and,
Rajiv Dhawan has recently said, 'the Constitution has fallen into lumpen hands'.
Tolerance, which is the basic postulate of the Hindu religion, as all sane people
understand it, is now being replaced by feelings of hatred, and physical annihilation or torture of those who favour a different path. Activities in the name of
religion are spreading the cancer of communal divide amongst the people. The
demolition of the Babri Masjid in 1992, which was an act of sacrilege and national shame, and was preceded by the *Rath Yatra* of a well-known political
leader, showed how communal passions could be roused, and how the nation
could be divided due to fundamentalist activities.

Recent happenings in Gujarat have shown how a minority community,
namely, Christians, has been treated ruthlessly on the plea of alleged forced
conversions. It is unbelievable that in a country which is supposed to be governed
by rule of law, a police official in a state (as has happened in Gujarat) can issue
a circular (as has been done) to his subordinates, to prepare a census report on
the Christians which, *inter alia*, directs them to seek information about the Christians, the place they live in, the location of the Christian missions, the foreign
countries which encourage them, the grants they receive from foreign countries

and how they use it, to ascertain the population of the Christians, district-wise, taluka-wise and village-wise and prepare a list of telephone numbers, addresses of their leaders, how many clashes were there between the Hindus and the Christians in the last five years, list of Christian offenders along with their dossiers and to indicate what type of trickery is being used by the Christian missionaries for defilement activities. One wonders whether we are living in a civilized society governed by a Constitution which enjoins a secular state. Fortunately, the legality of the Gujarat circular has been challenged before the High Court.

What was the reaction of the political rulers at the centre to the most gruesome murder of Dr Graham Staines and his two sons? Now that a judicial commission headed by a sitting Hon'ble Judge of the Supreme Court has been set up, one need not go into the merits of the incident or refer to the main suspects, but what is amazing is that the Home Minister of the country exonerated the suspected organization and its members of any wrongdoing on the plea of alleged absence of a prior criminal record. Another central minister attributes the gruesome killings to an alleged international conspiracy against the main ruling party at the centre, which is nothing but a crude diversionary tactic to deflect the course of the investigation. One can only hope that the truth will come out soon, but seeing the fate of reports of different judicial commissions earlier, one cannot but have serious doubts about the effectiveness of the exercise. The rejection of the Shri Krishna Commission Report by the Maharashtra government with the blessings of the central government, and the contemptuous reference made by leading functionaries of the state government to the learned judge who headed the Commission, show not only lack of respect for the judicial process, but the futility of such commissions, unless the concerned government is committed sincerely to ascertainment of the truth and taking appropriate follow-up action.

The 'Agenda for India' adopted by the Parliament in September 1997 gives primacy to the necessity of freeing political life and political processes from the impact of criminalization, towards transparency, probity and accountability in public life. Since then, there has been no visible attempt on the part of the government to achieve the said objective. Political parties and others talk of elimination of money power and muscle power, but although the Constitution was amended to deal with the cancer of political defection, methods have been found to avoid the same and indulge in the grossest forms of political corruption. Defectors have been rewarded with ministerships and plum assignments. Leading parties have been accused of giving bribes to legislators. Political defection takes place, not on the basis of change of political affiliation or political conviction, but due to bribery and monetary considerations. In the absence of political will, the recommendations made by different committees for electoral reforms have remained unimplemented. Unless we are able to completely eliminate the nexus between politics and crime, and also between politics and religion, the country is in danger of losing its identity. Today, the nation's soul cries out in agony, and our freedom is becoming a fissured one because of contrived division of the people. Innocent people are losing their lives because of their caste or religion.

There are well-calculated efforts to emphasize the so-called differences between the people on the basis of religion, caste, language and customs instead of emphasizing the commonality and unity between them. The concept of India's basic unity is being undermined for vested interests.

The above, no doubt, exposes a grim situation, and the time has come to ponder why a country with such tremendous resources, both natural and human, should be facing such daunting problems. People without shelter, food or employment, and begging on the streets of India, are most common sights, and there can be nothing more degrading for a human being.

Our Constitution contains lofty ideals: people have been given Fundamental Rights; many human rights have been mentioned to provide the principles of governance in the country as the Directive Principles of State Policy. Is there any lacuna in our organic law, or is it misfeasance, malfeasance and nonfeasance on the part of the rulers?

Recently a former Chief Justice of India, who is the Chairman of the National Human Rights Commission, asked in agony, 'Where did we go wrong?' He also observed, 'The country faces the ghastly illness of corruption and criminalization, which are like cancer, so the time to act is now.'

Of course, in spite of non-achievement in several areas of national life, the country, as a whole, has made progress in various sectors. Our young men and women, boys and girls, overcoming severe handicaps, have attained great proficiency in several fields. Our scientists have made significant achievements, and their efficiency and calibre are well-acknowledged. Our gross domestic product has increased, as has the standard of living of the people, though only of small sections of the people. In higher and technical education, there have been significant achievements. Our agriculture has also developed, and it would have been spectacular if land reforms had been implemented, as has been done only in some states. We have been able to maintain our parliamentary system of democracy, in spite of several aberrations and distortions. The voters of the country have shown remarkable maturity in spite of interference caused in the way of free and fair exercise of their franchise by people indulging in questionable tactics. We should not ignore or minimize the achievements, wherever and whenever made, though they have been for the benefit of only limited sections of the people.

Then where did we go wrong, as the former Chief Justice of India and many others are asking?

As mentioned earlier, many of the important basic human rights in the Constitution have only platitudinous content. Issues which concern the people in their everyday life for sustenance and development, namely, the right to work, right to free and compulsory education, right to secure justice and right to living wages to workers, which are contained in the Directive Principles of State Policy, should have been made enforceable to ensure accountability by the administration.

It is apprehended that more than half of the people in the country, or even more, are not fully aware of the provisions of the Constitution, particularly of the fundamental rights, which are enforceable. The intended beneficiaries have remained ignorant of their rights and privileges under the Constitution. Thus a proper review of the Constitution, particularly of Parts III and IV, is necessary to assess their actual application. It is ironical that due to lack of awareness and lack of resources, the most vulnerable sections of the community are unable to enforce, in many cases, their minimal rights, as provided by the Constitution.

In my view, one of the causes which has hindered our balanced development and progress is the imperfect federal structure of our constitutional set-up. The distribution of powers among the centre and the states shows that power is preponderantly located in the centre, and the states, who have been given the responsibility to look after the needs and welfare of the people, are starved of minimal financial resources and adequate constitutional authority. This has resulted in uneven development of the country, and has given rise to a feeling of alienation from the mainstream. The planning process, which is non-statutory, has, in most cases, accentuated the differences between different states and areas, and has failed to draw up proper priorities. Education, health care, minor irrigation and building of infrastructure, amongst others, are the responsibility of the state governments, but they are facing a perennial resource crunch; in the meetings of the National Development Council, the Chief Ministers of different states, irrespective of their political affiliations, have been demanding greater and greater allocation of funds. Though the Constitution provides for distribution of financial resources by the centre amongst the states, the amount distributed hardly meets the minimum needs of the people. There have been several demands for review of the centre–state relations and the Sarkaria Commission Report, which contains recommendations for change, remains largely unimplemented. A feeling of discriminatory treatment between states has given rise to the formation of regional political parties, and also to militancy and terrorism. The demands for formation of separate states and even secessionism are born out of feelings of discrimination and neglect, and this has affected the development of our country in a cohesive manner, as well as unity amongst the people.

Over-centralization of power in our country has also given rise to a hegemonistic attitude, and the crudest manifestation of its arbitrary use was the declaration of an internal Emergency in 1975. Political morality in the country reached its nadir during the traumatic months of the Emergency which lasted for over two years, when the biggest victim was the constitutional set-up itself.

In a country like India with myriad problems, with unequal development of different states and areas having specific regional problems that are not common to the country as a whole, with special urges and aspirations of different groups of people, it is essential that the true spirit of federalism pervades our constitutional set-up. Obviously, subjects like external affairs, defence, communications, etc., are to be left with the centre, but it is essential that meaningful and effective autonomy are given to the states, to frame their own policies, raise their own resources and make their own laws to meet their particular needs, according to their capacity. A new orientation should pervade our centre–state relations; it is high time that a closer look is given to the recommendations of the Sarkaria Commission, and those on which there is broad agreement, particularly relating to distribution of financial resources, should be implemented soon. Such an approach will lessen the tension between the centre and the states, and also between states and states.

Another provision of the Constitution which requires an immediate and close look is contained in Article 356; this Article has been the most misused in our country. As the Sarkaria Commission has pointed out, the provisions of Article 356 have been taken recourse to more for narrow political purposes than for any justified reasons; the time has come to decide about its continuance. Some recent attempts by the central government to impose President's rule in states governed by other political parties were thwarted by the sagacity of the President of India, but the scope of misuse always remains, as has been shown in the case of Bihar. India is no longer run by a single political party, as was the situation when the Congress ruled the centre and the states. Today, different states are ruled by political parties, some regional, which are different from the ruling party or the parties in the centre, and the central government cannot be made the arbiter of the fate of state governments ruled by different parties where they have popular support.

Many in this country consider that continuing a provision like Article 356 in the Constitution is an anachronism in a federal structure, and a source of friction between the centre and states, and between different political parties, and hence should be removed. A power-hungry central government which is intolerant of other political parties and their governments can disturb state governments for narrow political purposes by taking recourse to Article 356.

The Constitution of India provides that democracy and federalism are the basic features of our Constitution, and indeed its essential features. As the Supreme Court has itself observed in the case of S.R. Bommai, there are many provisions for the states in the Constitution: they have an independent constitutional existence; they are required to play an important role in the political, social, educational and cultural life of the people in their respective areas; they cannot be treated as mere agents or vassals of the centre. Provisions relating to declaration of Emergency and those contained in Article 356 of the Constitution are anathema to a proper federal structure. Although they may be treated as exceptions, the history of this country since independence has shown that the true intentions of the founding fathers have neither been respected nor adhered to, and measures which were intended to be resorted to only occasionally to meet the supposed exigencies of special situations, have been used with alarming liberality.

The prerequisite for the imposition of President's rule in any state by the centre under Article 356 of the Constitution is the satisfaction of the President, that is, of the central government, that a situation has arisen in which the governance of the state cannot be carried on, in accordance with the Constitution. Dr Ambedkar, the chief framer of the Constitution, had observed quite emphatically in the Constituent Assembly that the use of the Article would be confined only to breakdown of the constitutional machinery, which would be in very exceptional circumstances, and the exceptional provision contained in Article 356 should be applied only as the last resort. It was the hope of Dr Ambedkar that 'such Articles will never be called into operation and they would remain a dead letter'. How his hope has been belied is for all to see.

The assumption that the Presidential nominee, who, in effect, is the representative of the government in the centre, will necessarily be more concerned with the well-being of the people of the state than its elected government, is totally unacceptable both in principle and on the basis of the experience that has been gathered over the years. The history of the use of Article 356 is replete with instances of the grossest misuse, as has been very graphically pointed out by the Sarkaria Commission in its report. What was intended to be a matter of use in exceptional circumstances, as was contemplated by Dr Ambedkar and other founding fathers of the Constitution, has become a very convenient tool in the hands of politicians occupying the seat of power in Delhi, however tenuous be its majority, to destabilize governments belonging to their political rivals. The recent imposition of President's rule in Bihar while ignoring the critical situation in Gujarat and Maharashtra is a sickening spectacle of motivated use of the provision. I am sure Dr Ambedkar and his colleagues in the Constituent Assembly never imagined that central rule would, at a given time, necessarily be better rule. It was contemplated to be used in extraordinary situations like threat to the unity and integrity of the nation, and threat to the security of the state owing to external aggression, armed rebellion or such degree of internal disturbance as would have justified intervention under Article 355 of the Constitution. Article 356 cannot be utilized for the sake of providing better governance by displacing an elected government having majority support. The people of the state are best judges of the performance of the state government, and not the centre. Bureaucratic administration in place of a popular government is against the spirit of the federal Constitution. There can be no assumption that the central government possesses a greater degree of wisdom and patriotism as compared to state governments. Therefore, the time has come when a provision of the Constitution which has been grossly misused by vested interests should no more find a place in the Constitution, as the intention of the makers of the Constitution has been totally frustrated. There can be no President's rule in the centre, even if the central government is a non-functioning or malfunctioning one, or acts against the unity and integrity of the country. Then, why should such rights be conceded so far as the states are concerned by a liberal interpretation of Article 356, contrary to the intention of the founding fathers?

Ours is a pluralistic society and a true federal structure is necessary to reconcile the urges and aspirations of the people, and for the maintenance of national unity and integrity, which can only be achieved if the centre and the states consider themselves as partners in the important task of nation-building and providing the wherewithal to the people.

There can be no valid explanation why people in different regions and different areas should not enjoy the same state of development, why the per capita income of the citizens of the country should vary from state to state, and why there should be feelings of threat in the minds of some people regarding loss of their identity.

We have ample material to judge the appropriateness of the provisions of our Constitution. While, in most respects, the Directive Principles of State Policy have remained unfulfilled, and even though there are interferences with the exercise of fundamental rights by the people, the common people, and particularly the working class of the country, have shown great maturity in the face of serious handicaps. To my mind, India's unity can be maintained not by an overbearing centre but by evolving an attitude of cooperation.

Out of the misuse of the political system in this country and the failure to exercise governmental power for meeting the people's needs over the years, various aberrations have crept into our body-politic. If laws had been strictly and evenly applied, proliferation of black money in this country could not have taken place, because of government patronage to a small section of the people who have obviously been the benefactors of the powers-that-be. The use of unaccounted money has been the source of political corruption in this country. A political system can operate only with the dedication and sincerity of the people who operate the system. We have to wage a relentless battle to eliminate all forms of corruption, political and economic.

Political corruption and communal violence are seeking to engulf our very political and social system, and, as a result, the rights and privileges which are given to the people in the Constitution are under great strain. It is essential to bring back probity in our political and administrative functioning. Fortunately, there are parties and organizations who have not joined the bandwagon and are free from such distortions and aberrations. Due to the activities of some politicians, a question mark has been raised about the credibility of politicians as a whole.

All will have to work together for achieving the primacy of the constitutional goals, and for commitment to legal and constitutional methods. As a nation, we suffer from lack of accountability. There is an impression which has gained ground, that criminals with recourse to resource and influence can remain out of the reach of legal processes. There is also a question mark about proper enforcement of our criminal justice system. We have scores of scams and corruption of different hues. It is only by commitment to constitutional objectives that we can bring back probity into the system.

Those people who deserve to receive their entitlements under the Constitution have been waiting for long, and only by their efforts can accountability be enforced. Communalism, secessionism, corruption and divisiveness are anathema to the letter and spirit of the Constitution, and only united national endeavour can assure to the people what is justly due to them. Let us all commit to strive assiduously to fulfil the 'Agenda for India' contained in the unanimous resolution of Parliament adopted in the special session.

In view of the non-performance of many governments, including at the centre and the states, and as many provisions of the law for the benefit of the common people have not been duly implemented, our judiciary has evolved the process of what is called public interest litigation (PIL), to protect the people from the administration's wrongdoings, and also to achieve for them what the Constitution and the laws provide. As has been held by Chief Justice Bhagwati, large sections of the people in our country are unable to take recourse to legal proceedings on their own, to obtain what is due to them. In this circumstance, well-meaning individuals or organizations can approach the courts of law for their intervention, and the courts have generally played a pro-people role in securing for them their just due by striking at wrongful actions or inactions on the part of the government. PIL shows the vitality of our Constitution and the proactive role the courts can play. However, the Supreme Court itself has cautioned against too liberal and unjustified use of PIL jurisdiction, as the principle of separation of powers between the legislative, the executive and the judiciary should not be weakened. As a whole, the country is badly in need of comprehensive judicial reform; the criminal justice system has almost collapsed, with huge arrears in the numbers of both civil and criminal cases making dispensation of justice almost a mockery. In this area too, comprehensive steps have to be taken to remedy the situation.

For the last several years, this country has not had one-party rule in the centre; the government has been formed by a coalition of different political parties. In a vast country like ours with different degrees of development, different regional problems, urges and aspirations, the people have clearly expressed their views against one-party rule. It appears that we have entered into an era of coalition governments. But some pundits feel that such governments give rise to political instability, and advocate the introduction of the presidential form of government.

The state of political and constitutional developments indicates, by and large, that one-party rule in this country is no longer possible, and we have to evolve proper methods for the functioning of coalition governments. With a proper attitude of working together for the common good and with broad agreement on political, social and economic objectives to be agreed before the elections, there is no inherent difficulty in the functioning of coalition governments. West Bengal provides a model of a coalition government which has received overwhelming support from the people of the state in five successive general elections. One-party rule has not necessarily resulted in either stability of government or good performance. A presidential system will result in total lack of accountability and concentration of power in the hands of one person. This country has experienced that when power is concentrated in one hand, it results in stultification of democracy and the rights of the people. Protagonists of the presidential system of government are apparently more concerned with 'stability' than good governance. A stable government need not be a pro-people government or an efficient one, and in a country like ours with a pluralistic society, there is a great danger of the emergence of an authoritarian regime by dividing the people on the basis of religion. Our people, though faced with several problems, some of which are overwhelming, have shown great political maturity in the manner in which they have exercised their democratic rights, as has been seen during several elections when parties and governments which acted against the people and deprived them of proper exercise of democratic rights or failed to deliver the goods, have been unceremoniously removed.

The parliamentary system of government is one of the basic features of our Constitution, like democracy and federalism, and the endeavour should be not to change the system with the inevitable danger of authoritarianism thwarting democracy, but to make governments more accountable, where solution of the people's problems and providing them with wherewithal will be their primary responsibility.

After more than fifty years of freedom from colonial rule, we are unable to meet the basic needs of about four hundred million people who live below the poverty line, and who do not even have food, clothing, shelter, health care and education. In fact, the number of poor people in the country today is larger than the population of India at the time of independence, and these are our countrymen whose interests should have priority and primacy.

In view of the complexities of the problems facing the country and the people, to my mind, there is no alternative to parliamentary democracy with adult franchise and a federal set-up. To provide for the development of different states and regions, we have to strengthen our federal structure and remove the shortcomings that have already been identified. If the centre and the states can function without interference from each other in their specified areas, we shall be strengthening the basic unity and integrity of the country. Decentralization of administration up to the grassroot level has to be effectively implemented, the rights of the people have to be assured, and the minimum necessities of the people have to be ensured. India lives in its villages, as it is said, and the development of the rural areas, particularly of the rural economy, should have the highest priority, which cannot be achieved without implementation of land reforms. The experience of a few states which have faithfully implemented land reforms legislation, should inspire others to do so. The development of small-scale and rural industries will have to be given priority to accelerate growth of the economy. Science, technology and research will have to be encouraged. Steps have to be taken for the empowerment of women, who constitute half of our population. Their active participation in political and administrative affairs will make the development process more transparent and people-oriented. With the participation of workers in the management of industries and provision of living wages to them, there will be greater involvement of the workers, which will accelerate the process of development and strengthen the industrial base of the country. Necessary legislative measures will have to be taken to bring about electoral reforms so as to reduce, if not eliminate, the influence of money power and muscle power from our body-politic.

All these can be achieved by principled adherence to the constitutional provisions, amended as indicated, and by providing adequate executive and legislative power. To achieve the participation of women in legislative and administrative processes, for restructuring of centre–state relations, and for the removal of the Emergency provision in the Constitution except in cases of external aggression, necessary amendments should be made. We have had a large number of constitutional amendments; some have helped us, some have caused a setback to the cause of our democracy. In a free and democratic country, laws of preventive detention are anathema, and the sooner they are deleted, the better.

The common people of this country have waited long. The country has the resources and the ability to grapple with its problems: what is needed is a commitment to people's rights, to democracy and to a true federal structure. There can be no substitute to transparency and accountability, and a relentless war has to be waged against the nexus between crime and politics.

The constitutional provisions and the laws made thereunder are required to be implemented with commitment to serve the people for whom they are meant. The resources of the country and the development that takes place cannot be arrogated by small sections of the people for themselves. Our country can provide leadership to developing countries, provided there is commitment to the goals of our Constitution as contained in Parts III and IV thereof. Political parties with a common programme must develop the culture of working together, as the era of coalition is expected to continue. The fight against forces of disruption, communalism and fundamentalism, and against poverty, obscurantism and exploitation, will be long-drawn, but can be won with confidence in ourselves. There is no reason why the next millennium should not belong to this country.

Civil Society and the Good Society

André Béteille

Terms and Concepts

The main subject of the present lecture is civil society, and its distinctive features as a particular type of social and historical formation. Because the phrase has acquired a positive connotation, it is often used in public discussion today as a kind of synonym for the good society. I believe, on the other hand, that a distinction should be maintained between the two, and that nothing is added to our understanding of society by using two phrases where only one will do.

Being a sociologist, I would naturally like to approach the problem from the sociological point of view. Since I consider sociology to be mainly an empirical, rather than evaluative, discipline, I feel more at ease with the concept of civil society than I do with that of the good society. I believe that social theory has something useful to contribute to the understanding of civil society, but I doubt that the sociologist has much more to say on the good society than may be expected of any responsible citizen.

There are, and perhaps always will be, many and various conceptions of the good society. I doubt that the religious believer and the unbeliever can ever have the same conception of the good society; yet, it should be possible for them to agree on the basic characteristics of civil society. What I understand by civil society has little chance of growth in a totalitarian regime where a single and uniform conception of the good society is imposed from above. Civil society flourishes not under totalitarian regimes but under liberal, pluralist and secular regimes, and it is a defining feature of the latter that they accommodate diverse conceptions of the good society. A theocratic regime accommodates only believers, whereas a secular regime accommodates unbelievers as well as believers, and believers of different religions. A totalitarian regime accommodates partisans only of a particular political cause; a liberal regime accommodates partisans of different political causes.

Sociology is a comparative, rather than a generalizing, science. The comparative approach brings to the sociologist's attention societies of many

---

Twelfth Zakir Husain Memorial Lecture, 22 February 2000.

different kinds, each having its distinctive morphological features and its distinctive norms and values. The comparative and empirical approach characteristic of his discipline makes it difficult for the sociologist to declare that one and only one among the many societies in existence approximates best to a universal model of the good society. Not only have societies differed in their actual characteristics, but the ideals they have set before themselves have also been different. It will be futile to judge an agrarian society by the ideals of an industrial society, or a matrilineal society by those of a patrilineal one. The comparative approach discourages the expression of preferences in these matters, in the analysis of societies.

When I say that the concept of civil society is more amenable to sociological analysis, I do not mean that there is a single conception of it on which all sociologists are agreed, or even that it will be easy to arrive at such a conception. The discussion of the subject among social scientists uses a great variety of divergent conceptions, among which Gurpreet Mahajan, in a recent article (Mahajan 1999), has drawn attention to only two. In these discussions, there is little agreement on even what constitutes the core of civil society. Some would represent non-governmental organizations (NGOs), often funded or at least inspired by international agencies, as the core; others would regard assemblies of persons for ethical, moral and religious discourse as the core. Such formations, no matter how desirable in themselves, belong to the periphery rather than the core of what I consider to be civil society, whose core consists of, in my view, the open and secular institutions that mediate between the citizen and the state in modern democratic societies.

In drawing attention to the great divergence of opinion about civil society among social scientists in India, I do not mean to suggest that there is complete agreement about it among social scientists in the west where the idea first came into use. There have been at least two distinct usages in the west, among which the one that is better known in India is that which goes back to Hegel and Marx. Now, for both Hegel and Marx, civil society was not a universal but a historical category that they saw as emerging in the European societies of which they were members. They themselves gave little thought to extending the concept to societies outside the west.

It is doubtful that either Hegel or Marx would use civil society as a synonym for the good society. There is a distinctive feature of their usage, arising from the language in which they mainly wrote, to which I must draw attention. The German phrase actually used by both Hegel and Marx was 'Bürgerlichegesellschaft', which may be translated into English as either 'civil society' or 'bourgeois society'. Hegel did not regard Bürgerlichegesellschaft as the highest form of historical development, and I hardly need to point out that Marx had an ambivalent rather than positive attitude towards bourgeois society; he might consider it as a necessary stage in the historical development of the good society, but certainly not as the equivalent of it.

There is another term in German, 'Zivilgesellschaft', that corresponds much better to the specific sense conveyed by 'civil society' in English. But that is a new term, devised to meet a contemporary need for which the term *Bürgerlichegesellschaft*, used by Hegel and Marx, is no longer found suitable. It is, in fact, a neologism in the German language based on a direct adaptation of the English phrase. The new coinage is a belated acknowledgement by German writers of the need to distinguish between bourgeois society (or *Bürgerlichegesellschaft*) and civil society (or *Zivilgesellschaft*). It also indicates that we can get little guidance from either Hegel or Marx in the understanding of what has come to be widely regarded as civil society; they wrote about bourgeois society, and not civil society.

Marx, and to some extent Hegel as well, may be regarded as the inspiration for Gramsci's views on civil society which are, in many ways, fuller than those of either of his two predecessors. The value of Gramsci's contribution lies in his better appreciation of differentiation and mediation. But, while recognizing the great significance of civil society, Gramsci does not, by any means, regard it with unmixed approval. Gramsci's observations on state, civil society and political society, though much admired by the *cognoscenti*, are not easy for the uninitiated to unravel. His writings show an acute awareness of the interpenetration of state and civil society in what may be called the bourgeois democratic regime. That regime, according to him, exercises its grip not simply through the constituted authority of the state, but also, and more deeply, through the hegemony of civil society. To the extent that civil society is the site of hegemony, it cannot be viewed with unmixed approval.

An earlier and somewhat different perception of civil society may be found in the writings of the Scottish moral philosophers. Notable among these is Adam Ferguson's *An Essay on the History of Civil Society* (1966), first published in 1767. Here too, civil society is viewed not as a universal but as a historical category, in the process of formation. But on the whole it is viewed with sympathy, although there is both misgiving about the future and nostalgia for what civil society is displacing.

The Scottish moral philosophers did not have the principled antipathy towards bourgeois democratic regimes that came to characterize the work of Marx and, even more, of his successors. In eighteenth-century Britain, the bourgeois democratic regime was still at a nascent stage, and those like Adam Ferguson and Adam Smith looked forward to an era of continuing peace and prosperity under its aegis. In this tradition, the positive attitude towards civil society goes hand-in-hand with the positive attitude towards bourgeois society. Peace and prosperity went together in their conception of the emerging social order. A common contrast in nineteenth-century social thought, found in both Henri de Saint-Simon and Herbert Spencer, was the contrast between 'industrial society' and 'military society'. They saw the dark face of military society more clearly than the dark face of industrial society.

For Adam Ferguson, the development of civil society meant a movement away from barbarism. Civil society was not only the site for the pursuit of private interest, but also the site for the practice of civility. The contrast was between civil society and natural society. Civil society pulled man out of the state of nature in which untempered passion held sway, and it encouraged the orderly pursuit of interest through the practice of civility. Not surprisingly for a man of his time, Adam Ferguson believed that western Europe was the proper home of civil society.

The significance of the contrast between the passions and the interests has been brought out with remarkable effect by Albert Hirschman (1977). The eighteenth century abounded in arguments about the beneficial effects on society and polity of the expansion of commerce and industry. A world governed by the rational pursuit of interest would be a world characterized by constancy and predictability. A new legal order which respected the rights of the individual – as against the claims of clan and community – was essential for its success. But a change merely in the legal order would hardly suffice. What was needed in addition was a change in customs and manners; in other words, in society in the widest sense of the term.

But the change from 'rude' to 'polished' manners would not be without its costs, and no one perceived those costs more clearly than Adam Ferguson. Hirschman (1977: 119–20) has put the point nicely: 'As a member of both a Scottish clan and the group of thinkers who formed the Scottish Enlightenment, Ferguson was especially ambivalent about the advances "polished" nations had achieved over the "rude and barbarous" ones.' A society based on the division of labour was, for him, not preferable in every respect to one based on clan and community. His concept of civil society was specific enough for him to recognize that it was not a panacea.

A peculiar feature of the discussion of civil society is that there are many who use the term lavishly but hardly describe its content, while there are others who discuss that content extensively but use the term scarcely, if at all. Alexis de Tocqueville had a better understanding of the new social order that was emerging than Hegel, and he did not have towards it the kind of antipathy that marked so much of the writing of Marx. He showed a profound insight into the new social order – its strengths as well as its weaknesses – but he scarcely used the phrase 'civil society' to describe it. His key phrase was 'democratic society', which he contrasted with 'aristocratic society'. To put it in a nutshell, his conception of democracy was that it had two sides – a political side and a social side – and in his account of the latter, he ranged through the entire gamut of institutions, manners and customs – the 'habits of the heart', as he memorably called them – characteristic of what may be rightly described as 'civil society'.

Among contemporary authors broadly within the same tradition as de Tocqueville, Edward Shils (1997) has written about civil society with both insight and sympathy. His contrast is not between democratic and aristocratic societies, but between democratic and totalitarian societies. Civil society, in this view, is incompatible with a totalitarian regime; it can thrive only in a liberal democracy, although it is not identical with it.

Liberal democracy is a set of institutions. Civil society comprises the institutions of liberal democracy but it contains other institutions as well. It also comprises a pattern and standard of judgement without which the institutions of civil society cannot flourish. When that pattern of judgement and the relations it sustains are lacking, it is scarcely possible for civil society to exist at all. (Shils 1997: 70)

The interpenetration of institutions referred to above makes it difficult to give a clear and consistent account of civil society. In his characterization of civil society, Shils assigns some importance to the virtue of civility. There is more to this than the mere appreciation of good manners as a matter of form. Civility ensures the free and frank exchange of opinions among persons with divergent political attachments and, indeed, with divergent conceptions of the good society. It also ensures a certain basic equality in interchanges among persons occupying unequal positions in society and its institutions. Civil society cannot prosper unless its members are able to put themselves, at least to some extent, in the positions of their political opponents and their social inferiors. It is in this view of the subject, by no means the only or even the predominant one in contemporary western writing, that the idea of civil society comes closest to that of the good society.

The State and Social Movements

I have said enough in the foregoing to make the point that, whatever the case may be with the good society, civil society is a historical and not a universal category. This point is not sufficiently acknowledged in contemporary discussions of the subject in India, and if it is, it is done so only in a half-hearted way. Much of the discussion seems to be driven by either a radical disenchantment with the present or an insidious nostalgia for the past.

The disenchantment with the present that has led to the creation of an interest in civil society is in the main a disenchantment with the state and its institutions. There can be little doubt about the steady and continuous loss of faith in the Indian state in the last fifty years, particularly among the intelligentsia. What people have come to expect from the state has to be measured against what they expected of it fifty years ago when India became a republic. If they had not expected so much at that time, they would probably be less disenchanted today.

The new Constitution, adopted exactly fifty years ago, defined for the state a very ambitious and comprehensive role in the regeneration of society. The Directive Principles of State Policy ranged from free and compulsory education up till the age of fourteen to the ban on cow slaughter. The prolonged debates in the Constituent Assembly, lasting for over three years, show how keenly the leaders of modern India wanted the new state to be the handmaiden of social change. But if society was not yet ready to be regenerated so comprehensively, the entire blame for that cannot be laid on the state.

An important part of the state's effort for the regeneration of society was to be realized through economic planning. Shortly after the adoption of the new Constitution, a high-powered Planning Commission was set up with the Prime Minister as its chairman. From almost the very beginning, planning in India was based on the principle that the state should take over the commanding heights of the economy. Disenchantment with centralized planning had set in already by the mid-1970s, and it is by now widely recognized that the direct involvement of the state in every kind of economic activity has harmed the economy itself by stifling individual initiative and voluntary effort.

A more basic and palpable source of disaffection has been the runaway expansion in the bureaucratic apparatus of the state. When people think of the state today, they think of its bureaucracy; and it cannot be said that the Indian bureaucracy has, in the last fifty years, endeared itself to the Indian people. In all sections of the population, the feeling has grown that the bureaucracy does not serve society, it serves itself. And, certainly, a gargantuan bureaucracy is not anybody's idea of the good society, whether in India or anywhere else.

There has been disenchantment not only with administration, but, if anything, even more with politics. The state legislatures and, to some extent, even Parliament, have lost much of the dignity with which they were invested fifty years ago. Not only are legislative skills absent among many if not most legislators, some among them are of doubtful virtue while others have criminal records. It is not that there were no corrupt or uninformed legislators in the past, but, on the whole, they remained quiet. Today, the corrupt and the uninformed are also the most vociferous.

Political parties, too, have lost much of their credibility in the public eye. There was a time when the Congress party was an object of pride for its members and of admiration for many who were not its members. That time is now long past. In the city of Calcutta, where I grew up, the Communist party enjoyed considerable public esteem in the 1950s and 1960s, but no Communist party does so anywhere any longer. It seems as if a political party has to be in office for only a short while, for it to be dragged to the dust by its own members.

Many factors have contributed to the decline in the public esteem of political parties. There was an anarchistic element in Gandhian thought which came to the fore in the J.P. movement of the mid-1970s. It sought to give expression to the vision of a partyless democracy which devalued not only the executive and legislative branches of the government, but also the party system itself. In this vision, the driving force for the regeneration would come not from the state and the institutions associated with it, but from the social movement which has come to occupy a central place in some of the current conceptions of civil society.

State, Citizenship and Mediating Institutions

In a certain line of thinking that has acquired considerable influence in recent years, the state has come to stand for oppression and decay, and the social movement for freedom and regeneration. If one is looking for a turning point, one will find it in the repressive measures of the Emergency and the political disorder that preceded and followed it (Dhar 2000). In this line of thinking, civil society is identified with the social movement, and state and civil society are viewed in opposition to each other. I have taken some pains to sketch its background because I believe the argument underlying it to be confused, and the appropriation of the phrase 'civil society' to buttress it, an abuse of terminology.

In the perspective in which I view the subject, state and civil society are not antithetical or substitutable: they are complementary (Béteille 1999). Where the state was hostile to civil society, as it was in the USSR under Stalin or in Germany under Hitler, civil society shrank and withered. Where it was supportive of civil society, as it was in Britain and the Netherlands in the post-war years, it grew and prospered. But in a democracy, the state also requires support from civil society for its own health and well-being. If we believe that democracy has two sides – the social and the political – the one cannot grow without the other.

A notion that is not always clearly articulated is that civil society can be made to do the work that the state has failed to do. This, I consider to be a delusion. Those who have fixed their sights on people's movements have persistently attacked the state for being unfeeling and uncaring, oppressive and dehumanizing, alien and alienating, and, in sum, out of tune with the aspirations, sentiments and needs of the ordinary people. It should be put on the back burner and the real work of reconstituting the nation should be assigned to civil society. In the extreme case, the target of attack is not merely the state as it is or has been for the last fifty years, but the state as such, the very idea of the state itself. This kind of emancipationism is antithetical to the idea of civil society as I understand it.

I will not try to give a definition of civil society but, instead, sketch the context in which it may be meaningfully described. While doing so, I would like to repeat that civil society is a feature of the modern world, and it will serve little purpose to look for alternative forms of it in the medieval or ancient world.

The framework within which I seek to understand civil society has three basic components. These are: (*a*) state, (*b*) citizenship and (*c*) mediating institutions. Each has certain distinctive features, although they are homologous with each other. Their historical growth and, therefore, the historical growth of civil society may be understood only by keeping in sight the mutuality of their relations.

When I speak of the state in the context of civil society, I have in mind only the modern constitutional state based on the rule of law. There have been states of many different kinds in different times and at different places, and these have been described by political theorists, historians, sociologists, anthropologists and others. They include tribal states in Africa in recent times, feudal states in medieval Europe, imperial states in China and India, and totalitarian states in twentieth-century Russia and Germany. These states were associated with societies to which the term 'civil society' cannot be fruitfully applied.

The adoption of a republican constitution was a watershed in India's long and complicated history. We celebrated the golden jubilee of the republic a short while ago, but the celebrations were somewhat muted in comparison to what we had on the occasion of the golden jubilee of India's independence, or even the advent of the new millennium. Certainly, freedom from foreign rule is a great event, but so is the inception of a new republic. Perhaps we have been less successful in nurturing the new republic than in freeing ourselves from foreign rule.

The Constitution of India, which may be viewed as the charter of our democratic society and polity, is, I believe, the lengthiest and the most elaborate and detailed document of its kind. It also took a very long time in the making. One of the reasons why so much space and time were taken is that its makers knew that they were making a break into the past, and, therefore, what was being stated had to be spelt out clearly. No one felt this more keenly than Dr Ambedkar who piloted the document through the Constituent Assembly. But no constitution can provide for every contingency, and ours has had to be amended more than eighty times in less than fifty years.

As one would expect, the Constituent Assembly represented a diversity of points of view. But there was a consensus that the state should derive its authority from secular, rational and impersonal rules. Rules are secular when they are created by the actions of men and do not claim any divine origin; they are rational when there is a conscious and continuous effort to make them consistent with each other in accordance with some wider general principle; and they are impersonal when they are designed to apply to all without fear or favour. Lawyers were present in strength in the Assembly, and legal procedures were repeatedly invoked. There were some who wanted more feeling, more soul, more spiritual matter to be put into the Constitution; but the lawyers prevailed.

Clearly, Dr Ambedkar set a very high value on the kind of state he and his colleagues in the Constituent Assembly had set out to create. But, unlike many others, he had few illusions about the readiness for such a state of the society whose darker side he knew only too well. 'Democracy in India', he had said, 'is only a top dressing on an Indian soil which is essentially undemocratic' (*Constituent Assembly Debates* 1989: 38). If all has not gone well with the Indian state in the last fifty years, is the state alone to be blamed?

If the constitutional state does not emerge fully formed with the adoption of a Constitution, this is even more true of the second component in my triad, namely, 'citizenship'. Citizenship has distinct legal and social characteristics, present in some societies and absent in others. To be sure, the germ of the idea may be found in some societies of the past, but the idea of universal citizenship in the sense given to it in the Indian Constitution, as in other modern constitutions, is of recent historical growth. Its origin and development are intimately linked with the origin and development of the constitutional state.

The specific issue before the Constituent Assembly was the transformation of a nation of subjects into one of citizens. The British empire, in Nirad

Chaudhuri's memorable words, had 'conferred subjecthood but withheld citizenship' (Chaudhuri 1951: v). But citizenship, except in the purely formal sense, cannot be created overnight merely by inscribing a set of rights in a constitution. As sociologists since T.H. Marshall (1977) have shown, the development of citizenship in the substantive, as against the formal, sense was a slow and tortuous process that, in Britain, extended over more than three hundred years, and is still by no means complete. Many in the Constituent Assembly seemed to believe that citizenship was a part of their national heritage, of which they had been deprived by the colonial government.

While it is true that Indians were denied citizenship during British rule, the belief that they enjoyed citizenship before British rule is mistaken. Pre-British society was not a society of citizens or even of individuals: it was a society based on family, caste and community. Citizenship and caste are antithetical principles: one cannot grow without the other being, to some extent and in some respects, diminished.

There is a vague and unformed opinion that an alternative to the western form of civil society may be found among the traditional institutions of Indian society, and caste itself has been considered as a possible candidate. In a letter dated 4 February 1996, M.N. Srinivas urged me to consider such a possibility. He asked, 'Does not India provide a unique example of "civil society" providing stability and continuity for nearly two millennia?' In fairness, it has to be noted that he began with the remark, 'It may appear perverse to you but please think about it', and ended by saying, 'I am not convinced by what I have just said but it *may* bear thinking.' Few have had Srinivas' natural curiosity or his ingrained intellectual scepticism, and many have drawn conclusions where he would merely ask that a possibility be considered.

Although caste has been an institution of great strength and durability, providing linkages both within and between groups, that is not the kind of institution I have in mind when I speak of institutions that mediate between the citizen and the state in civil society. The institutions I have in mind are what I call 'open and secular institutions'. They are of a different genus from the institutions of kinship and religion.

What is an open and secular institution? A modern university, such as the University of Delhi or the Jawaharlal Nehru University, is an open and secular institution. It is open because admissions and appointments are made on individual merit, without consideration of family, caste or community. It is secular because teaching, research and other activities in it are free from regulation by religious authority and religious doctrine. Medieval Oxford and medieval Cambridge were not open and secular institutions, although they have become so for all practical purposes through a long and not entirely painless evolution.

The university is only one example of the many kinds of open and secular institutions mediating between citizen and state. There is a large variety of these, such as schools, libraries, newspapers, publishing houses, laboratories, hospitals, banks, political parties and numerous others. Some are organized mainly

for profit, others are funded mainly or solely by the government. But they all
serve to link individuals with each other and with the wider society through ties
of a very distinctive kind.

Mediating institutions of the kind described above constitute the back-
bone of what I understand by civil society. They have grown in every country
and may now be regarded as a distinctive feature of the modern world as a
whole. But their growth has not followed the same trajectory everywhere. It is
undeniable that their nursery was the western world where they have had the
longest and most continuous period of growth. India is one of the few countries
where they have grown more or less continuously since the middle of the nineteenth century. It is impossible to survey the social landscape of contemporary
India without paying serious attention to the institutions about which I am now
speaking.

Despite their almost continuous growth in size and variety in the last
century, it cannot be said that open and secular institutions have secured a firm
foothold in each and every case. This is true, whether we take universities, or
hospitals, or political parties. They have failed to meet the high expectations
placed on them at the time of independence. While this is true of modern institutions in general, it is particularly true of the ones in the public sector. It is being
increasingly said that they are alien implants unsuited to the Indian soil.

While the fragility and vulnerability of the open and secular institutions
mediating between the citizen and the state poses difficult, not to say intractable,
problems, it is not easy to take too seriously the bogey of foreign implants. If we
have to dismiss the University of Delhi, the National Library, the Presidency
General Hospital, the Indian Institute of Science and the Congress party as foreign imports, then we must also dismiss citizenship and the constitutional state
for the same reason. The present condition and the future prospects of these three
components are inextricably linked. While it is impossible to predict an absolutely safe ride into the future for any of them, it is difficult to see what kind of
alternative vehicle, if any, is available to carry us into the future.

Voluntary Action

Because of the disenchantment with the state and the mediating institutions that are its counterparts, attention is turning increasingly to what many
now say is the true motive force of civil society, namely, voluntary action. The
interest in voluntary action, voluntary movements and voluntary associations
has given a new lease of life by the concerned for the creation or revival of civil
society, particularly in the countries of Asia, Africa and Latin America. It has
acquired a global dimension. One very small but telling indication of the connection being made between the two is the recent redesignation of the Centre for
Voluntary Organizations in the London School of Economics as the Civil Society
Centre.

The significance of voluntary action in linking society and politics together, and in driving them forward in democratic systems, cannot be too strongly

emphasized. A democratic society cannot function properly, not to speak of its growing, if everything in it is left to the state or even to statutory bodies. Mere statutory action will be infructuous if it is not underpinned by voluntary action. The mediating institutions of which I have spoken would amount to little if they left no room for voluntary action and relied only on statutory action. It will be a travesty to regard the university, the library, the laboratory, the hospital, or even the bank, merely as statutory bodies from which all voluntary action has been banished by the long arm of the state. The state does not have such a long arm anywhere, and certainly not in India.

The significance of voluntary action and voluntary associations in the life of a democratic society has been brought to light by many, but by none more persuasively than Alexis de Tocqueville, as is well known, in presenting his account of democracy in America. Tocqueville repeatedly compared its fortunes in the United States to those in his own country, France. He attributed the success of democracy in America to the natural inclination, so to say, of Americans to form associations. As he puts it, 'Wherever at the head of some new undertaking you see the government in France, or a man of rank in England, in the United States you will be sure to find an association' (Tocqueville 1956, Vol. II: 106). Observers of American society, from outside as well as within, have repeatedly drawn attention to the number and variety of voluntary associations in it (Hsu 1963; Hunter 1998).

Tocqueville made a distinction between political and civil associations only to point to the ways in which they reinforced each other. 'In America', he said, 'the liberty of association for political purposes is unlimited' (Tocqueville 1956, Vol. I: 193). It must be remembered that in the early decades of the nineteenth century, this kind of liberty was, to some extent, a novelty in Europe. Tocqueville was shrewd enough to realize that liberty of association was a safeguard not only against the authority of the state, but also against the power of the people. 'At the present time the liberty of association has become a necessary guarantee against the tyranny of the majority' (ibid.: 194). He viewed populism not as a form of democracy but as a threat to it.

If Tocqueville thought of civil society, it is because of the great value he assigned to civil associations in democratic societies. He was impressed by the range and variety of such associations in the United States, in contrast to what he knew of them in his own country or in other European countries. 'In the United States associations are established to promote the public safety, commerce, industry, morality and religion. There is no end which the human will despair of attaining through the combined power of individuals united into a society' (ibid.: 192). It was not only their numbers which were important, but also their variety.

I hardly need to stress the contribution these associations make to the formation of citizenship. At the same time, civil associations do not emerge out of the blue, just anywhere, simply because we believe that they contribute so much to the growth of citizenship. If every soil is not equally conducive to the growth of open and secular institutions, it is not equally conducive either to the growth of civil associations. There was something in the character and personality of the Americans, a unique feature of their culture, that Tocqueville found particularly congenial to the growth of civil associations.

> The citizen of the United States is taught from infancy to rely upon his own exertions in order to resist the evils and the difficulties of life; he looks upon the social authority with an eye of mistrust and anxiety, and he claims its assistance only when he is unable to do without it. (Ibid.)

It is the same trait to which he referred elsewhere in his work as 'individualism'. If we now turn to the contemporary Indian scene, we will find that voluntary action and voluntary associations are of many different kinds. Just as the voluntary component is not entirely absent in what are formally statutory bodies, so also it is not equally present in every association considered to be a voluntary association. To the extent that a voluntary association is also an organization, its members have to conform to certain rules, whether or not they are statutory rules. The transition from a movement to an association, and from an association to an organization which seeks and secures statutory foundations, is familiar to all students of modern societies.

When a movement acquires an organizational form, it does not acquire the same form in every case. Even in a single country like India, one may see them at various stages of development, in various sizes, and with varying degrees of functional specification and differentiation. While these movements, associations and organizations, taken in their totality, undoubtedly contribute something to the life of civil society, it would be unwise to form a judgement about the nature and extent of their contribution without discriminating amongst them.

Non-Governmental Organization (NGO)

The last decade of the twentieth century may justly be described as the decade of the non-governmental organization or the NGO. The NGO has now become a part not only of the Indian social landscape, but also of the vocabulary of practically every Indian language and of languages in many parts of the world. There is now also a growing body of literature in which the nature and significance of the NGO and its contribution to economic development and social change is extensively discussed. Some of this takes the form of advocacy, calling for a wider appreciation of the transformative role of the NGO worldwide, and particularly in the countries of Asia, Africa and Latin America, where the state is corrupt and oppressive, and democratic institutions are fragile and ineffectual.

Advocates of the NGO have put forward the idea of the third sector in society, in which state and market are the first and second sectors (Jain 1995). The NGO is separate from the state because it is a 'non-governmental organization': it is separate from the market because it is a 'non-profit organization'. But while the idea of a third sector is appealing, it is by no means easy to specify. Are

NGOs only one component of the third sector, the core of that sector, or the whole of it? From the sociological point of view, it would be absurd to maintain that NGOs do or can fill the entire space in society not occupied by either state or market. Economists were justified within their limits to distinguish between the public sector and the private sector. But to extend that distinction, after adding a third sector, to the whole of society would be to set foot on shifting sands.

Autonomy in general and autonomy from the government in particular are, and ought to be, prized as values in any democratic society. The mediating institutions I spoke of earlier – universities, libraries, laboratories – are jealous of such autonomy as they have. The University of Delhi, to take but one example, is an autonomous institution under an Act of Parliament. But the autonomy of such institutions is always relative and never absolute. They have to constantly contend, not always successfully, with threats from the government to their autonomy. It would be a travesty to regard such institutions, however precarious their autonomy, as merely creatures of the government. And does an NGO escape regulation by the government simply by calling itself 'non-governmental', particularly if it has to look to the government for funding? An NGO may secure autonomy, including financial autonomy, from the government, but does it enjoy autonomy from the international agencies to which it has to turn for funds? In considering the vital issue of autonomy, we have to ensure that different standards are not used for the established institutions of society and the emerging body of NGOs.

Staying just a little while longer with the example of the university, India does not have private universities but the United States does. Will it be reasonable to describe such private universities as Harvard, Princeton and Stanford as organizations for profit, on a level with the business firm? The London School of Economics has been, at least for as long as I know, a limited company registered under the Companies Act in the United Kingdom, but it has also been a distinguished academic institution, some of whose faculty members have, moreover, contributed to the creation of the welfare state. It may well be the case that Harvard, Princeton and Stanford derive large incomes from which their presidents, deans and professors, in part, benefit, but that does not mean that they cannot contribute anything to civil society. It hardly makes sense to say that salaried professionals in universities, laboratories and hospitals work only for their individual profit, whereas salaried professionals in Oxfam, Action Aid and Acord work only for service to society.

To take a different example, is the Bar Council of India an organization of the government or is it an organization for profit? It would perhaps be true, though trivial, to say that in bourgeois society, every person works for his own profit. What is not true is that every person works only for his own profit and from no other impulse. The more important point is that in institutions, associations and organizations of the kind I have referred to in this section and the preceding one, it is extremely difficult to sort out the sheep who work mainly for service to others from the goats who work mainly for profit to themselves.

What evidence we have tends to suggest that the component of voluntary action in what are called voluntary associations or NGOs is highly uneven, and, in some cases, it is weak. In a detailed empirical study of Britain, published just after World War II, Lord Beveridge (1948) drew a distinction between the 'philanthropic motive' and the 'mutual aid motive' in voluntary action. While philanthropy is extremely important in any civilized society, what really counts in the life of civil society are the associations created and nurtured by the impulse of mutual aid.

In comparing Lord Beveridge's account of voluntary action in Britain with what little I know of the work of NGOs in India, I am struck by the strength of mutual aid in Britain and its weakness in India. The sheer range and variety of associations created by individuals acting together in pursuit of a common objective, without encouragement or support from outside or above, is truly remarkable. Typically, such an association began its career when a group of like-minded persons in similar circumstances got together to achieve a common purpose, raised money among themselves, arranged to meet periodically, and to have a meal together before or after the meeting. Having launched itself in that way, the association might cease to exist after a brief span of time; or it might continue broadly in its original form for decades; or it might expand, branch out and change its form.

Tocqueville was not wholly right when he said that a new undertaking was likely to be launched only in America by an association but in England by a notable. Voluntary associations set up and managed by individuals on the basis of mutuality were extremely important in Britain throughout the nineteenth century and well into the twentieth, until they were displaced, to some extent, by the welfare state. These associations were not only based on mutual aid and self-reliance, they also became schools for the cultivation of those qualities. It is, as yet, too early to determine how far education in the civic virtues of mutuality and self-reliance is being provided by the many NGOs that have come into existence in India.

The trajectories of many of the NGOs in India appear to be different from those of the voluntary associations observed by Tocqueville in America and described by Beveridge in Britain. The sources of their funds are different. It appears that the most successful NGOs in India, and elsewhere in Asia, Africa and Latin America, are the ones that are best able to ensure a steady flow of funds from the government or from international agencies. If the effectiveness of an NGO depends on its capacity to keep funds flowing in from foreign donors, then this must surely affect its contribution to the growth of civil society in India.

To me it appears that an NGO in India is often caught between the ideals of the social movement and the requirements of organized philanthrophic service. It is far from my intention to belittle either the philanthrophic impulses of foreign donors or the very highly creditable work that many NGOs in India are doing in the fields of health, education, childcare and so on. The bureaucratic apparatus of the government is ill-equipped to take care of many of the needs of the common people. If other agencies and organizations are able to do what the government was expected to do but failed to do, or do well, their efforts should receive public support and encouragement. But the question of what they contribute to the creation of civil society, and in what way, still remains open.

The NGOs in India are too diverse for them to have a single organizational form, and too new for them to have acquired a definite one. Many of them will, no doubt, fade and disappear, but, as a social phenomenon, the NGO is here to stay. It is difficult to predict the typical or predominant form they will acquire in course of time, but my feeling is that it will be well within the range of organizational forms already in existence; in particular, where it is large and successful. I doubt that the NGO will be able to dispense with bureaucracy, rational accounting and material incentives for its employees.

Once they take root, NGOs in India will undoubtedly acquire some of the social characteristics of the Indian soil on which they are growing. Even if they are able to escape the influence of caste, it is doubtful that they will be able to escape the influence of kinship. The claims of kinship are very strong in Indian society, much more so than in nineteenth-century America or in post-war Britain. Public bureaucracies have, so far, been reasonably successful in keeping those claims at bay, at least so far as recruitment and promotion at the higher levels are concerned. The more cosy environment of the NGOs, particularly the smaller ones, makes them more indulgent towards the claims of family and kinship, and they will find it easier, in a way more natural, to accommodate the wife, the nephew and the daughter-in-law than the civil service.

Religious Assemblies

If I have given the impression that Indians show very little initiative in voluntary action in comparison to the Americans or even the British, that impression now needs to be qualified. It is true that they appear to be excessively dependent on the government in running not only institutions such as universities, hospitals and laboratories, but also in establishing and maintaining 'nongovernmental organizations'. But there is one extensive and significant domain of social action in which they show genuine initiative, mutuality and self-reliance. And that is the domain of religious activity, in the widest sense.

The ease with which help and support can be mobilized in India in the organization of a religious event is remarkable. The enthusiasm may be observed and experienced in any contemporary Indian city when there is a marriage, a religious ceremony or a religious discourse. People from the neighbourhood come forward and offer help freely and ungrudgingly. They do it without seeking support from the government and without consideration of financial reward; they do it because they like it.

As a boy, I experienced this in the city of Calcutta. There, the most important social event of the school from which I matriculated, as of most such schools, was the annual Saraswati Puja. The entire event was organized with remarkable efficiency and good humour by teenaged boys. The main responsibility was with the boys in the senior year, and in my last year at school, I joined the others in collecting donations, selecting the idol, arranging the decorations and the music, and, most important of all, in ensuring that the food would be abundant and well-prepared. No doubt, some students believed that their piety would bring them good results in the forthcoming examinations, but that was not my motive and I doubt that it was the main motive of any of my fellow students.

On a later occasion, in the same city, a friend took me to the house next door to collect a donation for the local Durga Puja. These neighbours were Brahmos, and they were puritanical and straitlaced. The lady of the house told my friend that being Brahmos, they did not believe in idol worship, so she would not make any donation. My friend was indignant. He pointed to our house and said, 'Those people are Christians. Do you think they believe in idol worship? But they are not mean about money.' He then walked out of the house abruptly, leaving me speechless and embarrassed. Though born a Hindu, my mother had a principled objection to idol worship, but she would be appalled by the thought of turning away a neighbour's son who had come to collect money for the Durga Puja.

It may be said that great religious events such as Durga Puja in Calcutta, Ram Lila in Delhi or Ganesh Chaturthi in Mumbai bring people together for aid and support in collective action seasonally and not continuously. But they also have permanent effects. There is continuity in the membership of the bodies, now universally known as committees, who organize the events from one year to the next. If they are not institutions, many of them have at least the makings of institutions.

In some cities, the temple is used as a base for organizing seasonal religious events on a larger scale, and mobilizing support from its regular members as well as others. The secularization of India has not put an end to temple-building; if anything, there has been an increase in it. Unfortunately, we do not have good sociological accounts of the building of new temples in contemporary India. We need to know in what measure and in what ways philanthrophy and mutual aid come together in such activities. My surmise is that philanthrophic support flows more easily into temples than into universities, libraries or laboratories. Where there is philanthrophic funding of NGOs, it is likely to come from the rich countries of Europe and North America.

As I have already indicated, there is a great variety of religious activities, organized, unorganized and partly organized, that take place outside the temple which is a specifically religious institution. There are also semi-religious and quasi-religious activities. Among these are regular, occasional and sporadic assemblies of persons for discourses of a moral, ethical or spiritual nature. Hinduism as a system of religious beliefs and practices has been organized very differently from Christianity or Islam. It has left much room for activities that might be interpreted as either religious or non-religious, according to the inclinations of the individual. In that sense, though not in every sense, it has a closer affinity with secularism than Christianity or Islam. But Hinduism is changing and one significant change is its tendency to define itself in opposition to other religions, notably Islam.

There is sometimes a linkage, even if it is a loose one, between the assembly for moral, ethical and spiritual discourse, and a religious movement. India has been the land of religious movements and the energy that creates such movements is still very strong. A religious movement is also a social movement, but not all social movements are religious movements.

In conclusion, I can only raise a question which is a very important one, but, for lack of time and space, I cannot even attempt to answer it. How far do religious movements and assemblies for moral, ethical and spiritual discourses contribute to the formation of civil society? They may contribute a very great deal to the formation of the good society, depending, of course, on what one means by that phrase. But I have taken pains to distinguish between the good society and the civil society. I remain sceptical about what religious assemblies and religious movements can contribute directly to the formation of civil society, although their indirect contribution may be extremely valuable. Civil society requires the *separation* of open and secular institutions from the institutions of kinship and religion, although it does not require the *exclusion* of the latter from society as a whole.

References

Berger, Peter L., ed. (1998), *The Limits of Social Cohesion* (Boulder: Westview Press).
Béteille, André (1999), 'Citizenship, State and Civil Society', *Economic and Political Weekly*, Vol. 34, No. 36, pp. 2588–91.
Beveridge, W.H. (Lord) (1948), *Voluntary Action* (London: George Allen and Unwin).
Chaudhuri, Nirad C. (1951), *The Autobiography of an Unknown Indian* (London: Macmillan).
Constituent Assembly Debates (1989), *Official Report*, Vol. 7 (New Delhi: Lok Sabha Secretariat).
Dhar, P.N. (2000), *Indira Gandhi, the 'Emergency' and Indian Democracy* (New Delhi: Oxford University Press).
Ferguson, Adam (1966), *An Essay on the History of Civil Society* (Edinburgh: Edinburgh University Press).
Hirschman, Albert O. (1977), *The Passions and the Interests* (Princeton: Princeton University Press).
Hsu, Francis L.K. (1963), *Clan, Caste and Club* (Princeton: Van Nostrand).
Hunter, James D. (1998), 'The American Culture War', in Berger, *The Limits of Social Cohesion*.
Jain, R.B., ed. (1995), *NGOs in Development Perspective* (Delhi: Vivek Prakashan).
Mahajan, Gurpreet (1999), 'Civil Society, State and Democracy', *Economic and Political Weekly*, Vol. 34, No. 49, pp. 3471–72.
Marshall, T.H. (1977), *Class, Citizenship and Social Development* (Chicago: University of Chicago Press).
Shils, Edward (1997), *The Virtue of Civility* (Indianapolis: Liberty Fund).
Tocqueville, Alexis de (1956), *Democracy in America*, 2 vols (New York: Alfred Knopf).

Urdu and the Question of Its Linguistic Identity

Namwar Singh

> Hegel seems to me to be always wanting to say that things which look different
> are really the same whereas my interest is in showing that things which look like
> the same are really different.
>
> Ludwig Wittgenstein

Since this lecture has been organized in memory of Dr Zakir Husain, it
would be appropriate to begin by referring to his own article on '*Quami Zuban
ka Masla*' (The Issue of a National Language). This article is of the time when
Hindustani was being presented as the national language. Undoubtedly, the inspiration came from Gandhiji, but Zakir Sahib was amongst the first to go on
record on this matter. Those who supported this viewpoint included such
litterateurs and scholars as Munshi Premchand and Dr Tarachand.

It is worth noticing the style in which the article begins:

> The way we are involved in the debate over Hindustani reminds me spontane-
> ously of a character from Moliere, M. Joudain. This gentleman was restless to
> the extent of becoming a maniac to acquire all the knowledge a civilized man
> ought to have. He was very surprised when his master informed him that what
> he spoke was prose. For him, it was unimaginable that he himself had no
> knowledge of the fact that he had been speaking prose for forty years. . . . Our
> condition is somewhat the same; for us Hindustani is the same as what prose
> was for M. Joudain.

After this interesting preface, Zakir Sahib approaches the real issue:

> Hindustani is a language that is spoken and understood by lakhs of Hindus
> and Muslims of our country. In the northern regions of Hind, it is a language
> commonly used. In the rest of the country too, there are lots of people who
> know this language. Also, there are many such people who may not even speak
> this language but they do understand it.

Thirteenth Zakir Husain Memorial Lecture, 26 February 2001.

And then he responds to those who protest:

> People like M. Joudain will object and say that the language I am referring to is
> not Hindustani but Urdu. They are right. Hindustani is also Urdu. The distinc-
> tive feature about Hindustani is that none has any difficulty with it, neither the
> ones who speak Urdu nor those who speak Hindi.

Finally, he substantiates his point by referring to a comment by the eminent linguist, Maulavi Abdul Haq: 'While introducing Insha Allah Khan's way
of writing "Rani Ketaki", he has praised Hindustani in a beautiful way. It is
understood as easily by those who speak Urdu as the ones who speak Hindi. It is
a language that is current and clear, and it is called Hindustani.'

Needless to say, Hindustani has been supported in a strong way but the
example of Insha Allah Khan's 'Rani Ketaki' has something else to offer too.
Talking about his language, Insha makes the following comment in the beginning of his story:

> One day I was suddenly possessed by an idea, that I should tell a story in which
> there should neither be a departure from Hindi, nor a trace of any dialect; only
> then would my heart bloom into a flower. There should not be any intervention
> of any external/alien speech or rustic dialect. A very senior, shrewd and old
> scholar from amongst my acquaintances persisted in his tune of doubt . . . it
> doesn't look you will succeed in what you plan. That the Hindiness be in tact,
> and 'Bhakhapan' [Sanskrit] eliminated. That good people – the best of them –
> should continue to converse amongst themselves and everything should remain
> the same while there should be no one's shadow from the outside. This will not
> be possible.

The question is this: Is Insha's 'Hindustani' the same as the one that
Zakir Sahib calls 'Hindustani'? Insha vowed to keep his language free from three
kinds of vocabulary – external/alien vocabulary, rustic words and 'Bhakha'
(Sanskritization). By 'external', he meant Arabic, Persian, Turkish, etc.; rustic
would be Brajbhasha, Avadhi, etc.; and 'Bhakha' would mean literary Hindi
formed through its mixture with Sanskrit words. This is how Acharya Ram
Chandra Shukla understood the meaning of Insha's words.

Shuklaji goes on to make another critical comment on '*Rani Ketaki ki
Kahani*': 'While Insha escaped "Bhakha-ness" so neatly, in his sentence construction the impact of Persian does show itself here and there – For example, "*Sir
jhuka kar naak ragdta hon apne banaanewaala ke saamne*" (I bow and rub my
nose in front of those who created me).' Despite this, Insha's language is the most
spicy, metaphorical and smart amongst the earliest Hindi prose writers, such as
Lallooji Lal, Sadal Mishra and Munshi Sadasukh Lal. This has been freely acknowledged by the most important of critics. It was indeed generosity on the part
of Zakir Sahib too, that, despite his own distinctive style of writing, he presented
Insha's conversational Hindi as a good sample of Hindustani.

Actually, the language that Insha used for his own poetry was totally different from the language of '*Rani Ketaki ki Kahani*'. He wrote his couplets in the pure and proper Urdu of Lucknow, and in Persian he wrote prose such as the book titled *Darya-e-Latafat*. This is the book in which he included the story of the creation of Urdu in Shahjehanabad. He writes about the happy talkers/narrators who agreed on picking up good words from many languages, and then, using and adapting them in writings/narratives, created a new language different from other languages, which they called 'Urdu'.

One other title of '*Rani Ketaki ki Kahani*' is '*Udaybhan Charit*'. The language is Hindi but it has been written in the Urdu script. Subsequently it was published in both the Hindu and Urdu scripts, alternatively. In 1925, Babu Shyam Sunder Das published it in Hindi from Nagri Pracharini Sabha, and Maulvi Abdul Haq edited it in 1926 and published it in the *Risala-e-Urdu* of Aurangabad. Finally, in 1974, Dr Abdul Sattar published it in both the scripts from Mahatma Gandhi Memorial Centre, Bombay.

Clearly, Insha Allah Khan knew about the languages called Persian, Urdu and Hindi, but he was not familiar with Hindustani. For Zakir Sahib, Insha was, in one sense, M. Joudain.

Actually, that M. Joudain spoke prose is doubtful. According to Northrop Frye, prose is not equal to common speech – it is a refined version of everyday speech. The prose of common parlance is called prose because it does not *appear* to be different from prose. No matter whether it is Hindustani or not, Dr Zakir Husain's commentary on Hindustani is an excellent example of prose.

Supporting Zakir Sahib in the Hindustani movement was Premchand, the author who wrote both in Urdu and Hindi, and who was respected equally as the most eminent story-teller in both the languages. In the last phase of his life, between 1934 and 1936, Premchand toured Madras, Bombay, Nagpur, Allahabad and Lahore. In many gatherings, he lectured on the issues of national language, *Quami Zuban* and Hindi–Urdu Hindustani. Later, all these lectures were collected and published as a small book entitled *Kuchh Vichar* (Some Thoughts). Some of the issues in these lectures have been taken up repeatedly in different ways, with emphasis on different issues in different contexts.

In his essay 'Urdu, Hindi and Hindustani', Premchand clearly says:

> · The national language of Bharatvarsh is neither Urdu nor Hindi; but it is Hindustani which is understood everywhere in Hindustan and is spoken in a very large area. And yet it is not the written language anywhere. And if someone tries to write in it, the littérateurs of Hindi and Urdu outcaste him. In reality what is obstructive for the progress of Hindi and Urdu is their own distinguished lover. Whether we write Urdu or Hindi, we do not write for the common folk – we write for a limited class of people.

In his typically humorous style, he continues to make his point through examples:

> They love '*manushya*' but they hate '*aadmi*'. Even though the word '*darkhwast*'

is commonly used by people, for them its use is out of question; they wish to substitute it with '*prarthna patr*' even if people do not understand the word. In no way can they accept '*isteefa*'; in its place, they want to use '*tyagpatr*'. No matter how easily '*hawaijahaz*' may be understood, they would like to fly by a '*vayuyan*'. Urduwallahs are even more possessed by this tendency. They believe in '*Khuda*' but will not accept '*Ishwar*'. They commit a number of '*kusoor*' but never an '*aparadh*'. While they like '*khidmat*' very much, they cannot stand '*seva*'. In this way, we have created two separate camps for Hindi and Urdu. And no one from one camp can dare step into the other camp. From this point of view, as compared to Hindi, there is far more of rigidity in Urdu. Hindustani wishes to bring the boundaries down and create an interaction between the two, so that both can visit each other's house without any embarrassment, not merely in the capacity of a guest but as a member of the same family. (Premchand 1970: 97–98)

Premchand raised the question of a national script too when he said, 'I am fearful of raising this issue.' The answer to this question can be located in his article 'Rashtrabhasha Hindi and its Problems'. This was a speech delivered as a convocation address on 29 December 1934 at Dakshin Bharat Hindi Prachar Sabha, Madras. In this lecture, Premchand says:

The spoken language can somehow be one but how can the script be common? The scripts of Hindi and Urdu are poles apart. Muslims are as fond of the Persian script as Hindus are of the Nagri script. Those Muslims as well, who read and write Tamil, Bangla or Gujarati, even they look at Urdu with a religious faith. The Persian script is filled with their ancient pride, their culture, and historical importance. That is why they finally conclude, 'We are not going to discard the Urdu script. All we want is that our national script should be one. If the whole country has Nagri as its script, it is well possible that the Muslims will accept this. National spirit will not allow them to remain isolated for long. . . . We do not want to discard any script. We merely want that inter-religion communication should be done only in Nagri. (Ibid.: 122)

Premchand expressed his views on the question of script in another lecture as well. This lecture was delivered at the Rashtrabhasha Sammelan, Bombay, on 27 November 1934, a month before the lecture at Madras. It was about the national language and was published in the book *Kuchh Vichar* under the same title, 'Kuchh Vichar'. According to Premchand, 'The relationship between language and its script is so intimate that one cannot pick up one and drop the other.' At the same time, he also believed that the difference between the two languages does not diminish if the script were to be common. And yet finally what emerges is:

We may keep writing regional languages in regional scripts, there's no objection to this; but it is a matter of convenience that the Hindi script be used for Hindustani language. Not because we have some special attraction for the

Hindi script but because it has a vast spread, and also, there may not be much difficulty in learning this script. But the Urdu script is totally different from the Hindi one. And those who are used to the Urdu script, cannot be forced to use the Hindi script.

Premchand firmly believed that if the languages were to become one, the differences of the scripts would not be a matter of much significance. On the basis of such a faith, he declared,

> Time will take the decision on the issue of the script. The script with greater vitality will take the lead, the other one will be left behind. To touch the subject of the difference in script will actually mean, placing the cart before the horse. We have to go by accepting the condition that Hindi and Urdu are both national scripts, and that we have the right to choose any for our use. Our convenience, inclination and orientation will decide. (Ibid.: 141–42)

There was no specific persuasion in Premchand's mind regarding the nomenclature for the national language. In his lecture mentioned earlier, at Dakshin Bharat Hindi Prachar Sabha, he had said: 'Call it Hindi or Hindustani or Urdu, it is the same thing. We have no quarrel with the nomenclature. *Ishwar* is the same as *Khuda*, and in the context of national language, each one of them ought to get an equal amount of respect' (ibid.: 110).

Finally, it is as if Premchand puts his life's service to literature at stake when he says:

> I have a right to present something to my Muslim friends too, since I have spent all my life in the service of Urdu, and even today I write much more in Urdu than in Hindi. And since I am a Kayasth by caste and have practice of writing Persian since my childhood, Urdu comes to me more naturally than Hindi. What I want to ask is, why do you think of Hindi as a killer?

The destiny of Hindustani was decided on 24 April 1936, in Nagpur, at the Bharatiya Sahitya Parishad, on the occasion of its first convention. While the Congress session was going on, meetings of the Hindi Sahitya Sammelan and Bharatiya Sahitya Parishad too were organized. In *Premchand: Kalam ka Sipahi*, Amrit Rai gives a complete description of the meeting of the Bharatiya Sahitya Parishad. The meeting was chaired by Gandhiji. Leaders of great significance from literature and politics were present. The question raised by the organizing committee was regarding the language to be used for the proceedings. Gandhiji said that this language may be identified as Hindi or Hindustani. He got up after making his point, but the debate carried on. In fact, there was 'voting' over this issue in the session. Between Hindi and Hindustani, it was Hindi that received the majority vote.

After the session was over, Maulavi Abdul Haq wrote in his journal, *Urdu*:

> There was a day when Mahatma Gandhi wrote a letter to Hakim Ajmal Khan in

his own handwriting in Hindustani or Urdu language in Persian script, and today we have come to such a time as this when he doesn't even like to hear or write the word 'Hindustani' on its own, leave aside Urdu. . . . Till such time as Mahatma Gandhi and his associates had the hope that there would be some compromise with the Muslims, he kept calling out for 'Hindustani', which was like a good lullaby to pat people to sleep. But when he lost hope or when he did not feel the need for this compromise, he threw away the mask of hypocrisy, and became visible in his true colours. He is welcome to indulge in the propagation of Hindi. If he cannot leave Hindi, we too will not put aside Urdu.

In reply, Premchand said in a sad tone:

> We are pained to see these words coming from the pen of such a senior, wise and prudent person. He [Gandhiji] was sitting in a gathering which had a majority of Hindiwallahs. There were not more than three to represent Urdu. And yet, when there was a voting conducted, to choose between 'Hindi–Hindustani' and just Hindi, those in favour of Hindustani were less only by a small number. If I remember correctly, the division perhaps was between fifteen and twenty-five. In a gathering with the Hindi majority in which there were only three to represent Urdu, to have fifteen in favour of Hindustani, such a defeat is actually like a win. It is quite possible that in another meeting, the Hindustani side may have emerged stronger. And for the Hindustani that has so far not come to be in use, it is no surprise that more supporters have not surfaced for it. People who have been advocating the cause of Hindustani – and amongst them is also the writer of these lines – they too have not been able to project any specific form of Hindustani yet. (Rai 1962: 628–30)

There was no other meeting of the Bharatiya Sahitya Parishad held after this. The first one was also the last one. Everybody's enthusiasm for Hindustani cooled off. The Partition of the country happened in 1947 but Hindustani died its death ten years earlier. Maulavi Abdul Haq left for the new nation, Pakistan, but he did not take Hindustani with him. However, even if just for namesake, there are two institutions in India for Hindustani even now: one is Allahabad's Hindustani Akademy run by the state government, and the second one is Bombay's autonomous institution, Hindustani Prachar Sabha, which brings out regularly, even now, a magazine called *Hindustani Zuban*, both in Hindi and Urdu, in their own scripts. And yet, the truth is that Hindustani is now a thing of the past.

Then what is the purpose of narrating this story in such a detailed way? '*Kuredate ho jo ab rakh, justajoo kya hai?*' (When you are raking up the ashes now, what exactly are you looking for?) What I am searching for is an explanation for the fate of Hindustani. Does that history teach us any lesson? It is for us to learn or not to learn. As it is, these days a lot of interest in history is being demonstrated. Digging is going on even where it should not be.

If we go back into history, we will see that there was no language by the name of Hindustani. Undoubtedly, there was Hindustan, which survives in the song 'Saare Jahan se achha Hindostan hamara'. Hind too existed, which came to us as a legacy left behind by Subhash Chandra Bose through his slogan Jai Hind, and it was on the sheer weight of this that there was a language tradition in the name of Hindavi or Hindui, Hindi, and attached to this is also 'Hindu'. All of this existed earlier, but what was not there was Hindustani. It took birth suddenly in the last few years of the eighteenth century as a brainchild of John Gilchrist of Fort William College, Calcutta. It occurred to him that if the language spoken in England is called English, that in France French, and the one in Germany is German, then why not call the language of Hindustan, Hindustani. By this time, Hindvi/Hindi and Urdu had become quite prevalent. And yet Gilchrist liked the name Hindustani. From his point of view, Urdu was, in fact, Hindustani. The English dictionary of those times gave Urdu as the meaning of Hindustani. That is why it is not surprising that later, an Urdu supporter such as Maulavi Abdul Haq preferred Hindustani. After all, Hindi/Hindvi were the names given by people of Urdu/Persian to the common dialects of Hindustan. Vidyapati, Kabir, Tulsi and other poets composed poetry according to their own understanding of 'Bhakha', a language different from what was traditionally called Chhandas/Vedic.

But the Hindustani that Premchand suggested as the national language for the country remained a mere dream and an idea. Why else would he have said in his final speech, in 1936, '[We] have not yet been able to evolve any specific form of Hindustani.' At one time, Premchand was a follower of an ideal-istically inclined realism, specially during the time he was writing Premashram-Rangabhumi. That is to say, while his feet were firmly on the ground, in his eyes he kept the skies too in his vision. It is as though he followed the same principles of idealistically inclined realism in the domain of the language issue. Normally he wrote the first draft of his stories in Urdu since he was most adept at Urdu. Then, while putting it into Hindi, perhaps he would recall his ideal Hindustani. In the process, along with the script, the language too would somewhat change. Scholars have tried to show the difference by comparing the Urdu–Hindi texts of two of his well-known stories, 'Kafan' and 'Shatranj ke Khilari', but this is not the occasion to go into the details of this issue.

And yet, what is clear is that for Premchand, Hindi and Urdu are two separate languages – not 'one language and two scripts', but two languages and two scripts. His realism too has a similar claim. Despite this, if he was trying to make them come together as one, it was because of his idealism; and his ideal was national unity. That unity was essential for freedom. The idea was that linguistic unity could help national integration, although it now appears that this was a misconception. Language became a victim of politics. In politics unity is possible through new programmes, but the tool of language does not offer such an easy resolution.

Politicians' eyes are generally focused on similarities, while people work-ing in the field of language, literature, art and culture keep making efforts to perceive difference and distinction. Although there is a process of give-and-take in these areas as well, the emphasis usually is on distinction and difference. Call this a contradiction or a predicament, but it is true that difference in the cultural arena is in no way obstructive to political unity.

For the time being, it would be better to put aside this vast cultural area. If we limit our debate to the linguistic history of modern India and, within that, focus our attention on the Hindi–Urdu relationship, we would find that the Hindi litterateurs took Hindi and Urdu as two different languages.

Actually, the Hindiwallahs of those times persisted in demanding acceptance of Hindi as a language separate from Urdu because, in the earlier phase of the British rule, Urdu had virtually a hegemonic position, especially the Urdu script, in the courts and governmental offices. That is why, initially, it was the script-related Nagri movement that emerged. The first organization for Hindi was therefore called 'Nagri Pracharini Sabha', and its theatre was named 'Nagri Natak Mandali'.

That is to say, resistance to hegemony emphasizes 'difference'. In contrast, it suits the forces of hegemony to take shelter under the slogan of unity. In the beginning, Urdu too had stressed on difference, and that is why it adopted 'Urdu' as its name so that it could dissociate itself from the tradition of Hindvi coming down from Amir Khusrau. Later, in the third decade of the twentieth century, when the hegemony of Urdu, the language and the script, became weaker, a move was made on behalf of Urdu in the direction of unity between Hindi and Urdu through Hindustani. And, on behalf of Hindi, a voice of protest was raised against this Hindustani since, in the eyes of the Hindiwallahs, Hindustani was in reality Urdu.

After the Partition, the position of the languages on the linguistic map of India, changed completely. Hindi became the national language of this new nation, with English retaining its position alongside. It is definitely being propagated as a link language, even though not adequately. Urdu is the official language of the state of Jammu and Kashmir, and other languages are the official languages in other states. For the promotion of Urdu, the centre has established a National Council, and in several states, Urdu academies are functioning. Despite all this, the condition of Urdu is deteriorating day by day. Some of this can be estimated through this couplet by Nida Fazli:

> *Sab mere chahne wale hain, mera koi nahin,*
> *Mai bhi is desh main Urdu ki tarah rahta hoon.*
> (Everybody likes me, but I have no one of my own,
> I too, live in this country, like Urdu.)

The irony is that while Hindi is fighting for hegemony, Urdu is struggling for survival. The greatest danger is faced by the Urdu script. The rate at which Urdu books are being transcribed and published in the Nagri script of Hindi, one fears that Urdu books may soon start getting published only in the Nagri script. As Dr Ramvilas Sharma prophesized, 'In future, the works of Urdu writers will be published in Devanagri script' (Sharma 1977: 332). But

Dr Ramvilas Sharma thought of Urdu as the language of the 'cultural minority', and therefore his approach to Urdu has been patronizing.

Even though those who speak and write Urdu may be a 'cultural minority', by virtue of being citizens of this country, they have right to equality. They are neither dependent on the charity of the majority group, nor is such dependence appropriate for their self-respect. Its script is the special identity of the Urdu language, and nobody has the right to ask them to give it up. Those who want to write or publish Urdu literature in their own script to be able to read it may do so, for the sake of convenience, but that should not be taken as the inadequacy of the script. The Urdu script is identified with the Urdu language in the same way as Nagri is with the Hindi language. When there was so much protest against the Romanization of the Hindi language, then, today, why is there so much insistence on writing Urdu in the Nagri script? No script is in itself adequate and complete, not even Nagri. The Chinese script is the strangest, and yet no one has had the courage to ask the Chinese people to change or leave this script. Then why this proposal for Urdu? This amounts to sprinkling salt on wounds.

'What difference does it make?' – this may be just a popular response in Delhi today, but we all know that it does make a difference, particularly in today's postmodernist world when difference is celebrated the world over and many different identities are emerging – tribal identity, dalit identity, women's identity and, at times, the identity of linguistic groups on the margins. From amongst all of these, the linguistic identity of one community is the most secular and harmless; needless to say, in today's India, that linguistic community is that of Urdu.

Despite the linguistic revolution initiated by Saussure, the problem is that often people do not measure the importance of language adequately. It is language itself that speaks, not the identity of those who speak it. It is not for nothing that the poet Ghananand said, '*Log hain laagi kavitt banavat, mohin to mero kavitt banavat*' (There are people who are busy making poetry; as for me, it is my poetry that makes me). If poetry creates its poet, language too creates its speaker. It is, in fact, language which becomes the medium for the cognition of our identity. That is why there are times when a linguistic group is forced to stress its linguistic difference, if only to save its identity. When all is vanishing, one's language is the final treasure which has to be saved; the greatest threat, on such occasions, is from the language closest to it. The Urdu linguistic community today in India is going through such a phase, and it is experiencing its predicament with grave intensity. This is the reason why it is fearful of Hindi. Especially because, sometimes, alongside Hindu nationalism, there is also a danger of the homogenization of Hindi. After the demolition of the Babri Masjid and the brutal massacre of Muslims in Gujarat, why should there be surprise that Urdu is worried about its being? Finally, one can only say:

> *Jab tavakko he uth gai Ghalib*
> *Kyoon kisi ka gila kare koi?*
> (When hope itself has vanished, Ghalib,
> Why should one complain against anyone?)

References

Premchand (1970), *Kuchh Vichar.*
Rai, Amrit (1962), *Premchand: Kalam Ka Sipahi* (Allahabad: Hans Prakashan).
Sharma, Ramvilas (1977), *Bhasha aur Samaj* (second edition).

The Power Politics of Culture

Akbar Ilahabadi and the Changing Order of Things

Shams-ur-Rahman Faruqi

It is in itself an honour for one's name to be connected, even if indirectly, to Dr Zakir Husain. Having been formally associated with Aligarh Muslim University, I never had the privilege of coming in close contact with him, but his name, like those of Mahatma Gandhi, Abul Kalam Azad and Jawaharlal Nehru, on the one hand, and of Muhammad Iqbal and Hasrat Mohani, on the other, was a household name for those of us who were born in the 1930s, and who grew up amidst the bustle and clamour of our struggle for freedom. I still remember my thrill and awe when, as a young boy, I got to read Rashid Ahmad Siddiqi's short book called *Zakir Sahib*. The only thing that, to my mind, excelled the author's urbane wit and sparkling prose was the personality of Zakir Sahib himself, as depicted in that memorable book.

In his nationalistic outlook, his erudition, his sophistication, Zakir Sahib stood for all the best and noblest traits in the Indo-Muslim character. Akbar Ilahabadi too, in his own way, was the epitome of Indo-Muslim culture, and it seems appropriate to devote a Zakir Husain Memorial Lecture to Akbar Ilahabadi, especially at a time when many of our traditional values of liberal and secular thought are in a state of siege from two contradictory tendencies in our culture: blind, uncritical imitation of western styles of life and thought in the name of globalization, and determined efforts to impose neo-fascistic, totalizing ideas on education, culture and politics in the name of nationalism. I, therefore, hope this essay reads as more than just a homage to the memory of these two great Indians.

I

Most of us are familiar with the main circumstances of Akbar Ilahabadi's life. So I will recapitulate them here but briefly. Born as Syed Akbar Husain in 1846 at village Bara in the trans-Yamuna area of Allahabad district, young Akbar received his early education from Syed Tafazzul Husain, his father. They came from a family of Sayyids that had long settled in that part of the country. Conservative, middle-class and proud, they had preserved their traditions of classical learning but were not in the most prosperous of circumstances. Akbar Husain was obliged, in 1863, to find clerical employment with the builders who had contracted to bridge the Yamuna, not far from his native village. In the meantime, he acquired a good knowledge of English at home and sat the Lower Court Advocates' examination in 1867. He cleared that examination without difficulty, and in 1869 he was appointed *Na'ib Tahsildar*, a comparatively low-grade Revenue Department appointment under the British. He soon quit that job to sit the High Court Advocates' examination. He passed that examination too without difficulty, and enrolled as a lawyer at the High Court of Allahabad. In 1880, he was appointed *Munsif* (a medium-grade judge). He progressed steadily to become a Sessions Judge in 1894, and then acting District Judge at Banaras. In 1898, the British made him *Khan Bahadur*. It was a highly regarded title, considered just below that of a Knight of the Empire. He took retirement in 1903, and settled to a life of poetry and semi-reclusive comfort, though beset by poor eyesight and bad health, in a vast house built by him near the Kotwali in Allahabad.

Towards the end of his life, he was much attracted by Gandhi and his movement for political independence and Hindu–Muslim unity. He wrote a long series of brief poems called *Gandhi Nama* (The Book of Gandhi) to embody his ideas on these matters. He died in 1921, at the peak of his reputation as a powerful socially and politically engaged voice on the Indian literary scene.

II

Akbar has had bad press over the past five decades or so, though he had immense prestige and a commanding reputation during his lifetime. A list of his friends and admirers read like an Indian 'Who's Who' of the decades between 1880 and 1920. Despite Akbar's bitter opposition to his ideas and agenda, Sir Syed Ahmad Khan liked and respected him so much as to have him posted to Aligarh in order to be better able to enjoy his company.[1] Iqbal once wrote about a *she'r* of Akbar's that it encapsulated the central idea of Hegel's philosophy, 'condensing Hegel's ocean into a drop'.[2] Madan Mohan Malaviya had him write poems on Hindu–Muslim unity (Akbar Ilahabadi 1940: 154).

Akbar's poetry remained popular, and perhaps gained even more admirers and adherents, over the score or so years following his death. His *Kulliyat* (Collected Works) was published in three volumes during the period 1909–21. It was reprinted many times during and after Akbar's lifetime. The first volume had run to eleven printings by 1936, the second saw seven printings by 1931 and the third was printed five times by 1940. Yet things are very different today. The *Gandhi Nama* (1919–21) was printed only once, in 1948, and has long been out of print. Akbar was planning a fourth volume of his *Kulliyat*. But Volume III itself was a long time in coming and could be published only in August 1921, a few weeks before the poet's death. Ishrat Husain, his son and executor, did nothing to bring out the fourth volume, or even the *Gandhi Nama*. Muhammad Muslim Rizvi, Akbar Ilahabadi's grandson, published the latter in 1948. Some uncollected verses are to be found in *Bazm-e-Akbar*. Some of the unpublished poems appeared in an edition brought out by Sarvar Taunsavi from Maktaba-e-Shan-e-Hind, Delhi. Sadiq-ur-Rahman Kidwai used some of these in his selection from Akbar. According to Kidwai, a fourth volume of the *Kulliyat* did come out from Karachi in 1948. It does not seem to have reached many people in India, though, and has been long out of print in Pakistan as well.

The Maktaba-e-Shan-e-Hind edition is by no means authoritative or scholarly. The National Council for the Promotion of Urdu now proposes to bring out a comprehensive, though not critical and scholarly, edition. Akbar's fame as our greatest satirical poet remains undented but his readership has declined, and he has been almost uniformly criticized by Urdu critics for what is seen as his opposition to progress, science and the enlightened way of living and thinking.

There are at least two more reasons – one literary and the other non-literary – for Akbar's rough treatment at the hands of critics. The literary reason is the lowly place that comic and satirical verse occupied in the literary canon, in the eyes of Urdu critics. Doubtlessly, Urdu has an immensely rich tradition of such verse, but Urdu critics of the early part of the twentieth century were brought up to believe in Matthew Arnold's dictum of 'high seriousness' being the ineluctable quality of poetry. I well remember my chagrin and feeling of being let down when, as a young student of English literature nearly half a century ago, I read Arnold's pronouncement that Dryden and Pope were the classics of English prose, not of English poetry. Even if my teachers did not entirely endorse this opinion, they unhesitatingly held Dryden to be a poet of the second rank. This, coupled with the strictures of Muhammad Husain Azad on the satirical and scurrilous poetry of eighteenth-century Urdu poets, especially Sauda (1706–81), to the effect that it was offensive to good taste,[3] was enough to make Urdu critics suspicious of all satiric and comic verse. Akbar's passionate engagement with political and social questions in his poetry was not enough to redeem his position. It would be a rare Urdu critic today who would put Akbar among the first ten Urdu poets.

A.A. Surur is one of the few critics who acknowledged the seriousness of Akbar's purpose, and the force of his vision. In a perceptive early essay, Surur said, 'One may not agree with his [Akbar Ilahabadi's] ideas, but one can't help smiling at his verses, and being often obliged to give serious thought to them, and that's what he aimed at' (Surur 1942: 87). Yet, even Surur, in spite of a lifelong admiration for Akbar, was unable to commit himself on the place of Akbar among the greatest of Urdu poets.

The other reason has to do with the obvious cleavage between Akbar's life and political opinions. In his poetry, he presented himself as an implacable enemy of all things British. Yet he was a fairly senior member of the British official establishment, and was apparently quite proud of the high regard in which Thomas Burn, one-time Chief Secretary to the Government of UP, held him (Akbar Ilahabadi 1940: 157). He even wrote an adulatory *qasida* on the golden jubilee of Queen Victoria (1887), at the request of 'Mr Howell, Judge'

(Akbar Ilahabadi 1936: 207–08). He sent his son Ishrat Husain to England for higher education and, on his return, suffered him to enter the civil service under the Government of UP as Deputy Collector. All this sits ill with the humiliating scorn and trenchant castigation that he pours over the British, the west and their admirers.

It is possible that Akbar was conscious of the contradiction. Perhaps it was this sense of duality in his personal life[4] that made his denunciatory voice so much more vehement, his disavowal of western and British mores and systems so much more passionate. Certainly, he knew that no one could really swim against the current, but the tragedy, according to him, was that those who swam with the current too were drowned. The Indian, in trying to fashion himself like a modern [British] creature, gave up his past, his traditions, his belief systems, but could not really become the modern western individual that Macaulay had expected him to become. The following verse is poignant in its tragical bitterness:

> They became votaries of the Time
> And adopted the style of the West.
> In their ardent desire for a second birth
> They committed suicide. (Akbar Ilahabadi 1931: 30)

The Urdu original has a powerful ambiguity owing to a peculiarity of our grammar, which permits sentence construction without an explicit subject. So the original can be read as having any or all four of the subjects I, you, they and we. In a longer poem he expresses the same dilemma with a sense of personal defeat and loss, though the protagonist of this poem, too, could well subsume the whole Muslim community:

> Akbar, if I stick to the old ways,
> Sayyid tells me plain: This hue
> Is now sleazy. And if I adopt
> The new style, my own people raise
> A Babel of hoots and shouts.
> Moderation? It doesn't exist
> Here or there. All have stretched their legs
> Beyond all limits. One side insists
> One mustn't touch even a lemonade
> Bottle; the other side is keen
> To summon the Saki, 'Hey! A stoup of wine!'
> One side regards as unclean
> The whole book of management,
> Skill and sound policy. For the other,
> The bag of English mail is God's own word.
> Majnun's soul suffers from double trial:
> Laila's company and separation both
> Are catastrophic. (Akbar Ilahabadi 1936: 161, 162)

Hostile critics (and nearly all of Akbar's modern critics are hostile) ignore poems such as these, and stress only those which, according to them, show him up as a blind, unreasoning hater of the New Light, or deliberately perverse in his backwardness and love for a past that was generally unsavoury and, in any case, dead or dying. And these are the views not only of those who might have regarded the British rule as a blessing or a necessary stage in the march of historical forces, but also of those who were out of sympathy with the Raj.

The sub-text, and sometimes the explicit strain, in most modern criticism of Akbar is that he may have been a good poet of satire and extremely popular in his day, but the values, ideas and ideals that he held as valuable had suffered a decisive defeat in his lifetime itself. Thus, when the values that provide the prop of belief and conviction to his poetry are gone, his poetry must inevitably make room for others. Akbar's negative agenda and, therefore, his poetry, critics say, can have no strength or validity in the modern age.

But it is entirely false to reason that the defeat or demise of the group, party or ideals targeted by a satirist necessarily makes the satire invalid or obsolete. No satirical text from Aristophanes through Sanskrit and Arabic polemical poems and individual lampoons, to the poems and prose of Swift and Jafar Zatalli, would be intelligible or even extant today if the satire died with its subject. Another point to be noted here is that Akbar's attitude towards the issues of his day, and especially towards issues of 'progress', was not so unilinear and uncomplicated as his critics would like us to believe. He is a very complex poet and he cannot be read like the morning newspaper. All of Akbar's fears and dire predictions were not just the fancies of a diehard conservative.

Akbar was, in fact, one of the few to realize at that time in our history that Syed Ahmad Khan's reformist schemes had much in common with Macaulay's agenda. The 'Indian renaissance' was really a powerful current of shallow modernization. The Anglo-Oriental College at Aligarh had very little 'Anglo' and even less 'Oriental' about it. For all his strength of mind and good intentions, Syed Ahmad Khan was not equipped to create a unified system of modern scientific enquiry and religious faith. An independent intellectual adoption of the attitudes and world-view of the scientific–heuristic world of contemporary European enlightenment, so ably represented by the British, was something quite different from a servile, comprador approval of and active participation in the administrative–imperial apparatus of the colonial British. But British policy in India consisted in making sure that the two came together, as a package. This was a truth that may not have been apparent to many Indians of that time. Apart from Akbar and Iqbal, there is hardly anyone in our cultural history of the late nineteenth and early twentieth centuries who articulated this truth so eloquently. Akbar was relentless in his assertion that it was wishful thinking to believe that the two attitudes could be practised in mutually exclusive realms.

In his own way, Akbar admired Syed Ahmad Khan. He valued his sincerity, his industry and his devotion to the cause of education, especially the education of Indian Muslims. Contrasting Syed Ahmad with his 'sons', both physical and intellectual, Akbar found little to admire the sons, while the Old Man of Aligarh did often tug at his heart. It is not without reason, perhaps, that the very first piece in Akbar's *Kulliyat* is a *ghazal* which contains the following three verses:

> *Indeed, what a wonderful guide*
> *Our Master proved to be!*
> *He lost the way to the Ka'ba and the Church*
> *Was never found!*
>
> *Though the College kept intact*
> *The colour on his face*
> *In regard to hue of the heart,*
> *The son couldn't match the father.*
>
> *Sayyid rose, government Gazette in hand*
> *And came back with millions;*
> *Shaikh went round exhibiting the Qur'an*
> *And didn't get a penny.* (Akbar Ilahabadi 1936: 1)

As we can see, the first verse is a summing up of the entire Indian dilemma and the contradictions that the effort at resolution of the dilemma entailed. Syed Ahmad Khan is the obvious target, but there are larger social and moral implications here. The second verse pays oblique but clear tribute to Syed Ahmad Khan by implying that his heart was at the right place, and blames the sons for losing the spiritual and intellectual heritage of the father. The third indicts him for changing the Muslims' way of life and thought from Qur'anic to British.

In a short poem mourning the death of Syed Ahmad Khan (1898), Akbar stressed the dead leader's industry and integrity:

> *All of us do nothing but talk, Sayyid*
> *Was a man of action. Never forget*
> *The difference between one who talks*
> *And one who acts. Let people say, oh Akbar*
> *What they will. I declare: may God*
> *Have mercy upon him, he was a man*
> *Of many merits.* (Akbar Ilahabadi 1936: 199)

Soon after he became a judge of the High Court at Allahabad, Syed Mahmood, the son of Sir Syed Ahmad Khan, finding that Indian judges of the High Court were allowed pay and privileges inferior to those of the British judges, submitted a memorandum to the government demanding that for the purposes of pay, perquisites and conditions of service, he should be treated at par with British judges. He based his claim not on the principle of equity and fair play but on the fact that he was to all intents and purposes an Englishman, by virtue of his long sojourn in England, his English education, and his complete absorption of the English language, culture and ethos.[5] Akbar Ilahabadi, who was himself in the

Judicial Service of UP at that time, would have known or heard of this, and would have felt his worst fears realized in the conduct and mind-set of Syed Mahmood. He would also have known or heard of the later intransigencies of Syed Mahmood and the arrogant hostility to him of his Chief Justice, John Edge. Syed Mahmood was ultimately obliged to resign his judgeship.

All this would have amply vindicated Akbar in his own eyes. He would have been galled to see that Mahmood, scion of a distinguished and ancient family, who was brought up according to the best traditions of Indo-Muslim culture, and who had vast knowledge of Urdu, Persian and Arabic, should choose to stress the British side of his personality to the exclusion of the Indo-Muslim one. No wonder that Akbar's short poem on the death of Syed Mahmood in 1903, though briefly elegiac, has a bitter triumphalism too:

> *Neither (Theodore) Beck remains now*
> *Nor Sir Syed: a sigh arises*
> *From the hearts of friends. There was*
> *Some consolation so long as Mahmood*
> *Was there. Today he too departed this world*
> *For paradise. Admonition, weeping, said:*
> *To your senses! Oh you who are greedy*
> *For pomp and power and splendour,*
> *Obliterated is the stamp of Ahmad and Mahmood*
> *'There's no god but God' is all*
> *That remains.* (Akbar Ilahabadi 1936: 185)

Akbar's contradictions, thus, were of his age. And there is no doubt that towards the end of his life, he was groping towards a resolution of his inner paradoxes. He was, in the idiom of the age, a 'government servant' and then a 'pensioner judge' for most of his life, and did not find it in himself to enter active politics in open support of Gandhi and the freedom movement, though he never ceased to attack the British, their government and their cooperationists in no uncertain terms. A poet, after all, is not expected to wield a stick or lead a suicide squad. Many years before *Gandhi Nama*, he wrote in two separate verses:

> *Were Akbar not the Government's concubine,*
> *You would find him too among Gandhi's gopis.*[6]

For himself, Akbar uses the word *mandkhulah*, which means exactly what I say in translation: 'a kept woman'. For Gandhi's followers, he uses the word *gopi*, which means one of the myriad legendary female lovers of Sri Krishna, and thus suggests the extraordinary, almost superhuman charisma that Gandhi possessed. There are other meanings too, but I will mention just one here: Akbar sees Gandhi as the principle of fecundity and creative liberation, and India as the female principle, to be fecundated by Gandhi. Now the other *she'r*:

> *Little Buddhu too is with*
> *The Honourable Mr Gandhi; though he is*
> *But a pinch of dust on the road*
> *He is the storm's companion.*[7]

'Little Buddhu' (*Buddhu Miyan*) is one of Akbar's favourite metaphors for the Indian Muslim. Maulana Muhammad Ali is reported to have been slightly miffed at this *she'r*, suspecting that *'Buddhu Miyan'* here stood for him and that Akbar was making gentle fun of him. Akbar is reported to have disabused Muhammad Ali of this notion. There is a *she'r* in the *Gandhi Nama* which suggests that here *'Buddhu Miyan'* was none other than Akbar himself:

> *The word 'Buddhu Miyan' was actually*
> *A matter of prudence,*
> *What I actually meant it to mean*
> *Is hidden in my heart.* (Akbar Ilahabadi, *Gandhi Nama*: 45)

Akbar did not let *Gandhi Nama* see the light of day. He is reported by Maulvi Qamaruddin Ahmad to have said to him that he regarded open opposition to the British as both harmful and futile. 'And after all, what could my poems achieve, nothing', he is said to have added. Towards the end of his life (in February 1921), he remarked to Qamaruddin that he was not worried about losing his pension. If he wanted to earn money, he could earn more than his pension by devoting himself actively to the cause of the nation. It was just that he did not have the physical health and strength to stand the hardships of jail. He also quite candidly admitted that he did not have the fortitude to oppose the government, and that he was concerned about his son getting into trouble because of his nationalistic poetry (Qamaruddin Ahmad 1940: 146, 163–64, 164n). Yet, in the *Gandhi Nama* he lets himself go, putting the following *she'r* as its epigraph, declaring Firdausi's great epic *Shah Nama* (The Book of Kings)) to be obsolete and abrogated:

> *The revolution is here:*
> *Its New World, a new tumult,*
> *The Book of Kings is done*
> *It's the age of The Book of Gandhi now.* (Akbar Ilahabadi, *Gandhi Nama*: 1)

Akbar was strongly conscious of the immense fascination that the culture of the politically victorious has for the politically vanquished. As numerous examples in contemporary life and letters amply demonstrated, the vanquished people could be made to unconsciously strive for identification with the ruling elite by the insertion of popular and powerful icons of alien culture into their day-to-day life. The pulls and counter-pulls exerted themselves as much, if not more, through culture as through politics. Akbar's great insight was his early identification of the colonizer's culture with his politics, his administration and

his regulations. That is why he replied through his poetry, traditionally the greatest cultural weapon that one could command in Indo-Muslim society. That is
why he equates his *Gandhi Nama,* a series of short or very short and politically
overt poems with the *Shah Nama,* a literary masterpiece of an entirely different
kind. The *Shah Nama* is devoted to acquisition of space, and subjugation of
alien realms and peoples by kings; *Gandhi Nama* essentially celebrates the efforts of a subject people to drive out the conqueror from the space wrongfully
occupied by him.

It is fashionable today for us to talk of cultural and economic colonization of the third world by the capitalist–imperialist west in a post-colonial scenario of globalization. For all its trendiness, this notion of the cultural hegemony
of the west represents hard realities on the ground level in countries like India.
Akbar was, perhaps, the first to appreciate the political power of cultural icons:

> *Though Europe has great*
> *Capability to do war;*
> *Greater still is her power*
> *To do business. They cannot everywhere*
> *Install a gun, but the soap*
> *Made by Pears is everywhere.* (Akbar Ilahabadi 1931: 63)

Improved means of communication go side by side with improved ways
of doing business, and new ways of loving and living:

> *Nowhere now the hands*
> *Of frenzied love tear at the collar*
> *Separating thread from thread;*
> *Now it's Majnun's hands, and The Pioneer,*
> *And news despatched by wire.*
> *Shirin has contracted to supply milk*
> *At the commissariat; and Farhad*
> *Is building a railroad through the mountain.* (Akbar Ilahabadi 1931: 68)

> *Lovers of peris now*
> *Are enchanted by the Ms.*
> *Frenzy once made them rip their clothes*
> *They're now sewing blazers.* (Akbar Ilahabadi 1931: 15)

> *I took her to bed and later*
> *Took my leave, saying:*
> *'Thank you.* (Akbar Ilahabadi 1931: 54)

III

The mode of British rule in India was often described by the British
civil servants themselves as the rule of law, and as benevolent, though despotic.
One of the chief methods of despotism, however benevolent, is a pronounced

propensity for over-regulation. Akbar regarded the constricting effect of British over-regulation as cultural invasion as it forced the people to change their lifestyles. He often uses the English word 'License' as a metaphor for the over-regulation:

> *Eyes*
> *Watching every step,*
> *License*
> *Demanded at every turn,*
> *Oh Akbar, I finally gave up strolling*
> *In the Park.* (Akbar Ilahabadi 1931: 94)

> *Just the license is enough*
> *To give you honour on the road,*
> *Just have a license on you,*
> *Put away the sword.* (Akbar Ilahabadi 1936: 255)

> *Don't ask: 'Are you Piru, or*
> *Are you Harbans?' Whatever*
> *This slave is, he is*
> *Without license.* (Akbar Ilahabadi 1940: 84)

In Akbar's changing world, there is not just the sense of loss at things which are gone; the vanquished and subjugated Indian, becoming a part of the colonial administrative system, tries to out-Herod Herod, and shows himself up as even more oppressive than the British benevolent despot:

> *When buttons were stitched onto the waist-wrap*
> *And western pants grew out of the dhoti,*
> *A corporal and six was posted at every tree,*
> *And a law sprouted in every field.* (Akbar Ilahabadi 1940: 19)

Where Akbar's poetry has seemed most annoying to modern critics is his apparent rejection of even such obviously useful and progressive things as running water supplied to homes through pipes, the printing press, the newspaper and the railway train. A casual reading would indeed leave us puzzled, or sad, at Akbar's refusal to permit, far less welcome, even such essentials of modern life and enlightened living. But Akbar was not, in fact, protesting against the signs of progress: he was protesting against the signs of enslavement, and the destruction of Indian cultural values and lifestyles that such enslavement guaranteed above the putative guarantee of progress and improvement in the quality of life. In addition to the comfort (though it was enjoyable by only a few), he also saw water tax, and stagnating puddles and pollution, accompanying piped water. He saw the disappearance of wells, and the desuetude of the river as a source of water for day-to-day consumption as an undesirable sequel of the establishment of waterworks in the cities. He was also keenly conscious of the adverse environmental and economic effect of the new measures on urban life:

The plague, and the fever, the bug and the mosquito
Are all nurtured in the muck
That surrounds the municipal tap;
The flow from the municipal tap
Is something, cleanliness is
Something else again. (Akbar Ilahabadi 1931: 12)

Tears are such great things:
They do good to the heart's tillage:
Water tax is now proposed
To be levied on the weeping eye. (Akbar Ilahabadi 1931: 85)

Is it the flow and surge
Of civilization or the deluge?
What need is there for the tap
When there's a well in the house? (Akbar Ilahabadi 1940: 13)

The symbolism of the domestic well whose water is native, pure and controlled, against the municipal tap that supplies intermittent water to homes and street-corners, need not be laboured. What is more important to my mind is the cultural effect that the change portended for Akbar. Those of us who are familiar with our folklore about Krishna and Krishna's *gopis* at the well or riverbank, and with songs of drawing and conveying home the water from wells and rivers in general, will easily appreciate the feeling of cultural loss, the sense of desecration and denigration of community values and lifestyle, that commercially controlled and supplied water would have produced in the mind of anyone sensitive to those values.

The well was not just a well in the Indian mind, nor was the river just a river. For one thing, well water and river water was free. Even in the village, where caste segregation was common, those who were entitled to draw water from a well did so without payment, without let or hindrance. Then, both the quality and quantity of the water were within reasonable power of the drawer: it was not like the impersonal, unknown source from which tap water came, and on which there was no control of the consumer in terms of quantity and flow. And, lastly but perhaps most importantly, there was the religious, social and cultural value of the well and the river as a locus for emotional and spiritual commerce.

How important the well was even in large cities like Delhi is reflected in Ghalib's letters. In a letter of 1860–61 to Mir Mehdi Majruh, Ghalib wrote:

Qari's well has dried up. All the wells at Lal Diggi have suddenly become entirely brackish. So one could somehow drink the brackish water, but those wells now yield only warm water. Yesterday I rode out into the city to enquire into the state of the wells. . . . In brief, the city has become a wilderness. And now, if the wells disappear and fresh water becomes rare like a pearl, this city will turn into the wilderness of Karbala. (Khaliq Anjum, ed. 1985: 524)

Such was the state of Delhi after the destruction of buildings and monuments carried out by the British after they reoccupied Delhi in September 1857, and the demolitions effected by them in 1859–61 in the name of modernization and progress. Tap water could not replace all the wells, and was not tax-free like well water, anyway. The drying out or the disappearance of wells was not just inconvenience, it was the prelude to a new kind of dependency, a new kind of life where water could not be drawn at will but had to be awaited; the taps must flow for the water to reach the people. It was no longer a natural resource but a man-made artifact.

Akbar Ilahabadi once recited the following *she'r* of his to Qamaruddin Ahmad:

> None of the taps run, and the house
> Is on fire, one must run now
> There's no more time to think.

He then commented upon the *she'r* as follows:

> Some time ago fire broke out in some shops in the Chowk area. The taps were stopped at that time and the people suffered heavy losses by the fire. I was moved by that thought and composed my *she'r*. What can one say? The Sahib *Rules over food and water*.
> Had the wells been there, as there were in the former times, the fire could have been brought in control in good time. And just look at the altered organization of the cities: the ruling class and the rich are in the Civil Lines, for the poor to eke out their existence, there are squalid pockets of the city, set aside from the rest. The idea is that the rich and the poor should not be in the same place; thus they would have no fellow feeling, no empathy for each other's state.[9]

Rivers were even more dynamic sources of cultural strength and continuity in India. Water from different rivers was believed to have different properties and was valued, in terms of both sanctity and salubriousness. It was not unknown for people to hand-carry on their travels, the water from the Ganga, or any other river that they favoured. Even a hard-headed sultan like Muhammad Tughlaq (r. 1325–51) had his favourite Ganga water carried to him every day, a thousand miles away to the Deccan.[10]

The great Mughal emperor Akbar invariably drank Ganga water and it was carried to him every day, regardless of the distance, when he was far from the river itself. Abul Fazl tells us about waters from the Ganga and other rivers used in the emperor's kitchen.[11]

The Mughals were, in fact, apparently more conscious of issues relating to environment and water pollution than their European counterparts. M. Afzal Khan says that Akbar created the office of water taster on account of his 'predilection for good water'. In the early seventeenth century, we find Jahangir commenting adversely on the Gujarati practice of storing rainwater in underground cisterns (he called them *birka*), saying that water not exposed to fresh air for many months is bound to become unhealthy. He said, 'The evils of water to which air never penetrates and which has no way of releasing the vapour are evident.'[12]

Nearer our time and place, here is Ghalib, eloquently praising the water of the river near Rampur:

> How can I have the tongue to thank God for the water? There is a river, called Kosi. Holy is the Lord! Kosi's water is so sweet that anyone who drank it could imagine it was a lightly sweetened drink: clean, light, easy on the system, digestive, quick to be absorbed in the body.
>
> The water, Holy is the Lord! There is a river, just three hundred paces from the city. It's called Kosi. Doubtless some underground current from the stream of the Elixir of Life is a tributary of it. Well, even if such is the case, the Elixir only extends life, it could never be so sweet.[13]

It was the loss of these protocols and being deprived of these waters and their cultural reverberations that Akbar was lamenting:

> *Obliged to drink water from the tap*
> *And to read texts set in type.*
> *Suffering from the flux*
> *And conjunctivitis; Help!*
> *Oh Good King Edward, help!* (Akbar Ilahabadi 1936: 239)

The supreme irony of the appeal to King Edward VII is too good to need comment. The protest against typesetting the reading material is not just because the typefaces were generally small and harder to read than books calligraphed by expert calligraphers. The matter had to do more with mass production and quality control. In the pre-print age, one often commissioned books to be copied by a calligrapher, and one generally supervised the job personally. On account of the one-time nature of the work, the calligrapher could ensure uniformity of style, ink and general layout of the work that he was producing. More important, the copier or the commissioner made sure, at least in theory, of an error-free copy. With the advent of the printing press and mass production, errors became extremely numerous, for the quality control ensured by the author/commissioner's personal supervision was no longer there. The author or the commissioner of the printed work had no real control over it, but was still held liable for the numerous errors that printed texts now routinely contained.

Ghalib tried to maintain a measure of quality control during the printing of some of his works. His letters on that subject reflect his concern and his anguish over the printer's excesses:

'Let the ink be bright black, and uniform throughout,' Ghalib pleads to Har Gopal Tafta who was supervising the printing of *Dastanbu*.[14] Now this is about an edition of his Urdu *Divan*: 'I saw each and every proof. The copywriter was someone different from the middleman who used to bring the proofs to me.

Now I find all the errors are just as they were. That is, the copywriter didn't incorporate the corrections at all.'[15] In a letter to Junun Barelvi, Ghalib laments that people blame him for typos, and 'do not envisage the possibility of error in printed texts. The poor author is indicted for the copywriter's mistakes.'[16]

Thus, in his mock-protest against the typeset text, Akbar is actually protesting against the culture of mass production which lowers aesthetic standards, makes coldly impersonal what once was a work of art and mindlessly permits errors to proliferate. It is for these reasons that Akbar dislikes photographs and the phonograph too: they separate the subject from his/her attribute. Printed photographs are worse, for they are copies of a copy:

> *Now what occasion could there be*
> *For me to boast about my album?*
> *Your photograph has now become*
> *All too cheap: Even the painter cannot*
> *Have a sight of you. From just a photo*
> *Are now your pictures made.* (Akbar Ilahabadi 1940: 20)

> *Why wonder if my friends*
> *Are parted from me; in the age*
> *Of the phonograph, the voice*
> *Is parted from the throat.* (Akbar Ilahabadi 1940: 10)

A similar tension, or perhaps even worse, prevails with the telephone, for not only is it impersonal, but, in permitting avoidance of eye contact, it makes refusal of requests easy:

> *Now how could one hope*
> *For the eye of compassion, when*
> *The telephone is the only*
> *Means of Conversation?* (Akbar Ilahabadi 1940: 17)

Akbar saw the newspaper too, as a weapon of cultural invasion. He equated British business with British information. Worse still, by virtue of it being a vehicle for the promotion of commerce through advertisement and aggressive salesmanship, the newspaper was also a medium of disinformation. It was culturally deleterious in other ways too: it had immense even if false prestige, and made Indians eager to be seen in print on its pages:

> *Real goods are those that are made in Europe.*
> *Real matter is that which is printed in* The Pioneer. (Akbar Ilahabadi 1931: 62)

> *Okay, so give me nothing from your purse,*
> *But please do print my name in the paper;*
> *Whoever you look for, you find them*
> *Settled at the door of* The Pioneer:
> *For God's sake, Sir, do print me on some page!*

The true state is not hidden
From the eyes of the world:
Print in the paper whatever you please. (Akbar Ilahabadi 1936: 254)

The letter from home says: Yesterday
His fortieth day rites after death
Were done: The Pioneer *reports*
The patient is doing well. (Akbar Ilahabadi 1936: 68)

I have now no desire for Paradise and its Lote tree
Nor do I long for the heavenly spring of Kausar,
I lust only for publication
In The Pioneer. (Akbar Ilahabadi 1936: 226)

Give me too a couple of pages from the paper
But not the one that contains medicine ads.[17]

The last one is particularly interesting. With characteristic astuteness Akbar notes that the newspaper, by printing advertisements, in fact, deviates from its true function. Early newspapers in England were nothing more than accounts of parliamentary debates. It was only in the nineteenth century, in the shadow of the industrial revolution and because of the vast blue-collar readership that the revolution spawned, that newspapers began to contain 'sensational' news stories and reports of crimes, criminal trials and similar juicy stuff. Advertisements came still later, when the industrial revolution led to the assembly line and mass production and glut. Thus the newspaper, from being a politically educative medium, became a player in big business and aggressive salesmanship.

It seems that the feeling that a newspaper was not the proper place or medium for advertisements was shared by a number of Indians in the nineteenth century. Ratan Nath Sarshar's *Fasana-e-Azad* (1880) is a serio-comic narrative of the picaresque type in four volumes. It is not a text notable for being in sympathy with what the author apparently saw as the effete Indo-Muslim culture of the nineteenth century. In what is almost the opening scene of *Fasana-e-Azad*, we find Azad, the main character, talking to a 'nautch girl':

> *Azad*: Today Professor Locke Sahib is to give a lecture on the nobility and superiority of the holy Sanskrit tongue. This revered old gentleman is very holy, pious, a uniquely learned man, unmatched in the present times, and famous through all realms and cities.
> *Chhammi Jan*: May God protect me! Really, by the holy Lord, how uncouth you are. What bad taste indeed! Hey, what's all this about the Professor Sahib being famous? I have grown to this age and put me on oath if I ever at all hear his name. And is he in any case more famous than Dunni Khan? (Sarshar [1850] 1986: 15)

It does not need an Edward Said to read the sub-text here: The worth and value of Sanskrit (read Indian culture) is only as much as is determined by the European (read British) men of learning. Azad represents the modern man who has grasped this truth. The woman (read the effete Indian culture) is perverse and does not awake to its real worth, even when the European (read colonial master) takes pains to study and interpret that culture. In fact, this culture is stupid as well as decadent. It refuses to believe that the learned European savant could be more famous than a local music master.

These were some of the cultural–political presumptions that Akbar had to contend with. Going back to newspapers, later in the *Fasana-e-Azad* we find Bahar, Azad's friend, disapproving the appearance of a 'Situations Vacant' advertisement in a newspaper, and Azad explaining to him the uses of a newspaper:

> *Bahar*: May God grant you success. But say listen, is this not a newspaper? If so, what occasion could there be in it for complications like vacancies, emoluments, applications? A newspaper should contain accounts of battles and wars, or discussion and disputation on matters scientific and political, and not such kinds of complications and fuss.
>
> *Azad*: Then my dear Sir, you never did read a newspaper. Revered Master, a newspaper is an admixture of fragrances. It is the young people's tutor, affectionate adviser to the youth, touchstone of the experience of old men, chief member of the government, friend to the businessman, loyal companion to the manufacturer, advocate of the people, ambassador of the public at large, adviser to policy makers; a column full of banter about the affairs of the country, another column full of disputation on social matters; brilliant poems on some pages, notices and advertisements on another. English newspapers have things of myriad varieties and native papers imitate them. (Ibid.: 163)

Needless to say, here Azad is the modern man; he revels in the salesmanship, the jack-of-all-tradeness and the lack of privacy (note the bit about tutoring and advising the young and the very young) that mark the newspaper. It is for him a replacement for education, and a desirable engine of mind control. And those are precisely the reasons for Akbar's disapproval of the newspaper.

The newspaper, for Akbar, is essentially a materialistic device. (Note the 'this-worldliness' of the typical newspaper's contents listed by Azad to his friend above.) Its main purpose is not education; its main purpose is furtherance of business, and of the administrative and political interests of the colonizer. In a letter to Padam Singh Sharma, Akbar equated the newspaper with many other things which he said were divisive and fissiparous: 'Each and everyone is now absorbed with and drunk upon the wine of self-regard. Council, Committee, Police Station House, Newspaper, these things are everywhere. So what need there is for developing mutual love [between Hindu and Muslim] and practising brotherhood?'[18]

An even stronger embodiment of the British government's cultural/political/economic idea was the railway engine and the goods train:

> *Oh Akbar, those who place*
> *Their faith and trust in the*
> *Goods train, what fear*
> *Could they have of an overload of sin?* (Akbar Ilahabadi 1940: 8)

> *This age is an enemy*
> *To tranquillity and prayer;*
> *There aren't the wanted birds in trees*
> *Nor that youthful lush green look*
> *Upon the jungle. The holy man of the forest*
> *Is not below the railroad;*
> *In place of the tamarind tree, the signal's pole,*
> *And instead of the dove, the railway engine.* (Akbar Ilahabadi 1931: 56)

The poet's environmental concerns are at least as urgent as the cultural ones. Elsewhere, he parodies a famous *she'r* from a *ghazal*:

> *Someone passed this way a little while ago:*
> *The footprint's insolent beauty tells all .*[19]

This delightful verse becomes non-delightful but also somewhat grim parody:

> *A railway engine passed this way*
> *A little while ago. The darkness*
> *Of the air tells all.* (Akbar Ilahabadi 1936: 251)

The railway engine imparts an arrogance, an overweening confidence to modern man:

> *The Shaikh doesn't lend his ear*
> *To the discourse of the New Light,*
> *Blow into his ears the steam*
> *Of the railway engine.* (Akbar Ilahabadi 1936: 254)

> *What does the divine path count for*
> *Before the railway engine?*
> *What does the flute count for*
> *Before the water buffalo?* (Akbar Ilahabadi 1936: 243)

Akbar returned to the theme of railway engine again and again, reserving some of his bitterest satire for it. Clearly, he saw it as an extremely potent medium for exploiting the colonized people and for making a statement of power:

> *This one sweats and is softened*
> *By that one's vapour-steam,*
> *Europe has strapped Asia*
> *To the railway engine.* (Akbar Ilahabadi 1940: 104)

I have refrained from commenting upon the subtlety, the metaphoric reach and the outrageously funny word-play in Akbar's use of language, for it is difficult to put across, far less translate, in English. Yet I cannot resist saying a few words about the above *she'r* where Akbar has outreached even himself. A literal translation of the above-quoted *she'r*'s second *msra'* would be: 'Europe has put Asia to the railway engine.' Here 'put to the railway engine' is like the English 'put to the sword'. Its appropriateness is great because in Urdu one says *talvar/talvaron par rakh lena,* or *talvar/talvaron ki barh par rakh lena* (to put to the sword, or to put to the sharp edge of the sword). And, by extension, we have *banduqon/raiflon ki barh par rakh lena, golion ki barh par rakh lena* (to kill by sustained gunfire). Akbar extends the metaphor further: treating the railway engine as a weapon of destruction, he says, *injan pe rakh liya hai.* The creative ingenuity barely conceals the bitterness implicit in the metaphor.[20]

> Machines edged out the good people;
> Pigeons flew away
> At the hooting of the railway engine. (Akbar Ilahabadi 1931: 46)

> Our young people say:
> In the path of progress we don't need
> The guidance of Khizr over the routes
> Where the railway reaches. (Akbar Ilahabadi 1931: 98)

IV

Akbar Ilahabadi and Muhammad Iqbal are our first, and by far the greatest, post-colonialist writers. Both of them knew intimately the British system of life and thought, and neither found himself much impressed by the west. This is extremely remarkable, given the very nearly unqualified admiration for the west among late nineteenth and early twentieth-century Indian intellectuals.[21] Iqbal had first-hand knowledge of western culture and philosophy, and his opposition to the west was mostly on philosophical and intellectual grounds. Akbar too was not entirely a stranger to western philosophy and scientific thought, as his letters to Abdul Mjid Daryabadi amply demonstrate.[22] But his main concern was about practical matters relating to the social, political and religious issues of modern India. As against Iqbal, who thought he had practical and philosophical solutions to the predicament that the Indian, in general, and the Indian Muslim, in particular, found himself in, Akbar seems to have come to the conclusion that nothing much could be done. The cancer in the Indian body-politic had metastasized everywhere. On 2 November 1912, Akbar wrote to Padam Singh Sharma: 'You know the trend of our times. Avidity for false honour and deleterious pleasures rules everyone's heart. Under the name of national progress and development, effort is being made for things that are certain to cause fragmentation of the society' (Ahmad, ed. 1997: 119).

Some time in 1917, Akbar wrote to Syed Sulaiman Nadvi that the po-

ems were 'not meant to prevent the revolution; they were memorials of the revolution'. Then he quoted the following *she'r* of his:

> *Understand the poetry of Akbar to be*
> *The memorial to revolution:*
> *He well knows that whatever*
> *Was fated to come, couldn't be prevented.*[23]

'Fated to come' is my translation for *'a'hu'i'*, which is also used for
'death'. Akbar's use of it suggests that he regarded the coming as well as the
staying of the new order as inevitable. He felt that he was at best fighting a
rearguard action for an army that had already been routed, for a cause that had
already been given up as lost. This gives a poignancy as well as bitterness to his
voice. His opposition to western values, the western way of governance, and to
the insistence on modernization at the cost of radically modifying or even jetti-
soning the older norms and mores, was not the mindless opposition of a diehard
traditionalist. He certainly wanted his country to become modern and forward-
looking, but not at the price that the British were intent upon exacting: he did not
want the materialism, the commercialism, the Hindu–Muslim divide, the Urdu–
Hindi divide, the over-regulation, the loss of self-respect, the obsolescence of
values, and the perversion of history and religion that the British system of modernization entailed.

   Some of us today might still feel that, in some instances, Akbar Ilahabadi
was over-reacting or simplifying, but there can be no doubting his sincerity and
the basic soundness of his position: he was not against the railway engine, or the
newspaper, or what the British euphemistically described as 'public works, public instruction, public welfare'. He was against the destruction of our culture that
these things entailed, and he was against the political and economic hegemony
that these things stood for. Our subsequent history has vindicated him in many
ways.

   Sadiq-ur-Rahman Kidwai is an Urdu critic who takes Akbar's laughter
seriously. He says that when Akbar laughed at himself, the laughter was that of
the defeated person whose sense of defeat underlies his laughter, but there is also
the knowledge deep in him somewhere that his 'seemingly successful adversaries
were destined to face a worse defeat' (Kidwai 1999: 83–84). This may be stretching things a bit, for one need not credit Akbar with a prescience that he does not
need in order to be recognized as a great poet, but no doubt, his poetry, for all its
bitterness of defeat, does have the air of having been produced by a robust mind
and spirit. In his encounter with the new age, Akbar was no wilting lily.

   Ralph Russell also seems inclined to find in Akbar something of an image of his own cool and rationalistic mind when he says that Akbar Ilahabadi is
'a poet who looks at the conflict between the New Light and the Old, but refuses
to give indiscriminate support to either' (Russell 1995: 200). He and Kurshid-ul-
Islam are nearer the mark when they say that Akbar is *not* the wooden, unimagi-
native, obstinate conservative that some have made him out to be. . . . Essen-

tially, he is a man intensely aware of change, and the irresistibility of change'
(Russell and Khurshid-ul-Islam 1992: 175; italics as in the original).

The impression that Akbar's poetry finally leaves us with is that of a
poet who was sharply aware of the political import of things, of a person of great
wit and humour who wrote humorous and satirical poetry on social, cultural and
political issues with an almost unbelievable felicity of language and fertility of
invention. Also, even those who do not agree with his message cannot fail to be
struck by Akbar's passionate love for his country, and his intense dislike, even
contempt, of the west. During their early encounters with India, westerners often
described Indians as fastidious and proud, even arrogant, given to looking down
upon westerners. All this disappears by about the third quarter of the nineteenth
century. Most Indians, and certainly the intellectuals, now began sincerely to
believe that the intellectual, moral and artistic superiority of the Europeans,
especially the British, could not be overemphasized. Akbar Ilahabadi and Sir
Muhammad Iqbal stand out as exceptions in our literary history. Perhaps Akbar
disliked the European even more than Iqbal. There was certainly more pain and
overt passion in Akbar.

Akbar has a number of delightful verses on the Darwinian theory of
evolution which stipulates that man developed from the primates, and nothing
shows up his contempt for the European better than those poems:

Mansur said: I am God,
Darwin called out: And I, a monkey
A friend of mine laughed and said,
Everyone thinks up
According to his/her reach. (Akbar Ilahabadi 1940: 140–41)

The original is a four-line poem and its last line has been merrily appropriated from a *ghazal* by the great Hafiz Shirazi (1325?–98):

You, my friend are absorbed
In the thought of the tree of Paradise,
And I, in the thought of her noble stature,
Everyone thinks up
According to his/her reach. (Divan-e-Hafiz Shirazi 1949: 27)

A more delightful use of a love-poetry text for entirely non-love purposes
cannot be imagined. Akbar was, in fact, extremely skilful in making such appro-
priations. He routinely parodied poems and well-known phrases from prose texts,
or quoted them out of context, to create incongruity which is the soul of humour.

Coming back to Darwin, Qamaruddin Ahmad quotes from Akbar's conversation of 28 January 1921:

If Darwin's theory is correct and the primate was man's ancestor, the Europeans
at this stage of their civilization should have exemplified numerous high qualities of humanity. But I am sorry to see that such is not the case:

What kind of monkey are these, oh Lord?
They evolved and yet didn't become human.[24]

The wheel here has come full circle in the poetry of Akbar Ilahabadi: instead of the European looking down upon the Indian, it is now the Indian again who looks down upon the European.

Akbar was conscious of his status as a poet. He rarely acknowledged anyone's superiority or precedence in finding themes and images (Qamaruddin Ahmad 1940: 217–18). Later generations may have become inclined to dismiss him as a 'joking poet', but he knew his own greatness and rightly regarded himself as an artist with a serious purpose.

Akbar Ilahabadi may have been a blind enemy of progress and enlightenment, as many Urdu critics today believe (though wrongly, as I hope I have shown above), but apparently he had more self-respect and national pride than his denigrators. As a poet, he had a keen eye for detail, extremely sharp wit, a marvellous ear for Urdu poetry's rhythms and a technical mastery that could be rivalled in his time by Iqbal alone. As an observer and commentator of contemporary life, he evinced an intellectual vigour, an icy scorn and a searing anger which was unmatched in Urdu poetry since, at least, the eighteenth century. As a poet and a colonized Indian, he refused to be browbeaten by the promulgators of the new culture and power.

In spite of all this, his was a sad spirit. The loss of his history and culture was heavy over him, especially with the realization that he too was, in some sense, part of the forces that were taking away his heritage. Perhaps this *she'r* should stand as the most appropriate epitaph for him:

If you pass by this way you'll see
My village, laid waste
A broken mosque, and by its side
A British barracks. (Akbar Ilahabadi 1931: 48)

Note: Urdu and Persian texts have been translated into English by the author himself.

Notes

1. See Preface in Ahmad, ed. (1997: 18). This collection of Akbar Ilahabadi's letters was first published from Lahore by Muhammad Nasir Humayun, with a preface by Sir Shaikh Abdul Qadir. Sahil Ahmad has reissued it with additions and copious notes.
2. Iqbal's letter to Akbar Ilahabadi, dated 17 December 1914, in Barni, ed. (1991: 320).
3. 'Closing the eyes of modesty and opening the mouth of shamelessness, he [Sauda] said such wild things that even Satan would ask for a truce.' Azad (2001: 153)
4. A similar tendency to harbour self-contradiction can be seen in Akbar Ilahabadi's religious beliefs. He himself was a devout Sunni but his second wife, whom he loved to the exclusion of the first, was Shi'a. Still, he seems to have become more and more anti-Shi'a with age. On the other hand, he married his son Ishrat Husain to a Shi'a girl whose father was originally a Sunni but had converted to Shi'ism after taking a Shi'a wife. Akbar used to be exercised at rumours that Ishrat too had converted to Shi'ism. Ishrat Husain denied this to his father in a letter to him, written in English. Once Akbar requested the famous jurist and scholar Sir Shah Muhammad Sulaiman to

advise Ishrat Husain that he desist from imbibing the influence of Shi'ism. Shah Sulaiman gave an ambiguous reply, saying, 'I'll comply with this request of yours only when you broach the issue in Ishrat's presence.' Akbar wanted Muhammad Aqil, one of Ishrat Husain's sons, to go to the Nadva at Lucknow, a manifestly Sunni educational institution. Nothing seems to have come of this proposal. See Qamaruddin Ahmad (1940: 25, 27, 161) and Ahmad, ed. (1997: 24–25).

[5] See Lelyveld (2001).

[6] Quoted in Qamaruddin Ahmad (1940: 158). Akbar did not put this *she'r* in his *Kulliyat*, for obvious reasons, yet it is one of his most famous verses.

[7] Qamaruddin Ahmad (1940: 64). Akbar did not include this *she'r* too in his *Kulliyat*.

[8] Thank You' in English in the original.

[9] Qamaruddin Ahmad (1940: 132–33). The *she'r* in question is to be found in Akbar Ilahabadi (1940: 42). The line of verse that occurs in Akbar's conversation is in Akbar Ilahabadi (1940: 130).

[10] 'In 1327 when Sultan Muhammad Tughlaq established Daulatabad as the second capital of the Sultanate, he ordered Ganges water to be carried to Daulatabad, a distance of forty days' journey from North India, for his personal use.' See Ibn-e-Battuta (1953: 4).

[11] 'Whether at camp or on march, His Majesty drinks Ganges water. . . . In the cooking of food, water from the Jamna, and Chenab, and rainwater is used, mixed with a little of Ganga water.' Abul Fazl, *The A'in-e-Akbari*, Vol. I, edited by H. Blochmann, p. 51; reproduced in Moosvi (1998: 100). I am obliged to Professor N.R. Farooqi of the University of Allahabad for the information about Muhammad Tughlaq and the citation from Abul Fazl.

[12] Afzal Khan (2002: 104–05). I am grateful again to Professor N.R. Farooqi for bringing this text to my attention.

[13] Letter dated February 1860 to Hakim Ghulam Najaf Khan, and letter dated February 1860 to Mir Mehdi Majruh, in Khaliq Anjum, ed. (1985: 630, 517).

[14] Letter dated 7 September 1858, in Khaliq Anjum, ed. (1984: 292).

[15] Letter dated 8 August 1861 to Mir Mehdi Majruh, in Khaliq Anjum, ed. (1985: 521).

[16] Letter dated 8 May 1864, in Khaliq Anjum (1993: 1511). Note that for the calligrapher employed at the press, Ghalib consistently uses the term 'copywriter' (*copy nigar* in the original); he does not consider him a proper calligrapher, far less a calligrapher-artist, such as were people like Navab Fakhruddin Khan, Ghalib's regular calligrapher. I may mention here in passing that calligraphy was one of the noble arts in pre-modern India; Bahadur Shah Zafar himself was a calligrapher of excellence.

[17] Kidwai, ed. (1984: 153). This *she'r* does not find place in the *Kulliyat*.

[18] Letter dated 9 February 1913, in Ahmad, ed. (1997: 126).

[19] This is an extremely famous *she'r* but its provenance is not quite settled. Many people regard Hakim Momin Khan (1800–52) as its author. But it doesn't find a place in Momin's *Divan*. Arsh Gayavi relates an anecdote according to which the second *misra'* of the *she'r* was composed by Mir Husain Taskin, a disciple of Momin, who then composed the second *misra'* and gave it away to Taskin. See Arsh Gayavi (1990: 40). The book was originally published in AH 1347 [1928–29].

[20] A.A. Surur has commented upon Akbar's artistry and his brilliant use of language. This, according to Surur, is in itself justification enough for us to continue reading his poetry. See Surur (1996: 70–71).

[21] Iqbal's long Persian poems *Asrar-e-Khudi* and *Rumuz-e-Bekhudi*, translated into English by R.A. Nicholson, had been well received in the west. Akbar wrote to Sir Shaikh Abdul Qadir on 21 April 1921:
'I value Iqbal not because he is well thought of in the court of the West:
I desire a glance from my own heart,
I am not crazy about the adulation
Of friend or foe.'
See Ahmad, ed. (1997: 115–16). I could not find this *she'r* in the *Kulliyat*.

[22] In Ahmad (1997: 144–90).

[23] Ahmad, ed. (1997: 36–37). This *she'r* is to be found in Akbar Ilahabadi (1931: 83).

²⁴ Qamaruddin Ahmad (1940: 165). This *she'r* is not included in the *Kulliyat*. This must
have been an omission and not a suppression, or Akbar may have intended to put it in
his projected Volume IV of the *Kulliyat*.

References

Ahmad, Sahil, ed. (1997), *Ruqa'at-e-Akbar* (Allahabad: The Urdu Writers' Guild).
Akbar Ilahabadi (1931), *Kulliyat*, Vol. II (Lucknow: Adabi Press).
—— (1936), *Kulliyat*, Vol. I (Allahabad: Asrar-e-Karimi Press).
—— (1940), *Kulliyat*, Vol. III (Allahabad: Asrar-e-Karimi Press).
Akbar Ilahabadi, *Gandhi Nama*.
Ansari, A.A., ed. (2001), *Sir Syed Ahmad Khan, A Centenary Tribute* (Delhi: Adam Publications).
Arsh Gayavi (1990), *Hayat-e-Momin*, facsimile edition in a special number of 'Nigar-e-Pakistan', Karachi, August, edited by Farman Fatehpuri.
Azad, Muhammad Husain (2001), *Ab-e-Hayat*, translated by Frances Pritchett in association with Shams-ur-Rahman Faruqi (New Delhi: Oxford University Press).
Barni, Muzaffar Husain, ed. (1991), *Kulliyat-e-Makatib-e-Iqbal*, Vol. I (New Delhi: Delhi Urdu Academy).
Divan-e-Hafiz Shirazi (1328 / AD 1949) (Tehran: Shirkat-e-Nasabi Kanun-e-Kitab).
Ibn-e-Battuta (1953), *Rehla*, translated by Agha Mahdi Husain (Baroda: The Oriental Institute).
Khaliq Anjum, ed. (1984), *Ghalib ke Khutut*, Vol. I (New Delhi: The Ghalib Institute).
—— (1985), *Ghalib ke Khutut*, Vol. II (New Delhi: The Ghalib Institute).
—— (1993), *Ghalib ke Khutut*, Vol. IV (New Delhi: The Ghalib Institute).
Khan, Afzal M. (2002), 'Environment and Pollution in Mughal India', *Islamic Culture*, Vol. LXXVI, No. 1, January.
Kidwai, Sadiq-ur-Rahman, ed. (1984), *Intikhab-e-Akbar Ilahabadi* (New Delhi: Maktaba Jami'a).
—— (1999), 'Poet Who Laughed in Pain: Akbar Ilahabadi', in Oesterheld and Zoller, eds, (*Of Clowns and Gods, Brahmans and Babus.*).
Lelyveld, David (2001), 'Macaulay's Curse, Sir Syed and Syed Mahmood', in Ansari, ed., *Sir Syed Ahmed Khan.*.
Moosvi, Shireen (1998), *Episodes in the Life of Akbar: Contemporary Records and Reminiscences* (New Delhi: National Book Trust).
Oesterheld, Christina and Claus Peter Zoller, eds, (1999), *Of Clowns and Gods, Brahmans and Babus* (New Delhi: Manohar).
Qamaruddin Ahmad Badayuni (1940), *Bazm-e-Akbar* (Delhi: Anjuman Taraqqi-e-Urdu [Hind]).
Russell, Ralph (1992), *The Pursuit of Urdu Literature: A Select History* (London: Zed Books).
—— (1995), *Hidden in the Lute* (New Delhi: Viking).
Russell, Ralph and Khurshid-ul-Islam, 'The Satirical Verse of Akbar Ilahabadi', in Russell, *The Pursuit of Urdu Literature*.
Sarshar, Ratan Nath ([1880]1986), *Fasana-e-Azad*, Vol. I (New Delhi: National Council for the Promotion of Urdu).
Surur, A.A. (1942), 'Akbar, Shakhsiyat aur Art', in his *Tanqidi Ishare* (Aligarh: Nazir Ahmad and Sons).
—— (1996), 'Akbar Ilahabadi ki Ma'aviyat'.
—— (1996), *Kuch Khutbe Kuch Maqale* (Aligarh: Educational Book House).

The Hegemony of English and Modern Indian Literatures

Sisir Kumar Das

The English language in India is one of the greatest ironies of our contemporary history. It was the language introduced to us by our foreign masters little more than two hundred years ago, and by now it is the only language which unifies the whole of India. It is the mother tongue of many Indians and certainly the first language of a large number of people in the country. It is the language of the Indian elite, a language through which the national movement was propelled, and it is through this language our scholars and leaders spoke to the world about the greatness of our civilization. Most of the modern Indian literatures have received stimulus from English literary traditions; our critical literature still follows the canons set by the English language; our creative literature responds to every movement in the west. During the last two hundred years or so, we have also created a body of literature in the English language which claims international distinction, and, in fact, it is often considered by many, both in India and abroad, as the only true representative of Indian literature.

In some sense, English has become to many modern Indians what Sanskrit was to ancient India or Persian to medieval India. The number of speakers of English in India is not as large as that of speakers of most of our major languages, but English is spread all over the country cutting across the boundaries of states, and is spoken by the people who dominate our political, economic and intellectual life. There is hardly any educated Indian today capable of speaking his mother tongue without using English with ease and fluency. Rarely, rarely indeed, has such a thing happened in the history of any other people, where a foreign language has so completely overpowered it, dominating as it does, all walks of its life.

We know that the history of the spread of the English language was a part of the colonial project. Macaulay made the policy quite clear when he wrote: 'We must, at present, do our best to form a class who may be interpreters between us and the millions whom we govern; a class of persons, Indian in blood and colour, but English in taste, in opinions, in morals and in intellect.' The

Fifteenth Zakir Husain Memorial Lecture, 18 February 2003.

English education undoubtedly helped the creation of that class of people but Macaulay's dream of an anglicized Indian was only partly fulfilled. He did not realize that not only would one section of the group of English-educated people launch a movement against British rule in India, but even claim cultural superiority over the British. Many of these 'interpreters' were our cultural heroes.

However, the hegemony of English that was created in the nineteenth century, more precisely from 1835, was not exclusively through coercion or direct imposition of ruling ideas, but, to use the words of Gramsci, 'by winning and shaping consent so that the power of the dominant classes [in this case the power of the foreign government] appears both legitimate and natural'.

When English appeared in India, very few Indians, if at all, were aware of its rich literary and intellectual traditions. It did not come to us as the language of Shakespeare and Milton, but as the language of the East India Company. But a handful of Indians who came to the proximity of the traders and Company officers were quick to realize the economic prospects that the English language promised. Indians with a smattering of English became the subject of various amusing anecdotes. The Company took several decades to adopt a clear-cut language policy. Charles Grant and Lord Wellesely represented two distinct views in respect of the introduction of the English language in India, which resulted in the emergence of two contending groups – the Orientalists and the Anglicans. The latter ultimately triumphed in 1835, the year when Macaulay prepared his historic Minute. By the time English replaced Persian as the language of the court and administration, there was already a public opinion welcoming the change. Not only did an influential section of the Indian community want their children to be educated in English, but Ram Mohan Roy, in a letter to Lord Amherst in 1823, criticized the intention of the government to establish a Sanskrit College, and wanted the government to seriously consider 'to instruct the natives of India in Mathematics, Natural Philosophy, Chemistry, Anatomy and other useful sciences which the nations of Europe had carried to a degree of perfection that has raised them above the inhabitants of other parts of the world'. It is important to know that Roy was a distinguished Sanskrit scholar of his time and was also well-known for his learning in Persian–Arabic studies. Yet it appears that he pleaded very strongly indeed for the introduction of English education. 'If it had been intended to keep the British nation in ignorance of real knowledge,' wrote Roy,

> the Baconian philosophy would not have been allowed to displace the system of Schoolman, which was the best calculated to perpetuate ignorance. In the same manner, the Sanskrit system of education would be best calculated to keep this country in darkness if such had been the policy of the British Legislature.

Ram Mohan Roy did not talk about the English language as such. But twelve years later, when Macaulay pleaded for the introduction of English education as a corrective to 'false history, false astronomy and false medicine', he obviously emphasized the importance of the English language as opposed to

Sanskrit or Arabic or Persian. 'I have no knowledge of either Sanskrit or Arabic', wrote Macaulay. Yet, with unbelievable vehemence he declared, 'A single shelf of a good European library was worth the whole native literature of India and Arabia.' This arrogance never died out completely and has often surfaced, in a slightly different tone, even after fifty years of India's independence. Macaulay was certain about one thing. 'As at the close of the fifteenth and the beginning of the sixteenth century, all that was worth reading was contained in the writing of ancient Greeks and Romans', and 'what the Greek and Latin were to the contemporaries of More and Ascham, our tongue is to the people of India'. This was accepted by a powerful section of educated Indians in the nineteenth century, and this view of the superiority of the English language got strengthened throughout the colonial period; the number of Macaulayan children was so big and so strong at the time of independence that the possibility of discontinuance of English appeared absolutely absurd, if not suicidal. It was almost like dismantling the very mechanism that had kept the country politically and culturally united, and modernized it. The English language was allowed to continue.

But the English language, in fact any language, is not a neutral system of communication alone. It is a part of a value system, a carrier of a thousand thoughts and memories. With the continuance of the English language, the values it represented throughout the colonial period got perpetuated, its modernizing power notwithstanding. One of the most conspicuous features in the Indian literary history of the colonial period is the growth of Indian writings in English. This literature was born much before 1835, which is the official date of the introduction of English in India. The proto-history of this literature goes back to the first decade of the nineteenth century when Cavelley Venkata Boriah wrote *Accounts of Jains* in English in 1803. The second decade belongs almost entirely to Ram Mohan Roy who translated several Upanishads from Sanskrit, and wrote prolifically on social and religious issues. However, the Indian English writings were not confined to discursive prose alone. By 1830, Indians had experimented with poetry and drama as well, whatever be their quality. This body of writing was considered more as a literary curiosity than as something serious, more as an adventure than as an achievement. Despite being written in the prestigious language of the masters, the new literature hardly received respect either from the Indian readers or from the English critics, with occasional exceptions. Things changed, and changed very radically indeed, after independence, with the valorization of English in India and its transformation into a global language. Never before in the history of Indian literature of the last two centuries or so, had the Indian language literatures faced a situation which reinforced the hegemony of the English language and consequently of Indian writings in English.

The writers' meet at Neemrana Fort Palace in Rajasthan, organized by the Indian Council for Cultural Relations last year, brought together a large number of distinguished writers in Indian languages as well as in English. Sir Vidia Naipaul, a writer of Indian ancestry, was the star attraction in this gala gathering. In such conferences, writers in Indian languages hardly feel comfortable. It is not because of their inadequate command over the English language, which is naturally the language of communication in such an assembly, but more because of the relative obscurity of Indian language writers. Their reputation is more or less confined within their respective language areas, and many of them are not available in English translation. Any conversation between a writer in an Indian language and an Indian writer in English, not to speak of international celebrities like Sir Vidia or Salman Rushdie, is an exercise in embarrassment. The Indian writer is hardly known: he/she writes in a 'regional language' for a 'regional market'.

We do not know whether the Neemarana meet, where Sir Vidia was the chief attraction, generated enough light and heat to illumine the areas of darkness in our literary life. But what is beyond doubt is that it brought out the existing cleavage between the two groups of writers: one writing in English, a global language, and the other writing in the Indian languages, the *bhashas*. Mamoni Raicham Goswami, an immensely popular Assamese writer and recipient of the Jnanapith Award, the most prestigious literary prize of the country, said rather bitterly, 'There is nothing common between us, they write in English and we in the "regional" languages. We are different, our worlds are different.' Similar expressions of disquiet were also heard from several other writers including Mahasweta Devi, one of our tallest literary figures. The reference to this government-sponsored literary *mela* is not to malign either the sponsor or writers in the English language. Any comparative judgement of the relative merit of the two streams of literature, one in the Indian languages and the other in English, is outside the scope of this paper and beyond my capacity. This is only to underline a deep-rooted perception about these literatures present among our writers. This perception of difference can be further extended to larger spheres of life as well. This is what we have inherited from our colonial history, and it has assumed a new dimension in the post-colonial period.

No one can deny that there is a hierarchy among the Indian languages and consequently among the literatures produced in them. In a country like India, where several hundred languages are spoken – some by a vast number of people and some by less than a million, some with an unbroken literary tradition through the centuries and some almost without any written literary heritage – the hierarchy among them seems to be almost natural, at least as an unavoidable necessity. This is not because of any inherent flaw in their structures or any deficiency in their relative expressive power. Edward Sapir's words are worth remembering: 'Both simple and complex types of language of an indefinite number of varieties may be spoken at any desired level of cultural advance. When it comes to linguistic forms, Plato walks with the Macedonian swineherd, Confucius with the head-hunting savage of Assam.' They are all equal systems of communication and have the potentiality to cope with any situation of socio-economic development. However, every society always makes a distinction between languages and claims the superiority of one language over the other, mainly on the criteria of the economic and cultural progress of the speakers of that language.

This is clear in the case of the relationship between the standard language and the dialects. It is the power of the speakers that privileges a particular language. It is possible for a Clytemnestra to ridicule the language of Cassandra as 'strange and outlandish' even as a swallow's (*Agamemnon* 1050–51), and for the Greeks to call the speech of all non-Greeks *barboros*. The language of the rulers has either replaced a language from its position of eminence or relegated it to a subservient status. Its implications can be understood from the larger framework of hegemony. In fact, all languages operate under a hegemonic condition and that condition exists among the Indian languages too.

We have recognized the multilingual reality of our country, as well as the existing hierarchy among the languages in terms of their relative usefulness and areas of operation. The Constitution of India recognizes eighteen languages as national languages. One among them is Sanskrit. The criterion for selection of Sanskrit is not the number of speakers but its role in history. It is a befitting tribute to a great language, one of the greatest in human civilization. I am aware that a few thousand people have declared Sanskrit as their mother tongue. (A few years ago I saw a programme on television which informed us of the existence of a village in Kerala, a linguistic Shangrila, where everybody speaks this ancient tongue – not only scholars but the postman, the milkman, the grocer and the fisherman as well.) Apart from the major languages like Hindi, Telugu, Bengali and others recognized by the Indian Constitution, a few more languages have been recognized by the Sahitya Akademi. Prizes are given to writers in these languages. But there are many more which are yet to get recognition, either from the government or from learned bodies. Many of them are known as tribal languages. Writing has been introduced in them only recently, though some of them possess a substantial body of literature which is transmitted and preserved orally. Among such languages are Bhili, Gondi, Tulu, Santhali and Orao, which are spoken by more than one million people. Educated Indians are hardly aware of their existence, as most of the speakers of these languages are obliged to speak one of the major languages spoken in the area. Barring a few, most of these languages are dying slowly, and, by the end of the century, many of them will be extinct. David Crystal, in his work, *Language Death* (Cambridge University Press, 2001) informs that of the 6,703 languages of the world, the existence of almost half is threatened, and this a mainly because of a hegemonic language.

In a multilingual society, languages cannot operate in isolation. A hierarchy is constructed among them so that every language can find a distinctive role for itself. Before the introduction of English as the language of administration and higher education, different regions of India had their own linguistic hierarchy. The *bhashas*, that is, the languages of the people, were the languages of the private sphere, while the hegemonic languages – Sanskrit, Arabic and Persian – were of the public sphere. This may be too simple a generalization (as several languages – Tamil, Marathi, Assamese and Urdu – were also employed in public spheres in varying degrees), but pre-English India had maintained a three-tiered hierarchical situation: one language for religion, one for higher education and administration, and one for communication at an intimate level. This may be called a functional hierarchy which had accommodated several languages within it.

The hegemony of Sanskrit had been challenged, from time to time, by Pali and Arddha Magadhi in the ancient period. In the medieval period, younger languages, from time to time, tried to construct a counter-hegemony. Kabir describes Sanskrit as *Kupajal* (water of the well) while the *bhashas*, according to him, are 'the flowing water', almost anticipating as it were, the Bakhtinian ideas of monologism and dialogism, respectively. The Bhakti poets of Tamil Nadu created a vast body of poetic literature in Tamil, which became almost a metaphor for Siva. The hegemony of Sanskrit certainly created distinct stylistic stratifications which can be identified with reference to occupation, social status and gender. It must be remembered that except for Tamil, whose literary history goes back to the first century AD, if not earlier, all the other living Indian languages continued to experiment with the foreign language. It might have promised them a much wider audience, not only outside their respective language area within India, but also, with a bit of luck, outside the country. It was not only a choice between the mother tongue and the acquired tongue, but also between an international language and what was known in those days as vernaculars. Modern Indian literature grew more or less simultaneously with Indian English literature: one with the patronage of a vast number of peoples, and sustained by a many-centuries-old tradition or multiplicity of traditions; the other in search of a heritage as well as a well-defined market. The new literature was yet not very clear about its clientele. Was it for Indians or for Englishmen? For a certain period of time, it was considered as an offshoot of English literature, or an Anglo-Indian literature. English critics, of course, hardly cared for this Indian adventure in English. Occasional praises for a Toru Dutt or a Sarojini Naidu by English critics did not give this literature any special distinction. Till the time of the intense nationalist movement, the Indian English writer had almost no relation with the Indian language literature; Indian language writers, too, did not consider Indian English to be anything more than a substandard literature which was neither Indian nor English. It was the period of valorization of the mother tongue, a metonymy for the motherland, and the patriotic Indian even thought, rather unfairly, that its spirit was against nationalism. Soon after the publication of R.K. Narayan's *The Bachelor of Arts*, Pudumaippittan, the avant-garde Tamil short story writer, wrote:

> All Tamil people can take pride in what Shri R.K. Narayan has achieved. He has written a novel in English, called *The Bachelor of Arts*, which has been much acclaimed in England. However, it is to be regretted that an author who has been praised highly by renowned writers and critics such as E.M. Forster should remain a foreigner in his own land, Tamil Nadu. I admit that it is a great skill to be able to use a foreign language with complete ease. But it can be no more than an acquired dexterity, rather like a circus feat. The thoughts which are closest to

the life and being of a people can only be expressed in the language that is closest to their hearts. That alone becomes literature. However fine a testimony *The Bachelor of Arts* might be to Shri Narayan's skill, the story it tells will remain counterfeit. That is to say, Shri Narayan's attempt has only been to look at our country through English eyes.

I do not want to comment whether these observations are just or not. But they are important, coming as they do, from an extremely talented Tamil writer whose respect for R.K. Narayan is beyond doubt. The Indian writer's critical paradigm was conditioned by the dialectics of mother tongue and acquired tongue, between a national language and a foreign language. It was difficult for him to accept Indian English literature as a part of Indian literature.

There was a significant change in the status of English in India after 1947. The reorganization of the states created a new space for the Indian languages, and, almost simultaneously, there was a reinforcement of English too. The linguistic history of the last fifty years in India is a strange record of simultaneous attempts to empower the Indian languages and to perpetuate the hegemony of English. The class that Macaulay wanted to create has been finally born. The difference between the group that Macaulay thought would act as interpreters between India and England, and the group of the anglicized generation that emerged after independence, is that the new generation did not feel any linguistic tension in respect of their choice of language. Early Indian writers of English knew their mother tongue. The post-independence writers of English are monolinguals and, being a part and parcel of the elite, they have nothing to interpret. India, for them, is a subject, and a saleable one, in the international market.

The growth of a new English writing in India partly coincides with the recognition of the diverse varieties of English and the challenges to the centrality of British English, the English of the empire. It is significant to note that Robert Burchfield, the man who revised the Oxford Dictionary of English and compiled a four-volume supplement, quotes Salman Rushdie's pronouncement that 'English is no longer an English language, it now grows from many roots', as the epigraph in the first chapter of his book, *The English Language* (Oxford University Press, 1986). Indian English, along with other varieties such as African English, is no longer a substandard register of the British language but a legitimate style in its own right. English has become a world language par excellence. In a situation like this, the relation between English and the Indian languages is getting more and more precarious; it is clearly a pronounced struggle between a woolly cosmopolitanism and a vibrant parochialism, and between the global and the local. This is the time when a new generation of writers in English has emerged in India. Some of them are known as the Stephanian novelists, those who have announced their exalted presence in India thanks to the blessings of their foreign publishers. The globalization of the English language and the patronage of foreign publishers have greatly contributed to their success. Whatever be the merit of the new crop of writing, its social base is incredibly narrow. As Professor Harish Trivedi observes, 'Those who know only English are writing about only the tiny "English-medium fraction" of our vast and wide society.' In fact, one can go a step further in identifying the mark that separates contemporary Indian English writing, the absence of awareness of the vast and wide society that is ours. 'I write for Indians like myself', says Shashi Tharoor. In fact, that all writers do. But what makes their writing abiding is the very awareness of the vast and wide society in which they live. Despite its glamour and sophistication, Indian English writing is yet to acquire the status of a representative Indian literature. Unfortunately, however, it is often mistaken as the most important one and, at times, as the true representative of Indian literature, by the western world, because it is written in English.

Whether Indians will write in English or not is not a serious problem. Some Indians will write in English as a matter of choice. Some will write in English because they have no choice. The main problem is how to negotiate the hegemony of English. African writers like Ngugi or Chinua Achebe have tried to evolve their own strategies, the former by bidding farewell to English ('From now on it is Gikuyu and Kiswahili all the way'), and the latter by making English a different language ('A new language that will be able to carry the weight of my African experience'). I do not know whether our writers in English will follow them or not. We have a large number of languages, most of them nearly one thousand years old, with an uninterrupted literary history – carriers of myths and legends, memories of intense suffering and moments of great exaltation of our people. The question is, how long are they going to survive. Many languages, some of which were widespread, have died in the past, and there is no reason why some other languages will not meet a similar fate. With their vast number of speakers, our major languages do not have the fear of immediate extinction, but the gradual shrinkage of their spheres of operation is a matter of serious concern.

All over the world, there is a play of contradictory forces. While declaring Twenty-First February as Mother Language Day, the Secretary General of the United Nations, in his message declared: 'In an age of globalization and international cooperation, where a few languages have become global languages, it is imperative that we uphold the diversity of local languages.' The very epithets *global* and *local, national* and *regional, international* and *provincial, metropolitan* and *vernacular,* which have been used from time to time to designate languages, are all value-loaded terms, indicating the hegemony of English and the subservient status of the Indian languages. History also abounds in instances of struggles of languages against hegemony to assert their position. The case of Catalan or Galaico-Portuguese or Basque struggling to find a place in the Spanish-speaking world is probably only too well known. The strength of the Indian languages in their struggle against the hegemony of English is in their deeply rooted relations with a vast number of people and large territories. But the ultimate importance of a language depends not on the number of its speakers alone, or on the largeness of the area where it is spoken, not even on the philosophical and literary works written in it, but on its affiliation with political and military power. In this struggle of survival, our languages and literatures are almost defenceless.

Language is important to men for two main reasons: one, it gives them a sense of identity, two, its utility. Naturally, a global language, or what Harish Trivedi calls 'a multinational language', is more useful than an Indian language. If knowledge of English becomes a passport to high positions in life, why take the trouble to learn a language only for the sake of identity? A thoughtless journey towards a state of being free from the markers of identity, language being only one of them, is the greatest danger faced by all the Indian languages.

Globalization and Education

Defining the Indian Crisis

Anil Sadgopal

I have spent the best years of my life – almost twenty years – as a social activist in rural areas of Madhya Pradesh, working towards social transformation through education. It is only during the last decade that I got an opportunity to look at education in an academic perspective, rather than perceiving it primarily as an area of activism. This recent experience has made me realize that my earlier deep involvement with the Hoshangabad Science Teaching Programme in government upper primary schools, with rural development issues, with the people's science activities or with the struggle of the victims of the Bhopal gas disaster for justice, did not equip me with adequate intellectual tools for analysing education and its socio-political context. Yet, without this grassroots experience, my academic work would have lacked the necessary insight. To add to my travails is the fact that my university education was in science, and doctoral dissertation in molecular biology and biochemistry, which could hardly be an acceptable initiation into social science. This severe academic lacuna in my life – or if you permit me to take the liberty of calling it so, a sort of 'knowledge disorientation' – was partly made up by the opportunity the Government of India gave me twice to get involved in analysing the Indian education scenario and national education policies. This was first as a member of the National Commission on Teachers (the Chattopadhyaya Commission), in 1983–84, and then as a member of the National Policy on Education 1986 Review Committee (the Acharya Ramamurti Committee), in 1990. Both of these engagements were intense lessons for me to learn policy analysis, to begin with by evolving a methodology and a political perspective for undertaking analysis, and later using the analysis to 'read along as well as between the lines', thereby revealing the mind of the state and the social forces influencing it.

During the last thirteen years, I have focused attention on the impact of globalization on Indian education policy, especially in the area of elementary education. Incidentally, this concern allowed me to sharpen my tools of policy analysis and evolve an analytical framework for viewing policy changes. I

Sixteenth Zakir Husain Memorial Lecture, 10 February 2004.

propose to share with you the results of this study which, I have no hesitation in admitting, reflects a synthesis between my past social activism and recent academic incarnation.

But before I do this, I must share with you a preamble. I have had the opportunity to read through the lectures delivered by some of my illustrious predecessors in this lecture series. I have noted that, in his 1992 lecture, Professor P.C. Joshi deliberated upon Zakir Sahib's intellectually rigorous explorations during the late 1920s into the phenomenon of capitalism with reference to the Indian economy 'as an agrarian hinterland of the British empire'. Professor Joshi also dwelt upon Zakir Sahib's reflections in 1944–45 on European capitalism, wherein he noted not only the changes in the internal structure of capitalism but also the later assertion of the 'social conscience' that 'forces capitalism to subordinate itself to social purpose'. I will return to this critical insight of Zakir Sahib as I conclude my analysis.

I take the liberty of drawing your attention to the great educationist in Zakir Sahib which attracted the attention of Mahatma Gandhi during the National Education Conference held at Wardha in October 1937, as part of the freedom movement.[1] It was during this conference that Gandhiji introduced the nation to his revolutionary concept of integrating the 'world of work' with the 'world of knowledge' by weaving the curriculum around some form of productive work. This was Gandhiji's response to colonial education which, he was convinced, was detrimental to India's future. As noted later by Acharya Kripalani (1939), the Gandhian pedagogy – now known either as Basic Education (*Buniyadi Shiksha*) or *Nai Talim* – was so radical that it shocked both the learned in general and educational experts in particular, apart from confusing the revolutionaries of the time. For Gandhiji, however, Basic Education was conceived 'as the spearhead of a silent social revolution' for reconstruction of India in a non-violent developmental framework. The Wardha Education Conference constituted a committee under the chairpersonship of Zakir Sahib to give concrete shape to the curriculum of Basic Education.

The report of the Zakir Husain Committee became the basis of a resolution passed by the fifty-first session of the Indian National Congress, held at Haripura (Gujarat) in February 1938. The Haripura session resolved to 'build up national education on a new foundation' by committing itself to three principles, viz. (a) provision of free and compulsory education for a minimum of seven years (this was later extended to eight years) on a nationwide scale; (b) mother tongue as the medium of education; and (c) education to be given through some central productive work or craft, and all curricular activities to be organized around this central task, the productive work being selected on the basis of the child's socio-economic context. The Haripura session also resolved to establish an All India Education Board (also known as *Hindustani Talimi Sangh*), for which it requested and authorized Zakir Sahib (and his colleague, E. Aryanayakam, who was then experimenting with Basic Education at Sewagram, now in Maharashtra) 'to take immediate steps, under the advice and guidance of Gandhiji, to bring such a Board into existence, in order to work out in a consolidated manner a programme of basic national education, and to recommend it for acceptance to those who are in control of state or private education'. It is now universally known that Zakir Sahib set up one of the finest (and probably the most prestigious) experiments in *Nai Talim* at Okhla village in Delhi in 1938, as part of Jamia Milia Islamia. The experiment has been since extensively researched. One is struck by the rigour with which this historic educational experience and its pedagogy was documented and analysed under the academic leadership of Zakir Sahib.

It is a different matter that Zakir Sahib's experiment could not be sustained, as was the case with hundreds of other *Nai Talim* experiments around the country. This fate was inevitable as the government of independent India decided to retain the Macaulayian education system, thereby continuing the colonial (and, significantly, also brahmanical) practice of delinking knowledge from productive work and social reality. This lack of policy support to the Gandhian concept, concretized so powerfully by Zakir Sahib, led to slow but inevitable attrition of the commitment made to the nation at the Haripura Congress session. The betrayal of this unique educational heritage of the freedom struggle against British imperialism – admittedly without parallel in the freedom movements of other countries – was carried 'forward' by the Education Commission (1964–66) that recommended work experience as merely an *additional* subject. Unlike in Zakir Sahib's *Nai Talim*, work experience was to remain isolated from the knowledge structure inherent in the curriculum. The task of 'butchering' *Nai Talim* was completed by the Ishwarbhai Patel Committee (1978), which recommended that 'socially useful productive work (SUPW)' be added in the school curriculum as a separate period. The policy-makers went a step further. The marks for SUPW are now added as a marginalized routine in the last (almost literally) column of the mark sheet which no one cares to even read! Ironically, and most probably as a subconscious reflex action, the middle-class intelligentsia supported the government policy by reducing *Nai Talim* to mere vocational education for either the poor or low-performing children. This distortion resulted in *Nai Talim* being treated as something unrelated to the mainstream curriculum, rather than being perceived as a powerful pedagogy for liberating Indian education from the colonial-cum-brahmanical framework. This policy stance destined the education system to increasing irrelevance and alienation from the masses in the years to follow. But, more significantly, it also helped widen the socio-political faultline through which the forces of both the global market and communalism launched an epistemic (knowledge-related or knowledge-based) assault on the character of Indian education during the last decade of the twentieth century. And this is exactly the thesis that I now set myself to develop.

National Policies and the Neoliberal Agenda

In order to comprehend the dynamics through which the neoliberal agenda became operational in the Indian elementary education sector, it is necessary to refer to two sets of critical policy-related documents: one national and the other international. First, the *National Policy on Education 1986* (henceforth referred to as NPE 1986) and its companion document called *Programme of Action 1986* (henceforth referred to as POA 1986), approved by the Parliament in May 1986 and November 1986, respectively.[2] Both the NPE 1986 and POA 1986 were revised by the Parliament in 1992, and, as a result, are known as NPE 1992 and POA 1992 respectively. Second, the *World Declaration on Education for All* and its companion document called *Framework for Action to Meet Basic Learning Needs*, adopted by the World Conference on Education for All (EFA): Meeting Basic Learning Needs, held at Jomtien, Thailand, in March 1990 (these documents are referred to as the Jomtien Declaration and Jomtien Framework, respectively).

The Jomtien Conference was jointly convened by the UNDP, UNESCO, UNICEF and World Bank.[3] These international agencies continued to hold follow-up conferences at both the regional and global levels during the 1990s.[4] The decadal follow-up of the Jomtien Conference was held at Dakar, Senegal, in April 2000, wherein the progress made by various nations to achieve the EFA goals as set out by the Jomtien Declaration was reviewed. Just as the Jomtien Declaration guided educational planning throughout the 1990s, the Dakar Framework of Action (World Education Forum 2000) has now become the new policy-level international guidepost for the first fifteen years of the twenty-first century.[5]

We may recall here that the New Economic Policy, giving primacy to market forces in national development and 'integrating' India into the global economic order, was enunciated by the Government of India within a week of Prime Minister P.V. Narasimha Rao's assumption of power in July 1991. Along with this, however, another decision taken by the government in the same month did not attract much notice. This was with regard to the report of the National Policy on Education 1986 Review Committee, 1990 (NPERC), also known as the Acharya Ramamurti Committee, which had been tabled in both Houses of Parliament earlier in January 1991. The review report had made recommendations for significant changes in the National Policy on Education 1986 in consonance with the terms of reference which had directed the Committee to:

(a) make education an effective instrument for securing a status of equality for women, and persons belonging to the backward classes and minorities;
(b) give a work and employment orientation to education;
(c) exclude from (education) the elitist aberrations which have become the glaring characteristic of the education scene;
(d) lay special emphasis on struggle against (the) phenomenon of 'educational institutions . . . increasingly being influenced by casteism, communalism and obscurantism'; and
(e) move towards a genuinely egalitarian and secular social order.

(Excerpted from the Government of India's Resolution dated 7 May 1990 constituting the NPE 1986 Review Committee)

In the perception of the policy-makers, such policy changes would not have apparently resonated well with the New Economic Policy, especially with the NPERC's recommendations for elimination of the 'elitist aberrations' of NPE 1986 and ensuring universal access to education of *equitable* quality. In particular, the government was obliged to move urgently to neutralize the unambiguous advocacy by NPERC for establishing the Common School System which will eventually include private unaided schools as well. More specifically, these policy changes, as I hope to demonstrate, would have predictably come into conflict with the structural adjustment programme imposed by the IMF on the Indian economy, as well as with the World Bank policy imperatives in education. A 'democratically legitimate' method was, therefore, conceived to essentially dispose of all the crucial NPERC recommendations for policy changes. In July 1991, the government constituted a CABE (Central Advisory Board of Education) Committee on Policy to 'review the implementation of the various parameters of NPE, taking into consideration the report of the Committee for Review of the NPE and other relevant developments since the policy was formulated, and to make recommendations regarding modifications to be made in NPE.' The intention of the government stood exposed by the very brief given to the CABE Committee as this task had already been completed by NPERC six months earlier! Thus, the decision to constitute this Committee to purportedly review the NPERC report essentially amounted to *not* giving effect to the major education policy changes recommended therein. This step, taken concomitantly with the declaration of the New Economic Policy, was the only 'legitimate' option available to the government to carry forward the ongoing withdrawal from constitutional commitments, and to keep the doors open for international intervention in Indian education, especially in the area of elementary education.

The political and economic framework for subjugation by global forces in the education sector emerged soon after the announcement of the New Economic Policy, when the Indian government was 'persuaded' by the IMF and the World Bank to accept the twin concepts of *structural adjustment* and a *social safety net* in planning and budgeting for social sectors. There was no choice, the government told the people, justifying its apparent 'helplessness', since these were the preconditions set by the Bretton Woods institutions for extending further loans. Plainly speaking, these twin concepts implied that the government would, as part of the structural adjustment programme, incrementally reduce public spending on social sectors such as health, education and social welfare. Recognizing that such a reduction could lead to severe socio-political tensions, the IMF and World Bank 'offered' to create a social safety net by extending loans for the social sector on certain terms and conditions.

One would tend to take a position that, in the face of the powerful forces of globalization, there is no option for the educational system but to accept the larger framework dictated by the global economic order as *fait accompli*. It is with this mind-set that the policy-makers in India have unquestioningly accepted the hegemonic role of transnational corporate forces, the global market system and powerful international organizations such as the Bretton Woods institutions in directing not just the structure and accessibility, but also the very aims and quality of education (and also health). The Jomtien Conference laid the basic architecture for intervention by the international funding agencies in national educational structures and processes.

Probing the Policy Framework

Before I proceed further to unravel the neoliberal agenda in elementary education, I must take a detour in the recent history of policy-making to decipher the mind of the Indian state at the time of the Jomtien Conference. The National Policy on Education 1986 marked a watershed as it was the first policy-level acknowledgement since independence that elementary school education of *comparable quality* will *not* become available to all children of India in the 6–14 age group. The notion of education of *comparable or equitable quality* for all children, irrespective of their class, creed, caste, gender, linguistic or cultural background, or physical/mental disability, was clearly implied in the Constitution. Such an implication is seen when the original Article 45 (that is, free and compulsory education for all children up to the age of fourteen years)[6] of Part IV (Directive Principles of State Policy) is read in conjunction with Article 14 (equality before law), Article 15 (prohibition of discrimination on grounds of religion, race, caste, sex, place of birth or any of them), Article 16 (equality of opportunity in public employment) and Article 21 (protection of life and personal liberty), the latter four Articles belonging to Part III (Fundamental Rights).[7] The concept of equality in *educational opportunities* and *conditions of success* is further strengthened in Part IV of the Constitution by Article 38 (social order with justice and elimination of inequalities in status, facilities and opportunities), Article 39e, f (tender age of children is not abused; children are given opportunities and facilities to develop in a healthy manner and in conditions of freedom and dignity; childhood is protected against exploitation) and Article 46 (promotion with special care of the educational and economic interests of the weaker sections of the people, and in particular of the Scheduled Castes and Scheduled Tribes). However, despite such unambiguous constitutional provisions, NPE 1986 stated: 'A large and systematic programme of non-formal education will be launched for school dropouts, for children from habitations without schools, *working children* and *girls who cannot attend whole-day schools* (NPE 1986, Section 5.8; emphasis added). It further resolved:

> This effort (that is '*ensuring children's retention at school*') will be fully coordinated with the network of non-formal education. It shall be ensured that all children who attain the age of about 11 years by 1990 will have had five years *schooling*, or its equivalent through the *non-formal stream*. (NPE 1986, Section 5.12; emphasis added.)

As per the Acharya Ramamurti Committee Report (GOI 1990, Chapter 6, Section 6.2.3, Table 2), out-of-school children were almost half of the children

of school-going age at the time NPE 1986 was adopted. The above policy measure implied that these out-of-school children shall be provided non-formal education (NFE) – an educational stream that would be *parallel* to the *mainstream*
of formal school education. Most of the out-of-school children were working
children, whether paid wages or not.[8] Indeed, the notion of 'mainstream' emerged
in the Indian educational discourse during the 1990s only because NPE 1986
gave legitimacy to a parallel stream such as non-formal education, a layer *below* the formal school. Until then, in principle, there was only one officially
acknowledged, planned and financially supported stream in Indian education
(that is, government, local body and government-aided schools of comparable
quality), the relatively minor streams of private unaided schools (erroneously
called public schools) and Kendriya Vidyalayas (or Central Schools) notwithstanding.[9] Recognizing this, the Education Commission (1964–66) had strongly
recommended the establishment of a *Common* School System (often misunder-
stood as *Uniform* School System) through the instrumentality of Neighbourhood
Schools. The Common School System was accepted in the first National Policy
on Education 1968 (that is NPE 1968), in order to 'equalize educational opportunity' for all children and to promote 'social cohesion and national integration'.
In this sense, the policy imperative of non-formal education amounted to violat-
ing not only the Constitution and NPE 1968, but also NPE 1986 itself, which had
made the following commitment:

> The concept of a National System of Education implies that, up to a given level,
> all students, irrespective of caste, creed, location or sex, have access to educa-
> tion of a *comparable* quality. To achieve this, the Government will initiate ap-
> propriately funded programmes. Effective measures will be taken in the direc-
> tion of the *Common School System recommended in the 1968 policy*. (NPE
> 1986, Section 3.2 [also retained in the policy revised in 1992]; emphasis added)

Since non-formal education was designed to be provided largely through
evening centres, it was directed particularly to child workers. POA 1986 was
explicit on this point when it stated:

> . . . it has been assumed in the Policy that a large number of out-of-school
> children are unable to avail themselves of the benefit of schooling because they
> have to work to supplement family income or otherwise assist the family. NPE
> proposes taking up of a large and systematic programme of non-formal educa-
> tion for these children and children of habitations without school. (POA 1986,
> II.4)

The policy also had a special provision for afternoon centres for girls.
This implied the willingness of the policy-makers to adjust with, rather than
challenge, the gender stereotype of the role of girls in domestic chores and sibling
care. In this sense, NPE 1986 legitimized both child labour and patriarchy.
Significantly, however, the policy and POA 1986 emphasized that
NFE was designed to be distinct from the formal school system in being socio-

culturally and physically accessible, making the curriculum flexible and relevant, and recruiting 'instructors' (not teachers) who would have empathy for the weaker sections of the society. The policy-makers seem to be taking the curious position that all these desirable features of education must belong to NFE whereas the formal school system should continue to be afflicted with all the undesirable features! If this was not the case, why else would the policy not propose ways and means for incorporating these desirable features into the formal school system itself, and, thereby, begin the process of educational reforms for all children? Indeed, this flawed logic is contradicted in the policy itself by its conception of the NFE 'instructor'. All the above desirable features of education – organizational, curricular and pedagogic – as listed in the policy in relation to NFE, will be introduced by an 'instructor' whose levels of qualifications, teacher training, salary and other service conditions would be of much lower order than those of the regular teacher of the formal school system. Yet, these underqualified, essentially untrained and underpaid 'instructors' (without any stability in service) will, for some magical reason, turn out to be, as per NPE 1986 (Section 5.9), 'talented and dedicated young men and women', which, obviously the policy implies, their counterparts in the formal school system cannot be or, rather, should not be expected to be. Not just this. The NFE instructor, despite these handicaps, is expected by the policy-makers to have much greater initiative and skills in attracting the presumably 'unwilling' and hitherto out-of-school children, particularly girls and working children, to NFE centres, and then ensuring their effective, enjoyable and, more importantly, relevant learning – something the formal schoolteacher is not expected to do! All this will be achieved by the 'miraculous' instructor by holding NFE classes for merely two to three hours per day (in contrast to the formal school where classes are held for four to five hours per day), since the policy states that NFE's 'total duration is generally shorter than in formal education' (NIEPA 1990: 53). The expectations of the policy-makers from the NFE instructors do not end here. Since no provision for even thatched huts (let alone buildings) or the teaching aids available under the Operation Blackboard scheme (meant only for formal schools) is made for NFE, the instructor is expected to use her/his 'genius' to arrange for all these from the community, failing which what she/he is supposed to do, the policy prefers not to specify. This conceptualization of 'instructor' in the 1986 policy was no trivial matter. It was destined to become the 'para teacher' of the post-Jomtien phase, and one of the key instrumentalities for operationalizing the neoliberal agenda in elementary education.

The entirely flawed logic and internal contradictions in the policy and POA relating to NFE were noticed and questioned by NPERC,[10] which observed:

> The above listed highly desirable features of NFE are indeed relevant to formal schools as well and they are also the essence of the child-centred approach mentioned by NPE. The criteria mentioned by POA for selection of NFE instructors – being local, being already motivated, acceptable to the community, being

preferably from the weaker sections in society, having given some evidence of work in the community – are the criteria relevant to the selection of formal schoolteachers also. Therefore, it is unclear why the policy has advocated NFE, in effect, as a parallel system. (Government of India 1990, Section 6.4.6)

Based upon this logic, the NPERC recommended that the formal school system be transformed to include all the desirable features of NFE instead of setting up two parallel systems, one for children from relatively better-off sections of society and the other for poor girls and working children (ibid., Chapter 6: 169–72). The NPERC proposed specific policy changes and a detailed programme design for building up a responsive and relevant formal school system that can not only reach out to children from the marginalized social segments and remote habitations, but also be much more socio-culturally and pedagogically meaningful to children from the middle class and even the elite sections than is the prevailing formal school. In effect, NPERC seemed to be raising an uncomfortable question for the ruling Indian elite: whom is the formal school system designed for, if it is both inaccessible and unsuitable for almost half of India's children? NPERC, therefore, advocated a phase-wise ten-year programme to concretize the vision of the Common School System (ibid.: 92–93, 169–72, 182–84).

Policy's Vision of Social Engineering
Both NPE 1986 (Section 5.9) and POA 1986 (Chapter II, Section 2.5) insisted that NFE was designed in order to fulfil policy's over-riding assumption that 'NFE can result in provision of education comparable in quality with formal schooling'. It is indeed ironical that the policy first creates a layer of lower quality below the formal school, mainly for poor girls and child labour, and then claims to design features in it to make it 'comparable with formal schooling'. It prefers not to take any radical measures in order to transform the social and pedagogic character of the mainstream formal school system such that it will be able to attract child labour as well as children from remote habitations, particularly girls, while also ensuring that they enjoy learning and receive education that is relevant to their lives along with the rest of the children in their neighbourhood. The policy-makers offer the following lame excuse for not taking the radical measure of transforming the formal school system:

> Given the present condition of the schools in general, the challenges before the school system are many, for example, enrolling and retaining children who cannot afford to attend school regularly; a harmonious interaction with the community around; improving the infrastructure, quality and learning environment; and ensuring that every student acquires minimum levels of learning. *These challenges are daunting enough* and it *does not seem desirable to overload the school system* with yet another formidable challenge of meeting the educational needs of children with severe para educational constraints. (Government of India 1992a, Section 9.13; emphases added)

Three contradictions need to be noted in the above statement. One, the policy-makers do not regard the 'daunting challenges' listed above to be the central task of the formal school system, if not the very *raison d'être* of its existence. Two, these 'daunting challenges' do not seem to constitute 'the educational needs of children with severe para educational constraints'. One wonders what will. Three, the policy erroneously assumes that it is the child, rather than the school system, that is handicapped by 'severe para educational constraints'. Is the above lame excuse offered because of the lack of policy-makers' interest in either abolishing child labour or changing the role of girls from poor families in domestic chores and sibling care? This is obvious, since the timings of the NFE centres were adjusted to evenings for child labour and afternoons for girls, instead of ensuring that they come to a regular *day-time* formal school, thereby challenging the socio-cultural constraints operating on their lives, as has been successfully demonstrated by the M.V. Foundation in Andhra Pradesh and advocated by Sinha (2000). The fact is that the policy conceived of a parallel stream like NFE which, instead of helping to eliminate the practice of child labour and resist patriarchy, ended up adjusting with and reinforcing it.

The policy-makers were determined to institutionalize the newly emerging principle of social engineering through parallel layers of so-called educational facilities (not schools). As per this sociological principle, a separate parallel layer of educational facility would be provided for each socio-economically, culturally or ethnically distinct segment of society. NPERC's recommendation, therefore, to transform the infrastructural, social and pedagogic character of the formal school system such that children from different social classes can socialize together, did not find favour with the CABE Committee on Policy (Government of India 1992a, Sections 9.7–9.13), which reiterated the same flawed logic critiqued above.[11] NPE 1986 (as modified in 1992), accordingly, retained the parallel NFE stream for crores of working children (two-thirds of them being girls), without providing a feasible design in the modified POA 1992 for radically transforming or improving the formal school system. Extending this spurious logic, it was only natural for the CABE Committee on Policy to also reject NPERC's recommendation for building up a Common School System (ibid., Sections 6.1–6.6). This retrogressive stand of the CABE Committee on Policy with regard to NFE and the Common School System at least followed an internally consistent logic and thus enabled the state to clear the path, as we shall soon see, for the structural adjustment programme being then imposed on the Indian economy by the IMF and the World Bank.

A detailed analysis of the policy documents reveals that the policy-makers were not persuaded by the superior attributes conceived by them for NFE but by the perceived financial constraints. NFE was envisaged as a way out of the dilemma of providing education of equitable quality to almost half of India's children in the relevant age group. It did not matter much, as pointed out by a policy document, even if 'no systematic study of the effectiveness of Non-Formal Education [was] available' or if some educational planners did not see in this 'a viable alternative to school education'. After all, NFE was meant only for the marginalized children, not for the children of the middle class or of the ruling elite! However, in a democracy like India, one needed to exercise abundant caution. The camouflage of the rhetoric of the superior attributes of NFE was, therefore, cleverly designed and incorporated in the policy. The Government of India had no hesitation in presenting even the Jomtien Conference (1990) with the same camouflage. The international funding agencies and global market forces might have even welcomed this camouflage, since, as we shall see later, the Jomtien Conference was organized precisely for preparing the groundwork for forcing developing countries like India to minimize their expenditure on the social sector. It is a moot point whether NFE was an outcome of the financial constraints perceived by the Indian policy-makers or of a lack of commitment on their part to push forward the vision of egalitarian education inherent in the Common School System. Or, maybe it was designed to fit in the framework of the structural adjustment programme which might have been quietly operational in India well before it was publicly declared as an inevitable part of the New Economic Policy from July 1991 onwards.

This is an appropriate juncture to revisit the conclusions arrived at by Myron Weiner who analysed the views of a large number of policy-makers, bureaucrats, social activists, educationists and other academics with regard to child labour in India and their education:

> The central proposition of this study is that India's low per capita income and economic situation is less relevant as an explanation than the belief systems. . . a set of beliefs that are widely shared by educators, social activists, trade unionists, academic researchers, and, more broadly, by members of the Indian middle class. These beliefs are held by those outside as well as those within government, by observant Hindus and by those who regard themselves as secular, and by leftists as well as by centrists and rightists. At the core of these beliefs are the Indian view of the social order, notions concerning the respective roles of upper and lower social strata, the role of education as a means of maintaining differentiations among social classes, and concerns that 'excessive' and 'inappropriate' education for the poor would disrupt existing social arrangements. (Weiner 1991: 5)

It is thus clear that the twin trends of gradual abdication of constitutional obligation and steady dilution of policy relating to 'free education of *equitable* quality' that later marked the neoliberal agenda of the 1990s had its roots in the policy framework of NPE 1986 and the programme design of POA 1986 (as well as their revised counterparts of 1992). The policy was designed basically to promote exclusion of crores of children from elementary education and introduce inequality by institutionalizing low-quality multiple tracks or parallel streams of education. It was this character of NPE 1986 that provided both the foundation and the necessary socio-political space to international funding agencies, including the World Bank, to exacerbate abdication, accelerate the pace of exclusion and further marginalize people's aspirations for a Common School System and genuine Neighbourhood Schools.[12]

Post-Jomtien Phase of Indian Education

The Jomtien Conference proved to be a turning point in the history of education in India. The Government of India gave hasty concurrence to the Jomtien Declaration (UNDP, UNESCO, UNICEF, World Bank 1990), without even consulting the Parliament on its major constitutional and policy implications. This marked the beginning of the phase of gradual but systemic erosion of the Parliament's role in policy formulation in education, as well as of the Planning Commission and the Ministry of Human Resource Development in formulating the agenda of Indian education and setting its priorities. As provided for in the Jomtien Declaration (Article 10) and Jomtien Framework (Section 3.3), external aid from a host of international funding agencies, operating under the World Bank umbrella, was systematically allowed in the primary education sector *as a matter of policy* for the first time in post-independent India.[13] This policy departure coincided with the beginning of the New Economic Policy in July 1991 in India. With this, it became necessary for the government to accept the IMF–World Bank's structural adjustment programme as well as the Jomtien Declaration's policy framework for Education for All (EFA). The launching of the first World Bank-sponsored comprehensive District Primary Education Programme (DPEP) in 1993–94 was part of this requirement, and its attendant social safety net provided under IMF–World Bank design (Government of India 1993: 88). The serious implication of this new situation was recognized by the government. The Central Advisory Board of Education (CABE), at its forty-sixth meeting in March 1991, formulated a set of guidelines for externally aided projects which were reiterated at the forty-seventh meeting in May 1992. These guidelines sought to ensure that external assistance 'does not lead to a dependency syndrome' and remains 'an additionality to the [national] resources for education' while being in 'total conformity with the national policies, strategies and programmes' (ibid.: 89).

Yet, a series of policy-related documents were issued during the following years, each adversely impacting upon the policy in a significant manner: Education for All (Government of India 1993), DPEP (Government of India 1995, 1998), Education Guarantee Scheme (Government of Madhya Pradesh 1998: 9–12), Para Teacher scheme (Ed.CIL 2000; Government of India 2001a), Ambani–Birla Report (Government of India 2000), National Curriculum Framework for School Education (NCERT 2000), and Education Guarantee Scheme and Alternative & Innovative Education (Government of India 2001a). An outstanding example of policy dilution was DPEP itself which shifted the national policy's focus from *eight years of integrated elementary education* to only *five years (or even less) of primary education*,[14] and from ensuring *three teachers per primary school* under Operation Blackboard *to Multi-grade Teaching*. As a result, the minimum norms for school infrastructure and strength of teachers in a primary school, as specified in NPE 1986 (as modified in 1992), stand diluted for *Sarva Shiksha Abhiyan* and EFA National Plan of Action (Government of India 2002, 2003a; Tilak 2003; Sadgopal 2003c). Similarly, the policy relating to women's education was diluted – from empowering women to merely enrolling girls on school registers – in line with the Jomtien and Dakar Frameworks, as also reinforced by the monitoring parameters (for example, gender parity index, an index based on enrolment ratios alone) as formulated by UNESCO (Sadgopal 2003c). For none of these was it considered necessary to take the approval of the Parliament, even when these contradicted significant elements of the education policy approved by the Parliament.

During the post-Jomtien phase, the Indian education policy was diluted and distorted in significant ways, whether directly as part of externally aided projects (for example, DPEP) or otherwise (for example, *Sarva Shiksha Abhiyan*). These are analysed below.

Trivialization of Educational Aims

The educational discourse today is marked by almost complete absence of any reference to *aims* (read Dhankar 2002 on the distortions that crept into DPEP pedagogy as a consequence of ignoring educational aims). Major changes in programme designs or curriculum are introduced without as much as even a reference to how these would affect our pursuit of basic aims of education. The Jomtien Declaration's ambiguous category of 'Basic Education' and its preoccupation with *literacy*, rather than *education*, in defining 'Basic Learning Needs' has been instrumental, in large measure, in making education synonymous with literacy in the post-Jomtien phase (Sadgopal 1994). The Jomtien Framework (Section 6) uses the language of behaviourism when it prescribes 'observable and measurable targets' for 'objective evaluation of progress'. It is no mere coincidence that, in line with this notion of evaluation, the Ministry of Human Resource Development set up a committee to formulate minimum levels of learning (MLLs) concomitant with the Jomtien Conference (the committee worked from January 1990 to August 1990). Further, it was chaired by a former Director of the UNESCO Institute for Education in Germany, a partner in organizing the Jomtien initiative. The competency-based narrow framework of MLLs has been criticized for its market orientation as well as for viewing the cognitive domain in isolation of the affective and psycho-motor domains (Dhankar 2002; Sadgopal 2002b: 118–20). It is a matter of great concern that the education of girls has been viewed in terms of only reducing their fertility rates, slowing population growth or increasing their productivity (World Bank 1997: 1, 39, 53). The curricular and assessment framework is sought to be reduced to intelligent quotient (IQ), emotional quotient (EQ) and spiritual quotient (SQ), thereby trivializing knowledge (NCERT 2000; Sadgopal 2002b: 132–33). All of these measures of the post-Jomtien phase, though having apparently independent origins, seem to be acting together to reinforce the now discredited behavioural paradigm in Indian education.

Fragmentation of Knowledge

There is no place in the post-Jomtien view of curriculum for the 'world of work' being pedagogically integrated with the 'world of knowledge'. Similarly, while defining 'child-centredness', 'joyful learning' or 'multi-grade teaching' in DPEP literature, no attempt is made to envisage knowledge in the context of the social ethos. This is despite the dominant rhetoric of contextual education in DPEP (Government of India 1993). Such trends reinforce the brahmanical-cum-colonial character of Indian education.[15] The cognitive domain continues to be viewed in isolation of the affective domain and psycho-motor skills (for example, in MLL). The notion of knowledge is fragmented in so far as the curriculum of primary education is structurally delinked from the upper primary stage. This ignores the Indian concept of integrated elementary education of eight years, conceived as part of the freedom struggle (DPEP promoted such fragmentation even in those states/union territories where elementary education was an integrated programme).[16]

Withdrawal from Policy Commitment to
Build a Common School System

As stated earlier, the issue of improvement (or transformation, if necessary) of the quality and relevance of the formal school system in order to build a Common School System for all children was gradually defocused after NPE 1986, particularly in the post-Jomtien phase. Instead, institutionalization of multiple or parallel tracks of low-quality 'educational' facilities replaced the Common School policy as the key strategy for providing so-called education to crores of out-of-school children belonging to dalit and tribal sections of societies, several segments of other backward classes, cultural and linguistic minorities, and the physically and mentally disabled. Two-thirds of each of these sections facing educational discrimination comprised girl children. Apart from continuing with NFE in the post-Jomtien phase, the following multiple tracks or parallel streams were introduced: accommodating 9–14 age group children in adult literacy classes, as declared at the E-9 EFA Conference held in 1993 in Delhi (Government of India 1993: 51)[17]; Alternative Schools (Government of India 1998: 18); Education Guarantee Scheme (EGS) Centres (Government of Madhya Pradesh 1998: 9–12; Government of India 2001a; 2001b, Section 3.2.2.2); Multi-Grade/Multi-Level Teaching (Government of India 1995: 10, 16; 1998:18); Bridge Courses and Back-to-School Camps of *Sarva Shiksha Abhiyan* (Government of India 2001b, Section 3.2.2.2; 2002: 11); and correspondence courses for the 6–14 age group (NCERT 2000: 22–23; Government of India 2001b, Section 3.4.18; 2003a: 44).

Four sets of observations are made here to reveal the ruthlessness with which the state has pursued its agenda of promoting and institutionalizing inequality in education.

(a) EGS has no provision whatsoever for any infrastructure (not even a tent or thatched roof); its supposedly chief beneficiaries, viz. the dalit or tribal communities, are expected, as per the EGS design, to arrange for some sort of space for the EGS centre (Government of India 2001a)!

(b) In externally aided DPEP, Multi-Grade/Multi-Level Teaching has meant nothing other than one/two teacher(s) being trained to teach five classes simultaneously, out of sheer necessity. In spite of the confused rhetoric of the DPEP authorities, it is not designed to be the progressive pedagogy of 'grade-less teaching', as is the case at Digantar (experimental schools practising grade-less teaching) near Jaipur, Rajasthan. DPEP has thus violated the Operation Blackboard norms of NPE 1986 (as modified in 1992) for providing at least three teachers and three classrooms to every primary school. Dhankar (2002) analyses this DPEP policy aptly:

> The need and rationale for multi-grade teaching is either socio-political or managerial; and *pedagogical considerations are only grafted on to it*. . . . The real solution to the problem is to appoint more teachers. . . . But appointing more teachers costs money. Since most of the children in these schools belong to the weaker sections of society, easier and less expensive solutions are sought. Therefore, a pedagogical solution for this socio-economic problem is devised in the name of multi-grade teaching strategies. . . . As the (conventional) grade was used to manage children, now in a changed situation the idea of multi-grade is used for the same purpose . . . claiming that (it) is an effort for quality improvement, is *nothing more than making a virtue out of an ugly necessity* – ugly because the children who bear the brunt belong to the weaker sections of the society. (Emphases added)

The policy (Section 5.7) had stated that 'Operation Blackboard will be enlarged to provide *three reasonably large rooms* that are usable in all weather and . . . (a range of teaching aids)' and 'at least *three teachers* should work in every school, the *number increasing, as early as possible, to one teacher per class* . . . at least 50 per cent of teachers recruited in future should be women' (emphases added). To be sure, these norms were approved by the Parliament in May 1992. Through Multi-Grade/Multi-Level Teaching, DPEP has cynically attempted to justify single-teacher and two-teacher schools (almost two-thirds of all primary schools), instead of building up political pressure or legislative action or catalysing community demand for fulfilment of Operation Blackboard commitments. This violation during the late 1990s, touted as an interim strategy, apparently opened the doors at the beginning of this century for institutionalizing the dilution of Operation Blackboard norms from three teachers–three classrooms per primary school to two teachers–two classrooms per primary school in the *Sarva Shiksha Abhiyan*, Tenth Five Year Plan (2002–07) and EFA–National Plan of Action (2003). This dilution is now the basis of financial allocations (Government of India 2003a: 92, Table 9.3). It also explains, at least partly, how the government managed to reduce the Tapas Majumdar Committee's estimates by 30 per cent for the Financial Memorandum attached to the Eighty-Sixth Amendment Bill.

(c) NCERT (2000: 22–23) recommended correspondence courses (euphemized as Open Schooling or Open Learning System) for the 6–14 age group without any basis in educational research or experience whatsoever. Again, this proposal is in violation of NPE 1986 (as modified in 1992) which had restricted the role of the so-called 'open learning system' to secondary and higher education (Section 5.37). Yet, such a farcical pedagogic notion is already a part of the Tenth Five Year Plan (Government of India 2001b, Section 3.4.18) and EFA–National Plan of Action (Government of India 2003a: 44). The government has even planned to present it to the Parliament for legitimization (Government of India 2003b, c, Schedule A). Apart from legitimizing child labour, the introduction of correspondence courses for the 6–14 age group of children, most of them being 'first generation learners', implies that the girl child will be *officially* denied the *relatively* more liberating atmosphere offered by school than what she is likely to get at home, bound by patriarchal traditions (Sadgopal 2003c).

(d) Whenever faced with criticism throughout the 1990s, the policymakers claimed that these multiple tracks or parallel streams are merely *interim* or *transitional* arrangements in order to *eventually* mainstream all children to reach regular formal schools. This is precisely what the nation was told about non-formal education in the wake of NPE 1986 and in the years following NPE 1986 (as modified in 1992), which promised that the NFE scheme 'will be strengthened and enlarged' (Section 5.8). The EFA (1993) again assured that 'many measures are being adopted to further strengthen this scheme' (Government of India 1993: 51). In 1995, the externally aided DPEP asserted that it would 'strive for the development of an effective NFE system which can meet the diverse educational needs of children' (Government of India 1995, Chapter II, Section 17). In 1998, DPEP declared that 'every state is deciding to set up different forms of alternative schools to ensure participation of working children, street children, children of migrating communities, dropouts, etc.' (Government of India 1998: 18). To be sure, all the categories of out-of-school children mentioned in the DPEP of 1998 are same as those mentioned in the NFE scheme of 1986 policy. Continuing in the same vein, *Sarva Shiksha Abhiyan* (2002) informs that:

> Studies on the Non-Formal Education scheme have pointed out the lack of flexibility which impedes effective implementation across different States. Efforts to provide for a diversity of interventions have been made in the revised scheme that has been approved recently, such as setting up of Education Guarantee Schools, Alternative Schooling facilities, Balika Shikshan Shivirs, 'Back-to-School' camps etc. (Government of India 2002, Chapter III, Section 3.5: 35)

We should be prepared for yet another revision of the scheme in the near future since the target of *Sarva Shiksha Abhiyan* of 'providing universal enrolment by the year 2003' is far from being met.

An adult literacy class, a non-formal centre, the so-called 'alternative' school, a multi-grade class, the Education Guarantee Scheme (wherein a para-teacher will be appointed) and now the correspondence course for the primary school child (even the para-teacher will be replaced by a postman) – all have come to be accepted as adequate substitutes for school education, as long as it concerns the education of the poor. Needless to say, no policy-maker will ever be prepared to send her or his child to any of these *parallel* low-quality educational 'alternatives'! In this scenario, as was stated by the Lokshala document (Bharat Jan Vigyan Jatha 1995), one can envisage 'a girl child engaged in child labour as having been *Constitutionally educated* if she can be enrolled in a non-formal stream for three years and then in National Literacy Mission's adult literacy programme for the next two years, without even having stepped into the village school'! It is also evidence of the state's willingness to coexist with child labour (read *destruction of childhood*) in the twenty-first century while, at the same time, boasting of nuclear-cum-rocket capability and global leadership in infor-mation technology!

The above policy analysis shows that these multiple tracks or parallel streams are here to stay with us for as long as the policy-makers refuse to: (a) focus attention on transforming the mainstream formal school system; (b) build a Common School System; and (c) reprioritize the national economy to ensure adequate resources for this central nation-building task. Otherwise, the promise of making these multiple tracks into 'transitional schools' (Government of India 2004) – the latest name for the range of NFE schemes – will remain an elusive dream, if not a complete farce!

Lowering the Status of Schoolteacher

In unabashed violation of Sections 9.1 to 9.3 of NPE 1986 (as modified in 1992) which call for raising the status of teachers, the post-Jomtien *operating* policy has been to replace the teacher with underqualified, untrained (or undertrained) and underpaid persons appointed on short-term contracts, to be called para-teachers (Ed.CIL 2000; Government of India 2001a; Kumar *et al.* 2001; Sadgopal 2002b: 118 and 2003a: 15). The para-teacher is known by a variety of euphemisms in different states, viz. *Guruji, Lok Shikshak, Shiksha Karmi, Lok Mitra, Vidya Upasak, Vidya Volunteer*, etc., but care is taken not to call her/him a teacher. This policy of para-teacher is now being rapidly extended to secondary and higher education as well, clearly to facilitate privatization and commercialization of education.

Erosion of Women's Education Policy

NPE 1986 (as modified in 1992) provided for a sharp perspective on 'Education for Women's Equality' (Sections 4.2 and 4.3), as follows:

> Education will be used as an agent of basic change in the status of women. In order to neutralize the accumulated distortions of the past, there will be a well-conceived edge in favour of women. The National Education System will play a positive, interventionist role in the empowerment of women. It will foster the development of new values. . . . This will be an act of faith.

The entire credit for this progressive stance must go to India's women's movement which persuaded even the policy-makers to move away from the conventional notions. The only programme, however, that was designed to reflect this policy insight was *Mahila Samakhya*. Its objective was to enhance the self-esteem and self-confidence of women; build their positive image by recognizing their contribution to society, polity and the economy; develop their ability to think critically; enable them to make informed choices in areas like education, employment and health, especially reproductive health; and ensure equal participation in developmental processes (POA 1992, Chapter 1, Section 1.5.1). However, *Mahila Samakhya* remained marginal throughout the post-Jomtien phase. For every 100 rupees allocated for elementary education in the union budget, hardly 25 paise were given to it, and even this pittance came as external aid! In due course of time, as was expected, this miniscule programme too lost its basic direction.

Significantly, the Jomtien–Dakar Framework does not even refer to patriarchy as an issue, and essentially reduces girls' education to merely enrolling them on school registers and giving them literacy skills. This is exactly what happened when the World Bank-sponsored DPEP adopted *Mahila Samakhya*. The focus on collective reflection and socio-cultural action by organized women groups, as advocated by the policy, was abandoned. It became a *mere girl child enrolment* programme. Critical issues such as girls' participation in schools, gender sensitization of learning material, and teacher education and holistic educational aims were ignored. Unfortunately, the notion of gender parity (ratio of enrolment of girls and boys) in UNESCO's EFA Global Monitoring Report 2003–04 reinforces this confusion. Also, the World Bank diluted the goal of women's education to just raising their literacy levels and productivity (rather than educating or empowering them), and turning them into mere transmitters of fertility control, health or nutritional messages (World Bank 1997). The Jomtien–Dakar Framework has now added the ambiguous notion of life skills that seems to be yet another mechanism for social manipulation and market control of the adolescent mind-set, particularly that of girls. India, unfortunately, gave up its progressive policy on women's education in favour of the international framework which was guided more by considerations of the market than by women's socio-cultural and political rights.

Increasing Abdication by the State

We will only briefly touch upon this alarming post-Jomtien trend here, since it has been referred to elsewhere, as well as reflected in the various aspects of policy dilution and distortion listed above. What is needed is recognition of the relationship between these trends and the IMF–World Bank's structural adjustment programme which is accelerating the pace of moving Indian education towards privatization and commercialization, as proposed by the Ambani–Birla Report (Government of India 2000). However, we need to advance our understanding beyond the Ambani–Birla formulations which gave the false impression that it called for privatization only in higher education and partly in secondary education; the Report seemed to be saying that elementary education must be entirely a state responsibility. The post-Jomtien policy measures adopted by Indian policy-makers, however, have evidently enabled the state to rapidly withdraw even from the elementary education sector. This is reflected in the ever-reducing financial commitment for this sector, as discussed in detail below in the context of the Ninety-Third (now called Eighty-Sixth) Amendment. There is mounting evidence that the state is not ready to reprioritize the national economy in favour of education of the deprived sections of society, and has become dependent on external aid, as it seems to be refusing to provide for even the diluted policy measures and for the much-reduced financial requirement.[18]

External aid has had an adverse impact on the political will to reprioritize the national economy for mobilizing public resources for universalization of elementary education. Soon after the 1986 policy, we saw an upswing in the national effort to mobilize public resources for education. By 1989–90, almost 4 per cent of GDP was being spent on education, with little less than half on elementary education. Ironically, with the onset of external aid in primary education in the 1990s, the investment in education (including in elementary education) started declining steadily and was as low as 3.49 per cent of GDP in 1997–98, the same level as in 1985–86, just before the 1986 policy. Clearly, the political will to mobilize resources for elementary education weakened with the entry of external aid. It is only during the last two to three years that there has been some improvement, followed by a declining trend again in 2001–02, though the level of external aid was twice in this year than in 1997–98. This official stance is in clear violation of the CABE guidelines against 'dependency syndrome' and policy dilutions in relation to external aid (Government of India 1993: 89). This dependence of external aid, in fact, implies that *there need be no change in the priorities of the national economy* since additional funds will keep flowing in, as long as the Indian ruling elite is willing to adjust its educational policy to the conditionalities of the international funding agencies. These are matters of great concern for those of us who have been consistently questioning the role of external aid in elementary education.

The post-Jomtien MLL framework is suggestive of an 'Orwellian' basis for dividing the adolescent and the youth, that is, the 'product' of the educational system, in terms of their specific competencies, so that the emerging work force can be 'rationally utilized' by the market-oriented economy. It is in this context that each child will be assessed as a resource and be assigned a price tag accordingly! Such an inference is justified since the post-Jomtien focus is on extending the *utilitarian* framework of colonial (that is Macaulayian) education as a dominant trend of the future.

The following observation by Tomasevski, Special Rapporteur on the right to education to United Nations Commission on Human Rights, on the Jomtien Declaration and Framework will provide the necessary perspective for comprehending the adverse changes in Indian education in the post-Jomtien phase:

The language of the final document adopted by the Jomtien Conference merged human needs and market forces, moved education from governmental to social responsibility, made no reference to the international legal requirement that primary education be free-of-charge, introduced the term 'basic education' which confused conceptual and statistical categories. The language elaborated at Jomtien was different from the language of international human rights law. (Tomasevski 2001)

Taking an early cue from the Jomtien Declaration and foreseeing the political, historical and educational significance of this turning point, I proposed to view the post-independent history of education in India in two separate phases for the purpose of policy analysis, viz. the *Pre-Jomtien* and *Post-Jomtien phases* (Sadgopal 1994).

Legitimizing Exclusion and Inequality in Education

In November 2001, the government pushed The Constitution (Ninety-Third Amendment) Bill, 2001 in the Lok Sabha, purportedly to give education the status of a Fundamental Right for children in the 6–14 age group. Rechristened as the Eighty-Sixth Amendment Bill, it was approved by the Rajya Sabha in May 2002 and signed by the President in December 2002. This was despite widespread public protests, memoranda to the government and severely critical speeches by several MPs in both Houses of the Parliament. The Amendment Bill had the following four major lacunae:

(i) The Bill excluded almost 17 crore children up to 6 years of age from the provision of the Fundamental Right to *free* early childhood care and pre-school education. This was in contravention of NPE 1986 (as modified in 1992), which considered this support during childhood as being crucial for child development and preparation for elementary education (Sections 5.1 to 5.4). The implication was clear: early childhood care and pre-school education will be officially denied to not less than 40 per cent of the children in this age group, two-thirds of them being girls, whose parents barely manage to earn minimum wages. This will also prevent girls in the 6–14 age group, belonging to the same sections of society, from receiving elementary education, as they will be engaged in sibling care. The lack of guarantee of *free* early childhood care and pre-school education will not only result in underdevelopment of the deprived children during childhood, but will also adversely affect their learning capacity during school education.

(ii) The Bill made the provision of Fundamental Right to education even for the 6–14 age group children conditional, by introducing the phrase '*as the State may, by law, determine*' in the new Article 21A. The implications of this phrase will be discussed below.

(iii) The Bill attempted to shift the constitutional obligation towards 'free and compulsory education' from the state to parents or guardians by making it a Fundamental Duty of the latter under Article 51A(k) to '*provide opportunities for education'* to their children in the 6–14 age group. This purpose is now sought to be achieved by promoting and legitimizing *'community partici-pation'* in raising resources for elementary education (Government of India 2003b, c, 2004), yet another measure towards abdication by the state.

(iv) The Financial Memorandum attached to the Bill provided for only Rs 9,800 crore per annum (that is 0.44 per cent of GDP in 2002–03) over a ten-year period, for implementing the provisions under the Bill. This commitment was far from being adequate, as it was 30 per cent less than what was estimated by the Tapas Majumdar Committee in 1999 to provide elementary education to all out-of-school children through *'regular formal schools'*. This lower estimate was made possible by depending on low-quality parallel tracks of education, and lowering several other critically important infrastructural and pedagogic norms for deprived sections of society (Tilak 2003; Sadgopal 2003c).

The systematic move towards incremental abdication by the state of its constitutional obligations formed the core of the statement given by the Minister of Human Resource Development while presenting the Bill to the Lok Sabha on 28 November 2001. While acknowledging the criticality of early childhood care and pre-school education for children up to 6 years of age, the Minister was not willing to place this burden on the government. Yet, he contradicted himself by assuring the Lok Sabha that this stage of child development shall receive the government's full attention. As if to resolve this contradiction, the Minister in-vited *'all voluntary organizations and corporate houses'* to help the government in this sector. This plea of the Minister is tailormade to fit into the globalization agenda of reducing the role of the state and increasing the role of the market and the private sector, leading eventually to commercialization. This is where the government sees the space for NGOs too. The state will be happy to open its own coffers as well as to mediate funds from the World Bank, UN and other interna-tional donor agencies for those NGOs who would agree to legitimizing the government's pro-globalization agenda.

Detailed critiques of the Bill contended that the lacunae were deliberate, rather than being a result of an oversight (see Sadgopal 2001a, 2001b, 2002a; Swaminathan 2001). The amendment was being made, these writings sought to establish, not to make elementary education a Fundamental Right but to snatch away the educational rights already made available by the Supreme Court's Unnikrishnan Judgement (1993), and to fulfil the dictates of the IMF–World Bank's structural adjustment programme that demanded reduction in public expenditure on social sector. In particular, the above critiques focused upon the implications of the phrase *'as the State may, by law, determine'*. No such conditionality ex-isted in the original Article 45. It is contended that the phrase was introduced in order to legitimize the low-budget, low-quality, multiple or parallel tracks of so-called educational facilities for poor children, as well as other forms of policy dilutions and distortions discussed above. This phrase also lays the basic frame-work for increasing abdication by the state of its constitutional obligation towards ensuring elementary education of *equitable* quality for all children.

Indeed, the draft Free and Compulsory Education Bill, 2004, being processed at present for being taken to the Parliament, became possible only because of the space created by this conditional phrase in the amended Constitution. This is precisely what I had predicted on the day the Eighty-Sixth Amendment Bill was presented to the Parliament more than two years ago (Sadgopal 2001a, 2001b), but hardly anyone took me seriously.

To the agitated MPs from various political parties who criticized the Bill in both Houses of the Parliament, an assurance was repeatedly given by the Minister that the lacunae in the Bill would be taken care of by enacting a new law. How would a law take care of the lacunae introduced in the Constitution through an amendment? If the government intended to rectify the lacunae later through a law, why was it bent upon introducing these in the Constitution in the first place? The leadership of various political parties neither raised nor pursued such uncomfortable questions in the Parliament. The assurance of a law to be enacted later seemed to have led to a curious (or *convenient?*) consensus in the Parliament on the constitutional amendment, in spite of its unambiguous bias against crores of children (girl children in particular) belonging to various deprived sections of society (Sadgopal 2001b, 2002a), and violations of several provisions in the Constitution relating to Parts III and IV.

Free and Compulsory Education Bill, 2003–04

Let me also briefly examine the law that is now before us in the form of the draft Free and Compulsory Education Bill, 2003–04 (Government of India 2003b, 2003c, 2004, Drafts I, II and III respectively). This is the law that was promised by the government in Parliament presumably to take care of the lacunae in the Eighty-Sixth Amendment Bill. Ironically, careful scrutiny by several academics, teachers, advocates and voluntary organizations reveals that, instead of 'taking care of the lacunae' in the Eighty-Sixth Amendment, the aforementioned draft Bill increases the lacunae on several grounds (Social Jurist 2003). We will not go into all those issues at the moment, but it would suffice to refer to the relevant portions of Schedule A of the Bill (Drafts I and II) which provides for *three types* of centres for 'imparting education', specifying their minimum norms.

Schedule A
A. Regular School:
Provides for
- 'At least two teachers in primary school';
- 'At least one room for every teacher'; and
- Qualification of teachers 'as approved by the National Council of Teacher Education (NCTE)', that is, the prevailing minimum qualifications for regular, properly qualified and trained teachers.

B. EGS Centres/Alternate Schools:
- 'At least four hours of teaching every day';

- Qualification of teachers: Class X certificate (Class VIII in the case of women) along with mere 30 days' training will be adequate;
- Yet, the curriculum will be 'same as the curriculum prescribed for recognized schools'.

[In this specification on the curriculum, we have an uncanny reflection of the NFE discourse of the late 1980s, evident in NPE 1986 and POA 1986, as documented earlier. Also, as expected, there are no norms for physical infrastructure since the EGS Centres/Alternate Schools will be provided none!]

C. Open Schooling Centres:
Based on The Free and Compulsory Education for Children Bill Draft I (Government of India 2003b). The mind-set of the state is further revealed by comparing Drafts I and II (Government of India 2003b and 2003c respectively). Although Draft II of the Bill is likely to be replaced by Draft III (Government of India 2004), this comparison, at least, enables us to see the likely direction in which the legislation may be moving. Three points may be briefly noted in this regard:

• The minimum, though nominal, norm for training of 'at least 30 days' for teachers to be recruited for EGS Centres/Alternate Schools in Draft I has been further diluted in Draft II which states:
Training: Should have been trained for at least 30 days *either before or within 6 months* of appointment (emphasis added).
• The minimum norm of 'at least four hours of teaching every day' for EGS Centres/Alternate Schools in Draft I has been diluted in Draft II by replacing it with *'As may be prescribed in the approved scheme'* (emphasis added).
• Draft II places the provision of boundary wall or fencing, playground, *toilets and drinking water*, child-friendly elements (?) and sports equipment in the category called 'Desirable' even for the 'Regular Approved Schools' (emphasis added)!

The draft Bill is both ambiguous and weak on inclusion of physically and mentally disabled children in the regular approved schools. Its provisions will encourage as well as facilitate violation of the policy commitment for inclusive education, which is integral to the fulfilment of the constitutional obligation for equality in education and for building up the Common School System (Jha 2003). As noted by Jha (ibid.), the Bill might even promote privatization and commercialization of the education of the disabled.

The draft Bill, thus, fully legitimizes the discriminatory, low-quality, multiple and parallel tracks of education, already institutionalized in the *operating* policy and programmes, for the deprived sections of society. In a sense, the Bill will carry forward the process of abdication by the state of its constitutional obligation for which a legitimate space was created by the Eighty-Sixth Amendment by introducing the conditionality, that is, *'as the State may, by law, determine'*, for provision of free and compulsory education for children in the 6–14 age group.

The draft Bill, when passed by the Parliament, will fully protect and also 'guarantee' the exclusion and discrimination designed by the *Sarva Shiksha Abhiyan* in its following statement: 'All children in school, Education Guarantee Scheme (EGS) centre, alternate school, "back-to-school camp" by 2003' (Government of India 2003a: 27).

With this guarantee for protection, the Indian government persists in its refusal to reprioritize the national economy, and continues its campaign for seeking increased external aid, thereby further subjugating the nation's education system and policies to control by the global market.

Assault on the Character of Knowledge

As was the case with the Macaulayian approach to education, globalization also aims at using education as a tool for building up various skills and capacities that are useful to the global economy (recall the competency-based approach of MLL). We have already examined the post-Jomtien framework in which educational aims are being trivialized and curricular knowledge is either being reduced to mere literacy skills (for reading product labels and prices), or fragmented into bits of information or competencies (for reading factory instructions, punching keys at the computer keyboard or accepting the dictates of the market *uncritically*). This amounts to rejection of a holistic approach to building up an enlightened and humane society. In this paradigm, knowledge in the sciences, social sciences and humanities would need to be divested of its philosophical, historical, ethical, socio-cultural and aesthetic roots. Given the predominance of market forces in the globalized world, it can be predicted that only those courses, research programmes or training activities would receive financial support which have a saleable value in the global market. This is exactly what was proposed by the Ambani–Birla Report (Government of India 2000). The implication is clear. Any discipline, sub-discipline or even set of ideas which are not saleable will gradually wither away, unless supported proactively by public funds as part of a conscious social policy. Interlinkage between *knowledge* (which is viewed in the globalized world as being synonymous with *information*) and its epistemic roots may not carry any price tag in the market economy. It has, however, critical significance for social reconstruction and transformation. *In this sense, there is a fundamental conflict of an epistemological nature between globalization and social development.*

Alienation of knowledge from the social ethos is a logical outcome of globalization. Increasing preference for the internet as a source of *'knowledge'* (read *information*), and its screening or filtration by corporate forces on the basis of marketability, will lead to uprooting of a substantial proportion of knowledge from its social ethos. Those communities, sections of society or nations denied equitable access to digital technology or English, the dominant language of information technology, will neither share the digitalized knowledge nor be able to contribute their knowledge for human progress. Geo-cultural diversity will come to be largely ignored and eventually have little role to play in defining or

qualifying knowledge. This trend will, over a period of time, establish the hegemony of only globally acceptable (that is marketable) parameters of what is
worth knowing in the age of globalization. Strangely enough, this hegemony
provides a meeting ground between the 'free' market agenda of globalization
and the well-established centralizing tendency of NCERT, at least in the short
term.

   Commercialization of higher and technical education has been promoted
in the post-Jomtien phase under the false argument that *resources need to be
shifted from this sector to the primary education sector*, as strongly advocated by
the Ambani–Birla Report (Government of India 2000). It needs to be emphasized
that *knowledge is produced and communicated in institutions of higher learning*.
This holds true even for knowledge that is essential for improving the curriculum, pedagogy and quality of teacher education programmes for school education. If public expenditure in higher education is reduced, it will lead to the
following anomalies.

   (a) Only those disciplines or sub-disciplines will be allowed to survive that
       have a marketable value; the rest of the disciplines, irrespective of their
       socio-cultural or epistemological significance, will gradually wither
       away.
   (b) The lower middle class and the deprived sections of society are likely to
       be denied access to this knowledge as well as participation in generating
       and reconstructing it; this will lead to further reinforcement of elitist
       control over knowledge and its social application.
   (c) The entire higher education system will become oriented to only utilitar-
       ian goals, while any knowledge that might lead towards social develop-
       ment or transformation will be marginalized.

   The following somewhat humorous but scary futuristic description of
higher education may be cited from an epilogue I wrote four years ago at the
peak of former US President Clinton's visit to India:

> Year 2010. The ultramodern campus of the newly established 'Bill Clinton
> International University' near Delhi. Two women students meet. One calls out
> to the other, 'Come, let us go somewhere and relax'. The other student says, 'I
> have a packed day today. In the first period, there is Unilever practical in the
> Coca-Cola Physics Lab; in the second period, there is the Proctor and Gambles
> session on Western Dance Appreciation in the Pepsi Theatre; this will be fol-
> lowed by the Suzuki Lecture on Information Technology in the Microsoft Au-
> ditorium. And then the recess. Come, let us meet in the Kentucky Chicken
> Canteen in the Union Carbide Square.' (Sadgopal 2000: 257; excerpted and
> translated from Hindi)

   The above scenario may not be so fanciful as it might appear. The newly
opened G.G.S. Indraprastha University in Delhi started five B.Ed. colleges in one
lot in 1999. A seat in these colleges costs Rs 45,000 each. To counter any allega-
tion of the elitist orientation, half of the seats are termed 'free seats', costing

'merely' Rs 12,000 each! Compare this with the fee of approximately Rs 2,500 per seat in the UGC-subsidized Central Institute of Education (CIE) of the University of Delhi, where a lower middle class or even a poor student (including tribal students from Rajasthan villages) can hope to obtain a B.Ed. degree with dignity and as a matter of right. But pressure is on for institutions such as CIE as well to change or else just be wiped out, as the UGC support to higher education is threatened to be drastically reduced, if not withdrawn all together. We already have UGC's 'Model Act for Universities' before us attempting to achieve precisely this objective. Such measures will clearly be in violation of the value framework of the Indian Constitution which emphasizes equality and social justice. This violation is only indicative of greater dangers ahead. For instance, the constitutional review, which seems to have been presently put on the back burner for strategic reasons, can hardly be expected to resist the pressure of global market forces when the entire Indian polity has already begun to make major adjustments, if not succumb to these forces. Evidence of this trend (that is, the changing relationship between the state and market) was also provided by the Supreme Court in its verdict given in October 2002 in what is popularly known as the minorities case (TMA Pai Foundation vs. State of Karnataka) which, by essentially reversing the Unnikrishnan judgement (1993), helped 'to sustain the ethos in which private interests can boldly advance and the State withdraws' (Kumar 2003).

Deconstructing Policy Statements

We have earlier referred to the marginalization of geo-cultural diversities in the post-Jomtien framework while maintaining the rhetoric of being committed to promotion of plurality. The market economy demands that multicultural, multi-linguistic or multi-ethnic societies are homogenized so that the marketing of a product is facilitated. The greater the homogenization (also read, standardization), the greater will be the size of the market for a specific product. An editorial in a UNESCO Newsletter (October–December 2002) advocated 'commoditization of learning material' for reducing the cost of production. Although, for the corporate world, this immediate economic motivation is adequate ground for pushing homogenization, the long-term political gains in terms of dominance of market forces over global, natural and human resources also need to be kept in mind.

Indeed, globalization has the *hidden agenda* of minimizing cultural diversity even across national boundaries. A document released jointly by UNESCO's International Bureau of Education and CBSE (2000: 10) notes that globalization is leading to '*erosion of the power of nation-states*', concomitant with the '*transfer of sovereignty*' from governments to larger geo-political regional entities (for example, ASEAN, CIS, European Union, etc.). The same document further recognizes that the development of multinational corporations has contributed to a '*dramatic increase in trans-border exchanges*' (ibid.). With the increasing dominance of information and communication technology in the promotion of the 'knowledge industry', one can easily see how the process of globalization is leading towards irreversible homogenization of plural cultures, ethnicities and languages, with the objective of increasing the size of the market and enhancing the political dominance of corporate powers (McDonalds and Kentucky Chicken are not mere symbols but represent the substantive content of this homogenization agenda!). The inclusion of these concepts in an educational document (ibid.) shows that the international educational bureaucracy has readily accepted the ideological dominance of globalization, and, that too, with an undercurrent of admiration!

Let us now examine how the Indian state is preparing itself to support the impetus given by globalization to homogenization of plurality. There is concrete evidence in recent policy documents of strong centralizing tendencies, including in NCERT's National Curriculum Framework for School Education (NCERT 2000). These are reflected in concrete measures relating to curriculum formation, textbook writing, preparation of 'modular instructional packages' and 'encapsulated orientation materials', organization of teacher education programmes, and standardization of evaluative criteria and testing services (ibid., Sections 4.6, 4.7, 5.1.1, 5.1.4, 5.2.7).[19] The setting up of national-level mechanisms for testing 'products' of higher education, and assessment and accreditation of institutions are part of the market agenda for standardization and commoditization of education. Ironically, these tendencies contradict the claims in the same policy documents regarding the need for promoting both plurality and plural pedagogies. It is precisely for this reason that we have to learn to deconstruct the policy statements and not be carried away by the rising decibel of the rhetoric.

The Bretton Woods institutions and associated international forces promoting globalization have burnt their midnight oil before proposing that the phenomenon of 'erosion of the power of the nation-states' and 'transfer of sovereignty' from nations to transnational corporations will form the cutting edge of globalization. However, the phenomenon has to be couched in a language that would be politically acceptable. The policy-makers have, therefore, discovered that 'interdependence and interrelationships between peoples and cultures' is the major consequence of globalization (UNESCO and CBSE 2000: 5). The International Commission on Education's Report (the Delors Commission's Report) to UNESCO states that 'learning to live together' must be one of the pillars of globalized education (Delors et al. 1996, 1998: 22). We must enquire into the real reason behind this sudden respect for 'learning to live together', while the same forces also recognize that globalization is widening the gap between 'those who globalize and those who are globalized' (UNESCO and CBSE 2000: 12). What is so new in this concept that, all of a sudden, that is, in the late 1990s, an International Commission on Education, followed by a host of international agencies, has discovered in it the guidelines of critical significance for remoulding the curriculum of all nations, especially the developing ones? The age-old Indian concept of Vasudhaiva Kutumbakum ('It is the entire world that is a family') never seemed to excite the imagination of either the international or the Indian educational bureaucracy more than it does today!

In the paradigm of globalization, universities are being perceived as 'knowledge producers' and the students as 'knowledge consumers', with hitherto hallowed institutions like science museums playing the intermediary role of 'information brokers' (ibid.: 11). This perception provides the underlying principle of globalized education for turning knowledge into a mere commodity in the global market system. It is already envisaged, as also is the case with the recently proposed UGC's Model Act, that the task of producing and disseminating knowledge in the universities through information and communication technology, the so-called 'knowledge industry', will be increasingly commercialized and handed over to the transnational corporations in the near future. In light of these known outcomes of globalization, the *'producer–broker–consumer'* paradigm of knowledge will begin to define the hidden agenda of globalized education.

The Delors Commission's emphasis on 'learning to live together' and the 'producer–broker–consumer' paradigm of globalized education have provided the rationale to the International Bureau of Education, a UNESCO institute, to conclude that global attention must bear upon the curricular concerns of the member-states, and that there is enough room for adaptation of educational content of various countries to the demands of globalization. For this, an *'international platform of information on educational content'* will be built up through *'a number of regional and sub-regional cooperation projects'* for facilitating intervention in national education systems by global corporate forces (ibid.). Of course, all this will be euphemized as *'adaptation of content to the demands of globalization and the need for learning to live together'* (ibid.: 6). This is exactly what the Jomtien Declaration and its 'Framework for Action' also ordained. And this challenge of globalization is knocking right now at the doors of Indian education!

The Communal Assault

My analysis of the impact of globalization will remain incomplete if I do not refer to the recent assault by the forces of communalism and religious fundamentalism on the knowledge inherent in the school curriculum. I will prefer to be brief on this subject as it has been extensively debated and commented upon in the media and academic discourse during the last three to four years. Even the Parliament has devoted several hours to this issue. For a detailed account, one may refer to compilations by the Delhi Historians' Group (2001), SAHMAT (2001) and SAHMAT–Sabrang.com (2001).

In 1993, seven years before the recent, fresh but highly organized wave of communal assault on the school curriculum, I wrote a detailed analysis of a new textbook prescribed by the first BJP government of Madhya Pradesh in the previous year, as a compulsory text for the foundation course for the Bachelor degree programme in all the seven state universities (*Hans*, September 1993; reprinted in Sadgopal 2000: 124–35). In this account, I identified six features of the changes evident in the new text (also in school textbooks of a comparable period in Uttar Pradesh) that defined the basic framework of communalization of knowledge in subjects such as history, geography and civics. As one examines the nature of the recent changes in the National Curricular Framework for School Education (NCERT 2000), Guidelines and Syllabi (NCERT 2001) and NCERT textbooks (2002–03), one is struck by the similarity of frameworks that defined the communalization of texts in 1993 and 2000–03. I am tempted, therefore, to share the earlier six-point framework, as presented below, along with certain explanatory remarks.

(i) To perceive and present all those ethnic or cultural groups that had migrated to the Indian subcontinent from other parts of the world as 'aliens', even if the said migration is known to have taken place more than 2,000 years ago; this is precisely why it became necessary for the Sangh Parivar to make an issue out of the origin of Aryans, the presumed 'founders' of Hinduism, and to make the controversial claim that their roots can be traced to as far back as the Harappan age; this is also precisely why the Sangh Parivar envisages the history of the Indian freedom struggle to be more than 2,000 years old, presumably for 'liberating' the motherland from the migrated 'aliens'.

(ii) To view Hindu culture as something 'pure' or absolute and to perceive the influence of any other culture essentially as 'adulteration'; this view implies that culture is a non-changing and inert phenomenon; the protagonists of this view deny that culture has any dynamic relationship with socio-economic conditions since their claim of the 'pure' nature of what they call Hindu culture will become untenable if such a dynamic relationship is granted.

(iii) The above premise is also the basis of the communalized perception of values in education and religion being their only source, as, according to this view, values do not arise out of human experience and its interaction with social reality but out of a 'spiritual' vacuum; like culture, this premise allows one to look at values also as being absolute; the delinking of values from social reality seems to be central to Hindutva's[20] strategy for maintaining the hegemony of the upper castes and upper classes over the rest, and also to provide an 'escape route' to the ruling elite from issues of disparity, oppression and injustice.

(iv) The traditional brahmanical, patriarchal and hegemonic culture of India is presumed to be synonymous with the contemporary Indian culture. This incomplete and distorted perception allows Hindutva to deny the rich plural cultural heritage of India. In order to sustain this ahistorical view, it has become necessary for Hindutva to also deny the concept of composite culture, and to insist upon monocultural hegemony in contemporary Indian society.

(v) In the above cultural framework, there is no space for acknowledging the contribution made by any non-brahmanical, non-patriarchal or non-hegemonic (that is, all-encompassing, egalitarian and democratic) tradition to Indian history or the making of our present culture. As a corollary of this irrational view, the Sangh Parivar would prefer to ignore the historical contributions made by the tribals, particularly by those of the northeastern region, to the building of contemporary India. It also becomes necessary for the Hindutva forces to marginalize the role of the dalits and tribals, as well as of the other non-Hindu sections of society, in the freedom struggle, and also to perceive the latter more as a struggle for the defence of Hindu 'cultural nationalism' or creation of '*Hindu Rashtra*' than for liberating India from colonial oppression.

(vi) There is no space for class analysis in Hindutva thinking since such an analysis will reveal major socio-economic and cultural contradictions within Indian society through various stages of history, thereby demanding their scientific resolution on the principle of dialectical materialism. It is therefore necessary for Hindutva to view Indian history in isolation from the productive forces in society, and to deny class struggle as a historical phenomenon of social development.

(Adapted from Sadgopal 2000: 125–26)

The above six-point framework enables us to both predict and deconstruct the nature of the communal assault upon the curriculum. I will avoid the temptation to demonstrate this by taking concrete examples from the recent NCERT curricular material. However, as an illustration, let me refer to certain issues relating to gender and patriarchy. In October 2001, on directions from NCERT, the CBSE ordered deletion of certain portions of history texts, and directed the affiliated schools neither to teach nor even to discuss these in the classrooms! One of these referred to Emperor Ashoka (273–32 BC) who '*derided superfluous rituals performed by women*' which '*naturally affected the income of the brahmanas*'. The text had recorded that the '*brahmanas developed some kind of antipathy to him* [Ashoka] . . . *really wanted a policy that would favour them and uphold the existing interests and privileges*'. Clearly, the government did not want students to learn how the powerful brahmanas in ancient India exploited women by promoting superstition in the name of culture, or how they resisted the progressive state policy of Emperor Ashoka in favour of women. The policymakers must have been apprehensive of students becoming aware of the socio-cultural roots of patriarchy, as this might encourage them to question its practice in contemporary India too.

The Work Education programme in the NCERT syllabus for the secondary stage recommends two sex-stereotyped courses – one for rural girls and the other for urban girls (NCERT 2001: 95). Worse is NCERT's conception of pre-vocational activities for the upper primary stage as it includes sex-stereotyped activities such as 'maintaining cleanliness at home', 'keeping sources of water in the school and the community safe and clean', and, amazingly, 'helping parents in looking after younger children and old family members' (ibid.: 86–87). With the deep-seated gender bias in the curriculum framework and lack of any programme for women's empowerment in the *operating* education policy, it is easy to guess as to who would be assigned such sex-stereotyped pre-vocational activities in the schools. The syllabi for other subjects also lack a gender perspective. The gender bias can further be seen in the latest NCERT textbooks which refer to the contribution of women to Indian history and the making of contemporary India only marginally.

Let me also briefly mention the Hindutva denial of rationality and critical reasoning in education. The allocation of financial resources by UGC in 2001–02 for starting courses in *Jyotirvigyan* (that is, astrology, not astronomy) and *Paurohitya* (brahmanical *karmakand*) is not to be wished away as just a bizarre expression of an irrational world-view. Rather, this is precisely its preferred manifestation. What is more significant is the de-emphasis in the NCERT curriculum and texts on critical thought and a scientific temper concomitant with the rising expectation of uncritical acceptance of a revivalist world-view. Both Puniyani (SAHMAT 2001: 49–61) and Ahmad (2002: 82–91) have attempted a rational distinction between reform and revivalism, and documented historical and sociological evidence to show how critical reason became a powerful tool for the oppressed classes to challenge the hegemony of the upper castes and upper classes. Ahmad (ibid.: 88) observes that a common trait among the revivalist movements has been '*an anti-materialist conception of revolution, an anti-liberal conception of nationalism and an anti-rationalist critique of modernity*'.

At this juncture, it may not be out of place to raise the question, what is the linkage between globalization and communalization? Religious fundamentalism appears in different forms in different religious or cultural contexts, but the common thread in all kinds of fundamentalist ideologies has been a blind revivalist tendency. This tendency is then used to underline and strengthen a false consciousness of a narrow and exclusivist communal identity. In complex and plural societies like ours, Hindu fundamentalism (read, Hindutva of the contemporary Indian polity) can coexist and flourish alongside fundamentalist tendencies of other religions. In contrast, some of our neighbouring countries would exhibit monolithic fundamentalism. Irrespective of the specific religious or cultural context, communal politics and globalization seem to form an undeclared alliance in spite of their contradictory frameworks and roots. Ahmad (ibid.) contends that, while fundamentalism emerges out of an archaic, feudal and anti-scientific ideology, globalization *claims* to represent the 'liberal and scientific framework' which underlines the latter's ideology of 'modernity'. Significantly, Ahmad seeks to resolve this apparent contradiction by offering the following analysis of the 'anti-rationalist critique of modernity' as advanced by the revivalist movements:

> It is significant that this critique of Modernity was also very partial. It does not include, for example, a repudiation of the market, which has been so central

an institution of capitalist forms of rationality and modernity. Nor does it repudiate the sciences and technologies upon which modern industrial production is based, and which are so much the source of capitalist wealth. Rather it rejects ... the values of non-racial and non-denominational equality, the fraternity of the culturally diverse, the supremacy of reason over Faith, the belief in freedom and progress, the belief that the exercise of critical reason, beyond all tradition or convention or institution, is the fundamental civic virtue without which other civic virtues cannot be sustained. (Ibid.: 90)

With this analytical insight into the framework of coexistence of globalization and communalization, the latter with its roots in religious fundamentalism, it also becomes possible to unravel the nature of their collusion. The two ideologies support each other in so far as communalization can be used for stabilizing and enlarging the market. This is a reminder of the support extended by the British *Raj* to fundamentalist forces (Islamic as well as Hindu) in order to strengthen its colonial stranglehold. Similarly, when fundamentalism raises its ugly face, the forces of globalization would prefer to look the other way, as long as the former is kept within bounds to politically stabilize the market in the long run. Further, as globalization fails to generate adequate employment, it is expected that there will be a rapid rise in socio-economic tensions, eventually leading to even political unrest. This is exactly what communalization of politics achieves by diverting the attention of the masses from socio-economic issues to the perceived 'dangers' to their religious identity. This should explain why NCERT's new curricular material attempts to simultaneously promote both globalization and communalization through education.

Before I move on, I must also draw attention to the fascist tendencies emerging in education. It will suffice for me to reproduce the following analysis I wrote within three days of the release of NCERT's National Curriculum Framework for School Education in November 2000.

Over-Baked, Quarter-Baked and Unbaked Quotients: A curriculum framework for inequity, social fragmentation and cultural hegemony

On 14 November 2000 (Children's Day), the Minister of Human Resource Development presented the revised version of the National Curriculum Framework for School Education to the nation. Authored by an NCERT group, the document raises more new and perplexing questions than it answers. It is true that the document is not termed a policy and is cautiously called a *mere* curriculum framework in order to obviate the need to seek the sanction of the Parliament which will be necessarily preceded by an uncomfortable and embarrassing national debate (remember the storm in October 1998 when the same Minister tried to sneak in a new communalized educational agenda at the State Education Ministers' Conference and was persuaded to backtrack!).

This time, the attempt to achieve the same objective is not just well camouflaged but can be credited for being both tactful and suave. Yet, the new policy perspective reflecting the socio-cultural and political thinking of the dominant party in the central government is too evident to be hidden.

The rhetoric and the smokescreen need to be deciphered. For this, we need to construct a framework which will be defined by at least the following three major Constitutional concerns:

- universally accessible education of equitable quality for all children in order to build up a cohesive society and ensure Fundamental Rights;
- an ever-widening democratic space for the articulation and development of each community in the multilingual, multicultural and multi-ethnic Indian society; and
- a forward-looking educational system that will enable the unfolding of the holistic potential of each child (and not just those of the elite).

The NCERT document refers to the much-debated concept of Minimum Levels of Learning (MLL) which was introduced by NCERT in 1990 on the basis of a report hastily prepared by a handful of officially chosen 'experts' (out of whom two to three have since disowned its main recommendations). The MLL has been mechanically imposed on the primary schools of the entire country despite its highly questionable philosophical and pedagogic basis. This imposition also ignored the rich diversity of the country, which we all continue to claim must be the basis of planning curricula and preparing textbooks.

The MLL experiment has never been scientifically evaluated. As if this was not enough, the new document now talks of measuring children in terms of their Intelligent Quotient (IQ), Emotional Quotient (EQ) and Spiritual Quotient (SQ). IQ is an over-baked concept which was introduced at the beginning of the twentieth century in the west to presumably calibrate the intelligence levels of children. The concept was part of the attempt by western psychologists to provide a tool for categorizing children. This was then used to claim that low IQ levels are genetically predetermined and that poor children have low IQ levels not because of socio-cultural conditions but because of their genetics.

Later, IQ was also used to racially denigrate the blacks and all other non-white ethnic groups, and, further, to claim that any public expenditure on their education would be a waste since nothing can be done to change their IQ levels. Such distorted thinking has already been rejected by a majority of the academic community, but continues to be used for racial and fascist politics.

As far as Emotional Quotient (EQ) is concerned, there have been only descriptive records of what can be termed as desirable emotional attributes. Even here, the cultural framework of EQ is hardly understood, which makes such a concept totally inappropriate for a multicultural country like India. Given such a fluid basis of understanding, there is no question of having any scientific ground for talking of measuring the emotional attributes of children. Indeed, this concept cannot be called even quarter-baked.

Spiritual Quotient (SQ) has not even a fragment of descriptive research basis. There is no understanding, not even in a specified cultural milieu, of an acceptable definition of spiritual attributes.

Why, then, have the NCERT scholars proposed the use of such over-baked, quarter-baked and unbaked concepts for the evaluation of children? The only plausible answer will come from an understanding of a political agenda combining both globalization and religious fundamentalism. It is only in this paradigm that educational psychologists will be required to lend their services to calibrate, categorize, label and eventually marginalize the vast masses of poor children so that a stable globalized market can be built up in India for the benefit of 15 per cent of the nation's population. Fortunately for the promoters of the joint agenda of globalization and religious fundamentalism, 15 per cent of India's population will provide a market as big in size as the entire Europe! Clearly, the NCERT document is a declaration of a new education policy for strengthening globalization on the one hand, and religious fundamentalism on the other.

(Excerpted from Anil Sadgopal's article published in
Hindustan Times, 18 November 2000)

We may also recognize that the emergence of this design for the communalization of knowledge in the curriculum and promoting fascist thinking is not an isolated act of academic institutions such as NCERT, ICHR, ICPR or ICSSR alone. This design will be incomplete if it is not fully supported and coordinated with other branches of the state. Let me cite two pieces of recent evidence. I had earlier referred to the Free and Compulsory Education Bill (Draft I), which was in circulation since June 2003. Within six days of the announcement, on 4 December 2003, of BJP's electoral victory in three states, viz. Rajasthan, Madhya Pradesh and Chhattisgarh, the government introduced Draft II of the Bill. The new draft had the following two additional features:

(a) A 'Competent Academic Authority' which will mean 'an authority empowered by law or by the Central or an appropriate [that is state] government, or recognized by such government, for prescribing curriculum for the elementary stage' [Draft II, Section 2(1)(f)].

(b) A set of provisions for constituting elementary education authorities from the state level down to the level of district, block and even a village hamlet (termed habitation) that will be parallel to the constitutional authorities of the state government as well as the Panchayati Raj institutions or municipal bodies under the Seventy-Third and Seventy-Fourth Amendments (Draft II, Sections 16–20). This parallel structure will be fully empowered for the purpose of financing, promoting and planning, giving recognition, regulating, guiding, monitoring and providing academic or technical support to elementary education. The state-level parallel authority will be empowered for even 'formulation of policy, laying down of priorities . . . and mobilization and allocation of resources', and, of course, also for 'promotion of use of information technology and distance education' [Draft II, Section 20(3)(iii) and (vi)]. I need not comment on the 'hidden agenda'. It would now make it possible for the forces of communalization to marginalize the constitutional authorities and set up a parallel structure under their direct control to manipulate elementary education. In order to ensure that this provision is not used by secular political formations in various states, a clever mechanism has been built in for the manner of notifying the Bill. Section 1(3) of Draft II provides for the following: 'It shall come into force on such date as the Central Government may by notification in the Official Gazette appoint and different dates may be appointed for different provisions of the Act, *and for different parts of the country.*' (Free and Compulsory Education Bill, 2003, Section 1(3), Draft II dated 10 December 2003. *Note*: The phrase in italics was not there in Draft I. It was added in Draft II following the BJP's electoral gains in three states.

As if this was not enough, a third draft of the Bill was issued on 16 January 2004. This latest draft has provisions that will make it obligatory for the state governments or the Competent Academic Authorities to follow the National Curriculum Framework and 'essential levels of learning' notified by NCERT (Draft III, Section 30). As of today, due to the concurrent status of education, the state governments are under no such obligation and are free to follow their own curriculum framework and prepare their own text materials. This new provision aims at not just imposing a communalized curriculum but also at destroying, from the back door, the federal character of the Indian Constitution. This 'deconstructed reading' of the Bill reveals the intention of the state to push the joint agenda of globalization–communalization. For reasons that must be obvious, the government is waiting for more convenient circumstances to present the Bill to the Parliament, but the instrument for furthering the combined agenda of Hindutva-cum-market forces into Indian education is ready.

Transformative Education

Given the producer–broker–consumer paradigm that has begun to govern the relationship between the teacher and the students, there is hardly any space left in globalized education for 'liberative' (or, for that matter, even *liberal*) pedagogy. The search necessarily has to be for a pedagogy that leads to liberation from the framework of exploitation, subjugation and dehumanization, and, at the same time, enables construction of alternative frameworks. A 'liberative' pedagogy, critical for social transformation, would provide ample space for the students to be actively engaged in *reconstruction of knowledge*, and then, to begin with, in *questioning the world around them* and eventually in *attempting to transform it*. The transformative paradigm would resist all attempts to fragment or restrict the holistic vision of education dedicated to the creation of an enlightened and humane society. The resistance to fragmentation of such a holistic vision would have to be reflected in various dimensions including the education system and its structural aspects, epistemological issues and pedagogic (in its widest meaning) concerns.

The whole point is to explore how, given the constraints imposed by market forces, education can still be transformed to resist the ill-effects of globalization, rather than accepting it as the unchallenged destiny of crores of our children and youth. Let, therefore, the framework of a dialectical materialistic relationship between educational transformation and social change inform this discourse. We may pose the following questions:

Depending upon what is feasible in the present national as well as the global situation, what role can education play in preparing the society to deal with the adverse social, cultural and economic impacts of globalization?

What conscious steps would we have to take in order to transform the quality and direction of education for this purpose?

What implications does this view of the transformative role of education have for the following:

- aims of education;
- structure of the school (or higher education) system;
- community's relationship with the school/university;
- pedagogic relations between the teacher and the students;
- role of children and youth in reconstruction of knowledge;
- parameters of evaluation?

Each one of the above issues would require a detailed scrutiny of the concept of knowledge and society, and their inter-relationship, as reflected in the present curriculum. This should pave the way for undertaking an enquiry into the transformation process that the education system would have to undergo in order to acquire a truly 'liberative' character. Such an enquiry, however, cannot be accommodated here.

Globalization: An Epistemic Challenge

At the beginning of this essay, I referred to the concept of Basic Education as advanced by Gandhiji at the Wardha Conference in 1937 as part of the freedom struggle, and later concretized into an eight-year curriculum by the Zakir Husain Committee. The above enquiry into the combined assault of globalization and communalization on the sources, nature, accessibility, application, distribution and control of knowledge provides the necessary backdrop in which we will explore this matter. In proposing that knowledge should pedagogically emerge from productive work and that education be evolved as 'the spearhead of a silent social revolution', Gandhiji had, in a way, called for deconstruction and reconstruction of the epistemic character of Indian education.

For the next thirty years, the Indian political and educational leadership tried to grapple with Gandhiji's revolutionary proposal and to 'coopt' it in various forms within the colonial framework that it had decided to retain. Each official attempt at such cooption (for example, work experience, SUPW, *Shramdan* or social service as extra-curricular activities, 'learning by doing', etc.) further distanced the adapted version from the Gandhian concept. Throughout this period, Zakir Sahib was much sought after by official committees, educationists, teacher educators and the general public as the most articulate advocate of Basic Education. He would passionately explain the significance of 'essential educative conditions of work', the need to view schools as 'small educational communities with some common values' and the role of the mother tongue in Basic Education. As long back as in 1938, Zakir Sahib is reported to have protested to B.G. Kher, the then Premier and Education Minister of Bombay province (also chairperson of a CABE committee on educational reconstruction as per the Basic Education scheme), against the bifurcation of the school age into periods of five years (that is, primary) and three years (that is, upper primary), and pleaded for maintaining the integrated character of knowledge in elementary education (Mujeeb 2000: 224). Would today's proponents in India of World Bank and UN agencies, DPEP and external aid, which split elementary education into two unrelated stages during the 1990s with a tendency to reduce primary education further to two to three years of lower primary only, take note of this principled stand of Zakir Sahib? Ironically, Zakir Sahib had to contend with protests from some Muslim education bodies as well against the exclusion of religious instruction from the Basic Education syllabus and its entirely secular outlook, but his rational and humane approach eventually won their support, too, for both Basic Education and its secular basis (ibid.: 223, 225–26). It is important to recall these debates and to take inspiration from the ways in which our predecessors like Zakir Sahib dealt with the challenge to the democratic, secular and egalitarian conscience of education. I had earlier referred to Zakir Sahib's insight regarding how social conscience eventually 'forces capitalism to subordinate itself to social purpose'. In what Zakir Sahib did to promote Basic Education for almost three decades in his indomitable style, fighting essentially a losing battle, we see him playing his own historical role in the assertion of this social conscience.

Here is my understanding of what basically went wrong with the state policy regarding Basic Education. In contrast to the Gandhian notion, none of its official versions in post-independent India were designed to question either the philosophical, moral or socio-political basis of the colonial framework of education, or its epistemic character. In this sense, Basic Education was never even attempted to be implemented as a state policy for building the national education system. This perception leads me to the following thesis. The genesis of the post-Jomtien crisis can be traced to the failure of the Indian political and educational leadership in not being able to perceive the crisis in terms of the nature of knowledge and its social role, as reflected in colonial education. If it had proceeded to deconstruct the colonial framework and reconstruct the national education system on the core principles of Basic Education (or, for that matter, some other integrated philosophical framework rooted in the Indian ethos and contemporary social challenges), the forces of the market and communalism were less likely to find the political faultline through which to launch their assault. This thesis needs to be critically examined and tested. When we do this, it will become evident that basically it is the notion of knowledge itself that determines the social, structural and pedagogic character of education, as well as its relationships with the society.

Conclusion

I have sought to establish that the exclusion and discrimination inherent in the present *operating* education policy, though considerably exacerbated by the impact of globalization, has its roots in the national policies formulated well before the global market forces gained a dominant position in India. In this, we have a significant lesson: even as we must deepen our analysis to comprehend the nature and full dimension of the adverse impact of globalization on Indian education, we cannot exonerate our own policy-makers from accepting the primary responsibility for the collapse of the Indian education policy since independence. Indeed, the weaknesses and internal contradictions in our policy provided the necessary political space to the forces of globalization (and communalization) to intervene in Indian education. A corollary, but a critical, lesson is about the significance of evolving and sharpening the tools of policy analysis, and applying them for deciphering the mind-set of the state as well as global market forces. Also, this critical task must not be diluted by getting lost in the analysis of *implementation* of policy. Rather, attention must remain focused on analysis of the *character of the policy* itself.

I have also tried to build up evidence regarding the emergence of the following major alarming trends in the post-Jomtien educational scenario, and the need to reverse them through a political resolve rooted in effective policies.

The Parliament, state legislatures and the Planning Commission stand marginalized with respect to policy formulation and the laying down of priorities of the national educational agenda. This role needs to be re-established.

The state is rapidly abdicating its constitutional obligations towards provision of elementary education of *equitable* quality for all children.

The policy for improvement of access, quality and relevance of education in government, local body and government-aided schools has been essentially given up.

The promise in the policy for building up a Common School System with neighbourhood schools has been replaced by a policy of institutionalization of parallel low-quality educational streams for the deprived sections of society. The new guiding sociological principle in educational planning is *a separate educational stream for each section of society*.

Secondary and higher education is going to be steadily privatized and commercialized, for which the state will readily provide policy, legislative, financial and technical support.

Knowledge will be gradually trivialized, fragmented and alienated from its social ethos as well as its aim of social development. Its character will be determined by a collusion of the forces of the market and communal politics in a 'producer–broker–consumer' paradigm.

All deprived sections of society, viz. dalits, tribals, the majority of OBCs, cultural and linguistic minorities and the physically and mentally disabled, two-thirds of each section being girls, will suffer from further discrimination and exclusion in the education system.

Women will be turned into a marketable commodity, thereby further strengthening the patriarchal stranglehold. Girls' education will be aimed at turning them into mere transmitters of fertility control, health or nutritional messages, and making them 'efficient' producers for the global economy; their right to education and development as humans will be further marginalized.

The increasing dominance of information and communication technology in the promotion of the 'knowledge industry' will lead towards irreversible homogenization of plural cultures, ethnicities and languages, thereby increasing the size of the market and enhancing the political dominance of corporate powers in all sectors of life, including education.

The national economy will not be reprioritized for the purpose of allocating adequate resources for education and social development. Instead, dependence on external aid to fulfil constitutional obligation will rise and national education policies will be increasingly compromised under pressure from global market forces (these include Indian corporate houses).

An undeclared consensus has emerged among the political parties (and many prominent NGOs) on acceptance of the structural adjustment programme imposed by the IMF–World Bank on the Indian economy, and, therefore, also with regard to dilutions or distortions in education policy.

The Constitution and laws will be marginalized, amended and even tampered with, in order to fulfil the combined dictates of globalization and the revivalist world-view of the Hindutva forces.

Indian society will be reordered in an *Orwellian-cum-neo-brahmanical* perspective: (a) 60–70 per cent of the people with just enough literacy skills to be able to read advertisements and product labels, as unskilled or semi-skilled manual workers, barely earning minimum wages but forming the large mass of consumers; (b) 10–20 per cent of the people with secondary education, with capability to read, follow and, if necessary, even build upon instructions, who would comprise the skilled work force of technicians for industrial production; and (c) another 10–20 per cent of the upper castes/classes who would have access to higher, technical and professional education, and would '*participate*' (or *collude*, depending upon one's world-view) in the generation, distribution, application and control of knowledge and its social role for the benefit of the global corporate powers.

The basic design for attrition of the democratic, secular and egalitarian fabric of Indian society is thus almost ready. The project of these dark forces is to change the nature of the Indian state itself. Having understood the crisis of Indian education in this manner, howsoever tentative this understanding might be, we have a moral duty to ask the inevitable question to ourselves: What is to be done? I recently read a lecture delivered by Professor Aijaz Ahmad to a body of Delhi University teachers in February 1999, on these very problems. I will conclude by quoting him:

As Marx once put it:

In considering such transformations, a distinction must always be made between the material transformation of the economic conditions of production, which can be determined with the precision of natural science, and the legal, political, religious, aesthetic or philosophic – in short, 'ideological forms in which men become conscious of their conflict and fight it out'.

The battle over ideology and consciousness – the battle over all their forms, be they political, or aesthetic, or religious, or philosophic – is thus the central battle, because it is here, in these domains, not simply at the point of production, that human beings actually 'fight it out'. We, of course, know that, but they also know it, if they are to re-make India in their own image, they must first win the hearts and minds of our children. It is in this battle that we must engage, because without democratic teachers there shall be no democratic India. (Ahmad 2002: 90–91)

Let me add. The role of democratic teachers does not end here. We must also engage with and help build genuine grassroots movements, infused with a consciousness of the dangers inherent in the epistemic assault by the forces of globalization and communalization, in order to redeem India's freedom and re-assert national sovereignty in policy formulation.

This essay is based on a study I have undertaken since September 2001 as part of my work as Senior Fellow, Nehru Memorial Museum and Library, New Delhi. A substantial part of this essay, dealing with policy analysis with respect to non-formal education and the changes in education policy during the post-Jomtien phase, appeared in *Contemporary India*, July–September 2003. The essay also forms part of various chapters from my forthcoming book on the impact of globalization on education policy in India.

Notes
[1] It is recorded that, following Mahatma Gandhi's Presidential Address at the National Education Conference held at Wardha in October 1937, Dr Zakir Husain was the first one to stand up and courageously raise certain questions, particularly with respect to the self-supporting aspect of Basic Education. Mujeeb (2000: 219–20). The only other person who had the courage to similarly differ at the Conference was Professor K.T. Shah, an economist of repute. The rest of the participants uncritically submitted to the charismatic Gandhian personality, a fact that apparently was a cause of concern to Gandhiji himself. Fagg (2002: 55). Zakir Sahib's criticism of the Gandhian proposal, however, seemed not to have dissuaded Gandhiji from supporting Zakir Sahib's nomination as Chairperson of the Committee constituted at the Conference for preparing the Basic Education syllabus.
[2] NPE 1986 was preceded by NPE 1968, the first national policy on education, which was in the form of a Cabinet Resolution adopted by the Parliament.
[3] The Jomtien Conference was attended by representatives of 155 national governments (including the Indian government), twenty intergovernmental bodies and 150 NGOs.
[4] For instance, a follow-up Education for All Conference of nine high population-level countries was held in New Delhi in 1993. These nine high population-level countries

included Bangladesh, Brazil, China, Egypt, India, Indonesia, Mexico, Nigeria and Pakistan – collectively referred to as the E-9 countries. This group met recently in Cairo in December 2003.

5 As part of the Dakar Framework of Action, UNESCO now regularly monitors the progress made by each nation in the context of the Dakar Goals and issues an 'EFA Global Monitoring Report' annually. The EFA Global Monitoring Report 2003–04 focused on education of the girl child and was issued just before the EFA Conference held at New Delhi on 10–12 November 2003. The reports released in 2002 and 2003– 04 show that *India is amongst those countries which is unlikely to fulfil any of the six Dakar Goals* (only three out of six goals were assessed), *including the goal of gender parity, even by the target year of 2015.* The then Union Minister of Human Resource Development, Murli Manohar Joshi took strong exception to this negative assessment in the UNESCO report and claimed that it was based upon outdated data (*Hindustan Times, The Indian Express* and *The Pioneer,* 8 November 2003). However, the Minister's claim was unfounded, as shown by Sadgopal (2003 b and c).

6 The original Article 45 now stands substituted by a modified but diluted Article as a result of the Ninety-Third (now called Eighty-Sixth) Amendment to the Constitution. Compared to the original Article 45, the dilution is a consequence of: (a) delinking Early Childhood Care and Pre-School Education (ECCE) from elementary education, thereby not viewing the education of all children 'until they complete the age of fourteen years' as a continuum; (b) withdrawing the constitutional guarantee for provision of *free* ECCE; and (c) not including a specific time frame for fulfilment of the commitment.

7 Such a harmonious construction of Part IV with Part III of the Constitution was the basis of the historic Unnikrishnan judgement, giving education of children 'until they complete the age of fourteen years' the status of a Fundamental Right. Supreme Court (1993). In this judgement, Article 45 of Part IV was read in conjunction with Article 21 of Part III.

8 It is now widely acknowledged that all those children in the school age who are not in school are to be regarded essentially as child labour, even if they are engaged in domestic chores or outside work places to help their parents, including sibling care by girl children. This contention has gained credibility as a result of the work of M.V. Foundation in Ranga Reddy district, Andhra Pradesh, which led to the revealing sociological principle that 'all children out of school are, by definition, child labourers'. Sinha (2000: 168).

9 NPE 1986 (Sections 5.14 and 5.15) also gave birth to the Navodaya Vidyalayas – yet another parallel layer but *above* the formal school. Navodaya Vidyalayas, like non-formal education, also violate the principle of equality in educational planning and allocation of resources, but a discussion on this issue is beyond the scope of this essay. The NPERC Report analyses the policy relating to Navodaya Vidyalayas and shows how it amounts to a major policy distortion. Government of India (1990, Chapter 4E).

10 This author was a member of the seventeen-member NPE Review Committee 1990 (NPERC), and acted as the convenor of its sub-committee on 'Access, Equity and Universalization'. The sub-committee examined the policy on NFE and recorded in its deliberations this flawed logic, as well as these internal contradictions, in much detail. However, the final report included a rather diluted version of these deliberations due to the consideration shown to the hostile opposition to this analysis by the then Secretary, Ministry of Human Resource Development.

11 The CABE Committee Report, submitted in January 1992, fulfilled the objective of the government by rejecting essentially all the significant recommendations of the Acharya Ramamurti Committee for policy changes for promoting equity in elementary education and building up a Common School System. Accordingly, NPE 1986 was revised by the Parliament in 1992 with only minor modifications, mostly of shifting unfulfilled targets.

12 The Common School System and the concept of Neighbourhood Schools was recommended by the Education Commission (1964–66); see Sections 1.36–1.38, 10.05,

10.19, 10.20 (Government of India, 1966). While recommending a 'phased implementation of the Common School System within a ten-year time frame', the Acharya
Ramamurti Committee Report stressed the need for 'essential minimum legislation', a
common language policy for all schools, and a 'combination of incentives, disincen-
tives and legislation' to bring into its fold recognized but unaided private schools.
Government of India (1990, Chapter 4D: 91–93). The concept was further elaborated and enriched by Sadgopal (2000: 153–63; 2002b: 122–24; 2003a: 23–27).

13 Externally aided projects in primary education in Andhra Pradesh (APPEP) and Bihar
(BEP) preceded the Jomtien Declaration, but these were envisaged as special pilot
projects rather than a matter of policy. The possibility cannot be denied that the
international funding agencies might have used the Andhra Pradesh and Bihar pilot
projects in the pre-Jomtien phase to test the political waters in India, that is, the
political will of the ruling elite to stand by its constitutional obligations and policy.
The Indian political leadership obviously failed the test, as the externally aided projects
of the post-Jomtien phase led to major violations of the Constitution and dilutions of
the policy.

14 In the newly declared *Sarva Shiksha Abhiyan* in Bihar, the Education Guarantee
Scheme officially 'guarantees' merely *three years of primary education*. SIEMAT,
Bihar (2000).

15 The problem is probably inherent in the ambiguous notions of 'Basic Education' and
'Basic Learning Needs' in both the Jomtien and Dakar Frameworks. The ambiguity of
these notions, most likely deliberate, is what allows them to be used for merging of
'human needs and market forces', as noted by Tomasevski (2001). A discussion on this
issue is beyond the scope of this essay. It would be sufficient to point out here that
Jomtien's notion of 'Basic Education' must not be confused with the revolutionary
pedagogic concept of Basic Education (or *Buniyadi Shiksha*), as evolved by Mahatma Gandhi at the Wardha Education Conference in 1937 as part of the freedom
struggle, which was further elaborated by a committee under the chairpersonship of
Dr Zakir Husain as *Nai Talim*. The almost servile 'parroting' of Jomtien's narrow
notion of 'Basic Education' by Indian policy-makers in the post-Jomtien official
discourse amounts to denial of one of the most inspiring features of the heritage of the
freedom struggle, apart from further marginalizing the possibility of integrating the
'world of work' with the 'world of knowledge' as conceived by Mahatma Gandhi.

16 The concept of 'Basic Education' in the Jomtien and Dakar Frameworks is limited to
primary education of *five* years only. Elementary education of *eight* years, implied by
the Indian Constitution under the original Article 45 as well as the amended Article
21A as the minimum guarantee by the state, is non-existent in these Frameworks.
Interestingly, the Jomtien Framework concedes that 'these targets represent a "floor"
(but not a "ceiling")' and parenthetically provides for '(primary education) or whatever higher level of education is considered as basic' by a particular country [Sections
5 and 8(2), respectively]. It is indeed ironic that the Indian policy-makers, instead of
using these spaces in the Framework for persisting with India's constitutional and
policy imperatives, allowed the international funding agencies to dilute *elementary*
education to *primary* education as the dominant framework for educational planning
and financing in post-Jomtien India.

17 This scheme to accommodate 9–14 age group children in adult literacy classes was
announced with great fanfare by the then Prime Minister of India in his inaugural
address at the EFA Conference of E-9 countries held at New Delhi in 1993. Such
glorification of this policy measure is an evidence of *education being reduced to
literacy*.

18 According to 'Education for All: National Plan of Action' (Government of India
2003a), the total Tenth Plan requirement for UEE is Rs 52,280 crore (centre and state
shares combined). This amounted to an average of 0.47 per cent of GDP in 2002–03,
including the external aid component. Of the centre's share (Rs 39,760 crore), the
Planning Commission promised Rs 21,271 crore, that is, only 53.5 per cent of the
Tenth Plan requirement. This leaves a gap of at least Rs 18,489 crore. The gap in the
states' share is not yet reported. Recent press reports indicate that the Planning

Commission has further reduced its allocation to Rs 17,000 crore (that is, a mere 0.15 per cent of GDP), thereby increasing the gap. The story does not end here. The Prime Minister made desperate appeals to the international funding agencies at the UNESCO-sponsored 'Third High Level Group Meeting of EFA' held in New Delhi in November 2003, for increasing external aid for elementary education (*The Indian Express* and *Hindustan Times*, 11 November 2003); the Minister of Human Resource Development carried forward this appeal at the 'E-9 Ministerial-level Review Meeting on EFA' held in Cairo in December 2003 (*Rashtriya Sahara*, 21 December 2003). The Government of India seems to have got an assurance of additional external aid of Rs 15,000 crore for the Tenth Plan. However, as per press reports, the Ministry of Finance has 'asked the HRD Ministry to adjust Rs 15,000 crores in the original allocation of Rs 17,000 crores' (*Hindustan Times*, 17 December 2003)!

[19] NCERT's National Curriculum Framework, textbooks and other guiding material will soon become almost mandatory on states/union territories (it is only optional at present), if the draft 'Free and Compulsory Education Bill, 2004' is approved by the Parliament. Government of India (2004, Draft III, Section 30).

[20] *Hindutva* is not to be confused with *Hinduism*. It denotes politicization of Hinduism for espousing hatred against other religions, and fragmenting society along communal and casteist lines. Thus, Hindutva weakens the struggle of the masses by diverting their focus from the onslaught of global capital on their socio-economic and political rights.

References

Ahmad, Aijaz (2002), *On Communalism and Globalization: Offensives of the Far Right* (New Delhi: Three Essays).

Bharat Jan Vigyan Jatha (BJVJ), in collaboration with MACESE, Department of Education, University of Delhi (1995), *Lokshala Project for Universalization of Elementary Education: Demonstrating an Alternative Vision* (New Delhi: BJVJ), March.

Delhi Historians' Group (2001), *Communalization of Education: The History Textbooks Controversy* (New Delhi: Delhi Historians' Group, Jawaharlal Nehru University), December.

Delors, Jacques *et al* (1996, 1998), *Learning: The Treasures Within*, Report to UNESCO of the International Commission on Education for the Twenty-first Century (Paris: UNESCO).

Dhankar, Rohit (2002), 'Seeking Quality Education: In the Arena of Fun and Rhetoric', in *Seeking Quality Education For All: Experiences from the District Primary Education Programme* (New Delhi: The European Commission), June.

Ed.CIL (2000), *Para Teachers in Primary Education: A Status Report* (District Primary Education Programme, Department of Elementary Education and Literacy, Ministry of Human Resource Development, Government of India).

Fagg, Henry (2002), *Back to Sources: A Study of Gandhi's Basic Education* (New Delhi: National Book Trust).

Government of India (1966), *Education and National Development: Report of the Education Commission 1964–66* (Ministry of Education, Government of India).

—— (1986), *National Policy on Education, 1986* and *Programme of Action, 1986* (Department of Education, Ministry of Human Resource Development, Government of India), May.

—— (1990), *Towards an Enlightened and Humane Society: Report of the Committee for Review of National Policy on Education, 1986*, National Policy on Education Review Committee Report, NPERC, or Acharya Ramamurti Committee Report, (Department of Education, Ministry of Human Resource Development, Government of India), December.

—— (1992a), *Report of the CABE Committee on Policy*, Janardhan Reddy Committee Report (Department of Education, Ministry of Human Resource Development, Government of India), January.

—— (1992b), *National Policy on Education, 1986 (as modified in 1992)* and *Programme of Action, 1992* (Department of Education, Ministry of Human Resource Development, Government of India).

—— (1993), *Education for All: The Indian Scene* (Department of Education, Ministry of Human Resource Development, Government of India).

—— (1995), *District Primary Education Programme: Guidelines* (Department of Education, Ministry of Human Resource Development, Government of India), May.

—— (1998), *DPEP moves on . . .* (Department of Education, Ministry of Human Resource Development, Government of India).

—— (2000), *A Policy Framework for Reforms in Education*, Mukesh Ambani and Kumaramangalam Birla (Prime Minister's Council on Trade and Industry, Government of India), April.

—— (2001a), *Handbook for Education Guarantee Scheme and Alternative and Innovative Education* (Department of Elementary Education and Literacy, Ministry of Human Resource Development, Government of India).

—— (2001b), *Working Group Report on Elementary and Adult Education: Tenth Five Year Plan 2002–2007* (Department of Elementary Education and Literacy, Ministry of Human Resource Development, Government of India), September.

—— (2001c), 'The Constitution (Ninety-Third Amendment) Bill', 2001, Bill No. 106 of 2001 (as introduced in Lok Sabha on 26 November 2001).

—— (2002), *Sarva Shiksha Abhiyan: Framework for Implementation* (Department of Elementary Education and Literacy, Ministry of Human Resource Development, Government of India), June.

—— (2003a), *Education for All: National Plan of Action, India* (Department of Elementary Education and Literacy, Ministry of Human Resource Development, Government of India), June.

—— (2003b), 'The Free and Compulsory Education for Children Bill, 2003', Draft Bill dated 19 September 2003 (Draft I), posted on Ministry of Human Resource Development's website.

—— (2003c), 'The Free and Compulsory Education Bill, 2003', Draft Bill dated 10 December 2003 (Draft II), as circulated by the Secretary, Department of Education, Ministry of Human Resource Development, at a public discussion organized by NIEPA, New Delhi, on 15 December 2003.

—— (2004), 'The Free and Compulsory Education Bill, 2004', Draft Bill dated 8 January 2004 (Draft III), as circulated by the Secretary, Department of Education, Ministry of Human Resource Development, at a meeting of State/UT Secretaries of Departments of Education, held at New Delhi, 15–16 January 2004.

Government of Madhya Pradesh (1998), *The Madhya Pradesh Human Development Report 1998* (Government of Madhya Pradesh, Bhopal).

Hamid, Sayeda Saiyidain, ed. (2000), *Zakir Husain: Teacher Who Became President* (New Delhi: Indian Council for Cultural Relations).

International Bureau of Education, UNESCO and Central Board of Secondary Education, India (2000), *Globalization and Living Together: The Challenges for Educational Content in Asia* (Paris: UNESCO and New Delhi: CBSE).

Jha, Madan Mohan (2003), A Note for NIEPA Meeting on Free and Compulsory Education Bill, 2003, 15 December 2003 (unpublished).

Kripalani, J.B. (1939), *The Latest Fad: Basic Education* (Wardha: Hindustani Talimi Sangh, Sewagram).

Kumar, Krishna *et al.* (2001), 'The Trouble with Para-Teachers', *Frontline*, 9 November.

Kumar, Krishna (2003), 'Judicial Ambivalence and New Politics of Education', *Economic and Political Weekly*, 6–12 December, pp. 5163–66.

Mujeeb, M. (2000), 'The Adventure of Basic Education', in Hamid, ed., *Zakir Husain*.

NCERT (2000), *National Curriculum Framework for School Education* (National Council of Educational Research and Training, New Delhi), November.

NCERT (2001), *Guidelines and Syllabi for Primary, Upper Primary, Secondary and Higher Secondary Stages* (New Delhi: National Council of Educational Research and Training), November.

NIEPA (1990), *Education for All by 2000: Indian Perspective* (New Delhi: National Institute of Educational Planning and Administration), March.

Sadgopal, Anil (1994), Report of the Sub-Group on Education (Chair: Prof. Anil Sadgopal), in

National Consultation on Rights of the Child, organized jointly by Indian Council of
    Child Welfare, UNICEF and Department of Women & Child Development (Ministry
    of HRD, Government of India), November.
———— (2000), *Shiksha mein Badlav ka Sawaal: Samajik Anubhavon se Neeti Tak* (New Delhi:
    Granth Shilpi).
———— (2001a), 'Between the Lines: Writes and Wrongs in Education Bill', *The Times of India,*
    28 November.
———— (2001b), 'Political Economy of the Ninety-Third Amendment Bill', *Mainstream,* 22
    December (Annual 2001), pp. 43–50.
———— (2002a), 'A Convenient Consensus', *Frontline,* 4 January, pp. 107–08.
———— (2002b), 'Politics of Education in the Age of Globalization', in Thukral, ed., *Children in
    Globalizing India.*
———— (2003a), *Political Economy of Education in the Age of Globalization* (New Delhi:
    Bharat Jan Vigyan Jatha).
———— (2003b), 'Goal Posts Shifted', *Hindustan Times,* 11 November.
———— (2003c), 'Education for too few', *Frontline,* 5 December, pp. 97–100.
SAHMAT (2001), *The Saffron Agenda in Education – An Exposé* (New Delhi: Safdar Hashmi
    Memorial Trust), August.
SAHMAT and Sabrang.com (2001), *Against Communalization of Education* (New Delhi: Safdar
    Hashmi Memorial Trust), August.
Sinha, Shantha (2000), 'Child Labour and Education', in Wazir, ed., *The Gender Gap in Basic
    Education.*
Social Jurist (2003), 'Report of Consultative Meeting on Draft Free and Compulsory Education
    for Children Bill, 2003', (New Delhi, 29 November, unpublished).
Supreme Court of India (1993), Unnikrishnan, J.P. and Ors. vs. State of Andhra Pradesh and
    Ors., A.I.R. 1993, S.C. 2178.
Swaminathan, Mina (2001), 'Delegitimizing Childhood', *The Hindu,* 7 October 2001.
Thukral, Enakshi Ganguly, ed. (2002), *Children in Globalizing India* (New Delhi: HAQ, Centre
    for Child Rights).
Tilak, J.B.G. (2003), 'A Study on Financing on Education in India with a Focus on Elementary
    Education', Ministerial Level Meeting of the South Asia EFA Forum, Islamabad,
    Pakistan, 21–23 May.
Tomasevski, K. (2001), *Right to Education Primers No. 1: Removing Obstacles in the Way of
    the Right to Education* (Sweden: Lund).
UNDP, UNESCO, UNICEF, World Bank (1990), *World Declaration on Education for All* and
    Framework for Action to Meet Basic Learning Needs (The Jomtien Declaration),
    World Conference on Education for All: Meeting Basic Learning Needs, Jomtien,
    Thailand, 5–9 March.
UNESCO (2002), *'EFA Global Monitoring Report 2002: Education For All – Is the World on
    Track?'* (Paris: UNESCO).
———— (2002), 'Higher Education for Sale', by Daniel, J. in *Education Today,* UNESCO's
    Newsletter, October–December.
———— (2003), *'EFA Global Monitoring Report 2003–04: Gender and Education for All – The
    Leap to Equality'* (Paris: UNESCO).
Wazir, Rekha, ed. (2000), *The Gender Gap in Basic Education: NGOs as Change Agents* (New
    Delhi: Sage Publications).
Weiner, Myron (1991), *The Child and the State in India* (New Delhi: Oxford University Press).
World Bank (1997), *Primary Education in India* (Washington DC: The World Bank and New
    Delhi: Allied Publishers Limited).
World Education Forum (2000), *The Dakar Framework for Action,* adopted at World Educa-
    tion Forum's conference on 'Education for All: Meeting Our Collective Commit-
    ments', Dakar, Senegal, 26–28 April.

Contributors

P.C. JOSHI was formerly Director and Professor at the Institute of Economic Growth, Delhi. An eminent social scientist, he represents in his work a fusion of economics, political economy, sociology and social anthropology, in what he himself calls the Lucknow School of research in the social sciences. Professor Joshi graduated from Lucknow University in economics and sociology, and did his Ph.D. on the basis of intensive fieldwork with this spectrum of vision in the social sciences. His work on land reforms in India has been particularly influential. He was a leftwing activist in his student days and still identifies with the broadly leftist and secular movements in India. He has held senior academic positions at the Indian Statistical Institute, Kolkata; the Agro Economic Research Centre of the Delhi School of Economics; and the Institute of Economic Growth, Delhi. He has served as Chairman, Centre for Science, Education and Communication, University of Delhi; Chairman, National School of Drama; Member, Indian Council for Social Science Research; Chairman, Doordarshan Reforms Committee; and Chairman, Rural Labour Enquiry Committee. His published works include *Land Reforms in India: Trends and Perspectives* (1975); *Culture, Communication and Social Change*; *Secularism and Development: The Indian Experience*; *Gandhi and Development*; *Uttarakhand: Issues and Challenges*; and *Social Science and Development: Quest for Relevance*. Among his Hindi publications are *Aradhna ka Sankat*; *Bharti Gram: Sansthanik Parivartan aur Arthik Vikas*; and *Parivartan aur Vikas ke Sanskritik Ayam*. He has been awarded an *honoris causa* D.Litt. by the Rabindra Bharati University.

IRFAN HABIB was formerly Professor of History at Aligarh Muslim University. A Marxist scholar and historian, he has been a towering presence on the Indian intellectual scene for several decades. Professor Habib joined the History Department of Aligarh Muslim University (AMU) as a Lecturer in 1953. He went to Oxford for a D.Phil., which he duly obtained with his dissertation on *The Agrarian System of Mughal India*. This dissertation was published in 1963 and has since acquired the status of a classic on Indian history. He returned to AMU in 1960, where he taught, first as Associate Professor and then as Professor, for more than three decades. Although he retired in 1992, he continues to be the moving spirit behind a good deal of the historical research being conducted at that university. He has also served as coordinator and Chairman of the Centre for Advanced Study in History at AMU, and as Chairman of the Indian Council of Historical Research from 1987 to 1993. He was awarded the Padma Bhushan by the Government of India in 2005. Among his other major published works are *An Atlas of the Mughal Empire* (1982) and *Essays in Indian History: Towards a Marxist Perception* (1995). He is the General Editor of the ongoing series 'A People's History of India', initiated by the Aligarh Historians Society, in which he has authored *Prehistory*, *The Indus Civilization* and *Indian Economy, 1858–1914*, and co-authored *The Indus Civilization* and *Mauryan India*. He has also co-edited *The Cambridge Economic History of India, Vol. 1* and the *UNESCO History of Central Asia, Vol. V*.

PRABHAT PATNAIK, a Marxist political economist, is Professor at the Centre for Economic Studies and Planning, Jawaharlal Nehru University, New Delhi. Professor Patnaik earned an M.A. degree in economics from the University of Delhi, following which he was awarded a D.Phil. from the University of Oxford in 1973. He has taught at the University of Cambridge and been a Visiting Professor at the University of California, Riverside and School of Oriental and African Studies, University of London. He has served as Dean, School of Social Sciences, Jawaharlal Nehru University; Member, Economic Advisory Council, Chhattisgarh state; and is currently Vice-Chairman, Kerala State Planning Board. He was awarded the V.K.R.V. Rao Award in 1985 and elected as Conference President, Indian Society of Labour Economics in 2005. His major publications include *Time, Inflation and Growth: Some Macroeconomic Themes in an Indian Perspective* (1988), *Economics and Egalitarianism* (1990), *Whatever Happened to Imperialism and Other Essays* (1995), *Accumulation and Stability under Capitalism* (1997), *The Retreat to Unfreedom* (2003) and *The Value of Money: A Critique of Economic Theory* (2007).

UPENDRA BAXI was formerly Vice Chancellor (1990–94) of the University of Delhi, and is currently (since 1996) Professor of Law in Development, University of Warwick, UK. Professor Baxi graduated from Rajkot (Gujarat University), read law in University of Bombay, and holds LLM degrees from the University of Bombay and University of California at Berkeley, which also awarded him a Doctorate in Juristic Sciences. He has been awarded Honorary Doctorates in Law by the National Law School of India University, Bangalore, and the University of La Trobe, Melbourne. His areas of expertise include law and science, comparative constitutionalism and the social theory of human rights. He has written extensively on the changing paradigms of human rights within development discourses and the new social movements, and on public and international law remedies available to the victims of mass social disasters caused by multinational corporations. His publications include *The Indian Supreme Court and Politics* (1980), *The Crisis of the Indian Legal System* (1982), *Towards a Sociol-*

ogy of *Indian Law* (1985), *Liberty and Corruption* (1990), *Marx, Law and Justice: Some Indian Perspectives* (1993), *Inhuman Wrongs and Human Rights: Some Unconventional Essays* (1994) and *Mambrino's Helmet? Human Rights for a Changing World* (1994). He has also edited (with Oliver Mendelssohn) *The Rights of the Subordinated Peoples* (1994) and a trilogy of works on the Bhopal catastrophe.

ROMILA THAPAR, Professor Emeritus in History at Jawaharlal Nehru University, New Delhi, is one of the world's foremost experts on ancient Indian history whose work has consistently combated chauvinism and narrow nationalism in intellectual and public spheres. She was educated at Punjab University and then London University, from where she earned her Ph.D. in 1958. She has taught at London University, University of Delhi and Jawaharlal Nehru University, New Delhi. Professor Thapar was President of the Indian History Congress in 1983, and has held the Nehru Memorial Fellowship (1976–77), Bhabha Senior Fellowship (1992–94) and National Fellowship of the Indian Council of Social Science Research (1989–90). She achieved recognition as a Fellow of the Royal Historical Society and Honorary Fellow of Lady Margaret Hall, Oxford, and has been awarded Honorary Doctorates from the University of Chicago and Peradeniya University, Sri Lanka. She has been Visiting Professor at Cornell University, University of Pennsylvania and Collège de France in Paris. In 1999, she was elected as a corresponding Fellow of the British Academy. Her major publications are *Asoka and the Decline of the Mauryas* (1961), *A History of India, Volume 1* (1966), *Ancient Indian Social History: Some Interpretations* (1978), *From Lineage to State: Social Formations in the Mid-First Millennium* BC *in the Ganga Valley* (1985), *Sakuntala: Texts, Readings, Histories* (2002) and *Somanatha: The Many Voices of History* (2005).

M.S. SWAMINATHAN, a scientist of rare recognition, has been described as the 'Father of Economic Ecology'. A plant geneticist by training, he graduated from the University of Cambridge with a Ph.D. in genetics. Professor Swaminathan's contributions to the agricultural renaissance of India have led to his being widely referred to as the scientist leader of the green revolution movement. His advocacy of sustainable agriculture leading to an evergreen revolution makes him an acknowledged world leader in the field of sustainable food security. He has been awarded by the International Association of Women and Development for promoting technological empowerment of women in agriculture and for mainstreaming gender considerations in rural development. He was awarded the Ramon Magasaysay Award in 1986, the first World Food Prize in 1987, the Volvo Environment Prize in 1999, the Padma Vibhushan in 1989, and the Franklin D. Roosevelt Four Freedoms Award in 2000. He has been a Fellow of many leading scientific academies in India and the world, including the Royal Society of London and the US National Academy of Sciences. He has received 45 Honorary Doctorate degrees from universities around the world. Recently, he was elected as the President of Pugwash Conferences on Science and World Affairs. He currently holds the UNESCO Chair in Ecotechnology at the M.S. Swaminathan Research Foundation in Chennai, and is Chairman of the National Commission on Agriculture, Food and Nutrition Security of India.

SOMNATH CHATTERJEE is a veteran parliamentarian, a leading public figure, a statesman, an eminent intellectual and lawyer, a political activist and a well-known trade unionist. He is currently the Speaker of the 14th Lok Sabha of India. He was educated at the University of Calcutta and University of Cambridge, and became barrister-at-law from the Middle Temple, UK. Somnath Chatterjee began his career as a lawyer and joined active politics in 1968, when he became a member of the Communist Party of India (Marxist). He has been one of the party's leading spokesmen. His association with national politics began when he contested and won the elections to the Lok Sabha in 1971; since then, he has served as a Member in all successive Lok Sabhas. In recognition of his immense contribution towards strengthening India's parliamentary set-up, he was honoured with the Outstanding Parliamentarian Award in 1996 by the President of India. During his terms in Parliament, he has been chairman of various important parliamentary committees, and has represented India in foreign delegations and at the United Nations. He has also brought his legal acumen to bear, with considerable impact, on shaping legislation in diverse areas within the Parliament.

ANDRÉ BÉTEILLE, Chairman of the Indian Council of Social Science Research (ICSSR) since March 2005, is one of the foremost social scientists of India. Having acquired an M.Sc. degree in anthropology from Calcutta University and a Ph.D. in sociology from the University of Delhi, he became one of the founding faculty members of the Department of Sociology at the Delhi School of Economics in 1959. He was Professor of Sociology there till 1999 and is currently Professor Emeritus. Professor Béteille is also Chancellor, North-Eastern Hill University, Shillong; Chairman, Centre for Studies in Social Sciences, Kolkata; and Trustee of Sameeksha Trust, the Institute of Economic Growth, the National Foundation for India and the New India Foundation. He has lectured at many universities, and is a corresponding Fellow of the British Academy and an Honorary Fellow of the Royal Anthropological Institute. He was awarded the Padma Bhushan in 2005. With Indian society as his focus, he has examined, in his writings, the nature and types of inequality in human societies in general. He has authored many books, including *Caste, Class and Power: Changing Patterns of Stratification in a Tanjore Village* (1965), *Studies in Agrarian Social Structure* (1974), *Inequality among Men* (1977), *The Idea of Natural Inequality and Other Essays* (1983), *Antinomies of Society: Essays on Ideologies and Institutions* (2000) and *Equality and Universality: Essays in Social and Political Theory* (2002). *Anti-Utopia: Essential Writings of André Béteille*, was published in 2005.

SHAMS-UR-RAHMAN FARUQI is an eminent literary critic, poet and theorist, who has nurtured a whole generation of Urdu writers after the 1960s. Regarded as the founder of the new movement in Urdu literature, he has formulated fresh models of literary appreciation. With rare skill and clarity, he absorbed western principles of literary criticism and applied them to Urdu literature, but only after adapting them to address literary aesthetics native to Arabic, Persian and Urdu. Professor Faruqi obtained his M.A. in English in 1955 from the University of Allahabad. He served in the Indian Post Office and in other departments of the Government of India from 1958 to 1994. He was Adjunct Professor in the South Asian Studies Center at the University of Pennsylvania, Philadelphia, from 1991, and has held the Khan Abdul Ghaffar Khan Chair in the Faculty of Humanities at the Jamia Millia Islamia University, New Delhi (1999–2001). He has been the Editor of the influential Urdu journal, *Shabkhoon*, since 1966. Professor Faruqi's books include *Early Urdu Literary Culture and History* (2000), whose Urdu version came out from both India and Pakistan; *Lughat-e Rozmarrah*, a critical compendium of modern Urdu usage, published simultaneously from New Delhi and Karachi (2003); and *She'r-e Shor Angez*, a four-volume study of the *ghazals* of Mir Taqi Mir, which won him the Saraswati Samman for 1996.

The late SISIR KUMAR DAS was a scholar, linguist, poet, critic, playwright, children's writer and literary historian. He was Tagore Professor, Department of Modern Indian Languages, and Dean, Faculty of Arts, at the University of Delhi, and also a Secretary of the Sahitya Akademi, New Delhi. Professor Das held Doctoral degrees from the Universities of Calcutta and London, and was a post-doctoral fellow in general linguistics at Cornell University. He was also part of the teaching faculty at the School of Oriental and African Studies, University of London, for three years. During his distinguished career of teaching and writing in Bengali and English, Professor Das earned several awards and honours. These include the Nehru Award from the Federal Republic of Germany for his work *Western Sailors, Eastern Seas*; the Tagore Memorial Prize for his publications *Shadow of the Cross: Hinduism and Christianity in a Colonial Situation* and *The Artist in Chains: The Life of Bankim Chandra Chatterjee*; and the Kamal Kumari award from the Government of Assam for his contribution to Indian literature. He edited *Rabindranath Tagore's Writings in English* in three volumes, and *A History of Indian Literature* in two volumes, for the Sahitya Akademi.

NAMWAR SINGH is a distinguished Hindi writer, critic and Marxist scholar. He has been in the vanguard of progressive writing in Hindi, and his contribution to Hindi literature, language and linguistics, and as modernizer of a rich tradition is widely recognized. He studied at the Banaras Hindu University from where he received his Ph.D. He has held several teaching positions including Professor of Hindi and (Founder) Chairman of the Centre of Indian Languages, Jawaharlal Nehru University, New Delhi. Currently Professor Emeritus at that university, he has been recently appointed as Chancellor of the Mahatma Gandhi International

Hindi University, Wardha. He has also been a former Council member of the Sahitya Akademi. Among his published works are *Hindi ke Vikas Mein Apabhramsh ka Yog, Chhayawad, Bakalm Khud, Doosri Parampara ki Khoj Mein* (a study of Kabirdas), *Kavita ke Naye Pratiman* (winner of the 1971 Sahitya Akademi award), *Vad Vivad Samrad* and *Alochak ke Mukh Se*. He is the Editor of the prestigious Hindi journal *Alochana*. He has received many awards, including the Sahitya Akademi award, the Shalaka Samman, the Hindustan Academy Samman and the Bharat-Bharati honour from the Uttar Pradesh Hindi Sansthan.

ANIL SADGOPAL is Professor of Education at the University of Delhi. His work is marked by a strong plea for making elementary education a fundamental right in this country. Professor Sadgopal did his Ph.D. in biochemistry and molecular biology in 1968 from the California Institute of Technology, USA, after which he joined the Tata Institute of Fundamental Research, Bombay in 1968. He resigned from TIFR in 1971 to organize a rural education and development programme through Kishore Bharati in Hoshangabad district, Madhya Pradesh. He helped initiate the Hoshangabad Science Teaching Programme (HSTP) and co-founded Eklavya in 1982, which extended HSTP to almost 1,000 schools in 15 districts of Madhya Pradesh, wherein more than a lakh children learned science through an inquiry-oriented, experiment-based pedagogy. He has been active in the people's science movement and the movement for civil liberties and democratic rights. He was on the Supreme Court-appointed committee for overlooking rehabilitation schemes for the Bhopal gas victims. He was National Convener of the Bharat Jan Vigyan Jatha, an all-India people's science network, and conceived the Lokshala programme to work for social intervention in the government school system. Professor Sadgopal has also served as Dean, Faculty of Education, University of Delhi, and been a Senior Fellow of the Nehru Memorial Museum and Library, New elhi. He is the author of two books in Hindi: *Sangharsh aur Nirman* (on the movement of the Chhattisgarh mine workers led by Shankar Guha Niyogi) and *Shiksha mein Badlav ka Sawal*.